Urban Slavery in Colonial Mexico

Using the city of Puebla de los Ángeles, the second-largest urban center in colonial Mexico (viceroyalty of New Spain), Pablo Miguel Sierra Silva investigates Spaniards' imposition of slavery on Africans, Asians and their families. He analyzes the experiences of these slaves in four distinct urban settings: the marketplace, the convent, the textile mill and the elite residence. In so doing, *Urban Slavery in Colonial Mexico* advances a new understanding of how, when and why transatlantic and transpacific merchant networks converged in Central Mexico during the seventeenth century. As a social and cultural history, it also addresses how enslaved people formed social networks to contest their bondage. Sierra Silva challenges readers to understand the everyday nature of urban slavery and engages the rich Spanish and indigenous history of the Puebla region while intertwining it with African diaspora studies.

Pablo Miguel Sierra Silva is Assistant Professor in the History Department at the University of Rochester, New York.

T0370902

Other Books in the Series

(Continued after the index)

Urban Slavery in Colonial Mexico

Puebla de los Ángeles, 1531–1706

PABLO MIGUEL SIERRA SILVA

University of Rochester, New York

CAMBRIDGE
UNIVERSITY PRESS

CAMBRIDGE
UNIVERSITY PRESS

University Printing House, Cambridge CB2 8BS, United Kingdom

One Liberty Plaza, 20th Floor, New York, NY 10006, USA

477 Williamstown Road, Port Melbourne, VIC 3207, Australia

314-321, 3rd Floor, Plot 3, Splendor Forum, Jasola District Centre, New Delhi - 110025, India

79 Anson Road, #06-04/06, Singapore 079906

Cambridge University Press is part of the University of Cambridge.

It furthers the University's mission by disseminating knowledge in the pursuit of
education, learning and research at the highest international levels of excellence.

www.cambridge.org
Information on this title: www.cambridge.org/9781108412186
DOI: 10.1017/9781108304245

© Pablo Miguel Sierra Silva 2018

First published 2018
First paperback edition 2019

A catalogue record for this publication is available from the British Library

ISBN 978-1-108-41981-9 Hardback
ISBN 978-1-108-41218-6 Paperback

Cambridge University Press has no responsibility for the persistence or
accuracy of URLs for external or third-party internet websites referred to in
this publication, and does not guarantee that any content on such websites is,
or will remain, accurate or appropriate.

For Felipe Monsón y Mojica

Contents

Figures and Tables

Figures

Tables

Acknowledgments

This project began in the fall of 2006 when I arrived as a graduate student at the University of California, Los Angeles. The faculty and staff of this wonderful institution always made me feel a part of a greater academic community that challenged my thinking in ways I could have never foreseen. To my doctoral advisor, mentor and dear friend, Kevin Terraciano, I can only offer my utmost gratitude. I am just as indebted to Robin Derby, Andrew Apter, William Summerhill, Christopher Ehret, Brenda Stevenson, Teófilo Ruíz, Juan Gómez-Quiñones and many other UCLA historians. The seminars, independent studies and candid advice on the academic profession have proven invaluable. I must also extend a heartfelt "thank you" to Professors Mark Sawyer, Edward Telles, Claudia Parodi and Anna More for making me a better scholar. To my cohort, Dana Velasco-Murillo, Brad Benton, Verónica Gutiérrez, Xóchitl Flores, Peter Villela, Zeb Tortorici, Phillip Ninomiya and Sabrina Smith, *mil gracias*. I am especially in debt to my wife, best friend and colleague, Molly Ball. This project simply would not have been possible without you.

This book is also the product of the rich debates and conversations fostered at several academic conferences. My first paper was delivered at the Annual Meeting for the Society of Ethnohistory. The members of this vibrant community have always welcomed me into their midst, and for that I am grateful. Throughout the years, Matthew Restall, Susan Schroeder, Lisa Sousa, Laura Matthew and Camilla Townsend have offered insightful suggestions at Ethnohistory conferences. To Ben Vinson, Nicole von Germeten, Paul la Chance, Sherwin Bryant, Evelyn Jennings, Roquinaldo Ferreira, Joseph Miller and all of the commentators for the chapters that have gradually morphed into this book, thank you. Robert Schwaller contributed valuable insights for Chapter 1. Anne MacPherson and the members of the New York State Latin America History Workshop (NYSLAHW) have offered constructive criticism for Chapter 3. Tatiana Seijas has helped me understand the slave market of Mexico City, while David Wheat and Marc Eagle have been instrumental in expanding my understanding of the transatlantic slave trade and Spanish circum-Caribbean. Alex Borucki, this book simply would not have been possible without you. Thank you for sharing your time and knowledge.

I am honored to publish this study as part of Cambridge University Press's Latin American Studies Series. Debbie Gershenowitz saw this project through from a few chapter samples to a finished product. Kristina Deusch put all the pieces together to complete this colonial puzzle. Thank you to both! Kris Lane and Matthew Restall, thank you for your time and invaluable support as series editors. It means the world to me. I would also like to thank this book's anonymous reviewers for their insightful commentaries and suggestions. I hope I have matched your expectations.

I am greatly indebted to the University of Rochester, where I have been warmly received as a member of the academic community. Matt Lenoe, Mike Jarvis, Laura Smoller, Ryan Prendergast, Margarita Guillory, Jennifer Kyker and all my colleagues at the U of R, thank you for making the transition from graduate student to assistant professor such an enjoyable experience. The wonderful maps found in this book are the careful work of Benjamin Gerstner and Tim O'Brien. I also hold a debt of gratitude to all the wonderful graduate and undergraduate students who have challenged my thinking during these first years of teaching. Tucker Million, many thanks for indexing this project. I owe an especially effusive "thank you" to Anna Jarvis for her copyediting and suggestions during this project's final phase.

Funding for this project came from several generous institutions. A Fulbright-Hays DDRA Fellowship supported research in Puebla and Mexico City. The UCLA School of Graduate Studies supported summer research in New Orleans, while UC-Mexus also contributed a grant to further fieldwork during my final year of doctoral research. An internal fellowship at the University of Rochester's Humanities Center provided valuable time to complete the manuscript and funded research in Seville. Further financial support from U of R made additional research in Lisbon possible.

I must express my gratitude to the gatekeepers of Puebla's archives, María Antonieta Esquivel Torres, Gabriela Rivera Carrizosa, María Aurelia Hernández Yahuitl. To the parish priests of Analco, San José and El Sagrario, and to the staff and directors of Puebla's Municipal, Notarial and Historical Judicial archives and many others: *mil gracias*. I will always be indebted to Blanca Lara Tenorio for her willingness to share handwritten archival notes, unpublished papers and the treasures found in the Centro INAH-Puebla. Through the years, Lidia Gómez García has provided a blueprint for the selfless researcher, mentor and colleague that I hope to become. *Gracias*, Lidia! Miguel Ángel Cuenya Mateos opened the doors of the Casa Amarilla library and the greater BUAP research community to me. I will always be indebted to Isis Zempoaltecatl, Guillermo García

Rodríguez, Gustavo Mauleón and Rafael Castañeda García for their camaraderie and support.

Finally, this book would not have been possible without the care and support of my loving family (spread out across many lands and nations). *Familia, muchas gracias*!

Archival Abbreviations

ACCP   Archivo del Cabildo Catedralicio de Puebla
AGI   Archivo General de Indias, Sevilla
AGMP   Archivo General Municipal de Puebla
AGN   Archivo General de la Nación, México
AGNP   Archivo General de Notarías de Puebla
AHJP   Archivo Histórico Judicial de Puebla, INAH
AHN   Archivo Histórico Nacional, España
AHU   Arquivo Histórico Ultramarino, Lisboa
APSJ   Archivo Parroquial del Señor San José
ASAC   Archivo del Santo Angel Custodio (Analco)
ASMP   Archivo del Sagrario Metropolitano de Puebla
BNE   Biblioteca Nacional de España
FAJML   Fondo Antiguo José María Lafragua, Puebla
LAL   Latin American Library, Tulane University

Introduction

On 14 December 1650, a young black man by the name of Baltazar de los Reyes was sold to an illiterate Spaniard in the city of Puebla de los Ángeles. News of the sale quickly reached the entire community of the San Pedro hospital, where de los Reyes worked alongside his mother, Sebastiana Paramos. Nurses, servants, cooks, both enslaved and free, had all been embroiled in the contentious dispute between de los Reyes and Alonso Fernández, the hospital's administrator. In early September, a disagreement between Fernández and de los Reyes escalated to the point of violence. The administrator claimed that the young man attacked him with a weapon. In retaliation, Fernández threatened to sell the young man out of the city and into a sugar plantation (*ingenio*).[1] As administrator of the San Pedro hospital, Fernández was well within his rights to sell an undisciplined slave. He held power of attorney for this particular corporation, one of many slave-owning hospitals, colleges and convents in Puebla.

Shortly after their confrontation, Baltazar de los Reyes fled for Antequera (modern-day Oaxaca City), some 200 miles to the southwest. The archival record does not reveal why he chose to flee in that direction or whom he was seeking. Regardless, flight was a dangerous proposition for an enslaved youth. De los Reyes was now removed from the circle of family, friends and workplace acquaintances that had provided safety and community in Puebla. It effectively transformed him into a runaway slave, an *esclavo huído*, subject to corporal punishment and imprisonment by authorities with no ties to his community or the San Pedro hospital. Bounty hunters along the Puebla-Antequera road would be informed of his escape and remunerated for his capture. Sure enough, by early December, bounty hunters had captured de los Reyes and sent him to the Antequera jail. He would soon be sold *in absentia* by two men 200 miles away.

The bill of slave purchase signed by Alonso Fernández on 14 December 1650 might seem like just another harrowing, but all too common, slave

---

1 Archivo General de Notarías de Puebla (hereafter, AGNP), Not. 3, Box 101, 1650 December, 27r.

transaction in a Spanish American archive. After all, some 20,000 bills of slave purchase are archived in the city of Puebla for the seventeenth century alone. In this case, a runaway slave had been captured and sold in exasperation to a new master. This type of transaction was fairly common in the urban centers of colonial Mexico, especially when slave owners were unwilling to pay the cost of recovering their human property from a distant location. At first glance, this was exactly what happened to Baltazar de los Reyes. One master transferred the rights to a slave's labor, body and the prestige conferred by his ownership to another master. In a paper-centric society, the buyer and seller each received a notarized original of the transaction, while the local notary retained a triplicate for record-keeping.

Paradoxical as it may sound, the sale of Baltazar de los Reyes to another Spaniard represented a true triumph for an enslaved family.[2] Despite her legal status as an enslaved person and a single mother, Sebastiana Paramos orchestrated the entire transaction. Despite his status as an imprisoned runaway slave, de los Reyes secured a new life in a notarial process in which he was transacted as chattel. And despite the threats of the hospital's administrator, a son would return home, close to his mother. True, Baltazar de los Reyes would remain enslaved, but he would not, under any circumstance, become a fieldhand in some forlorn plantation. He would remain in Puebla, surrounded by friends, siblings, patrons, acquaintances, foes and former masters, as well.

In her quest to keep her son close, Paramos enlisted the aid of numerous allies: nurses, church ministers and her other unnamed sons. As an experienced hospital worker, she understood that any hospital administrator could be held accountable to the bishop and the seventeen other members of Puebla's cathedral council. Despite its medical services, the San Pedro hospital was ultimately a religious institution under the jurisdiction of the bishop and his auxiliaries. Appealing to such powerful religious figures was a particularly useful approach for a worker in the San Pedro Hospital. The cathedral complex was just three blocks south of her workplace, a five-minute walk at most (see Figure 0.1). In an undated statement (*memorial*), Paramos appealed to the bishop for assistance. She "and her sons had served the poor for many years" as hospital workers under other administrators, all of whom had treated them better.[3] In defending her right to remain close to her son, Paramos also claimed the moral high ground of motherhood and responsibility. De los Reyes could have never attacked or even feigned to harm Fernández for a simple reason: "As his mother and in the time of other [hospital] rectors, I have always disciplined him severely." Paramos boldly discredited the administrator's accusations as nothing more than "a sinister account."

2 AGNP, Not. 3, Box 101, 1650 December, 27r.   3 Ibid.

Puebla de los Ángeles, 17th century

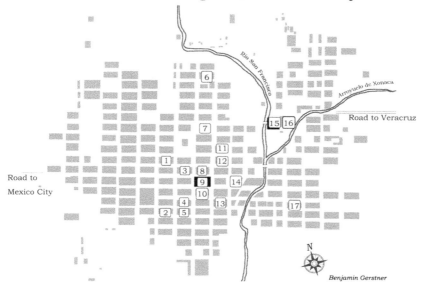

Figure 0.1 Map of Puebla de los Ángeles, seventeenth century. Created by Benjamin Gerstner

Key

1 - Convent of Santa Catalina
2 - Convent of Santa Inés
3 - Convent of the Santísima Trinidad
4 - Convent of La Limpia Concepción
5 - Church of Santa Veracruz
6 - Church of San José
7 - Convent of Santa Teresa (Carmelites)
8 - Municipal Palace (Cabildo)
9 - Public Plaza & Slave Market until 1624

10 - Cathedral
11 - Convent of Santa Clara
12 - Hospital of San Pedro
13 - Convent of San Jerónimo
14 - Jesuit College
15 - Slave Market after 1624
16 - Convent of San Francisco
17 - Church of Analco
    (Santo Angel Custodio)

Sebastiana Paramos went one step further. "If it is necessary to sell him, I will find a master for him in this city," she stated. On 6 December 1650, the members of Puebla's cathedral chapter ruled in favor of Paramos and de los Reyes.[4] A week later, Toribio Hernández, the hospital's illiterate head nurse, became Baltazar de los Reyes's nominal owner for 300 pesos. Hernández would travel to Antequera in order to secure his newly purchased slave and return him to Puebla (and to his mother). However, several clauses within the bill of purchase stipulated that de los Reyes could not serve his

4 Archivo del Cabildo Catedralicio de Puebla (ACCP), Actas de Cabildo, Tomo 12, 311r–313v.

new owner and that the latter "could not have the slave within the said hospital."[5] If not Hernández, who would de los Reyes serve? Did Paramos somehow provide the head nurse with the funds to recover her son? The historical record goes no further.

Instead, we are left with the remarkable story of a black family and their resilience. We are forced to reconsider what it meant to be enslaved in a Mexican city where the enslaved wove expansive social networks. Paramos would serve as a godmother for an enslaved child in 1655 and for a free child the very next year.[6] She was clearly a respected person in her urban community and benefited from her connections to the San Pedro Hospital. Certain spaces, such as hospitals, provided greater access to patrons and allies who could help trump, or at least mitigate, slaveholder power. In other city settings, such as the textile workshop, the brutality of slavery was exacerbated by the acceptance of localized violence. How different then was slavery in the convent, the elite household, or the marketplace? Could space define slavery? Or could the enslaved push back on the spatial limitations of their bondage? If so, what can Puebla tell us about the daily negotiation of bondage in colonial Mexico?

During the mid-1990s and early 2000s, sociologists, art historians, anthropologists and historians directed their attention to the history and contemporary experiences of people of African descent in Mexico. Among Mexican historians, the 1994 publication of *Presencia africana en México*, signaled the beginning of a new wave of academic scholarship on Afro-Mexicans.[7] A decade later, Ben Vinson III and Bobby Vaughn published *Afroméxico*, an important study that took the pulse of this emergent scholarship and situated it in relation to a growing body of scholarship produced in the United States. As a result, today the black communities of the Costa Chica (along the modern states of Guerrero and Oaxaca) and Veracruz are well known through studies that privilege Mexico as an emerging area of study within the African diaspora.[8]

Yet as Christina Sue makes clear in her study of contemporary Veracruz, understanding blackness in Mexico is often an exercise in exposing

5 AGNP, Not. 3, Box 101, 1650 December, 27v. "E tanbien se lo bendo con condission q. no a de servir a el dho toribio hernandes ni tener en el dho hospital el dho esclabo..."

6 Archivo del Sagrario Metropolitano de Puebla (ASMP), "Bautismos de negros y mulatos," 26r, 39v. Baltazar de los Reyes also served as godfather in this last baptism.

7 Luz María Montiel, ed. *Presencia Africana en México* (Mexico City: CONACULTA, 1994).

8 Gonzalo Aguirre Beltrán, *Cuijla: Esbozo etnográfico de un pueblo negro* (Mexico City: Fondo de Cultura Económica, 1989); Bobby Vaughn, "Los negros, los indígenas y la diáspora" in Ben Vinson III and Bobby Vaughn, eds., *Afroméxico* (Mexico City: Fondo de Cultura Económica, 2004), 75–96; Laura Lewis, "Modesty and Modernity: Photography, Race and Representation on Mexico's Costa Chica (Guerrero)," *Identities: Global Studies in Culture and Power*, 11, no. 4 (Fall 2004), 471–499; Anita González, *Afro-Mexico: Dancing between Myth and Reality* (Austin: University of Texas Press, 2010).

discourses of *mestizaje*, nonblackness and, ultimately, racism.[9] Simply put, blackness outside of modern Mexico's coastal regions is often interpreted as a phenotypical marker of foreignness. Until 2014, Mexico's National Institute of Geography and Statistics (INEGI) refused to consider Afro-Mexicans as members of a distinct and disadvantaged minority with a history dating back to 1520.[10] This historical neglect has come to an abrupt end. In the spring of 2015, Mexico's National Council Against Discrimination (CONAPRED) launched a groundbreaking campaign, *Soy Afro: Cuento y Me Reconozco*, in order to support federal initiatives in favor of *afrodescendiente* communities.[11] The 2015 census, which finally allowed individuals of African descent to recognize themselves as such, compiled information on 1.38 million *afrodescendientes*.[12]

While *afrodescendientes* from Veracruz, Oaxaca and Guerrero increasingly reject the national assimilationist ideology of *mestizaje* (developed by José Vasconcelos in the 1920s),[13] the same cannot be said for residents of modern Puebla and many other Central Mexican states and urban centers. Modern-day Puebla's population of African descent is minuscule. Accordingly, posters and other images for the CONAPRED *Soy Afro* campaign exclude several states within Central Mexico as spaces inhabited by people of African descent. Projected onto the colonial past, the city of Puebla emerges as a site of mestizoness and whiteness. Research on colonial indigeneity in the city has begun to challenge these ideas, but blackness remains a foreign concept.

Indeed, most Poblanos openly express surprise, shock or dismay when learning that a numerous population of African descent called their city home throughout the colonial period.[14] Invoking that population's enslavement and subsequent freedom in Puebla is met with disbelief. The same

---

9 Christina A. Sue, *The Land of the Cosmic Race: Race Mixture, Racism, and Blackness in Mexico* (New York: Oxford University Press, 2013).

10 This contradictory stance by INEGI has tangible socioeconomic consequences for the inhabitants of the Costa Chica, where indigenous communities often receive federal funding for infrastructural and cultural projects. Recently, Mexico's National Autonomous University, UNAM, has been moderately successful in raising awareness for Costa Chica communities through its *México Nación Multicultural* Program.

11 The CONAPRED campaign is specifically directed at children and young people. Digital posters with images of José María Morelos and Vicente Guerrero are accompanied with the Twitter hashtags #SoyAfro. For more on this initiative, which is backed by the Secretary of State (SEGOB), see the official website for the program: www.conapred.org.mx/index.php?contenido=noticias&id=5363&id_opcion=108&op=214 (accessed 2015/02/27).

12 INEGI, "Resultados definitivos de la Encuesta Intercensal 2015, www3.inegi.org.mx/sistemas/saladeprensa/noticia.aspx?id=2288 (accessed 2016/01/19).

13 José Vasconcelos, *La raza cósmica* (Madrid: Agencia Mundial de Librería, 1925).

14 In informal, everyday conversations during my research, I was told that slavery certainly took place in Cuba, Brazil, the United States, and maybe even in Veracruz, but the concept of chattel slavery is thoroughly incompatible with the historical narrative of Puebla.

incredulity applies to the experiences of enslaved Asians, although extolling "la china poblana" (literally, "the Chinese woman of Puebla") has tempered the public's rejection of a historic Asian presence. Local schoolchildren might know a thing or two about Catarina de San Juan, the enslaved Asian woman who achieved a quasi-saintly following among the city's working poor during the colonial period. However, *why* she was a slave in Puebla has never been explained to these children, their parents or their grandparents.

Instead, Puebla is profoundly associated with Baroque architecture, ceramic pottery, a rich gastronomy and the Cinco de Mayo battle of 1862. Slavery plays no part in the city's cultural imagination. Today, the slave market of yesteryear is nothing more than a lively plaza with benches for an easy Sunday stroll or for a political rally. And yet, thousands upon thousands of people, mostly Africans, were sold in Puebla (many on that precise plaza, just below the current municipal palace) during the seventeenth century. In the following chapters, I explain why, when and how colonial Poblanos invested in urban slavery. I also examine the ways in which enslaved people negotiated their bondage, laid roots in the city and eroded the foundations of slaveholder power.

This book is a sociocultural history of slavery in Puebla de los Ángeles, the second-largest city in the viceroyalty of New Spain (colonial Mexico). It traces the importation of Africans to Puebla since the mid-sixteenth century and analyzes early municipal ordinances in relation to the development of urban slavery. It also advances a new understanding of how, when and why transatlantic (and transpacific) slaving networks converged in Central Mexico and, specifically, Puebla throughout the seventeenth century. Based on this research, it is evident that the Mexican demand for slave labor was not satisfied by 1640. Slaveholders turned to American-born slaves, and the slave trade resurged intermittently during the late seventeenth century. As a regional approach to understanding the motivations of the enslavers and the enslaved, the book focuses on the social dynamics of a single city situated between the viceregal capital, Mexico City, and the principal port of entry, Veracruz.

Studying Puebla resolves many questions regarding the slave trade to Mexico. For instance, it is now clear that the densely populated towns and cities of the Central Mexican highlands represented lucrative markets for Portuguese slave traders based out of Cape Verde, São Paulo de Luanda (Angola) and Cartagena de Indias (Colombia). *Encomenderos de negros*, locally based slaving agents with transatlantic contacts, understood Puebla to be an essential node in a transimperial web of slaving interests. Despite their virtual absence from the historiography of slavery, these agents established profound ties with the city's political and merchant elites by extending credit. Artisans, small business owners and widows also came to depend on *encomenderos de negros* and their financing. Thus, addressing the specific motivations of Poblano slave owners is essential to advancing a more complete understanding of slavery and the economy of the region.

Urban Slavery in Colonial Mexico also engages the motivations and social networks of the enslaved by tracing multigenerational family histories across the seventeenth century. I contend that the particularities of Puebla's archives allow the experiences of enslaved families to be reconstructed (albeit imperfectly) through careful quantitative research and qualitative analysis. Thus, this book may at times read as a collection of statistically informed microhistories that illustrate how a family endured or transcended its enslavement or a particular space of bondage. In acknowledging the contributions and limitations of empiricist methodologies and historically imaginative research, I pursue a middle ground that borrows from both social and cultural history. In doing so, this book reflects the experiences of enslaved African and Asian parents, their Mexican-born children and grandchildren and their Spanish, mestizo and indigenous friends, foes and acquaintances in the city of Puebla.

I am especially interested in understanding how the social networks of slaves and masters were enhanced, circumscribed or otherwise affected by specific urban settings. To speak of urban slavery in seventeenth-century Puebla is to describe innumerable modalities of bondage so varied that they often defy effective analysis. The mobility of the urban setting undoubtedly made slavery more tolerable for some than others. However, many of the cases in this book speak to the "violent and spatially confining" versions of urban slavery found throughout the Americas and Caribbean.[15] Puebla's *obrajes*, or textile mills, were notorious as sites of confinement, punishment and coercion. Thus, understanding specific physical settings within the city allows for a more fruitful engagement with the expectations, limitations and possibilities that the enslaved and their captors confronted on an everyday basis. The cloister and the marketplace featured different dangers, respites and gendered dynamics. These spaces of slavery were not static, unchanging entities. Textile barons adapted their infamous mills and workforces to the fluctuations of the slave trade, political demands and slave reproduction. But adaptability was not the exclusive domain of the slaveholder.

This book makes a simple argument: throughout the course of the seventeenth century, enslaved people in Puebla increasingly transcended their bondage because their social networks surpassed specific spaces and relations of slavery. By cultivating strategic alliances and intimate relations in indigenous barrios, local parishes, elite residences and innumerable public

---

15 Marisa J. Fuentes, *Dispossessed Lives: Enslaved Women, Violence and the Archive* (Philadelphia: University of Pennsylvania Press, 2016), 8.

settings, the enslaved gradually expanded their ties to free people and the latter's resources. These social bonds were then validated at the local parish, a crucial arena through which to contest slaveholder power. This multigenerational process slowly but surely eroded the foundations of slavery in the colonial city. By 1700, many individuals of African and Asian descent were still owned in Puebla, but most of their kin were not. Slavery would die a slow and unremarkable death over the course of the eighteenth century.

Misrepresentations and Silences

Throughout the colonial period, Puebla emerged as the viceroyalty's second city and site of the richest bishopric. Approximately 100,000 people of all backgrounds, ethnicities and skin colors lived in the city by the 1680s.[16] While contemporary historians have convincingly discredited the myth of Puebla as an exclusively European space ("ciudad de españoles"), local histories simply do not recognize the social, cultural and political importance of the African and Asian populations that toiled as slaves. To date, only one English-language study of slavery exists for Puebla, and that article examined the 1540–1556 period.[17]

This considerable dearth of secondary studies has distorted our understanding of Poblano slavery, but also impacted historians' claims with regard to the operation of the transatlantic slave trade to Mexico. Simply put, we do not know enough about the transatlantic slave trade. We do not understand the extent and profitability of the slave trade in African children and American-born individuals. We especially lack an adequate understanding of how enslaved people navigated the routes that led to slave markets, especially outside of Mexico City. The overrepresentation of Mexico City – perhaps the most unrepresentative of all urban spaces in the Western Hemisphere[18] – has come at the expense of secondary cities, namely Puebla, Querétaro, Guadalajara, Morelia (Valladolid) and Oaxaca (Antequera).[19]

16 Miguel Ángel Cuenya and Carlos Contreras Cruz, *Puebla de los Ángeles: Una ciudad en la historia* (Puebla: Océano/BUAP, 2012), 80.

17 Peter Boyd-Bowman, "Negro Slaves in Colonial Mexico," *The Americas* 26, No. 2 (Oct. 1969), 134–151.

18 Jorge E. Hardoy and Carmen Aravonich, "Urban Scales and Functions in Spanish America toward the Year 1600: First Conclusions," *Latin American Research Review* 5, no. 3 (Autumn 1970): 60. Founded in 1325, Mexico City is unmatched in its concentration of political, economic and religious resources throughout the prehispanic, colonial and modern periods.

19 By contrast, historians of colonial Ecuador and Perú have demonstrated far greater interest in exploring questions of slavery, identity, interracial interactions, and the formation of diasporic communities within smaller settlements. For a sampling of such work see Rachel Sarah O'Toole, *Bound Lives: Africans, Indians and the Making of Race in Colonial Peru* (Pittsburgh: University of Pittsburgh Press, 2012); Sherwin K. Bryant, *Rivers of Gold, Lives of Bondage: Governing through Slavery in Colonial Quito* (Chapel Hill: University of North Carolina Press, 2014); Jean-Paul Tardieu, *El negro en el Cuzco: los*

Throughout this book, I make the argument that the study of slavery in provincial cities, such as Puebla, allows for more useful comparisons of the African diaspora across space and time. Puebla was neither a capital nor a port, yet its entanglement with transatlantic slaving networks is significant. How does our understanding of the slave trade change when we situate Portuguese ship captains and intermediaries outside of ports? Certainly, we expect to find powerful slave trading agents or factors in Veracruz. But what do we make of their continuous presence inland? Such questions can and should be extended to other colonial cities with smaller Spanish and larger indigenous, African and mixed-raced populations, reduced credit markets and fewer governmental institutions vis-à-vis colonial capitals.

Urban Slavery in Colonial Mexico also challenges us to understand the complex negotiation of urban bondage within spaces typically defined as Spanish, indigenous or both. Africans, like their Iberian contemporaries, never constituted demographic majorities in the highlands of Central Mexico. Cognizant of the centrality of indigenous people to the region, this book urges us to consider the history of Afro-indigenous interactions despite the paucity of materials that specifically describe the encounter between Nahua populations and groups of African and Asian descent. Within the Central Mexican context, it is insufficient to understand urban slavery solely from the perspective of the slaveholder and the enslaved. We must also account for interactions between these groups with diverse, urban indigenous populations clustered around specific parishes and barrios.

As Paul Lokken has noted for rural Guatemala, the foundations of slavery were notably eroded through Afro-indigenous interactions during the seventeenth century.[20] This study examines that same dynamic in a city with a diverse indigenous population of displaced native migrants, Chichimec war captives, tribute-paying Nahuas and locked-in textile workers (*encerrados*). Understanding how these loosely defined "indios" interacted with enslaved people and their masters becomes possible within Matthew Restall's proposed framework of informal interculturation.[21] The interplay between slavery and freedom in marketplace interactions, social gatherings and festivities acquires an additional dimension by considering the indigenous experience. By focusing on the enslaved populations that lived, worked,

caminos de la alienación en la segunda mitad del siglo XVII (Lima: Pontificia Universidad Católica del Perú, 1998); Charles Beatty-Medina, "Between the Cross and the Sword: Religious Conquest and Maroon Legitimacy in Colonial Esmeraldas" in *Africans to Spanish America: Expanding the Diaspora*, eds. Sherwin K. Bryant, Rachel Sarah O'Toole and Ben Vinson III (Urbana: University of Illinois Press, 2012), 95–113.

20 Paul Lokken, "Marriage as Slave Emancipation in Seventeenth-Century Rural Guatemala," *The Americas* 58, no. 2 (Oct. 2001): 175–200.

21 Matthew Restall, "Black Slaves, Red Paint" in *Beyond Black and Red: African-Native Relations in Colonial Latin America* (Albuquerque: University of New Mexico Press, 2005), 4–10.

married, bartered, fought, played, cleaned, bathed, cooked or otherwise simply called Puebla home, I raise new questions about Afro-indigenous relationships, cultural mixture and coexistence among enslaved and nominally free groups.

Race and Slavery

Although discussions on race necessarily factor into this investigation, the focus of this study is not on *race* per se, but on the spaces where urban slavery predominated and the specific mechanisms used to enhance or mitigate slaveholder power. My intent is not to reify the association between slavery and African and Asian populations, but to present a new understanding of how slavery operated and how it was challenged in urban Mexico. Historians understand that most (but not all) slaveholders were Spaniards and that they benefited enormously from the labor and prestige that owning other human beings signified. What to date has not been properly analyzed are the relationships that emerged between enslaved people of African and indigenous descent and the interactions of enslaved Asians with both of these groups.

Of course, race and slavery are inextricably intertwined, although there is considerable dissent on what exactly the first term signified in the seventeenth century. In the Mexican colonial context, "race" does not refer to the pseudoscientific classifications that came to the fore in the eighteenth and nineteenth centuries. Moreover, the term *raza* is virtually absent from the documentation used for this study. What is race, then? James Sweet argues that Iberians' notions of racial difference stemmed from medieval ideas that sub-Saharan Africans' "inferior culture implied a biologically inferior people."[22] In turn, skin color served as "an insignia of race . . . an indelible marker of cultural, and thus, racial inferiority." For Rachel O'Toole, colonial caste categories (such as *negro, mulata,* or *indio*) "did the work of race" by articulating difference and power among indigenous people, Africans and Spaniards.[23] Sherwin Bryant contends that race should be studied as a "colonial practice of governance" that "circumscribed black social life and interiority."[24] By contrast, Douglas Cope posits that race was not the driving principle of social organization among plebeians, but "a shorthand summation" of an individual's social network.[25]

22 James Sweet, "The Iberian Roots of American Racist Thought," *William and Mary Quarterly* 54, no. 1 (Jan. 1997): 144–145.

23 Rachel Sarah O'Toole, *Bound Lives*, 164–170.

24 Sherwin K. Bryant, *Rivers of Gold*, 47, 162 n. 9.

25 Douglas R. Cope, *The Limits of Racial Domination* (Madison: University of Wisconsin Press, 1994), 82–83.

I offer no sweeping revision of these authors' conceptions of race or racial difference, other than to note that all of the definitions above factored into slavery in Puebla. Most slaveholders in Puebla were Spaniards, who indeed believed they were culturally superior to the darker-skinned people they possessed. These beliefs needed to be supported through laws and ordinances that codified governance and slavery, "one of the most extreme forms of the relation of domination," in order to constrain the claims of the enslaved to personhood and family.[26] The genealogies of captives born in Africa and Asia were disregarded in order to render them individuals subject to enslavement. As in most Spanish American domains, slavery in colonial Mexico followed the Roman concept of *partus sequitur ventrem* by which a child inherited the mother's legal status. The relative stability of this model of slavery is not in question. In the Poblano context, however, slavery itself was malleable and highly contingent on the spaces in which enslaved people were expected to operate. Thus, I contend that space must be factored into discussions of race, caste and urban bondage.

In this book, I follow Alex Borucki's engagement of racial categories or caste labels for Spanish America in the sense that "people subjugated by slavery . . . acted and expressed themselves according to the categories available to them" during the sixteenth and seventeenth centuries.[27] Enslaved and free people manipulated these categories at different times and settings to advance specific objectives. Ben Vinson refers to these strategies as "racial pluralism," by which one same individual could live multiple "racial lives."[28] In Puebla, slaveholders consistently made use of the terms *negro, negra, mulato* and *mulata* to identify individuals whom they deemed enslaveable, even if the latter or their children secured their freedom later on. Free people of African descent consciously adopted competing labels (*pardo, parda, moreno, morena*) to distance themselves from the stigma of enslavement.[29] In seventeenth century Puebla, these labels denoted freedom. Individuals claiming "pardoness" are therefore largely absent from notorious slave spaces, such as textile mills. By contrast, slaveholders used the terms *chino* and *china* through most of the seventeenth century to describe enslaved people of Asian descent. Free Asian people

---

26 Orlando Patterson, *Slavery and Social Death: A Comparative Study* (Cambridge, MA: Harvard University Press, 1982), 1.

27 Alex Borucki, From *Shipmates to Soldiers: Black Identities in the Río de la Plata* (Albuquerque: University of New Mexico Press, 2015), 19.

28 Ben Vinson III, "Estudiando las razas desde la periferia: las castas olvidadas del sistema colonial mexicano (lobos, moriscos, coyotes, moros y chinos), in *Pautas de convivencia étnica en la América Latina colonial* (Mexico City: UNAM/CCyDEL/Gobierno del Estado de Guanajuato, 2005), 262–272.

29 Although common in the Andean region to identify people of Afro-indigenous parents, use of the term *zambo* or *zambaigo* was infrequent in colonial Mexico.

did not make use of a competing label because many adopted the *indio* or *india* labels instead.[30]

In Puebla, the *indio* and *india* category quickly came to identify people with civic rights and tributary obligations as members of the "República de Indios." Lidia Gómez has demonstrated that *indio* did not specify an ethnic identity,[31] but in Central Mexico it did mark people who theoretically could no longer be legally enslaved after 1550. The terms *español* or *española* firmly marked people whose combined ancestry, skin color and social standing exempted them from slavery. Individuals falling in to the *mestizo, mestiza, castizo* or *castiza* categories were typically assumed to be of partial Spanish and indigenous ancestry and thus also unenslaveable. Other racial categories were decidedly unstable (*morisca, lobo, coyote*) and could not firmly denote slavery or freedom, which perhaps explains why they appear far less frequently in slavery-related documentation. Vinson has established the malleable, socially contingent nature of all the terms above and especially for less common designations.[32]

In the following chapters, however, my focus is on the enslaved, with little regard for their ascribed racial or caste labels. While highlighting the colonial experiences of people of African descent, I nonetheless intend to respect the overarching cultural, juridical and social differences that led certain of these individuals to be differentiated and to differentiate themselves from one another. I therefore use the term "Afro-Poblano" cautiously and only when a particular set of circumstances generally affected all people of African descent in Puebla (municipal decrees, purity of blood statutes and so forth). My intent is not to downplay the importance of an individual's "race thinking," but to highlight the significance of linguistic fluency, religious organization, social networks and local barrio politics among enslaved people.

The focus on people subjected to slavery and their families (as opposed to members of ascribed racial categories) means that I adopt an alternative approach to discussions of exogamy, cultural reproduction and political consciousness. I am not interested in rates of *mulato-mestiza* or Angolan-Kongolese marriage, but in interactions between free grooms and enslaved brides and vice versa. When describing interactions between Africans and Asians, I highlight the commonality of their experiences as enslaved people, which in turns helps explain the historiographical conflation

30 Tatiana Seijas, *Asian Slaves in Colonial Mexico: From Chinos to Indians* (Cambridge: Cambridge University Press, 2014), 171–172.
31 Lidia E. Gómez García, "El impacto de la secularización de las parroquias en los pueblos indios del obispado de Puebla, siglos XVII–XVIII," in *Palafox, Obra y Legado: Memorias del ciclo de conferencias sobre la vida y obra de Juan de Palafox y Mendoza* (Puebla: Instituto Municipal de Arte y Cultura de Puebla, 2011), 216 n. 8.
32 Vinson, "Estudiando las razas."

of both groups. By focusing on a single city and thousands of locally rooted actors and documents, I address the formation of families within slavery.

During the seventeenth century, slavery in Puebla became dependent on harnessing the reproductive capabilities of enslaved females, and especially of Afro-Poblanas. Jennifer Morgan's study on enslaved women, childbirth and the ensuing "web of expectations" in colonial South Carolina and Barbados urges us to consider how these sexual dynamics operated elsewhere – in this case, in Mexican urban centers.[33] In Puebla, textile mill owners attempted to influence their laborers' marital choices and profit from the reproductive capabilities of enslaved women. Simultaneously, enslaved men of all colors and backgrounds sought out free women as spouses and as mothers of freeborn children. The latter process accelerated the growth of free families to an unprecedented degree. Thus, securing the freedom of childbearing women and prepubescent girls became of paramount importance for enslaved families. Enslaved men and women within the same city, household and family encountered different slaveries, limitations and expectations.

As a study of a specific urban center through time, I propose an alternate understanding of the mid-to-late seventeenth century in colonial Puebla based on the experiences of enslaved families. Slaves of African and Asian descent successfully challenged their bondage during the 1660–1700 period. I emphasize the actions of nuclear and extended families in making strategic use of flight, marriage, baptism, birthright and manumission by cross-referencing thousands of notarial and parochial references with highly detailed judicial and Inquisitorial files. At times, these strategies and practices coincided with those of slave owners. For instance, both slaveholders and enslaved parents benefited by securing formal apprenticeships for free and enslaved boys who would become journeymen and, perhaps, master artisans. More frequently, however, enslaved families pursued a combination of liberating strategies across two or more generations that allowed them to eliminate or, at the very least, significantly reduce their ties to a slaveholding household. Securing the trust of parish priests was essential to this end.

Spaces of Slavery

To study Poblano slavery is to engage differing, site-specific modalities of bondage. Space impacted the opportunities and motivations of the enslaved and their masters. Churches, elite residences and hospitals (to

---

33 Jennifer L. Morgan, *Laboring Women: Reproduction and Gender in New World Slavery* (Philadelphia: University of Pennsylvania Press, 2004), 4.

name but a few) codified urban interactions far more than ineffective viceregal decrees or municipal ordinances. All these spaces and the social interactions embedded within them became settings for distinctly Spanish American forms of slavery. In Puebla, the first documented encounter between native people and enslaved black men took place in the marketplace. Interaction between African and indigenous groups intensified within the confines of textile workshops (*obrajes*), infamous spaces characterized by overexhaustion, lack of sleep and corporal punishment. A similar dynamic of confinement also operated in the city's convents, although the inner workings of both spaces were radically distinct. Thus, rather than producing a chronologically ordered study, I have opted for a spatially configured perspective of slavery in seventeenth-century Puebla.

This study privileges four urban arenas: the textile mill, the convent, the marketplace and the elite residence. These spaces were scattered throughout the city, although the *traza* (central blocks radiating from the city square) concentrated a higher proportion of slave-owning settings. I have deviated from following a parish-centric approach, often used to study baptismal and marital patterns.[34] These are tried and tested models for demographic history, but often not the best approach to studying the experiences of enslaved families, whose religious records are often dispersed across two or three parishes at a time. Instead, I propose understanding Puebla as a fragmented ensemble of slave communities occupying elite houses, textile workshops, nunneries and places of commerce. These were not necessarily contiguous spaces, as many Poblanos did not own slaves and many workplaces did not make use of slave labor. In other cases, however, an affluent, slave-owning family lived alongside a convent staffed by dozens of enslaved cooks and servants. The enslaved and their masters understood the varying constraints offered by each setting and its occupants.

At times, these spaces of slavery overlapped. For instance, an enslaved domestic working in an elite household would be expected to frequent the marketplace as part of her routine obligations. Her path might take her past a notorious *obraje* in the San José neighborhood or the Limpia Concepción convent, but she would likely not interact with the enslaved workers in either space. Within the marketplace she would encounter enslaved food vendors and coachmen, alongside recently arrived African captives. This was a space of opportunity or debasement depending on the individual actor and his or her social networks. For some, such as the fish vendor María de Terranova, the marketplace represented a space in which to outcompete former masters and contest her bondage. For others, it was nothing more than

---

34 I have also opted not to follow studies of the colonial city as a set of ecological zones, see Rosalva Loreto López, "Los artífices de una ciudad: Los indios y sus territorialidades, Puebla de los Ángeles 1777," in *Los indios y las ciudades de Nueva España* (Mexico City: UNAM, 2010), 255–277.

yet another public venue in which overbearing men and women prodded their bodies prior to purchase.

In Puebla, the physical presence of the enslaved was not restricted to a specific neighborhood or parish, just as their social interactions were rarely hindered by racially specific ordinances. Most female slaves of African and Asian descent enjoyed considerable spatial mobility within city limits, whereas men were allowed wide latitude outside of Puebla as muleteers and coachmen. As the seventeenth century progressed, ex-slaves and freeborn people gradually moved out of Puebla's central parishes and bought lands or requested urban plots in peripheral indigenous neighborhoods, such as Analco. The spatial motivations for such initiatives are clear. Free people left spaces of slavery for more neutral sites, which also offered lower rents and accessible plots of land. Establishing the residential patterns of the formerly enslaved, however, is only possible by piecing together thousands of shreds of evidence from many different archives.

Methodology

Since the early 2000s, research on the Afro-Mexican experience has certainly moved into the realm of cultural history and a more anthropological approach that questions the motivations, biases and power embedded in the archive.[35] Herman Bennett, in particular, argues that a new approach focused on black community formation is necessary, even as it disrupts or contradicts nation-centric narratives. In his perspective, slavery was simply one aspect of the multifaceted lives of individuals of African descent in Mexico. By drawing on ecclesiastical sources and Inquisition cases, Bennett convincingly demonstrates that enslaved Africans and their descendants wielded a tripartite identity as royal vassals, personal property and people with souls.[36]

In the opening vignette to this book, Sebastiana Paramos certainly presents herself as far more than an enslaved person. Yet, as an unwed person, she is all but invisible in the city's marital registers. Her story reaches us through the mundane transactions of the notarial archive. Thus, attempts to decenter narratives of slavery from the Afro-Mexican experience have the collateral effect of eliding sources that reveal priceless fragments of negotiation and resilience. In the case of this book, many of these sources

---

35 Joan Cameron Bristol, *Christians, Blasphemers and Witches: Afro-Mexican Ritual Practice in the Seventeenth Century* (Albuquerque: University of New Mexico Press, 2007); María Elena Martínez, *Genealogical Fictions: Limpieza de Sangre, Religion and Gender in Colonial Mexico* (Stanford, CA: Stanford University Press, 2008); Laura Lewis, *Chocolate and Corn Flour: History, Race and the Making of Place in the Making of "Black" Mexico* (Durham, NC: Duke University Press, 2012).

36 Herman Bennett, *Africans in Colonial Mexico: Absolutism, Christianity and Afro-Creole Consciousness, 1570–1640* (Bloomington: University of Indiana Press, 2005).

are drawn from a vast notarial archive, a problematic one to say the least. To borrow from Vincent Brown, "our data are debased, compiled from the records of the slavers, the racists, the exploiters and their bureaucrats."[37] The bureaucrats in this book are certainly the notarial scribes, whose "paper proved the condition of bondage and made it legally meaningful" in Iberia and Spanish America.[38] Most of Puebla's bills of slave purchase, manumission letters and promissory notes are indeed the mediated work of slavers and exploiters.[39] But that alone must not keep scholars from reconstructing the motivations of slave holders or the positionality of the oppressed. In following Joseph Miller, "I want also to acknowledge, robustly, the historical contexts in which both parties, masters and slaves, were trying to influence not only the other but also others around them."[40]

Reconstructing the motivations of captors and captives is undoubtedly difficult and requires documentary breadth and depth. Fortunately, the Puebla archives contain such materials. In order to recover the fragments of information on enslaved people, I built a notarial database with 9,295 entries. Each entry features an individual's age, birthplace or provenance, occupation, familial relations and owners.[41] These references are not restricted to bills of slave purchase, but also consider promissory notes, apprenticeship contracts, inventories and testaments. By looking past the Puebla slave market, these sources allow us to understand patron-client relationships, the emergence and empowerment of freedmen and the cycle of debt-labor that characterized the lives of many ex-slaves. The notarial database is also helpful in tracing the motivations of slave owners, their dismemberment of enslaved families and the cold economic rationale behind many of their decisions.

My calculations on the slave market derive from the six local notarial offices found in the Archivo General de Notarías de Puebla (AGNP) that preserve an uninterrupted history of real estate purchases, bills of slave purchase, rental agreements and manumissions. Given the hundreds of uncatalogued boxes of extant colonial documents, I reduced the material consulted

37 Vincent Brown, "Mapping a Slave Revolt: Visualizing Spatial History through the Archives of Slavery," *Social Text* 125 (2005): 138.
38 Nancy E. van Deusen, *Global Indios: The Indigenous Struggle for Justice in Sixteenth-Century Spain* (Durham, NC: Duke University Press, 2015), 128.
39 Brown, "Mapping," 138.
40 Joseph C. Miller, *The Problem of Slavery as History: A Global Approach* (New Haven, CT: Yale University Press, 2012), 19.
41 During my time in Puebla, I was fortunate to encounter Prof. Guillermo A. Rodríguez Ortíz in the notarial archive. Together we digitized thousands of documents related to slavery in Puebla, many of which were used to construct this notarial database and to create an informal finding guide of sorts. For his historical demography of the city, see "El lado afro de la Puebla de los Ángeles. Un acercamiento al estudio sobre la presencia africana, 1595–1710," Doctoral dissertation (Benemérita Universidad Autónoma de Puebla, 2015), 175–231.

by studying one out of every five years within the notarial archive for the period 1590–1700.[42] The end result was a 20 percent sample of Puebla's six notarial offices. In this manner, my analysis of the years 1600 and 1605 can be used to represent the period 1600–1609 and so forth. By pointing out trends in slave purchases, I move past the traditional periodization of the Portuguese slaving licenses (1595–1639) and the poorly studied slave trade that followed (1640–1700). I am cognizant of the limitations of such an approach. For instance, fluctuations in slave purchases and prices undoubtedly took place within years between my observations. Nonetheless, this methodology has been useful in producing an extended perspective that approximates Poblanos' continued dependence on slave labor throughout the seventeenth century.

Urban Slavery in Colonial Mexico complements analysis of notarial sources with municipal, judicial, ecclesiastical and inquisitorial documents. The parochial sources used in this study represent only a fraction of the information available on enslaved people in colonial Puebla. Still, I have amassed considerable data by analyzing 4,407 marriages and 3,330 baptisms from 1585 to 1700. Through three years of on-site research, I was able to gain access to the records of the Sagrario Metropolitano, Santo Angel Custodio (Analco) and San José parishes. I focused my parochial research on marriages and baptisms, but did not attempt to produce a demographic history of Asians or Afro-Poblanos. Most of the references to enslaved individuals surface in racially segregated registers such as the "Book of black, mulatto and chino marriages" or sometimes, simply as "Black baptisms." In cases where parochial registers for Puebla's black or Asian population are missing, I have located scattered references to freedmen and their children in "Spanish" and "Indian" registers. Unfortunately, the Archivo del Provisorato, the repository that presumably contains the bishopric's marital petitions, confraternity records and other priceless documents, remained closed to the academic community during the years (2009–2012) in which this research was conducted.

The Archivo General Municipal de Puebla (AGMP) holds official information on city ordinances, municipal matters and viceregal taxation and, as such, represents the unrealized ideal of urban planning and governance. In many ways, the Archivo Histórico Judicial de Puebla (AHJP) holds an opposite type of evidence. Within its collections, enslaved people sue abusive owners, negotiate letters of liberation, or contest their innocence when accused of crimes. Many testaments produced by free men and women are found within its collections. The combination of municipal, parochial and judicial sources with notarial data has allowed me to partially reconstruct

---

42 Tulane University's Latin American Library also holds a series of seventeenth-century notarial documents from Puebla that were used to complement my research in the AGNP.

the lives of free and enslaved people and their families. Only by patching together the fragments found in local archives are we able to learn about remarkable freedmen and women such as Felipe Monsón y Mojica and María de Terranova (see Chapter 6).

Whenever possible I have also included references from documents produced in the Nahuatl language. Although my knowledge of Nahuatl remains rudimentary, I find that including information culled from translated *xiuhpohualli*, or indigenous annals, is an essential element of this academic exercise. These annals often contain information that Spanish chroniclers opted to ignore in their retelling of local history. Scholars of the Puebla-Tlaxcala Valley are fortunate in that an entire family of Nahuatl annals have survived and, thus, provide an explicitly urban, indigenous perspective of colonial life.[43] Thus, the Nahuatl transcriptions and translations of Susan Schroeder, Lidia Gómez García, Camilla Townsend and other ethnohistorians are of paramount importance to this project.

Outline

In Chapter 1, I describe a growing black population that entered colonial Mexico within the context of extreme indigenous depopulation. As smallpox and typhus epidemics decimated native groups during the sixteenth century, Spaniards demanded ever-larger numbers of slaves to compensate for indigenous losses. Within central Mexico, the arrival of thousands of African captives soon gave way to concerns over Afro-indigenous interactions, particularly between enslaved black men and free native women. Elite Spaniards articulated these anxieties through municipal decrees and ordinances that reflected a simultaneous fear and dependence on slave labor. Puebla's slave registry, the *Caja de negros*, reveals a significant commitment to defining slavery in relation to people of African descent.

Chapter 2 examines how slavery, confinement, interethnic relations and coercion were intermeshed in the *obraje* or textile mill. Beginning in the late sixteenth century, *obrajes* dominated the local economy and connected Puebla to a vast Spanish American trade network. In the harshest urban setting, Asian and African slaves worked, slept and ate along exploited indigenous migrants and debtors. This chapter seeks a new understanding of the culture and politics of the *obraje*. How, for instance, should we understand the sacrament of matrimony in such a coercive setting? We must also situate the shifting expectations that textile mill owners had for enslaved

---

43 Frances Krug and Camilla Townsend, "The Tlaxcala-Puebla Family of Annals," in *Sources and Methods for the Study of Postconquest Mesoamerican Ethnohistory*, eds. James Lockhart, Lisa Sousa and Stephanie Wood (electronic version: http://whp.uoregon.edu, 2008), 1–11.

women as Portuguese independence temporarily closed off the transatlantic slave trade. Finally, I contend that the gradual shift to all-slave workforces in textile mills was politically motivated and directly tied to inclusivity in municipal governance.

In Chapter 3, I explore the demands of elite society for enslaved servants in Puebla's nunneries. In focusing on these sacred micro-societies, I suggest that slavery formed a cultural expectation among affluent novices and nuns of the black veil. Enslaved girls and women toiled alongside hundreds of free servants, laywomen and white-veiled nuns in female convents, but their status as human property complicated nuns' vows to poverty and withdrawal from the secular world. Moreover, I seek to answer the following questions: How did urban slavery differ within the confines of the convent (*intramuros*)? Did unfree servants enjoy greater spatial mobility than their cloistered mistresses? Finally, I expose the contentious negotiations between nuns as representatives of slaveholding families and convents as religious corporations bent on retaining the enslaved servants of deceased nuns at the end of the seventeenth century.

Chapter 4, based on an extensive notarial database, proves that at least 20,000 men, women and children were sold on the Puebla slave market during the seventeenth century (1600–1700). After studying the actions of the *encomendero de negros*, a specialized slaving agent-on-comission, I propose several revisions to the historiography of the slave trade to Mexico. Puebla became an essential inland node for transatlantic slaving networks because Lusophone slave traders extended credit to elite and middling members of society. In turn, slave sales only peaked in the 1620s and 1630s, decades in which West Central Africans and smaller groups of Asian captives were forced into the city in large numbers. Poblano demand for slaves did not end with Portuguese independence in 1640. Instead, slaveholders turned to creole (American-born) slaves to produce and demonstrate wealth and power. By the 1680s, a reinvigorated trade in creole slaves and, to a lesser degree, Lower Guinean captives saturated the city's notarial registers once more.

Chapter 5 focuses on the complex social, economic and religious interactions that enslaved people in Puebla sustained among themselves and their free counterparts in elite residences and other non-confining spaces. I examine questions of spatial mobility, gender and trust to analyze family life in the difficult years after the 1612 slave conspiracy. Afro-Poblano social networks largely counteracted the discriminatory decrees of the 1620s and 1630s. Through mid-century interactions with local priests and religious brotherhoods, enslaved people secured claims to family (motherhood, fatherhood and godparentage) within slavery. By the late 1670s, these familal and religious bonds paved the way for generations of freeborn children.

Chapter 6 suggests that the colonial marketplace also served as a space of opportunity for enslaved people. In a profit-driven society, enslaved men and women fractured slaveholder power by outperforming competitors and seeking the highest bidder for their services. Based on three detailed case studies, I demonstrate how slaves and freedmen catered to diverse, multiracial constituencies in the public plaza and in the *baratillo* (second-hand marketplace). Whether selling fish, chile peppers or indigenous textiles, slaves and freedmen secured financial security and social stability for themselves and their families. For enslaved men, strategic marital alliances were essential to these commercial interactions. Finally, the Epilogue lays out the structural limitations of slavery at the dawn of the eighteenth century in Puebla and proposes new avenues for understanding freeborn populations in colonial Mexico's urban settings.

Early Puebla and the Question of Labor, 1531–1570

First, your illustrious grace should know that to date 288 blacks have been registered in this city's caja before us . . . your grace should know that some of the blacks that are registered in this caxa have escaped, they are being procured and bounty hunters are needed for this effect . . . we beg your grace to decree and order that the blacks that are brought from Spain, or Guinea or other parts of this New Spain be registered once more in the cajas of the cities where they will reside.[1]

– Puebla municipal council to Viceroy don Luis de Velasco, 1553

During Puebla's formative years (1531–1570), several hundred enslaved men and women provided the labor needed to maintain its first European households and workshops. In theory, they should not have been there. From its inception Puebla was supposed to be a space free of slaves, especially indigenous slaves. Religious men and government officials planned the city to combat the excesses of the *encomienda* – a system by which the Spanish Crown extended lifetime grants of native laborers and tribute to successful conquistadors. Instead, the colonizers conceptualized Puebla as a space for self-sustaining Spanish nuclear families. A foundational experiment devised by Franciscan and Dominican missionaries and backed by New Spain's Second Audiencia suggested that such an urban utopia might actually succeed. In April 1531, the act of settling (literally, "la puebla") was carried out on an uninhabited plain along the Atoyac River to great fanfare. By 1536, however, Puebla's first residents had already demonstrated a penchant for slave ownership as municipal authorities expressed concern over interactions between free indigenous women and enslaved black men. The fierce debates surrounding the enslavement of indigenous commoners did not extend to black men, women, or children, even in a city designed and committed to antislavery ideals.

---

1 Efraín Castro Morales, ed., *Suplemento de el Libro Número Primero de la Fundación y Establecimiento de la Muy Noble y Leal Ciudad de los Ángeles* (Puebla: Ayuntamiento del Municipio de Puebla, 2009), 162–164.

This chapter draws on personal letters, missionary accounts, and municipal documents to outline the appeal of coerced labor during Puebla's early decades. In avoiding *encomienda* labor, the city's first colonizers developed the *indios de servicio* labor arrangement to access indigenous laborers, while simultaneously investing in the early transatlantic slave trade. In turn, the trade in African captives was complemented by an irregular flow of indigenous slaves, captured and enslaved as rebels throughout northern and western Mexico. Thus, a diverse enslaved population lived in Puebla during the city's first decade despite the ideological commitment to the eradication of indigenous slavery. Although the New Laws of 1542 acknowledged the humanity of Central Mexico's indigenous commoners and gradually allowed for the recognition of some rights, they did nothing to prevent the dehumanization of a growing black population. By the early 1550s, the *caja de negros*, an early slave registry and tax (with its accompanying bounty hunters), betrayed the simultaneous demand for and fear of African captives in early Puebla. Indigenous workers could still be coerced to work for specific individuals, but this chapter argues that the creation of the *caja* established Africans' uncontested permanency as non-indigenous servants and status symbols.

The Foundation of Puebla: A Standard Narrative

Colonial chroniclers and modern historians have produced (and are still revising) numerous versions of just how, when, and why the city of Puebla was founded.[2] The foundational myth remains polemic to this day,[3] although there is relative certainty that thirty Spanish settlers ventured from Mexico City in 1531 to establish a new town on the southeastern side of the Popocatepetl-Iztaccihuatl mountain range. The two dominant religious orders, through the Dominican Fray Julian Garcés and the Franciscan Fray Toribio de Benavente (alias Motolinia), played an influential role in the settlement plan. The conception and execution of the city's founding is generally attributed to Dr. Juan de Salmerón, a trusted advisor to Charles V and an influential member of New Spain's

---

2 The city's colonial chronicles were heavily dependent on municipal documentation, particularly with respect to land and water grants and religious institutions, thus privileging the notion of pious, dual, and all-encompassing Spanish and Indian republics. For republished examples of the genre, see Mariano Joseph Antonio Fernández de Echeverría y Veytia, *Historia de la fundación de la ciudad de la Puebla de los Ángeles en la Nueva España, su descripción y presente estado* (Puebla: Ediciones Altiplano, 1962); Miguel de Alcalá y Mendiola, *Descripción en bosquejo de la imperial cesárea muy noble y muy leal ciudad de Puebla de los Ángeles* (Puebla: BUAP/Fomento Editorial, 1997); Pedro López de Villaseñor, *Cartilla vieja de la nobilísima ciudad de Puebla* (Puebla: Secretaría de Cultura, 2001).

3 For analysis of the numerous accounts and errors related to the city's foundation, see Leopoldo A. García Lastra and Silvia Castellano Gómez, *Utopía angelopolitana: La verdadera historia de la fundación de Puebla de los Ángeles* (Puebla: Secretaría de Cultura/Gobierno del Estado de Puebla, 2008), 73–84.

Second Audiencia. Salmerón provided the official backing and support for a project that threatened the conquistador class and the merchants of Mexico City. He envisioned a neat, efficient city – one that would stand apart from the rest of New Spain in its rejection of the exploitative *encomienda* system.[4] The enslavement of local indigenous populations would not be tolerated. Puebla was to provide a new, Christian model of urban development based on the self-sufficient labor of Spanish nuclear families.

The city's establishment on an uninhabited plain between the indigenous city-states of Tlaxcala and Cholula had a variety of purposes. Logistically, there was the urgent need to settle a population of former conquistadors, military auxiliaries, and servants in a place other than the viceregal capital, Mexico City–Tenochtitlan. Moreover, transforming that floating island-city into a proper European space presented formidable engineering and hydraulic challenges.[5] The appeal of constructing a new, grid-lined city on firm land was obvious. In 1530, Fray Julián Garcés, bishop of Tlaxcala, lamented that not a single Spanish village existed in his entire see, despite the agricultural potential of the surrounding valleys.[6] The plains that separated Tlaxcala, Cholula, and Huexotzingo were soon imagined as an ideal starting place.

The members of New Spain's Second Audiencia advanced the foundation of Puebla along the same humanistic and ideological current that led them to attack the holders of *encomienda* grants. In a 1531 letter to the Crown, the Audiencia characterized Puebla as an ambitious sociopolitical experiment: "For the perpetuity of this land, we have striven to design several models of republics and polities with hopes of correctly choosing one which does not hold Indians in *encomienda*, although everyone, except for the friars, considers this quite difficult to accomplish."[7] In order to succeed, these new models required the physical separation of European and indigenous populations through the creation of two republics. The latter would theoretically inhabit the *república de indios*, while the former would confine themselves to the more city-dependent *república de españoles*.

In practice, such a system could never come to fruition, given the colonizers' dependence on indigenous laborers and tribute. Nonetheless, in the early 1530s, the Puebla experiment aligned nicely with the dual-republic

---

4 Julia Hirschberg, "An Alternative to Encomienda: Puebla's *Indios de Servicio*, 1531–1545," *Journal of Latin American Studies* 11, no. 2 (Nov. 1979), 242–244.

5 John F. López, "'In the Art of My Profession'": Adrian Boot and Dutch Water Management in Colonial Mexico City," *Journal of Latin American Geography* 11 (Spring 2012), 35–36.

6 François Chevalier, "Signification sociale de la fondation de Puebla de los Angeles" *Revista de Historia de América* 23 (1947 Junio), 109–110.

7 Chevalier, "Signification sociale," 112–113. The members of the Audiencia took on other radical, utopian, and *encomienda*-free enterprises, such as the establishment of the Royal College of Tlatelolco for the education of noble indigenous youths and the hospital-town of Santa Fe during the early 1530s.

model that threatened to curtail conquistador power. As *encomienda* holders, the conquistadors attempted to derail the project.[8] Yet the Audiencia members were resolute. Only creating a separate urban center for Spaniards would mitigate the exploitation of the indigenous people. Following Bishop Garcés' pleas, the ideal location was chosen: Cuetlaxcoapan, an uninhabited plain between the indigenous city-states of Tlaxcala and Cholula. Each Spanish head of household would receive twenty indigenous workers, whose temporary labor would be limited to a three-month period.[9] Thereafter, the city's Spaniards would apply themselves to their own destiny, tilling their own crops and building up a new agro-urban model of colonial settlement.

Despite their profound rivalry, the Franciscan and Dominican orders supported the utopian initiative, which granted them greater control over indigenous communities at the expense of the *encomendero* class. On 16 April 1531, the Franciscan Motolinia performed the first mass to celebrate the settlement's foundation on an uninhabited plain along the eastern bank of the San Francisco River. Only thirty-three Spanish men and one widow participated in Puebla's establishment,[10] but an estimated 8,000 natives from Tlaxcala and smaller contingents from Huexotzingo, Calpan, Tepeaca and Cholula also helped erect the city's first houses for a week.[11] Their efforts would be in vain. Heavy rains and a flooding Atoyac River wiped out the settlement later that year, forcing the abandonment of the town.[12] In the fall of 1532, the surrounding communities once more provided the Spaniards with the labor needed for Puebla's second foundation.[13] By this point, the utopian project had been completely written off. Each Spanish household would receive the labor of thirty Indians to build their residences and another twenty to cultivate their fields.[14] Whether this new distribution of labor for construction and agriculture differed in any way from *encomienda* practices is unclear. That a Spanish *vecino* in 1532 could control up to fifty indigenous workers at a time suggests that, in scale at least, there was little to distinguish such a colonizer from a traditional *encomienda* holder.[15]

---

8 Francico del Paso y Troncoso, ed., *Epistolario de Nueva España* (Mexico City: Antigua Librería Robledo de J. Porrúa, 1939), Vol. 3, Doc. 139, 100–101.

9 Chevalier, "Signification sociale," 113–114.   10 Ibid., 23–25.

11 Fausto Marín Tamayo, *La división racial en Puebla de los Ángeles bajo el régimen colonial* (Puebla: Centro de Estudios Históricos de Puebla, 1960), 8–10; Francis Borgia Steck, *Motolinia's History of the Indians of New Spain* (Richmond: Academy of American Franciscan History, 1951), 92.

12 Carlos Contreras Cruz and Miguel Ángel Cuenya, *Puebla de los Ángeles: Una ciudad en la historia* (Puebla: BUAP/Océano, 2012), 15–25. Cuenya and Contreras offer the most complete synthesis of the diverse foundational stories of Puebla.

13 Hirschberg, "Alternative to Encomienda," 245–246.   14 Marín Tamayo, *La división racial*, 15.

15 José Miranda, *La función económica del encomendero en los orígenes del régimen colonial* (Mexico City: UNAM/Instituto de Investigaciones Históricas, 1965), 34–40. Miranda found that when

As unsuccessful as various aspects of the Puebla experiment proved to be, the new settlement did introduce a number of reforms in relation to the use of native laborers. Between 1533 and 1545, Puebla received a weekly, rotating service of 1,200 to 1,300 indigenous workers from Cholula and Tlaxcala, with smaller contingents arriving from Calpan, Huexotzingo and Totimehuacan.[16] Known as *indios de servicio*, these coerced laborers were delivered to a high-ranking official (*corregidor*) in the city on Mondays and Thursdays before being distributed to Spanish heads of household.[17] The system, originally supposed to run for a four-year period (1533–1537), was innovative in that it did not favor the powerful conquistador class in the allotment of indigenous labor. Instead, *indios de servicio* were strategically and temporarily distributed to married Spanish men, preferably those who did not hold political office and had not participated in the military conquest of the region.[18] The initial round of experimentation with the system was successful, as representatives for the Puebla municipal government were able to secure the program's renewal for two further terms (1537–1541 and 1541–1545).

Native laborers in Puebla were not subjected to outright slavery under the *indios de servicio* system, although working conditions approximated it. In 1539, New Spain's viceroy (acting on instructions from Madrid) ordered Puebla's early colonists to treat their indigenous workers "as men and not as beasts."[19] The order also stipulated that *indios de servicio* were to be properly fed by Spaniards, suggesting that the workers had been required to procure their own meals during the previous six years. By 1541, the city's municipal authorities entered an agreement with those of Cholula. The former agreed not to demand night work from their weekly allotment of indigenous laborers.[20] In order to prevent or at least mitigate these abuses, specialized judges (*jueces de indios*) were appointed to oversee labor arrangements in Puebla during the 1540s. In 1545, the Crown officially ended the *indios de servicio* system, perhaps a reflection of a growing commitment to the ideals behind the New Laws of 1542.

---

establishing commercial partnerships with one another, *encomienda* holders routinely contributed between 50 and 100 slaves as their portion of the investment.

16 Hirschberg, "Alternative to Encomienda," 252–253.   17 Ibid., 247.

18 Ibid., 255–256. Approximately 67 percent of the Spanish men receiving *indios de servicio* were married, another 11.3 percent were widowed. Single men accounted for only 2.6 percent of the total. In many cases this meant establishing formal, Church-sanctioned unions with noble indigenous women, as Spanish brides were particularly scarce at this time. For the inclusion of mestizo children women into Puebla's early "Spanish" population, see Elizabeth Anne Kuznesof, "More Conversation on Race, Class, and Gender," *Colonial Latin American Review* 5, no. 1 (1996), 129–134.

19 AGI, México, 1088, 113v cited in Hirschberg, "Alternative to Encomienda," 253.

20 Ibid., 254.

In theory, Fray Bartolomé de las Casas led the successful fight against the enslavement of Mexico's native populations and the abolition of the *encomienda*, which culminated with the New Laws of 1542. The laws established that the indigenous inhabitants of Spanish America were to be treated as subjected vassals, not slaves. They were to pay tribute to the Crown, but were entitled to legal protections, specialized law courts, and attorneys. Enforcing the humane application of the New Laws proved an entirely different matter. Indigenous resistance to Spanish rule in Western Mexico led to the Mixtón War of 1540–1542, which produced 4,700 native war captives.[21] Viceroy Antonio de Mendoza personally participated in the suppression and subsequent distribution of these slaves. Several of these captives were sold in Puebla during the early 1540s, many of them labeled as "Jalisco" slaves.[22] In this regard, the appointment of Sancho Ordoñez's as Puebla's *corregidor* in 1541 likely facilitated the acquisition of indigenous slaves. Ordoñez had personally assisted Mendoza in "the last pacification of Jalisco."[23] Although data for these early years is fragmentary, Blanca Lara Tenorio located sales for thirty-nine indigenous slaves in Puebla for the 1545–1552 period.[24]

The abolishment of indigenous slavery and the application of the New Laws would be difficult to accomplish during the mid-1540s in Puebla and throughout the viceroyalty. The Puebla city council even gathered funds in April 1544 to fund Mexico City's efforts to have the laws repealed.[25] In late 1546, Las Casas was forced to reassert the importance of immediately abolishing indigenous slavery before Viceroy Mendoza and Francisco Tello de Sandoval, a powerful inspecting official.[26] Actual changes were very slow in coming to the viceroyalty, but by the mid-1550s it became clear that Crown officials would challenge indigenous enslavement. This did not mean that native people were exempt from coerced labor. The Nahuas of central

21 Andres Reséndez, *The Other Slavery: The Uncovered Story of Indian Enslavement in America* (Boston: Houghton Mifflin Harcourt, 2016), 68–71.

22 Blanca Lara Tenorio, *La esclavitud en Puebla y Tepeaca, 1545–1649* (Mexico City: Cuadernos de los Centros INAH, 1976), 46.

23 Salvador Cruz, *Alonso Valiente: Conquistador de Nueva España y poblador de la Ciudad de Puebla de los Ángeles* (Mexico City: H. Ayuntamiento del Municipio de Puebla, 1992), 114.

24 Lara Tenorio, *La esclavitud en Puebla*, 46–47.

25 Efraín Castro Morales, ed., *Suplemento de el Libro Número dos de el Mismo Establecimiento y Dilatación de la Ciudad* (Puebla: H. Ayuntamiento del Municipio de Puebla, 2010), 205–207.

26 Reséndez, The Other Slavery, 68–70; Isacio Pérez Fernández, *Fray Bartolomé de las Casas, O.P. De defensor de los indios a defensor de los negros* (Salamanca: Editorial San Esteban, 1995), 36–37, 42–43, 73, 92–93, 130–131. Even as he agitated for the end of indigenous slavery, Las Casas requested and received the rights to transport 24 black slaves to his newly appointed bishopric in Chiapas (southern New Spain) in 1543. Yet, by 1555, the Dominican had retracted his call for substituting indigenous slaves with Africans as he found the latter's captivity equally unjust. Five years later, Las Casas laid out a stern critique of the early transatlantic trade in his *Historia de las Indias*.

Mexico would still be subjected to the weekly rotation of *repartimiento* work and outright captivity and enslavement if considered to be in rebellion. However, according to Rik Hoekstra, the *repartimiento* was used sparingly in Puebla. "Only religious constructions – especially the cathedral – in Puebla and the farms in the valley of Atlixco were regularly supplied with [repartimiento] labourers" during the late sixteenth and early seventeenth centuries.[27]

Over the course of the 1540s and 1550s, thousands of Tlaxcalans and Cholulans established themselves in makeshift ethnic neighborhoods surrounding the Puebla's central neighborhood, or *traza*. Drawn by the possibility of earning wages and evading tribute obligations, native people gradually consolidated these areas into formal neighborhoods (*barrios de indios*) with their respective ethnic affiliations and churches. The Tlaxcalans settled the eastern side of the city near the Franciscan convent and other residential areas, while migrants from Cholula and Huexotzingo settled the San Agustín neighborhood. The indigenous constituted the bulk of a permanent urban workforce by the late 1550s, but would not satisfy the demands of absolute and permanent servitude so desired by the colonizers. As nominally free people with rights, wages, and political representation, the indigenous residents of Puebla began to distinguish their experiences from those of enslaved Africans.[28]

Slavery, Power and "Vecindad"

Despite innovating with the *indios de servicio* system, Puebla's early settlers were also consumers and distributors of slave labor. A close reading of Puebla's early municipal ordinances suggests that the city founders sought to define the gendered and racialized contours of slavery as early as 1536. In other words, enslaved black men were present in Puebla no less than four to five years after its foundation. The earliest evidence of an enslaved population in Puebla also serves as the first direct reference to a population of African descent. These municipal minutes, or *Actas de Cabildo*, document an elite Spanish perspective on colonial urban life, race relations, and social hierarchies and, as such, should be treated with caution. Local councilmen would have been especially concerned with portraying the city's treatment of indigenous people in a favorable light in order to renew the *indios de servicio* system. It is at this intersection that council members offered their first portrayal of black men in Puebla:

27 Rik Hoekstra, *Two Worlds Merging: The Transformation of Society in the Valley of Puebla, 1570–1640* (Amsterdam: CEDLA, 1993), 130–131.
28 Marín Tamayo, *La división racial*, 34–37; Lidia Gómez García, "Las fiscalías en la ciudad de los Ángeles, siglo XVII," in *Los indios y las ciudades* (Mexico City: UNAM, 2010), 177–181.

In the City of Angels of this New Spain on the twenty-eighth day of February 1536, the members of the city council ordered that as far as the city's tianguiz [marketplace] is concerned, it is noted that ~~spaniards~~ and black men go to it and cause great harm and rifts, and that the market's indian women are harmed, therefore it is to be proclaimed that no ~~spaniard~~ nor black man may go to the tianguiz. A fine of one gold peso from the mines will be charged [to the infractor], a third of which will be given to the accuser, one third to the city's [public] works, and the other third to the sentencing judge. This is understood [to apply] ~~to the neighbors~~ and residents of this city. The lieutenant shall see to it that if a ~~spaniard~~ harm the indian women in the tianguiz he shall pay the said fine and that if the owner of the black man does not desire to pay the fine, then he [the black man] will be given fifty lashes in the plaza.[29]

This initial reference to an African presence in Puebla is significant for a number of reasons. First, the ordinance, one that protected indigenous women in the marketplace, targeted both black and white men. Over an unspecified period, the general condemnation of male behavior became a racially specific law with differing penalties and consequences. Within the document, the term Spaniard was crossed out in every instance (see transcription above).[30] We do not know when the document was altered or by whom. Nor can we confirm that the alteration affected the towncrier's proclamation of the 1536 ordinance in front of the municipal palace. What is uncontestable, however, is that this first legal reference to black men in Puebla assumed that *negros* were slaves. Only a slave owner could pay the fine to liberate a black man. The ability to pay or not pay for a perceived marketplace aggression was not conceptualized as a possibility for black men.[31]

Second, the 1536 ordinance envisions the male black body as subject to corporal punishment in contrast to the monetary fines imposed on Spanish men for the same crime. The public nature of these "fifty lashes" fall within the theatrical displays of violence that characterized conquest society. Just

29 Archivo General Municipal de Puebla (AGMP), Actas de Cabildo, Vol. 4, f. 137/135r, 1536/02/28. "En este dia los dichos señores ordenaron y mandaron que por quanto en el tianguiz de la ciudad los ~~españoles~~ y negros que a el van hacen mucho daño e bellaquas y las yndias del tianguiz reciben daño, por tanto mandaron que se pregone publicamente que ningun ~~español~~ de la çiudad ~~ni~~ negro en ninguna manera vaya a el dicho tianguiz, so pena de un peso de oro de minas, la tercera parte para el acusador, y la tercera parte para obras de la dicha ciudad, y la otra tercera parte para el juez que lo sentenciare. Y esto se entiende ~~a los vecinos~~ y estantes en la dicha ciudad y veráel tenientedesde el dia que sea pregone y si algun ~~español~~ hiciere daño a las yndias en el dho tianguiz que pague la dicha pena y que si su amo del negro no quisiere pagar la pena le den cincuenta azotes en la plaza."
30 Ibid. The term *vecino* only appeared once in the document, but it was also crossed out. The fact that "*residente*" was left intact hints at the possibility of outsiders disrupting the market's operations.
31 How this ordinance would have affected free black, mulatto, mestizo, or indigenous men is uncertain.

as the burning and dogging of indigenous priests in nearby Cholula was intended to instill dread and obedience in Nahua populations,[32] the whipping of black men served as a cautionary tale for other males of African descent who frequented the marketplace. Comparable municipal laws from Quito, Ecuador, suggest that similar punishments were enforced on black men frequenting indigenous villages and marketplaces outside of Mexico during the mid-1530s.[33] In 1555, another Puebla municipal ordinance stipulated that indigenous, black and mestizo men caught purchasing or selling adulterated *grana cochinilla* (cochineal) would receive 100 lashes in public, in addition to paying a 200-peso fine. Spanish men prosecuted for the same offense would only pay the monetary fine. In this sense, the absence of corporal punishment for Spanish males suggests that the white body would not be subjected to such public debasement (at least within the framework of municipal justice) during the mid-sixteenth century.[34] The misbehavior of Spanish men merely carried a fine, one that would theoretically benefit the city, accuser, local judge, and victimized indigenous women. No such benefit could be expected from the lashes inflicted on an enslaved black man. Evidently, most slaveholders would go to significant lengths to prevent such crippling punishment upon their human property. What is significant here is the early institutionalization of corporal punishment for black men.

The gendered overtones of the 1536 ordinance also foreshadow the authorities' concern over Afro-indigenous interactions at the local level. The ordinance identified blacks as male (*negros*) and natives as female (*indias*). This characterization of Puebla's African and indigenous populations may have in fact been accurate within the boundaries of the marketplace (*tianguiz*). However, the absence of indigenous men in the 1536 ordinance poses a vexing problem. Are we to assume the early colonial *tianguiz* was devoid of indigenous men? Were native women not harassed by native men in the marketplace? Or is it possible that native men were simply expressing their grievances to a compliant municipal council? This last scenario is plausible when taking into consideration Puebla's 1537 lobbying for a renewed grant of the *indios de servicio* system. Moreover, in that same year, the municipal council appointed an indigenous official (*alguacil de tianguis*) to oversee the marketplace and mitigate abuses.[35] In order to retain the weekly allotment of laborers, Puebla municipal authorities had to

32 Lori Boornazian Diel, "Manuscrito del aperreamiento (Manuscript of the Dogging): A 'Dogging' and Its Implications for Early Colonial Cholula," *Ethnohistory* 58, no. 4 (Fall 2011), 585–611.

33 Sherwin K. Bryant, *Rivers of Gold, Lives of Bondage: Governing through Slavery in Colonial Quito* (Chapel Hill: University of North Carolina Press, 2014), 29. The Quito town council decreed 100 lashes for any "Blacks found in the indigenous marketplace."

34 Echeverría y Veyta, *Historia de la* fundación, I, 298.

35 AGMP, Actas de Cabildo, Vol. 3, f. 240 cited in Marín Tamayo, *La división racial*, 35.

prove to the Crown and governing elites of Cholula and Tlaxcala that native people were being treated well within city limits. The symbolic extension of an ordinance protecting native women from black interlopers would have shored up support for Puebla's original mission and signaled a commitment to indigenous rights at a crucial moment in the city's development.

During the mid-sixteenth century, elite Spaniards struggled to govern Afro-indigenous dynamics. New Spain's viceroys would even attempt to curtail harmonious interactions between both groups.[36] The growing presence of black men (and women) in the viceroyalty complicated an illusory dual-republic model that was never adapted to accommodate a third, black republic. Given the lack of an official stance by the Crown or the viceroy on such matters, municipal governments had free rein to craft their own racially defined ordinances and punishments. More often than not, the results were lamentable. Suffice it to say that the earliest legislation on Puebla's African-descent population defined black men as criminal slaves subject to corporal punishment.

If the 1536 ordinance identified black men as enslaved people, it failed to account for free Afro-Poblano individuals who would have bristled at the decree's connotations. On the other hand, there is the very real possibility that free people of African descent simply could not be found in Puebla when the ordinance was proclaimed.[37] The first municipal reference to a free black man dates from 1539, when the municipal council acknowledged "Juan de Ordáz, negro" as a *vecino*, a title of municipal residency with accompanying civic rights.[38] Acquiring *vecindad*, the status and privileges of formally acknowledged residency, carried great significance during Puebla's foundational years. In a struggling settlement that desperately needed permanent residents, *vecinos* could petition the council for plots of land on which to erect their residences or cultivate orchards. This is precisely what Juan de Ordáz did. He emerges at least twice in the historical record, on both occasions selling the urban plots that he had been granted by the municipal council. In 1546, Francisco Díaz, a black freedman, was also included on the city's list of registered residents.[39] Two other black men, Juan de Montalvo and Diego Monte, had their *vecindad* formally acknowledged in 1550 and 1571, respectively.

The experiences of Puebla's first black *vecinos* suggests that despite a growing association between blackness and slavery, a minority of African descent was able to claim the benefits of urban citizenship during the mid-sixteenth century. Although their cases cannot be considered representative of the early Afro-Poblano experience, their status as

---

36 David Davidson, "Negro Slave Control and Resistance," *Hispanic American Historical Review* 46, no. 3 (Aug. 1966): 239–240.

37 My thanks to one of the book's anonymous reviewers for this insight.

38 López de Villaseñor, *Cartilla vieja*, 286.   39 Ibid., 290, 295.

officially recognized residents and landowners tempers the overwhelmingly negative connotations found in the 1536 municipal ordinance. What exactly allowed these men to earn *vecino* status? Judging from the limited cases at hand: freedom and a wife. Ordáz received a 200-peso dowry from his wife, Catalina Díaz. Montalvo, who worked as Puebla's towncrier, was married to a woman in Guatemala.[40] By 1555, he had secured enough money to send one Pedro de Padilla all the way to Guatemala in order to bring his wife back to Puebla. Although his own position in colonial society was modest at best, Montalvo's standing as a free black *vecino* with connections to elite Poblanos distinguished him in a city where the overwhelming majority of people of African descent were enslaved.

Other notable black men undoubtedly spent time in Puebla during its formative decades, but Pedro López de Villaseñor's listing suggests that very few were able to claim *vecindad*. For instance, the black conquistador Juan Valiente was unsuccessful in navigating the growing ethnocentrism that characterized life in Mexico's colonial urban centers. Born on the African mainland around 1505, Valiente was purchased by Hernan Cortés's cousin and fellow conquistador, Alonso Valiente.[41] The latter took Juan Valiente to Puebla shortly after its second foundation in 1532. None of the original settler accounts mention the African man, although he lived in Puebla by 1533. In an emerging settlement defined for its anti-conquistador stance, it is not altogether clear that he benefited from his owner's social standing. Rather than remain in the struggling town, Juan Valiente asked his owner to grant him four years "to seek opportunity" as a conquistador in Pedro de Alvarado's expedition to Guatemala. Remarkably, his owner agreed. By 1534, the black conquistador had made his way to Guatemala and Northern Peru. He would fight for Diego de Almagro in Chile the following year. Over the next two decades, Juan Valiente received an estate near Santiago de Chile, married Juana de Valdivia, and even received an *encomienda* for his military feats.[42] However, at the time of his death in 1553 Alonso's family in Puebla still technically owned Juan.

Local Conquistadors, Local Slave Traders

During the 1540s and 1550s, the simultaneous expansion of the transatlantic slave trade and New Spain's northern frontier resulted in an accessible pool of Upper Guinean and Chichimec captives for Poblano

---

40 James Lockhart, *Spanish Peru, 1532–1560: A Social History* (Madison: University of Wisconsin Press, 1994), 217–218. Many free blacks also became towncriers in early colonial Perú.

41 Matthew Restall, *Seven Myths of the Spanish Conquest* (Oxford: Oxford University Press, 2005), 53–54.

42 Matthew Restall, "Black Conquistadors: Armed Africans in Early Spanish America," *The Americas* 57, no. 2 (Oct. 2000), 187.

masters. Indigenous war captives from the Mixtón War were sold in Puebla precisely at the same moment that Upper Guineans began to appear in larger numbers.[43] This is an important point – one that is often lost in acrimonious debates on the *encomienda* system. For the purposes of this study, understanding the actions of conquistadors-turned-colonizers is particularly important because these men bridge the supposed divide between indigenous and African slavery in New Spain's history. Despite the anti-*encomienda* ideology of Puebla's foundation, thirty-five conquistadors had settled in the city by 1534.[44] Alonso Valiente, the previously mentioned conquistador and slaveholder, was also recognized as a *vecino*. As a relative and vital ally of Hernán Cortés, Valiente took part in the military expeditions against the indigenous inhabitants of Michoacán, Pánuco, and Honduras.[45]

The prestige associated with his early participation in the conquest allowed Alonso Valiente to settle in Puebla and subsequently claim political office between 1536 and 1555. For these services to the Crown and for preventing the enslavement of the natives of Guanaja, Valiente received a coat of arms in November 1547. However, only two years later Puebla's municipal magistrates investigated his ownership of an indigenous slave, Elvira, alias "La Campeche," whom he had purchased twenty years before.[46] Elvira's testimony was damning. The conquistador's wife, Doña Juana de Mancilla, had ordered Elvira's face to be branded in order to establish her servitude to Valiente and her family.[47] The former conquistador's ownership of indigenous slaves should not surprise us. In 1528, Fray Juan de Zúmarraga accused the same conquistador of loading a ship full of slaves in Pánuco (along the northern Gulf coast), in exactly the same manner as Nuño de Guzmán and his cronies.[48] Valiente's ennoblement, perhaps a measure of the influence Hernán Cortés wielded at the time, conveniently effaced his previous exploitation of the native Huastecans of Pánuco.

If ownership of indigenous slaves became a contentious issue after the New Laws of 1542, investing in enslaved Africans was not. Successful conquistadors, starting with Cortés himself, understood the value of

43 Lara Tenorio, *La esclavitud en Puebla*, 46–47. Van Deusen, *Global Indios*, 192–199.

44 Del Paso y Troncoso, *Epistolario de Nueva España*, III, 138–140.

45 Antonio Paz y Meliá, *Nobiliario de conquistadores de Indias* (Madrid: Imprenta de M. Tell, 1892), 124–126. Also see, Echeverría y Veytia, *Historia de la fundación*, 139–142.

46 Daniel García Ponce, "Indian Slavery in Sixteenth-Century New Spain: The Politics and Power of Bondage," M.A. thesis (University of Texas at Austin, 2013), 34–35.

47 For the significance of "proper" branding as legitimation of indigenous slavery, see van Deusen, *Global Indios*, 107, 133–136.

48 Juan Manuel Pérez Zevallos, *La visita de Gómez Nieto a la Huasteca, 1532–1533* (Mexico City: CIESAS, 2001), 28–29.

litigation-free laborers.[49] The conqueror of Mexico-Tenochtitlan owned no fewer than 123 African slaves on his sugar plantation in 1549 and had "contracted for the delivery of 500 slaves to work on his sugar plantations" seven years before.[50] His cousin soon followed suit. In 1551, Alonso Valiente sold thirty-one black slaves, twenty load-bearing horses, and various mining instruments to Toribio de Bolaños, a resident of Guadalajara, for the stunning sum of 7,000 gold pesos.[51] Valiente's actions illustrate the demand for skilled and unskilled slaves and Puebla's early role as a distribution center for black captives. Only a few of the twenty-one men were identified with specific occupations at the time of their sale: a tailor, a cowboy, a goat herder, two muleteers, and "Juan, a blacksmith, with his forge and its instruments."[52] The ten women included in the bill of sale likely labored as cooks and domestic servants. They were not singled out for specialized tasks of any sort.

What can we infer from Alonso Valiente's participation in the New Spain's early slave trade? First, it is clear that conquistadors resorted to the enslavement of an alternate population, Africans, once local government rendered indigenous slavery impractical. In other words, the individuals who imposed Iberian forms of slavery on indigenous people were the very same people who then facilitated the introduction of African captives. Brígida von Mentz suggests this process crystallized in Central Mexico during the 1550s and 1560s.[53] Second, Puebla's proximity to the viceregal capital and the principal port of entry incentivized the ownership of black slaves. In more remote places where royal control was weak and indigenous enslavement rampant, investing in black slaves could be delayed until Crown officials found sufficient allies to challenge the powerful *encomendero* class.

La Caja de Negros: Property, Rebellion and Racialization

If by the mid-1530s the early Afro-Poblano presence was already associated with slavery, in the two following decades such connotations would grow

---

49 Brígida von Mentz, *Trabajo, sujeción y libertad en el centro de la Nueva España: Esclavos, aprendices, campesinos y operarios manufactureros, siglos XVI a XVIII* (Mexico City: CIESAS, 1999), 184.

50 Colin Palmer, *Slaves*, 67. Philip D. Curtin, *The Atlantic Slave Trade: A Census* (Madison: University of Wisconsin Press, 1969), 98.

51 Von Mentz, *Trabajo*, 184. The ethnonyms of four male captives can be used to established possible provenance zones: Francisco Biafra, Francisco Mandinga, Juan Manicongo, and Francisco Manicongo. The remaining captives were identified by profession, relation (widow, husband, or similar), or a Hispanicized first name.

52 Ibid. The remaining 15 men would probably perform arduous manual labor in the silver refineries that dotted New Spain's western and northern regions.

53 Ibid., 71–72.

stronger with the expansion of the transatlantic slave trade. In turn, municipal councils throughout New Spain established slave registries known as *cajas de negros*.[54] The following discussion is based on the survival of Puebla's 1553 *caja*, although this administrative body had been in existence since 1540.[55] In practice, the *caja* was nothing more than a municipal list and tax that financed the retrieval of escaped slaves. These operations were managed by two judges, a scribe, and two bounty hunters (*cuadrilleros*) with the specific purpose of chasing down escaped slaves (*esclavos huidos*).[56]

In many ways the *caja de negros* was simply the local manifestation of a Spanish anxiety that reached regional, viceregal and, at times, continental dimensions. In a land bereft of external military enemies, Spaniards projected their fears onto the very society they had created. Nowhere is this more evident than in the colonizers' paranoia toward black slaves (thought to be) in rebellion. In what is still a poorly understood event, large numbers of insurgent black men allegedly launched two coordinated rebellions in late September 1537 in Mexico City and the Amatepec silver mines (125 miles to the southwest of the viceregal capital). According to Viceroy Antonio de Mendoza, the rebels had elected a king and concerted to kill all Spaniards and take over the land.[57] The 1537 rebellion exacerbated the racial tensions already manifest in Mexico City and catalyzed the need to count, regulate and establish ownership of black slaves throughout the viceroyalty. In Puebla, this policing mechanism was fulfilled through the *caja*.

The officials responsible for the *caja* were charged with producing a register of all "negro, mulato, and morisco" slaves over the age of 15.[58] *Morisco* or Moorish slaves were rare in seventeenth-century Puebla, though they may have been more commonplace during the early conquest period. However, the Crown strove to prevent practitioners of Islam (and Judaism) from arriving there. No native slaves were to be registered in Puebla,

54 Gonzalo Aguirre Beltrán, *La población negra de México: Estudio etnohistórico* (Mexico City: Fondo de Cultura Económica, 1972), 206. In his pioneering study on Mexico's black population, Beltrán lamented the loss of these municipal registers, which would have preserved the memory of an early African settlement in New Spain (and modern Mexico). Historians have been unable to locate other *cajas* outside of Mexico City and Puebla, although Perú's viceroy established one in 1549.

55 Rodríguez Ortíz, "El lado afro," 190.

56 Efraín Castro Morales, ed., *Suplemento de el Libro Número Primero de la Fundación y Establecimiento de la Muy Noble y Muy Leal Ciudad de los Ángeles* (Puebla: Ayuntamiento del Municipio de Puebla, 2009), 162–164. Each bounty hunter would receive 50 gold pesos annually for his services.

57 Graham W. Irwin, ed., *Africans Abroad: A Documentary History of the Black Diaspora in Asia, Latin America and the Caribbean during the Age of Slavery* (New York: Columbia University Press, 1977), 324–326.

58 Castro Morales, ed., *Suplemento de el Libro Número Primero*, 162–164. Also see Karoline P. Cook, *Forbidden Passages: Muslims and Moriscos in Colonial Spanish America* (Philadelphia, PA: University of Pennsylvania Press, 2016), 69–70.

evidence of an ideological commitment to eradicating indigenous slavery.[59] The fact that Chichimec war captives were not considered within the *caja*'s registry speaks to the racialization of slavery in Puebla and Central Mexico. The political battles waged in favor of indigenous freedom would have prevented Spaniards in Central Mexico from listing indigenous individuals as slaves in an official municipal register.[60] By contrast, Africans and their descendants were increasingly understood to be enslaveable at mid-century.

Puebla's *caja* was active and well funded during the 1550s. Though the actual registers are lost, a copy of the register for 1553 or 1554 survives in the city's first municipal volumes.[61] Officials reported that the *caja* contained 576 pesos derived from 288 slaves that year. This number only referred to those enslaved men and women over the age of fifteen whose owners had actually gone through the trouble (and cost) of having them registered. The children of slave unions, in addition to an undetermined number of enslaved children born of black women with Spanish, mestizo, or indigenous men were not included in the listing. Although producing an exact calculation of just how many children of full or partial African ancestry lived in Puebla is impossible, by mid century the Afro-Poblano population 1550 would have actually consisted of well over 300 individuals.[62]

Most references to enslaved Chichimecs in Puebla date from the 1540s and 1550s, precisely when the *caja* was operational and, presumably, most efficient. Their absence from the municipal register is, therefore, notable. In Puebla, sales of indigenous people from the viceroyalty's western and northern frontier fluctuated depending on the success (or lack thereof) in

59 In the neighboring city of Tlaxcala, indigenous slaves were still present in 1552. That year the native municipal council manumitted two *"yn omen tlacohtin indiome."* See Arthur J. O. Anderson, Frances Berdan and James Lockhart, *The Tlaxcalan Actas: A Compendium of the Records of the Cabildo of Tlaxcala, 1545–1627* (Salt Lake City: University of Utah Press, 1986), 77; Camilla Townsend, "Don Juan Buenaventura Zapata y Mendoza and the Notion of Nahua Identity" in *The Conquest All Over Again: Nahuas and Zapotecs Thinking, Writing, and Painting Spanish Colonialism* (Brighton, UK: Sussex Academic Press, 2010), 163–164.

60 During the early 1530s, Cuba's governors had established similar registries with squadrons of bounty hunters to capture "wrongdoers and escaped slaves or indians." The Cuban institution functioned on the premise that black and indigenous people would, at all times, carry a document certifying that they were not runaways or else face imprisonment. See Jose Luis Cortés López, *Esclavo y colono. Introducción y sociología de los negroafricanos en la América española del siglo XVI* (Salamanca: University of Salamanca, 2004), 306–307.

61 Castro Morales, ed., *Suplemento de el Libro Número Primero*, doc. 135, 245r–245v. The copyof the register is undated, but is located between municipal minutes for 1553 and 1554 and features regents and aldermen active in the early 1550s.

62 By comparison, the city of Antequera held 150 slaves in 1569 despite its establishment a few years before Puebla's. See John K. Chance, *Race and Class in Colonial Oaxaca* (Stanford, CA: Stanford University Press, 1978), 53.

pacifying these communities. For instance, in 1552, thirty-one *Jalisco* Indians were sold for 3,752 gold pesos in a single transaction.[63] In 1570, Rodrigo, a 15-year-old Chichimec slave, was sold on condition that he "remain handcuffed."[64] Sales for Chichimec captives continued into the 1590s, as in the case of Diego, an indigenous man of unstated age, to a Poblano for 125 silver pesos.[65] It was expected that Diego would be "taught the things of our Holy Catholic faith." This religious language was absent in bills of sale for enslaved blacks and mulattos. Chichimecs were further distinguished by virtue of their temporary enslavement.[66] Because they were framed as rebels, not naturally born slaves, Chichimecs received ten- or twenty-year sentences for their criminal behavior. Their "service" was redeemable and transferable only during this set amount of time. While individuals of African descent were born and sold into slavery, Chichimecs were captured and temporarily transferred. In practice both groups may have been treated, whipped, and overworked equally, but the ideological implications of Chichimec captivity are significant at a time when slaveholding was being racialized in relation to the black body.

Puebla's *caja* allows us to situate the racially driven fears of local slave owners, bounty hunters and municipal officials within a broader viceregal context. In 1548, Viceroy Mendoza issued the "Ordenanza de Esclavos," which forbade selling weapons to free or enslaved people of African descent and Indians. In addition, *negros* and *moriscos* were forbidden from socializing in groups of three or more, or even from walking through the street a half hour after evening prayer.[67] By 1555, the Spanish fear of black rebellion had reached such a degree that Motolinia urged the king to allow the construction of a fortress in Puebla, there being "no better situated place in new Spain."[68] In the Franciscan's words, "defense is needed though it were only because we are here in an alien land, and there are many blacks, who have at times conspired to rebel and kill the Spaniards."

---

63 Lara Tenorio, *La esclavitud en Puebla*, 46–47.

64 Archivo Histórico Judicial de Puebla (AHJP), Exp. 16.

65 Archivo General de Notarías de Puebla (AGNP), Not. 4, Box 36, 1590 December, ff. 513v. Chichimecs could still be found in Puebla's Augustinian convent at start of the seventeenth century. See Mariano E. Torres Bautista, "Fulgor y final del Convento de San Agustín de Puebla," in *Estampas de la vida angelopolitana: Ensayos de historia social del siglo XVI al siglo XX* (Tlaxcala: El Colegio de Tlaxcala/BUAP, 2009), 67.

66 Diego, for example, would only serve Alonso de la Torre "the time remaining on his title."

67 David Davidson, "Negro Slave Control and Resistance in Colonial Mexico, 1519–1650" *HAHR* 46, no. 3 (August 1966), 243–244; Luis González Obregón, *Don Guillén de Lampart: La Inquisición y la Independencia en el siglo XVII* (Tours: E. Arrault & Cie., 1907), 243–245. Mendoza's successor, Don Luis de Velasco, expanded these limitations with new ordinances in 1551 and 1558.

68 James Lockhart and Enrique Otte, *Letters and People of the Spanish Indies* (Cambridge: Cambridge University Press, 1976), 234.

Despite the perceived need to control the viceroyalty's black population, a number of structural factors rendered Puebla's *caja* unviable by the last two decades of the sixteenth century. The black and mulatto population of the surrounding region was simply expanding at a much greater rate than could be controlled by such a small administrative body. If a minimum of 300 slaves of African descent lived in Puebla in the early 1550s, the cosmographer Juan López de Velasco estimated a black population of 500 (most of them enslaved) by 1574 in addition to an unspecified population of *"muchos mulatos."*[69] Many of these mulattos would have been born of Afro-indigenous unions.[70] According to the cosmographer, 3,000 indigenous people lived in the city along with 500 Spanish *vecinos.*[71] The growth of Puebla's population of African descent would only accelerate during the early seventeenth century, when a massive influx of African-born slaves overwhelmed the *caja*'s capabilities. By that point, Afro-Poblanos would have composed the bulk of a slave population numbering in the thousands. Furthermore, it was not a passive population. The *caja* hired bounty hunters who continually brought in runaway slaves from Mexico City. By the 1550s, enslaved people navigated the Puebla-Mexico City corridor, which afforded them anonymity among the ever-larger African-descent population.

The officials responsible for Puebla's *caja* were also aware that a significant number of slave owners were eluding their efforts and asked the authorities to resolve this problem. In their 1553 report, they alluded to the fact that it was very difficult for them to maintain a reliable registry with the increasing number of slaves brought in daily from "Spain, Guinea or other parts of New Spain."[72] Even the natural growth of Puebla's black population appeared problematic, as Spanish masters were supposed to register slave children with the authorities as soon as they reached fifteen years of age. Clearly, there were a number of financial and social incentives not to do so. Slave owners could easily prove ownership of a child born to one of their enslaved women by presenting a baptismal certificate. Why incur the additional expense of registering that child before the municipal

---

69 Juan López de Velasco, *Geografía y descripción universal de la Indias* (Madrid: Establecimiento Tipográfico de Fortanet, 1894), 208–209. It is not clear if López de Velasco was referring to "mulatos" as Afro-indigenous children, commonly known as *zambaigos* in Perú, or the offspring of Spanish men and black (likely, enslaved) women. López de Velasco also refrained from using the term "mestizo" in his assessment of Puebla.

70 Robert Schwaller, *Géneros de Gente in Early Colonial Mexico: Defining Racial Difference* (Norman: University of Oklahoma Press, 2016), 175–177. Schwaller's observations on Afro-indigenous *mulatos* have enormous implications for a term that has traditionally been used to describe the children of Spanish-African relationships.

71 The estimate of the Spanish population by *vecino* would place the city's white population somewhere between 2,400 and 3,000 people for the early 1570s.

72 Castro Morales, ed., *Suplemento de el Libro Número Primero*, doc. 135, 245r–245v.

authorities? Finally, Puebla officials also suggested extending the *caja*'s jurisdiction to Orizaba and Tehuacán, thereby indicating a significant and potentially menacing, African population to the south and east as early as the mid-sixteenth century.[73]

Despite its obvious flaws and early downfall, the *caja de negros* established an important number of paradigms for the study of race relations in Puebla. First of all, it defined slavery as an institution that could legally bind people categorized as *negro*, *mulato*, or *morisco*. Catholic anxieties over *moriscos* and their Muslim ancestry faded over time in New Spain, while African ancestry became the most important signifier in this characterization. Asian slaves were still not considered within the jurisdiction of Mexican slavery at this point, although they would be included by the end of the sixteenth century. Second, the *caja* institutionalized masters' rights and obligations over enslaved adults and youths fifteen years of age or older. In other words, children born to enslaved mothers in Puebla were not immediately subjected to a municipal register that defined them as slaves and taxable property. The age limitations of the *caja* found a ready parallel to the tribute payments expected of indigenous adolescents "from fourteen years and upward" in Puebla circa 1568.[74] Black and indigenous youths (fourteen and younger) inhabited ambiguous legal and fiscal territories. Spanish masters may have easily enacted restrictions on them regardless, but the nature of urban servitude suggests a certain malleability in their relationships. Most importantly, the *caja* registers allow us to definitively state that hundreds of black men and women lived within the city of Puebla during the mid-sixteenth century.

Enslaved Africans in Mid-Sixteenth-Century Puebla

Africans would become increasingly visible as human property in the notarial archives of Puebla during the mid-sixteenth century. Peter Boyd-Bowman's pioneering study of these sources confirms that the institutionalization of African slavery was well underway in Puebla by the 1540s. In his influential article on early Poblano slavery, Boyd-Bowman located bills of slave purchases for approximately 240 men and women of African descent

---

73 Ibid. "Es nescesario que los negros que hay por manifestar en la comarca desta ciudad, ansí en el ingenio de Oliçaba [Orizaba], y en Teguacan [Tehuacan] y en las otras partes que son más cercanas a esta ciudad que a la de México, Guaxaca [Oaxaca], a la de Veracruz, se manifiesten en la caxa desta ciudad conforme a las ordenanças de vuestra señoría ilustrísima."

74 C. Raymond Beazley, ed., *An English Garner: Voyages and Travels mainly during the 16th and 17th Centuries* (New York: E. P. Dutton and Co.), I, 266. According to John Chilton, who traveled to New Spain in 1568, "Indians [*at Puebla de los Angeles*], from fourteen years old and upwards, pay unto the King for their yearly tribute one ounce of silver . . . and a hannega . . . of maise, which is valued among them commonly at 12 Rials of Plate."

for the years 1540 through 1555.[75] Of these enslaved people, only thirty-three were considered *ladino*, or conversant in Castilian language (and culture). By contrast, forty-six slaves were classified as *bozales*, the term used to identify African slaves who had recently arrived from their homelands and had little understanding of Spanish society.[76] Another five were labeled "between bozal and ladino" as if to recognize their increasing, but still limited, familiarity with the colonial scenario. No further information was available for the remainder of the slaves sold in the city, but considering the timeframe, it is safe to say that a majority of them would have been recent African arrivals.

During the mid-sixteenth century, the transatlantic slave trade to Puebla primarily operated through Lisbon and Seville by way of Cape Verde. In fact, "residents in New Spain [had] contracted directly to obtain slaves in Cabo Verde" since the mid-1520s.[77] During the first sixty or seventy years of the sixteenth century, Portuguese merchants traded for Upper Guinean slaves that they would later resell throughout the Iberian Peninsula. Most of these captives hailed from territories comprising modern-day Senegal, Guinea-Conakry, Guinea-Bissau, Sierra Leone, and Liberia.[78] The ethnonyms of those sold in Puebla (*Bran, Biafara, Zape* and so on) confirm distinctly Upper Guinean origins.[79] A smaller group of captives was identified as hailing from the island of São Tomé, although in all likelihood they had merely been transshipped there from the African mainland.[80] No "Angola" slaves and only ten "Kongo" individuals from West Central Africa surface in Boyd-Bowman's research – an indication of the funneling of this early slave trade through Cape Verde. By contrast, during the period 1595–1639, when the Spanish Crown sold Portuguese merchants the required licenses to the Spanish American slave trade, most slaves sent to Mexico hailed from West Central Africa (see Chapter 4).

Slave prices fluctuated considerably during the mid-sixteenth century in Puebla. The average price for both male and female slaves at this time was around 105 pesos, a fraction of what they would cost fifty years later. Considering the scarcity of Spanish artisans and craftsmen at the time, skilled slaves of African descent would have been placed at an especially high premium. In Mexico, prices for African-born slaves would rise artificially

---

75 Boyd-Bowman, "Negro Slaves in Early Colonial Mexico," *The Americas* 26, no. 2 (Oct. 1969), 136.
76 Ibid., 137.
77 Toby Green, *The Rise of the Trans-Atlantic Slave Trade in Western Africa, 1300–1589* (Cambridge: Cambridge University Press, 2012), 192.
78 Gwendolyn Midlo Hall, *Slavery and African Ethnicities in the Americas: Restoring the Links* (Chapel Hill: University of North Carolina Press, 2005), 158–159.
79 Lara Tenorio, *La esclavitud en Puebla*, 16. The first four extant slave purchases in Lara's study include three West African slaves (2 Biafra and 1 Bran) and a couple from Puerto Rico.
80 Boyd Bowman, "Nego Slaves," 140; Lara Tenorio, *La esclavitud en Puebla*, 59.

after a 1556 law associated "a slave's origins" and price to a specific West African region.[81] In response, Mexican slaveholders soon began to receive enslaved Africans by way of the contraband Caribbean trade (one that would continue throughout the seventeenth century). During the 1560s, the port of Ocoa, along Hispaniola's southern coast, received unlicensed slave ships that would often continue toward Mexican ports.[82] Considering Cuba's close commercial relationship with both Veracruz and Campeche,[83] it is likely that the contraband slave trade also gained strength through those maritime routes as well.

Within a context of severe indigenous depopulation and aggressive anti-*encomendero* policies, Spaniards soon came to value enslaved blacks as unalienable property. The former imagined the latter as epidemic-resistant workers, a priceless attribute as the Central Mexican indigenous population was decimated by several smallpox and typhus epidemics.[84] In certain native communities, the combination of disease, overexhaustion, and military deaths led to 90 percent depopulation rates.[85] Within this diseased context, questions of just enslavement became largely superfluous to the colonist invested in the permanency of an African captive. But not all were convinced. From a religious perspective, the transatlantic slave trade raised troubling moral questions that required answers.

In 1560, the archbishop of Mexico, Fray Alonso de Montúfar, attempted to expose the ideological contradictions of allowing Africans to be enslaved and sold in the viceroyalty. In an audacious letter to Philip II, Montúfar argued that there existed no cause "for blacks to be any more captive than indians," nor had any scholars detected any legitimate reasons for their enslavement.[86] This posture reversed an Iberian logic of justification already well in place when the first African slaves made their way to the Caribbean first, and then into the central highlands of Mexico.[87] The archbishop argued that Africans did not "wage war on Christians," perhaps an

81 Green, *Trans-Atlantic Slave Trade*, 274.   82 Ibid., 213–214.

83 Alejandro de la Fuente, *Havana and the Atlantic in the Sixteenth Century* (Chapel Hill: University of North Carolina Press, 2008), 44–45.

84 The alleged African resistance to the epidemics that struck Mexico during the colonial period is a topic that remains severely understudied. Between 1579 and 1581 "many Negroes" died a result of the great *cocoliztli* epidemic that began in 1576; see Peter Gerhard, *A Guide to the Historical Geography of New Spain* (Cambridge: Cambridge University Press, 1972), 23.

85 Woodrow Borah and Sherburne Cook, "Conquest and Population: A Demographic Approach to Mexican History," *Proceedings of the American Philosophical Society* 113, no. 2 (April 1969): 180–182.

86 Manuel Lucena Salmoral, *Regulación de la esclavitud negra en las colonias de América Española (1503–1886): Documentos para su estudio* (Alcalá: University of Alcalá de Henares, 2005), 52–54, "Carta del obispo de México, Fray Alonso de Montúfar, al rey sobre los escrúpulos existentes por esclavizar a los negros después de haberse liberado a los indios."

87 James Sweet, "The Iberian Roots of American Racist Thought," *William and Mary Quarterly*, 54 (Jan. 1997): 155–164.

offhand reference to the continued struggles with the Chichimec populations of the northern frontier. Moreover, enslaved Africans had consistently demonstrated their "good will in receiving the Holy Gospel."[88] The significance of such criticism cannot be understated. Iberians had historically linked Africans with Islam, thereby equating skin color with a politico-religious adversary. Montúfar argued that such generalizations lacked validity as Africans in New Spain had constantly proven to be worthy neophytes and thus deserved just as much freedom as their indigenous counterparts.[89]

The Mexican archbishop proposed shutting down the slave trade altogether. In an unprecedented critique, Montúfar noted that despite the "causes that the holy and Catholic doctors use to explain [African] captivity, it does not appear that these excuse the wars that some blacks now wage on others."[90] Moreover, he continued, by "ceasing this captivity and business as it has been led up until now by ransoming their bodies, there will be greater care in taking them the preaching of the Holy Gospel, that in their lands they may be free in their bodies, but more so, in their souls by bringing them to the true knowledge of Jesus Christ." The archbishop's letter attacked a lucrative transatlantic slave trade that was becoming increasingly profitable with the Crown's endorsement. Between 1544 and 1550, Portuguese traders entered agreements to purchase 14,000 slaves on the West African coast and deliver them to the Spanish Indies.[91] By 1550, even the incoming viceroy of New Spain, Don Luis de Velasco, had arranged the delivery of 100 slaves (exempt from the requisite taxes) to Mexico by way of Cape Verde.[92]

Montúfar adopted a scathing tone against Portuguese slave traders, "their conquests" on the African coast, and the profits made in Mexico. According to the archbishop, the slave trade was "no mean business" (*no es la menor granjería*) in New Spain. Moreover, he argued that the "spiritual

---

88 Lucena Salmoral, *Regulación*, 52–54.

89 The Jesuit Francisco Calderón followed a similar line of reasoning in referring to blacks as "indios orientales" and Catholic neophytes. See Úrsula Camba Ludlow, *Imaginarios ambiguos, realidades contradictorias: Conductas y representaciones de los negros y mulatos novohispanos, Siglos XVI y XVII* (Mexico City: Colegio de México, 2008), 49.

90 Lucena Salmoral, *Regulación*, 52–54.

91 Maria de Graça Mateus Ventura, *Negreiros portugueses na rota das Índias de Castela (1541–1556)* (Lisbon: Ediçoes Colibri, 1999), 68.

92 María Justina Sarabia Viejo, *Don Luis de Velasco, virrey de Nueva España, 1550–1564* (Mexico City: Editorial CSIC, 1978), 132–133, 281–282. Considering the traditional rivalry between viceroys and archbishops in New Spain, it is possible that Montúfar condemned investing in the slave trade as a public slight against Velasco. This scenario is all the more likely when considering that the archbishop's own brother, Martín de Montúfar, had trafficked twenty enslaved black men from Spain and sold them for a handsome profit in Mexico. See Ethelia Ruíz Medrano, "Los negocios de un arzobispo: El caso de Fray Alonso de Montúfar," *Estudios de Historia Novohispana* 12, no. 19 (1992), 70–71.

and corporal benefits" that Africans received once in Christian captivity were negligible, as in most cases the enslaved were forced to relinquish their families and wives in Africa for lives of bigamy and concubinage in New Spain. Unsurprisingly, Montúfar's pleas fell on deaf ears. The archbishop's rationale clearly deserved consideration and, in fact, followed many of the lines espoused in the fight against indigenous slavery.

From the colonizers' perspective, the extreme demographic decline of Mexico's native populations (coupled with the discovery of the Zacatecas silver mines in the late 1540s) required the introduction of a new workforce. Based on Caribbean precedents, the Spanish Crown viewed black slave labor as a historically viable alternative to labor shortages. No efforts were made to remedy the religious perils that slavery imposed on the African men and women sent to New Spain after 1560, and as a result "shiploads from every part of Guinea" would continue to arrive in greater and greater numbers.[93]

The Demands of Domesticity

With the military phase of the conquest complete in Central Mexico, colonizers also turned to the transatlantic trade for enslaved female workers. In fact, elite Poblanos had exerted considerable demand for African women since the mid-sixteenth century. As cooks, laundresses, itinerant vendors, and sexual partners, but especially as status markers, enslaved domestics became a permanent fixture of the colonial city. Their roles were largely defined by the 1550s and 1560s, precisely the decades in which Spanish women began to arrive in the viceroyalty in greater numbers, bringing with them new cultural, familial, and social expectations. Unfortunately, studies on colonial servitude have rarely addressed the question of how, why, or when enslaved black domestics became rooted in Mexican society. In Puebla, it is not altogether clear what or who triggered the call for imported domestic laborers. Were established Spanish men living in Puebla calling for black domestic slaves or were these the demands of incoming Spanish women?

Judging from the corpus of extant personal letters written between Spaniards on opposite sides of the Atlantic, established men in Puebla often asked their relatives to bring along black domestic slaves. In 1559, Antonio Pérez wrote to his brother, Francisco Gutiérrez in Albuquerque, Castile, giving him precise instructions on how to properly prepare for his upcoming move to Puebla.[94] Pérez stressed that Gutiérrez should bring

93 Lucena Salmoral, *Regulación*, 52–54.
94 Enrique Otte and Guadalupe Albi Romero, eds., *Cartas privadas de emigrantes a Indias* (Mexico City: Fondo de Cultura Económica, 1993), 146–147.

along his wife and children, along with his marriage certificate, as this document was required by the Sevillean authorities. In the meantime, Pérez had made arrangements to send his brother money "and a black woman who would serve him on the sea." Once in Puebla, the Gutiérrez family would reunite with Pérez, his wife, and their other (unnamed) sibling and their four children.

In April 1563, the Puebla municipal council addressed the issue of black and indigenous domesticity in passing, and only because one Juan Ruíz presented a complaint. According to Ruíz, black and indigenous women habitually washed clothes in the water conduit (*alcantarilla*) on the street corner that faced the house of a resident named Diego Cortés.[95] Ruíz argued that these practices were "detrimental," but the municipal scribe did not detail what specific aspect (location, use of water, involved parties) was so inconvenient to the affected party. Still, the city regents ordered the towncrier proclaim that "no black woman or indian woman wash in said *alcantarilla*, under penalty of fifty lashes." The motion clearly targeted black and indigenous laundresses, who apparently were not joined by Spanish women in these activities. Municipal ordinances such as these reinforced the idea that black and indigenous bodies, both male and female, were subject to corporal punishment. However, unlike the 1536 ordinance that defined black men as criminal slaves and aggressors of indigenous women, the 1563 decree suggests that black female domestics were not necessarily enslaved and that indigenous and black women performed overlapping domestic roles in common urban spaces. For the laundresses of early colonial Puebla, the water conduit represented a working space, but also an arena of conviviality that was apparently off-limits to their Spanish mistresses.

By the second half of the sixteenth century, wealthy Poblanos had invested in and produced a slave-owning culture that combined the ostentatious demands of elite urban society with the practical needs of a region suffering from indigenous depopulation. In 1560, Catalina Rodríguez and her future husband received twelve black slaves – eight men and four women – as part of her dowry.[96] With the establishment of a mature, urban colonial society and the ensuing arrival of Spanish women from the Peninsula, female slave labor in Puebla became highly valued. Consider the following 1566 letter from Luis de Córdoba, a resident of Puebla, writing to his wife in Seville and persuading her to make the trip across the Atlantic.

95 AGMP, Actas de Cabildo, Vol. 9, 5r.
96 Blanca Lara Tenorio and Carlos Paredes Martínez, "La población negra en los valles centrales de Puebla: Orígenes y desarrollo hasta 1681," in *Presencia africana en México*, ed. Luz María Martínez Montiel (Mexico City: CONACULTA, 1994), 31.

Therefore, sell what you own over there . . . and buy the service of two slave women and a [male] black slave that they may serve you on the sea [voyage], make sure these three pieces be of very good quality, as they are what is most needed here.[97]

The notion of buying enslaved women for company and security along the voyage across the Atlantic appears frequently in the letters written by Spanish emigrants to their relatives back on the Peninsula. Yet Luis de Córdoba's letter represents a shift in the reasoning behind the demand for African slaves, both male and female. During the 1530s, enslaved blacks served as military auxiliaries and in the following two decades as replacements for indigenous laborers. By the 1560s, however, there was nothing more needed or valuable than an enslaved African in the city of Puebla.

Conclusion

For all of the continuities between the phases of African and indigenous slavery in colonial Mexico, key differences emerged during the 1530s and 1560s. The majority of involuntary laborers entering the viceroyalty now hailed from the Upper Guinea via the ports of Iberia and Cape Verde. Whereas conquistadors and *encomienda* holders previously sold the indigenous captives they had captured themselves, the acquisition of black slaves depended on the actions of the sailors, ship captains, creditors, and merchants who controlled Atlantic commerce. Despite the ongoing struggle against the Chichimec communities of the northern and western frontier, Spaniards turned away from indigenous slavery. Chichimec captives continued to be sold in the city throughout the century, but Puebla's municipal ordinances and *caja de negros* signaled an ideological commitment to African slavery. Even the religious plea for the humanity of African souls and spouses fell on deaf ears as the transatlantic slave trade intensified throughout the mid and late sixteenth century.

97 Otte and Albi Romero, eds., *Cartas privadas*, 147–149. "Así que, por tanto, señora, vended lo que allí tenéis, y cobrad lo que debe el rey, pues que decís que no lo habéis cobrado, y comprad servicio que os sirva por la mar de un par de esclavas y un esclavo negro, tres piezas que sean muy buenas, que es lo que más acá es menester."

2

Ambition and Agency in the *Obraje*

He heard him say, "I deny God," which angered this witness, and as he was irritated with the black [boy] he slapped him a few times and made his mouth bleed. When asked where he had learned such utterings and falsity, the [boy] answered that he had heard them from several others in the obraje of his [previous] owner Gabriel Carrillo. This witness then said he would take [the boy] where he would be burned. And because this took place, this witness did not lash the boy, nor has he lashed him since he bought him.[1]

– Don Manuel Alonso Mozarabe, merchant and *vecino* of Puebla (1687)

Accustomed to seeing slaves, prisoners, and apprentices whipped and beaten for minor offenses, Alonso learned since a young age that a blasphemous cry could interrupt or at least delay physical punishment. He did not forget these life lessons when he was sold out of Gabriel Carrillo's textile mill (*obraje*) in December of 1686 and purchased by Don Manuel Alonso Mozarabe. When accused of breaking an expensive clock in his new master's house and threatened with a lashing, the twelve-year-old resorted to a religious crime which he had learned to deploy as a survival strategy in the *obraje*. Tragically, the immediate effect of his outburst led him back to a textile mill where he presumably spent several months suffering the same punishment he had hoped to evade. For the Holy Office of the Inquisition, cases such as these held little relevance by the late seventeenth century. A year and half after Mozarabe's accusation, the inquisitors decreed that Alonso "should be punished for blapheming and denying God, and taught the Christian doctrine if he did not know it."[2]

Alonso's story sheds light on the routine brutality of domestic and *obraje* slavery, but it also reveals textile mill owners' dependence on non-indigenous laborers and enslaved children in mid- to late-seventeenth-century *obrajes*. The fact that a 12-year-old was sold from Carrillo's *obraje* at the end of the seventeenth century suggests that his mother had also worked there as well. The boy's sale also indicates that mill owners'

1 AGN, Indiferente Virreinal, Box 4380, Exp. 47, 3v–4v.   2 Ibid.

experiments with the slave trade and natural reproduction had not necessarily translated into economic success. As we shall see, mill owners (*obrajeros*) invested in slavery with commercial and political motivations. Unfortunately, we do not know what happened to Alonso, as he entered adulthood with a quick tongue and a healthy aversion to lashings. By contrast, the fate of Puebla's *obrajes* is well known. By the early eighteenth century, the city's textile mills lay in shambles.

In Puebla, the most violent, spatially confining variety of slavery was found in *obrajes*. Thirty to forty of these textile mills operated in Puebla's central parishes during most of the seventeenth century. Of course, *obrajes* served as sites of textile production, but also as jails for convicted criminals and holding houses for slaves and indebted laborers.[3] As spaces of coercion, *obrajes* were notorious for concentrating large, multiracial coerced workforces under the most extreme physical conditions. Overseers developed their own distinctive regimen of punishment within these spaces. In fact, brutal floggings and beatings were so common that Inquisition officials learned to disregard the blasphemous cries that could often be heard coming from a given *obraje*.[4] By the late seventeenth century, these were largely the cries of enslaved people.

In the following pages, I analyze the transition from *obraje* workforces of nominally free indigenous laborers to that of enslaved African and Asian workers from 1580 to 1706. I contend that Puebla's transition from free to enslaved workforces needs to be situated within local contexts of enslavement, commercial expansion and political power. This means grappling with the social and economic impact of transatlantic and transpacific slaving, contextualizing slave marriages and situating individual mill owners' motivations within Puebla's political landscape.[5] An earlier generation of historians suggested that New Spain's textile workshops were continually staffed by indigenous workers, and eventually mestizos, due to the exorbitant cost of purchasing black slaves.[6] This chapter revises that view by

3 In this regard, Mexican *obrajes* are comparable to the "architecture of terror" found in Bridgetown's "cage." See Marisa Fuentes, *Dispossessed Lives*, 38–42.

4 Javier Villa-Flores, "'To Lose One's Soul': Blasphemy and Slavery in New Spain, 1596–1669," *Hispanic American Historical Review* 82, no. 3 (Aug. 2002): 465–466.

5 While the historiography of colonial *obrajes* is extensive, the relationships between enslaved laborers, indigenous workers and slave owners remains nebulous. See Carmen Viqueira and José Urquiola, *Los obrajes en la Nueva España, 1550–1630* (Mexico City: CONACULTA, 1990); Richard Salvucci, *Textiles and Capitalism in Mexico: An Economic History of the Obrajes, 1539–1840* (Princeton, NJ: Princeton University Press, 1987); Brígida von Mentz, *Trabajo, sujeción y libertad en el centro de la Nueva España: Esclavos, aprendices, campesinos y operarios manufactureros, siglos XVI a XVIII* (Mexico City: CIESAS, 1999).

6 Charles Gibson, *The Aztecs under Spanish Rule: A History of the Indians of the Valley of Mexico, 1519–1810* (Stanford, CA: Stanford University Press, 1964), 243–244; Jan Bazant, "Evolución de la industria textil poblana." *Historia Mexicana* 13, no. 4 (Apr.–Jun. 1964), 495–498; Manuel Miño Grijalva, "¿Proto-industria colonial?" *Historia Mexicana* 38, no. 4 (Apr.–Jun. 1989), 802–805.

tracing the dependence on enslaved workforces in Puebla's mid-seventeenth-century textile mills. In this regard, I agree with Frank Proctor's interpretation of Mexican *obrajes* as increasingly "black spaces" during the mid-seventeenth century, although Asian laborers (*chinos*) must also be considered an important element of enslaved textile workforces.[7]

Textile production generated an enormous documentary corpus as the city's preeminent economic activity. Crown officials led inspections against abusive *obrajeros* and their overseers in the 1580s, 1600s and 1620s, and 1700s.[8] These campaigns aligned with the Crown's concern over the legal status of indigenous people and, in theory at least, were intended to improve the latter's working conditions.[9] These same concerns were not extended to non-indigenous slaves. *Obrajeros* responded to this pressure by reluctantly complementing their indigenous workforces with enslaved people of African descent during the last decades of the sixteenth century. Enslaved Asians followed their African counterparts during the 1610s and 1620s. Evidence of these enslaved *obraje* populations and their interactions with indigenous workers has been preserved in mill inventories, bills of slave purchase, marital and baptismal registers, and Inquisition files.[10]

The chapter also considers petitions written by Puebla's *obrajeros* in their dealings with local government and the viceroy in Mexico City. Mill owners formed part of the city's political elite, but securing an influential position in the Spanish municipal government (*cabildo*) was contingent upon renouncing *obraje* ownership. Alternatively, mill owners could demonstrate that they no longer employed indigenous wage laborers. Mid-seventeenth-century *obrajeros* came to understood slave ownership as an avenue toward political power, not merely commercial success. Black, mulatto and *chino* bodies, and especially those of enslaved women, became the instruments by which to secure this power by the 1650s (if not earlier).

---

7 Frank T. Proctor III, "Afro-Mexican Slave Labor in the *Obrajes* de Paños of New Spain, Seventeenth and Eighteenth Centuries." *The Americas* 60, no. 1 (Jul., 2003), 33–58. For studies that address *obraje* slavery tangentially, see Javier Villa Flores, *Dangerous Speech: A Social History of Blasphemy in Colonial Mexico* (Tucson: University of Arizona Press, 2006); Solange Alberro, "Juan de Morga and Gertrudis de Escobar: Rebellious Slaves" in David G. Sweet and Gary B. Nash, *Struggle and Survival in Colonial America* (Berkeley: University of California Press, 1981), 165–188.

8 The Archivo General Municipal de Puebla (AGMP) holds records of *obraje* inspections or *visitas* for 1583–1584, 1609, and 1622–1623.

9 For a mercantilist interpretation of New Spain's *obraje* inspections, see Asmáa Bouhrass, "El intervencionismo en el desarrollo de los *obrajes* mexicanos" in *Estudios sobre América, siglos XVI–XX* (Seville: AEA, 2005), 994–997.

10 Three parochial archives were consulted for this chapter: the Archivo del Sagrario Metropolitano de Puebla (ASMP), the Archivo de la Parroquia del Señor San José (APSJ) and the Archivo del Santo Angel Custodio-Analco (ASAC). Bills of slave purchase, *obraje* leases and inventories were culled from the Archivo General de Notarías de Puebla (AGNP) and the Archivo Histórico Judicial de Puebla (AHJP).

Harnessing the reproductive abilities of *obraje* women facilitated the creation of all-slave workforces, which in turn allowed mill owners to claim coveted political positions. In order to renounce their indigenous workforces, *obrajeros* encouraged slave matrimony and reproduction. These insidious *obraje* dynamics force us to consider the importance of specific urban spaces, especially confined spaces, in the everyday lives of the enslaved and their owners.

Indigenous Workers and the Men from Brihuega

Since the early colonial period, enterprising Spaniards introduced European textile workshops to Central Mexico, Quito and Perú.[11] Importing Spanish textiles to these American dominions proved to be too expensive, especially because clothing and rough cloths could be easily produced in areas with well-established textile production. Indigenous expertise was central to this development. During the prehispanic period, the dominant city-states of the Nahua region often imposed tribute in cotton blankets and other textiles. Textile production was just as important to Puebla's political and commercial development under the Spanish. No other city would concentrate more *obrajes* in New Spain until the mid-seventeenth century.[12] Along with the towns and cities in the immediate region (Cholula, Atlixco, Tepeaca, Tlaxcala and Huexotzingo), Puebla formed a powerful textile conglomerate dependent on access to indigenous laborers during the late sixteenth and early seventeenth century.

Although the first "*obraje* de hacer paños" in Puebla was established in 1539, textile production remained relatively unimportant because its success depended on hefty capital outlays, a constant supply of wool, a stable worker population, and a reliable purchasing public.[13] These factors had not coalesced in the Puebla-Tlaxcala Valley prior to the 1560s. The scarcity of permanent labourers was problematic even in areas under greater Spanish control. Viceroy Antonio de Mendoza, for instance, staffed his textile mill in Texcoco, just to the east of Mexico City, with over 100 Chichimec slaves that had been captured in the Mixtón War.[14] In what was one of the first *obrajes* built in New Spain, the viceroyalty's highest-ranking political figure made use of the very indigenous slave labor he intended to deny a growing

11 Kris Lane, *Quito 1599: City and Colony in Transition* (Albuquerque: University of New Mexico Press, 2002), 179–183.

12 María de las Mercedes Gantes Tréllez, "Aspectos socio-económicos de Puebla de los Ángeles (1624–1650)," in Carlos Contreras Cruz and Miguel Ángel Cuenya Mateos, eds., *Ángeles y constructores. Mitos y realidades en la historia colonial de Puebla, siglos XVI y XVII* (Puebla: BUAP/Fomento Editorial), 295.

13 Bazant, "Evolución," *Historia Mexicana* 13, no. 4 (Apr.–Jun. 1964), 477.

14 Ethelia Ruíz Medrano, *Reshaping New Spain: Government and Private Interests in the Colonial Bureaucracy, 1531–1550* (Boulder: University Press of Colorado, 2006), 127.

Spanish population. More importantly, Mendoza effectively established and legitimized the use of slave labor for textile production.

Puebla only emerged as a significant center for textile production with the arrival of several hundred *briocenses*, Spanish immigrants from the town of Brihuega, during the 1560s and 1570s. In *Transatlantic Ties*, her masterful examination of the point-to-point migration that defined the *briocense* community, Ida Altman notes that these migrants settled quickly in Puebla and "obtained grants to build fulling mills at key sites along the San Francisco and Atoyac Rivers" with considerable ease.[15] As expert textile producers, *briocenses* found a profitable, untapped market in a relatively stable urban setting. The availability of thousands of displaced indigenous people from surrounding communities guaranteed mill owners a steady supply of textile workers. By the last decades of the sixteenth century, between 2,000 and 3,000 indigenous commoners labored as textile producers in Puebla's thirty-seven *obrajes*.[16] Lured in through spurious cash advances, jail sentences, or outright kidnapping, considerable numbers of indigenous workers came to owe the men of Brihuega much of their lives. "At any one time in the years between 1565 and 1620 the majority of the *obraje* owners in Puebla were *briocenses* by origin or descent," although their acceptance into the city's social and political elite would be fiercely contested by the older landed families.[17] The unsavory nature of *briocense* economic success certainly did not advance their social standing.

By the 1570s, slave ownership in Puebla's *obrajes* played a dual purpose for *briocense* families invested in textile production. It formalized their control over permanent, non-indigenous laborers and enhanced their social status as slaveholders. As Spanish migrants established themselves in Puebla they reported their successes, failures, needs and wants to their relatives on the other side of the Atlantic. It is through private correspondence of this sort that we learn of the link between enslaved blacks and the city's *obrajes*. For example, in 1572, Juan de Brihuega wrote his brother, Pedro García, "glory to God, things are going well for us [in Puebla], I have a textile mill with twelve looms, and the people that are needed [to staff] it, and four black men and one black woman, and we are well disposed to earn our keep, if God wills it."[18] As in other documents of this genre,[19] a successful

---

15 Ida Altman, *Transatlantic Ties in the Spanish Empire: Brihuega, Spain & Puebla, Mexico 1560–1620* (Stanford, CA: Stanford University Press, 2000), 51–52.

16 Bouhrass, "El intervencionismo," 998; Viqueira and Urquiola, *Los obrajes*, 108.

17 Altman, *Transatlantic Ties*, 52.

18 Enrique Otte and Guadalupe Albi Romero, eds., *Cartas privadas de emigrantes a Indias* (Mexico City: Fondo de Cultura Económica, 1993), 154.

19 For the recruitment of able-bodied Spaniards to "the Indies" by family members (especially uncles calling for nephews), see James Lockhart and Enrique Otte, eds., *Letters and People of the Spanish Indies* (Cambridge: Cambridge University Press, 1976).

immigrant lures his sibling to join him with the promise of a steady income, wealth, and the service of five workers of African descent.[20] Should Pedro García accept the invitation he would immediately find employment "running the fulling mill and the carding [of the wool]" since his brother could barely find enough journeymen for these tasks. In light of the scarcity of skilled Spanish carders and fullers, *obrajeros* turned to black laborers to fill skilled occupations. These skilled black men replaced the young apprentices that traditionally worked the looms in the smaller workshops of the Iberian peninsula. Puebla's *obrajeros* valued black laborers because "their permanence made it worthwhile to train them,"[21] which could not be said for Chichimec war captives or Nahua debtors.[22] However, from the perspective of the Spanish entrepreneur, the inexpensiveness of indigenous labor trumped all other considerations. Captive, indebted, or free, the native inhabitants of Central Mexico were simply too accessible to Spanish colonizers.

Despite the presence of a black minority, during the 1580s indigenous workers constituted the overwhelming majority of the textile workforce. Within a context of severe indigenous depopulation, Crown officials attempted to improve the working conditions affecting natives working in Puebla's mills by conducting *visitas*, or official inspections.[23] In 1583 royal officials inspected the *obraje* of Francisco de Brihuega, another of Juan de Brihuega's siblings. Francisco owned a textile mill with 117 workers, 115 of whom were indigenous. Only two individuals of African descent surface in the register, "Diego Hernández, mulato" and "Antón, mulato," although the list allegedly only included "yndios e yndias."[24] For our purposes, the register serves as a head count for a nominally free, indigenous, wage-earning population. A close reading of the first and last names of these indigenous workers reveals that the *obrajeros* were recruiting men and women from neighboring indigenous communities. By interpreting last

20 Altman, *Transatlantic Ties*, 160. It is not entirely clear from this particular letter if these black men and women were enslaved, although Altman confirms they were not free people based on a 1579 partnership contract.

21 Altman, *Transatlantic Ties*, 57–58.

22 While rare, the service of Chichimec war captives was still being sold in Puebla during the 1590s. However, these were service contracts for "the time remaining on [their] titles" and not bills of slave purchase per se. See AGNP, Not. 4, Box 36, 513v.

23 Silvio Zavala, *Ordenanzas del Trabajo, Siglos XVI y XVII* (Mexico City: Editorial Elede, 1947), 139–145, 157–168. These efforts can be traced back to 1569, when viceroy Don Martín Enriquez proscribed the practice of locking up native workers, paying them in cloth, charging them for medicine, etc. During the last decade of the sixteenth century, viceroy Luis de Velasco was particularly active in restricting the notorious exploitation in New Spain's *obrajes*.

24 Archivo General Municipal de Puebla (hereafter, AGMP), Expedientes, Tomo 221r, 1r–2v. In fact, these two men may have been part of that small slave community owned by Juan de Brihuega in 1572. The inspection also reveals the presence of thirty-two indigenous women in the *obraje*.

names as toponymic indicators (as in "Bernabé de Tlaxcala"), we can deduce that at least one-fourth of Francisco de Brihuega's workforce was composed of indigenous migrants.[25] Almost all of these migrants hailed from the Puebla-Tlaxcala Valley, and particularly from Tepeaca, Huexotzingo, Cholula, and Tlaxcala.

Space, Confinement and Abuse

The confinement and physical abuse of textile workers became a distinguishing element of life in Puebla's late-sixteenth-century *obrajes*. People were so commonly enclosed in these settings that they came to be categorized as *"encerrados"* (locked-in people) in *obraje* inspections. Within Francisco de Brihuega's textile mill, indigenous *encerrados* were further identified by toponymic last names. By contrast, the few native laborers who could enter and exit the *obraje* held Spanish patronymics or the names of Puebla's emerging indigenous barrios. The names of peripheral indigenous neighborhoods where free wage-earners lived now served as identity markers. Andrés de San Pablo, Juan de San Francisco and "Joaquín Matías yn face de San Pablo" and seventeen others could all exit the confines of the *obraje* after completing their daily labor.[26] That none of these men invoked ties to surrounding indigenous city-states (*altepemeh*) distinguished them from the migrants-in-enclosure that conformed the majority of the mill's workforce.

Well over 100 and women, worked, ate, slept and essentially lived within the walls of Francisco de Brihuega' mill in 1583. More than half of all workers in the Rivas, Angulo and Castillo *obrajes* also labored in confinement (see Table 2.1). *Encerrado* workers throughout New Spain lived a de facto slavery by virtue of their permanent confinement. These conditions also extended to Puebla's bakeries (*panaderías*), where royal inspectors described indigenous workers as *encerrados*, "who are held like slaves."[27] In the late sixteenth century, coerced and confined urban laborers were commonplace throughout New Spain. During the 1570s even captured Englishmen sentenced to hard labor in Texcoco *obrajes* noted that they had worked "among the Indian slaves."[28] Workers were expected to remain

---

25 Ibid. This represents a minimum figure as many workers with Spanish or indigenous last names could have also migrated from rural settlements. Thirty of Francisco de Brihuega's locked-in workers held toponymic last names and most originated from the Puebla-Tlaxcala valley: Huexotzingo (2), Tepeaca (3), Tlaxcala (7), Tetela (4), Topoyango (1), Cholula (2), Cuautinchan (2). Workers from outside the Puebla-Tlaxcala Valley: Tecalco (1), Atizapan (1), Mexico (2), Tulancingo (1), Texcoco (1).

26 AGMP, Expedientes, Tomo 221r, 1r–2v.

27 Silvio Zavala, *Ordenanzas*, 218–219. Inspectors also held jurisdiction over tanneries and milliners' workshops in order to free *encerrados*.

28 Gibson, *Aztecs under Spanish Rule*, 243–244.

Table 2.1 *Workforces in inspected textile mills, 1583–1584*

Obraje	Workers	Men	Women	Assessed Fine
Francisco de Brihuega	115	20 free 62 locked-in	32	35 pesos
Alonso Gonzalez & Hernan Perez	77	27 free 24 locked-in	25 free 3 locked-in	n.a.
Francisco del Castillo	40	12 free 21 locked-in	7 free	30 pesos
Pedro de Angulo	30	6 free 18 locked-in	6 free	20 pesos
Juan de Rivas	111	84 locked-in	27	20 pesos

Source: Archivo General Municipal de Puebla, Expedientes, Tomo 221, ff. 2r-135v

in confinement, except for a privileged few. Francisco de Brihuega, for instance, nonchalantly admitted that only "ten or twelve Indians, more or less" were free to enter and leave the premises of his mill at any given time.[29] Moreover, he remarked, some worked from their homes while others had escaped his control, although he failed to mention why.

Since the objective of these official inspections was to corroborate whether indigenous workers were being confined or mistreated, a Nahuatl interpreter always accompanied the inspector on his tours of a given facility. By taking down the workers' testimony in their native language, an illusion of justice could be maintained for an otherwise terribly exploited population. While sixty-two men testified that they were in fact locked in the *obraje*, only two risked exposing the coercive conditions they all suffered. Besides confirming his confinement, Miguel Chapol accused that the mill's administrator "had mistreated him a few times by hitting him with a rod because of his *tiquio*," the Nahuatl term for labor.[30] For his part, Francico Tetela accused the administrators of making him work through the night. As a result of these transgressions, Francisco de Brihuega was forced to pay a symbolic 35-peso fine.

The inspections carried out in 1583–1584 reveal that while the New Laws of 1542 and the Ordinances of 1569 had theoretically provided the indigenous groups of Central Mexico with a series of rights, these were largely unenforceable within the textile mills of Puebla. By the late sixteenth century, the notoriety of *obrajes* as sites of rampant abuse was well established. For instance, Gabriel de Angulo, the brother of yet another *briocense* textile mill owner, Pedro de Angulo, was accused of hanging a "worker by his feet over a fire of burning chile peppers."[31] It is clear that *obraje* life

---

29 AGMP, Expedientes, Tomo 221r, 1r–2v.   30 Ibid.

31 Altman, *Transatlantic Ties*, 98. Curiously, this was a prehispanic punishment that had been traditionally doled out to disrespectful Nahua children. Unfortunately, establishing when and why

was characterized by corporal punishment, lack of sleep, insufficient food and a general disregard for human life. The abuse was succinctly captured in the sentencing of Pedro de Angulo. After inspecting the former's mill, a visiting judge ordered Angulo to

allow free entry and exit to the Indian men and women who are not forcibly subjected [*forçosos*]. He is to treat them well and will not awaken them before dawn or make them work through the night or during feast days.

He is to provide them with blankets with which to sleep and cover themselves and will satisfactorily provide cemita [bread] and meat rations. He is not to pay them in coarse cloths, or in kind of any sort, but only in [silver] reales.

This will be done under penalty of losing said money and the fines imposed by the ordinances against the aforementioned [Angulo] will be followed with all the rigor of the law.[32]

The Crown was theoretically committed to upholding the rights of indigenous people as free vassals, although in practical terms this was nearly impossible because textile production relied on confinement and coerced labor. Subjected workers, criminals or indebted people were offered no guarantees by even the most zealous inspectors.

Nonetheless, in urban centers like Puebla, officials could at least attempt to uphold basic rights if the affected parties were not overly influential. This is exactly what happened in Puebla as an insular political elite began to resent the immigrants from Brihuega.[33] As the latter consolidated their social standing in the city, Puebla's political elite launched a calculated attack on the *briocenses'* economic lifeline: the textile mills. The prosecution of the *obrajeros* was effective because it was common knowledge that indigenous workers lived in conditions resembling slavery within the workshops. More importantly, *briocenses* realized that they would always remain vulnerable to different political factions as long as they remained excluded from the Spanish municipal council and dependent on coerced indigenous labor.[34] The acquisition and exploitation of African and Asian slaves would resolve both of these problems.

---

these Spanish immigrants incorporated indigenous disciplinary techniques into Puebla's textile mills is beyond the scope of this study. See Matthew Restall, Lisa Sousa and Kevin Terraciano, eds. *Mesoamerican Voices: Native-Language Writings from Colonial Mexico, Oaxaca, Yucatan, and Guatemala* (Cambridge: Cambridge University Press 2005), 219–223.

32 AGMP, Expedientes, Tomo 221, 107 r.

33 In 1582, the *briocense* community of Puebla successfully convened an open council to discuss the election of "procuradores del común," who would be able to prosecute the established (read, non-*briocense*) members of Puebla's Spanish cabildo. See Altman, *Transatlantic Ties,* 94.

34 AGNP, Not. 4, Box 36, ff. 205r–206r. In May 1590, seven of Puebla's textile mill owners, six of whom were *briocenses,* granted power of attorney to Gabriel de Angulo and their attorney, Francisco de Herrera, to lobby their cases before Don Luis de Velasco, the viceroy and the Real Audiencia of Mexico.

Enslaved workers of African descent were especially at risk within the *obrajes*. Even though they formed a conspicuous minority, royal inspectors were not concerned with their well-being. According to Javier Villa-Flores, slaves "renounced God to provoke the intervention of the Inquisition as a strategy to gain at least temporary freedom from the brutal working conditions they endured."[35] Evidence of physical abuse against slaves is, thus, mostly found in blasphemy cases investigated by the Holy Office of the Inquisition. For instance, in 1596, Juan Carrasco, an enslaved black creole, "renounced god and his saints" after receiving "ten to twelve lashes" in a carding room (*enborriçadero*) of Marcos Rodríguez Zapata's *obraje*.[36] After being accused of this religious crime by another *obraje* slave, Carrasco was promptly processed by the Puebla's commissary for the Inquisition, sent to Mexico City in chains and sentenced to an additional 200 lashes. Two years later, the *obrajero* Cristóbal Jiménez's beat Juan Bautista, a slave of his, "applied hot pitch" to Juan's wounds and "then forced a firebrand into the slave's mouth." At this point, Bautista blasphemed in hopes of ending this dehumanizing abuse, but the beating continued.[37] Evidently, news of the case still reached the Inquisition's headquarters in Mexico City, even as Bautista's utterings failed to end the abuse.

By the 1620s, Mexico City's inquisitors consistently condemned *obraje* slaves to additional lashings (back in Puebla) in order to curb their desperate use of blasphemy. In a 1626 case that resulted in a 100-lash sentence, the inquisitors ordered that the punishment be inflicted "in the presence of all the people of said *obraje*."[38] The performance of these "public punishments" mattered immensely to Inquisition officals, even when they recognized that the everyday demands on textile workers were excessive (*si bien en los obrajes aprietan demasiadamente*).[39]

Over time, overseers even developed their own distinctive regimen of punishment within Puebla's textile mills. In the *obraje* owned by Juan López Paez de la Baña, enslaved workers suspected of stealing wool (or anything else) were punished in *arrobas*. Typically a unit of weight or measurement, an *arroba* became the equivalent of twenty-five lashes in the *obraje* context. In one harrowing case, Nicolás Rincón, a convicted *obraje* worker, admitted to having whipped the slave Pascual "six arrobas, minus five lashings, and this is the manner in which they are counted in the *obraje*."[40] Rincón's casual confession was confirmed by several other men, suggesting that

35 Javier Villa-Flores, *Dangerous Speech: A Social History of Blasphemy in Colonial Mexico* (Tucson: University of Arizona Press, 2006), 128.

36 AGN, Inquisición, Vol. 145, Exp. 12, 233r–252r.   37 Villa-Flores, *Dangerous Speech*, 127.

38 AGN, Inquisición, Vol. 356, Exps. 18, 19, and 20. Two other *obraje* blasphemy cases from Puebla resulted in lashing sentences that same year.

39 AGN, Indiferente Virreinal, Exp. 43, 1r.

40 AGN, Inquisición, Vol. 1551, Exp. 46, 618r–620v.

brutal punishments of this sort were not unique to this particular textile mill. In fact, this and other cases suggest that physical punishments of this sort were typically meted in the ground-level workspace (by the dyeing cauldron, in the carding room and so forth), but not in the residential areas of the *obraje*.

If *obrajes* became spaces of slavery and punishment during the long seventeenth century, such abuse was profoundly irrational. After all, the purchase of an enslaved person represented hundreds of pesos. Maiming or killing that same individual amounted to destroying an *obrajero's* human property, even if whippings effectively terrorized the mill's remaining population into submission. While no slave was above the threat of a whipping, slaves held in deposit for third parties, such as the aforementioned Pascual, were especially vulnerable in the mill.[41] The *obrajero* had not purchased them and they did not belong to the mill's slave community. Deposited slaves were outsiders; the cost of brutalizing their bodies did not weigh on an *obrajero's* personal relationships or financial calculations.

Cocoliztli and Debt

During the 1590s, Puebla's mill owners invested in the Portuguese-led transatlantic slave trade, albeit reluctantly. Three local interrelated factors accelerated this process: first, the decimation of the urban indigenous workforce due to epidemic disease; second, the political persecution of successful immigrant mill owners; and, third, a notable increase in the scale of *obraje* workforces. An examination of the multiple inventories and transactions of Alonso Gómez, Puebla's preeminent mill owner of the early seventeenth century, illustrates how all of these factors coalesced into a greater dependence on enslaved laborers by the end of the sixteenth century.

In December 1590, Alonso Gómez leased his mill, eleven black slaves and the debts of 130 native workers to Marcos de la Cueva, another Puebla resident.[42] Six of these enslaved men (Hernando, Gaspar, Baltazar, Bartolomé, Anton and Diego) labored as *tundidores*, or skilled shearsmen. Within the *obraje* context, these men had the specific task of trimming and leveling the coarse hairs off the woolen textiles produced on the looms.[43]

---

41 Ibid, 616. Pascual belonged to a Córdoba sugar plantation owned by Don Lope de Yribas. He was considered a slave held in deposit (*depositado*) in López Paez de la Baña's mill, but the *obrajero* could not even remember Pascual's name when presenting his testimony to the inquisitors.

42 AGNP, Not. 4, Box 26, 600r–603r. The three-year arrangement was a lucrative opportunity for the *obrajero*. Gómez would receive 16,000 pesos for the four-year lease, but more importantly, he would be able to serve on Puebla's powerful municipal council in 1593.

43 In 1579, Puebla's *obrajeros* successfully lobbied the viceroy for the right to employ skilled shearers who were not "examined masters" in their mills. The viceroy's approval effectively enabled enslaved journeymen to monopolize the task of *tundidor* for the next century. See Zavala, *Ordenanzas*, 150–151.

As the penultimate step in the textile process, shearing required considerable skill and significant training – much more than the carding and spinning of wool, for instance.[44] Nonetheless, Gómez made use of slave labor at practically every step of his operation. An enslaved fuller (*batanero*), carder (*cardador*) and dyer (*tintorero*) complemented the work of his indigenous laborers. María, an enslaved black cook, also played a crucial role in the mill. She was responsible for feeding more than 140 workers daily and was likely assisted by a number of indigenous women.[45] Only the activities of a loaned or pawned slave, "Dieguillo, Espinosa's negro" are unknown to us. Perhaps because of the sheer cost of acquiring and training each of these men, Gómez took the time to clearly establish each captive's name, occupation or alternate ownership. But he did not do the same for his indigenous laborers, even though they composed the overwhelming majority of the workforce. Their only distinguishing characteristic was their collective debt of 4,000 pesos, approximately 31 pesos each.[46]

A series of clauses within the lease of the Gómez mill expose the ideological underpinnings that differentiated the labor of indigenous workers from that of enslaved blacks. As the proprietor of eleven black bodies, Gómez assumed all of the financial risk associated with the death of his slaves during the three-year contract. Moreover, should the *obrajero* ever "want to remove one or two blacks" from the mill, he would be free to do so at any time.[47] By contrast, the lessee, Marcos de la Cueva, was to be held responsible for the death or flight of any of the 130 indigenous debtors, with one notable exception:

Should a notable cocolistle cause the death of many Indians, in that case [the lessee] has no obligation to replace them. Likewise, if the Justices [of the city] were to remove a few Indians as people wrongly held in the *obraje*, Marcos de la Cueva has no obligation to return them.[48]

In other words, death, especially among a coerced workforce numbering in the hundreds, was a constant of *obraje* life. Spaniards racialized their diverse worker populations based on their perception of epidemic disease.[49] In the document above, death by *cocoliztli* is imagined as a certainty for Nahua laborers (and indeed, is contractually written in as a potential warranty), just as a perceived biological immunity is simultaneously projected onto black workers. An equally damning conceptualization is evident in the idea

---

44 For a detailed breakdown of specialized *obraje* occupations, see Salvucci, *Textiles and Capitalism*, 47–52.

45 AGNP, Not. 4, Box 26, 600r–603r.   46 Ibid.   47 Ibid.   48 Ibid.

49 *Cocoliztli* could refer to any number of epidemic diseases (including smallpox and measles). A reported 1595 outbreak was especially deadly in Central Mexico. See Rebecca Dufendach, "Epidemic Contact: Nahua and Spanish Concepts of Disease, 1519–1615," (Ph.D. diss., University of California, Los Angeles, 2016), 117–164.

that natives could be "wrongly held" (*mal abidos*), whereas black slaves were owned and possessed in uncontested legimitacy.

Obrajeros and lessees anticipated that local authorities would rescue exploited indigenous workers just as the latter would succumb to epidemic disease. Enslaved black men and women would not find their time in the mill truncated by either scenario. This startling biological and legal juxtaposition of a single workforce leads us to question what type of social, material and spiritual conditions these men and women encountered in Puebla's *obrajes*. After all, the inspections of the 1580s made it perfectly clear that most workers, whether legally enslaved or not, spent the entirety of their days within the mill's confines.

Creating Urban Slaves by Decree

Although Crown officials began enforcing pro-indigenous legislation during the 1580s, the first concerted attack on *obrajero* power was only leveled in 1599. That year Viceroy Don Gaspar Zuñiga y Acevedo decreed that henceforth textile mills would only operate in four urban centers: Puebla, Valladolid (Morelia), Antequera (Oaxaca City) and Mexico City.[50] The decree represented a significant restructuring of textile production in New Spain. By 1597 *obrajes* could be found in at least twenty settlements throughout the viceroyalty – many of them deep in the indigenous hinterland and others in scarcely populated areas, where enforcing better working conditions was next to impossible.[51] Zuñiga's urbanization of textile production concentrated *obrajes* in "the cities and *cabezas* of the bishoprics" and increased surveillance. This was both a secular and religious enterprise: the viceroy noted that "prelates invested with his authority" and concerned with "the spiritual good" would aid in seeking "the remedy of the miserable indians."

Urban textile barons largely benefited from viceregal decrees that forced their competitors in smaller towns to relocate at great personal expense. The owners of emerging *obrajes* in Tepeaca, Tecamachalco, Huexotzingo, Cholula, Atlixco and Tlaxcala would now have to petition for viceregal exemptions or move their operations to Puebla.[52] In practice, mill owners from these surrounding settlements succesfully resisted these efforts by petitioning for exemptions. The most notable effect of Viceroy Zuñiga's efforts was not the centralization of textile operations, but the concentration of non-indigenous enslaved workforces in the largest urban

---

50 Zavala, *Ordenanzas*, 169–171.   51 Viqueira and Urquiola, *Los obrajes*, 107.

52 Zavala, *Ordenanzas*, 172–180. A similar process would have taken place the outskirts of Mexico City, Antequera and Valladolid.

centers.[53] As city residents with greater access to creditors and slave trading networks, Poblano mill owners invested in the transatlantic slave trade (albeit, reluctantly). A greater concentration of Crown officials and inspectors in Puebla may have also provided greater incentive to comply with royal mandates.

For native laborers confined within the *obrajes*, significant changes would only arrive with the dawn of the seventeenth century. In 1602, viceroy Zuñiga finally enforced King Philip III's decree ordering the release of all indigenous workers (illegally retained or not) from textile mills and their replacement by black slaves.[54] This unprecedented measure, to be implemented in four months, forced New Spain's mill owners into the transatlantic slave trade. Puebla would be particularly affected by these measures, and a flurry of letters of appeals soon reached the viceroy. The Crown's initiative, however, achieved its desired effect. *Obrajeros* purchased approximately 500 enslaved people in Puebla between 1590 and 1639.[55] Evidently, this was an insufficient number. If 2,000 to 3,000 indigenous workers had toiled in the city's *obrajes* prior to Philip III's decrees, a much greater investment would have to be made in the transatlantic slave trade. Nonetheless, Philip III's humanitarian stance toward the indigenous people of Central Mexico created a new, localized demand for African and Asian slave labor in Puebla and other textile centers.

The hundreds of slaves purchased by *obrajeros* during the early seventeenth century may erroneously suggest that mill owners looked favorably on chattel slavery. In fact, most did not. In 1616, Puebla's *obrajeros* pressured the municipal council into drafting a formal proposition to be delivered to the viceroy. The mill owners attempted to rationalize their resistance to replacing indigenous workers with slaves of African descent. In their own words,

the black [slaves] are not suited for such labor because they are clumsy and lack the required ability and skill. Furthermore, they cannot be had as many as are necessary because they are very expensive and many die, and if the Indians were to go missing so would the *obrajes* . . . and the royal sales tax and his Majesty's duties

53 Carlos Arturo Giordano Sánchez Verín, *Obraje y economía en Tlaxcala a principios del siglo XVII, 1600–1630* (Mexico City: Archivo General de la Nación, 2002) 40–41.

54 Zavala, *Ordenanzas*, 181–189.

55 AGNP, Not. 3, Boxes 12, 31, 50, 62–74, 75–77; Not. 4, Boxes 36, 41, 98–102, 102bis, 122–124, 137–139, 150–152; AHJP, Exp. 713 & 823. Slave sales for 99 workers were identified in a quinquennial sample of the AGNP's second, third, fourth and sixth notarial offices for the 1590–1639 period. This would lead to a conservative projection of at least 500 *obraje* slave purchases. This calculation excludes data on enslaved people who were leased into textile mills. *Obrajeros* from Tlaxcala, Atlixco and Cholula purchased seventeen slaves, while Poblano *obrajeros* account for eighty-two slaves. This sample does not include milliners, who were often described as owners of "hat-making *obrajes*." It also does not account for slaves sold out of *obrajes*.

would decrease, and this Republic and its neighbors would suffer great needs and labors.[56]

Obrajero resistance to slave purchases centered on three points. The first objection, related to Africans' alleged inability to produce quality textiles, can be easily dismissed. During the second decade of the seventeenth century, most enslaved people in Puebla hailed from the Kongolese and Angolan hinterland – areas well known for their elaborate textiles. Seventeenth-century Central Africans expertly combined raffia, cotton and vegetable fibers to produce clothing items for high-ranking individuals in their home societies.[57] Moreover, the adoption of European clothing by Kongolese elites served as a significant class marker by the late sixteenth century. According to Duarte Lopes, "only the common people . . . who cannot make clothing in the Portuguese fashion for themselves, retained their unchanged customs."[58] Lopes's observation suggests that Kongolese weavers were experimenting with Iberian cloths and techniques just as the transatlantic slave trade to Mexico and Spanish America intensified. The alleged technical inferiority of Kongolese and Angolan weavers was little more than a preamble to *obrajeros'* financial concerns regarding the acquisition of enslaved Africans.

Based on their second objection, Puebla's textile barons were especially concerned about the cost and mortality of black slaves in their mills. Despite an imagined immunity to disease, slaves of African descent suffered considerably from the epidemics that devastated the indigenous populations of Central Mexico.[59] New African arrivals had to contend with a new disease environment at 7,000 feet above sea level in addition to the terrible filth and working conditions of the *obraje* itself. On their end, *obrajeros* had a vested interest in providing medical treatment for all workers, but especially for purchased slaves. For instance, in 1611 the surgeon Alonso Domínguez filed a formal complaint against Juan de Ortega for 51 pesos in wages for four years of "cures" in the latter's *obraje*.[60] These expenses were the remainder of a larger unspecified amount that Ortega had paid Domínguez.

56 AGMP, Actas de Cabildo, 1616/06/28, Vol. 15, ff. 111r–111v.

57 Cécile Fromont, *The Art of Conversion: Christian Visual Culture in the Kingdom of Kongo* (Williamsburg: Omohundro Institute, 2014), 95, 123–132. Kongolese textile workers had been exposed to European clothing and regalia via the Portuguese since 1482.

58 Fromont, *The Art*, 112. For a discussion of Central African weaving techniques, see Jeremy Coote, "A Textile Text-Book at the Pitt Rivers Museum," *African Arts* 48, no. 1 (Spring 2015): 66–68.

59 Don Domingo de San Antón Muñón Chimalpahin, *Annals of His Time*, edited and translated by James Lockhart, Susan Schroeder, and Doris Namala (Stanford, CA: Stanford University Press, 2006), 27; Peter Gerhard, *A Guide to the Historical Geography of New Spain* (Norman: University of Oklahoma Press, 1993), 22–25.

60 AHJP, Exp. 851, 3r.

From the perspective of mill owners, medical care was an additional expense to consider in addition to the thousands of pesos spent on slave purchases. On average, Puebla's *obrajeros* paid 321 pesos for enslaved textile workers – not an insignificant sum of money.[61] By contrast, a nominally free indigenous worker could be secured for a 20- to 30-peso cash advance during the same period. Of course, employing indigenous workers attracted the attention of Crown inspectors, who repeatedly liberated them. Perceptions of technical skill were irrelevant to *obraje* owners when the cost of staffing their looms grew ten or fifteen times over. By 1597, the average textile mill in Puebla relied on seventy workers.[62] Such a workforce could be acquired by amounting to an expenditure of 1,400 to 2,100 pesos for an all-indigenous workforce with an average debt of 30 pesos. An identical workforce of seventy enslaved laborers would have represented an investment of no less than 22,470 pesos. Most mill owners would have been forced to reduce the size of their workforces considerably in transferring to all-slave laborers. In this respect, *obrajeros* were correct in highlighting the damaging effect of royal decrees on textile production. They tied this concern to their third objection, one close to the municipal council's interests: the diminishment of sales taxes.

Despite their financial lamentations, *obrajeros* did benefit from slave ownership in that enslaved men could be used for clandestine purposes outside of the textile mill. *Obrajeros* would occasionally release a few trusted slaves from their confinement for specific purposes. In 1607, a group of *obraje* slaves invaded a contested water hole (*ojo de agua*) and its adjoining lands. When the affected party asked who had authorized such a project, "an old black slave of Pedro Gómez . . . said that his master Pedro Gómez had told them to make a ditch."[63] More severe cases involved sending enslaved men and free employees to kidnap indigenous people for *obraje* labor. In a 1603 case, a diverse group of men affiliated with Sebastián Tomellín's *obraje* attacked and bound an indigenous man from Pachuca who was then forced to accept a cash advance from the mill owner. The case led to a wider investigation that revealed how Tomellín's men repeatedly kidnapped *indios* and then "sold" them to him for "fifteen to twenty pesos each."[64] In a similar incident from 1620, a Spaniard, two mestizos and Juan Alonso, a mulatto slave of Pedro del Río, seized an 8-year-old indigenous girl and took off on

---

61 See note 55 for this chapter. The 99 purchases for which prices are included amounted to a total of 31,821 pesos. Sixteen transactions involved skilled slaves who were bought for more than 400 pesos each.

62 Viqueira and Urquiola, *Los obrajes*, 139.

63 AGI, Escribanía, 168A, 1v. The affected party was the grandson of the conquistador Francisco de Oliveros, leading to another legal case between Puebla's old landed families and *briocense* textile barons.

64 AHJP, Exp. 643, 2r, 17r.

horseback. The child was later found in del Río's *obraje*, but was only freed after her mother produced an order of release (which had to be obtained in Mexico City).[65]

Cases such as these demonstrate that early-seventeenth-century *obrajeros* sought to acquire indigenous laborers by any means necessary, even requiring enslaved men to commit serious crimes. Mill owners and free overseers deployed male slaves in this capacity in order to protect themselves from criminal charges. For the enslaved, criminal prosecution led to imprisonment, a slightly different form of confinement than the one they usually experienced in the texile mill.[66] *Obrajeros* were more than willing to pay small fines for the release of their imprisoned slaves, especially if such penalties allowed the former to acquire cheap indigenous workforces. Despite the scandal generated by these kidnappings, it is important to keep in mind that most enslaved textile workers never left the confines of the mill. Urban mobility was the domain of only a privileged few *obraje* slaves, and these were disproportionately female. We now turn to their experiences.

Gender, Mobility and Companionship

During the course of the long seventeenth century, Puebla's *obrajes* operated as sexually unbalanced spaces demographically dominated by men. However, enslaved women were also active participants in the mills as cooks, domestic servants, messengers, mothers and wives. The spatial and occupational divide of the *obraje* complex (upper/domestic and lower/textile) complicated the socialization of enslaved people, even if on paper they all represented human property. By necessity, slave women had greater access to the kitchen, pantry and sleeping quarters that were found on the second floor of most *obrajes*.[67] For instance, in 1622, two slave women worked in the mill and residence of Pedro Gómez. Ana, a black woman "who serves in the bedroom," and a *china* named Gracia worked in the owner's living quarters upstairs ("del servicio de arriba").[68] Ana and Gracia were bound to the demands of the *obrajero's* wife, which presumably entailed cooking and cleaning, but also attending church services, delivering messages and purchasing provisions at market.

Another enslaved woman, Isabelilla, performed crucial tasks in and outside of the Gómez textile mill. In 1623, Isabelilla was responsible for delivering several payments throughout the city for Lázaro Gómez, the mill's overseer.[69] Lázaro exhibited a great deal of trust in his enslaved messenger. "On April 26, I sent Doña María thirty pesos with Isabellilla, the black

65 AHJP, Exp. 1054, 2r–4r.   66 Ibid., 5r–6r.
67 Salvucci, *Textiles and Capitalism*, 34–37.   68 AHJP, Exp. 1235, 22v.
69 AHJP, Exp. 1235, 411r. Many thanks to Blanca Lara Tenorio for sharing her notes on this case.

woman," read a common entry in his ledger. He sent Isabelilla on at least another nine deliveries for 25 to 50 pesos at a time. Some of these funds were the monthly wages of the mill's free weavers. The enslaved woman was so important to the *obraje*'s operations, in fact, that Lázaro twice referred to her as "my black administrator" (*mi negra administradora*).[70]

Despite their importance within the Gómez textile mill, enslaved *obraje* women remained relatively scarce in Puebla during the early seventeenth century. Pedro de Hita's textile mill circa 1607 provides a good example of this severe gender imbalance. Out of Hita's 189 textile laborers, nine were slaves, and of these, only three were women. That the twenty-year-old María "Angola" worked as a corn grinder (*moledora*) suggests that mill owners associated some enslaved women with food preparation. Another enslaved María did not have a specified occupation, as was the case with Magdalena, the thirty-five-year-old wife of Jerónimo. Magdalena's status as a married woman allowed her to identify with the numerous indigenous wives in the mill. She likely also sustained some contact with a free, married *mulata* by the name of Ana Hernández, who worked as a wool spinner. The inclusion of these two married women in Hita's 1607 inventory is suggestive of slaves' need and desire for companionship.[71]

These interactions force us to look past *obrajes* as more than sites of textile production and corporal punishment. Altman has suggested that "the *obraje* can also be understood as an institution that facilitated the integration of members of several groups into a new society and introduced them to a new form of productive enterprise."[72] Puebla's textile mills produced varying levels of socialization that cut across gendered, racial, ethnic, linguistic and judicial lines. To borrow Mary Louise Pratt's "contact zones" concept, *obrajes* where spaces, in which "cultures meet, clash, and grapple with each other, often in contexts of highly assymetrical relations of power."[73] This was certainly the case in Puebla, where the victims of the seventeenth-century slave trade negotiated the rigors of the textile mill alongside their indigenous counterparts.

The experiences of Asian men and women as textile workers are particularly important to this discussion, given the extreme gender imbalance among this group. Labeled as *chinos* and *chinas*, enslaved individuals from the Bay of Bengal, Goa, Malacca and other South Asian ports and provinces (often described as "the Indies of Portugal") entered the viceroyalty of New Spain via the port of Acapulco during the seventeenth century.[74]

---

70 Ibid., 278r, 279v.

71 Six other enslaved men, apparently single, formed part of this community, which would have also included two free, but indebted, mulatto weavers and forty-seven indigenous workers.

72 Altman, *Transatlantic Ties*, 80.

73 Mary Louise Pratt, "Arts of the Contact Zones" *Profession* 91 (New York: MLA, 1991), 33–40.

74 Tatiana Seijas, "Transpacific Servitude: The Asian Slaves of Colonial Mexico, 1580–1700," Doctoral dissertation (Yale, 2008), 38–41.

Numerous references to this minority population suddenly appear in Puebla's textile mills during the early 1620s, at the same moment the transatlantic slave trade to New Spain peaked. In 1623, for instance, twelve Asian slaves worked alongside eleven enslaved blacks and mulattos in the *obraje* of Pedro Gómez.[75] Another fifteen enslaved *chinos* toiled in the Carrillo family's mill in 1655.

An almost overwhelmingly male transpacific slave trade meant that Asian men in *obrajes* would have to seek companionship among women from different backgrounds.[76] For the same reason, references to *chino* children are exceedingly rare in seventeenth-century Puebla. The very absence of Asian women simultaneously nullified the possiblity of natural slave reproduction for this specific population. In a colonial setting in which slavery was contingent upon the enslaved woman's womb, Asian women should have represented a valuable alternative to the importation of African women. In practice, they did not.

Obraje Dynamics: Marriage, Coercion and Slave Reproduction

Obraje slavery must also be studied in relation to the "the web of expectations about childbirth held both by black women and men and those who enslaved them."[77] Although "women's lives under slavery in the Americas always included the possibilites of their wombs," *obrajeros* in sixteenth-century Puebla did not systematically purchase enslaved women for their "future increase" as they did in eighteenth-century Barbados and South Carolina.[78] Mill owners' relative indifference toward enslaved women's reproductive potential would begin to change in the 1630s.

During the mid-seventeenth century, Puebla's *obrajeros* invested in slave marriage as a method of ensuring the procreation of *obraje* slaves. Although Puebla's mill owners never maintained balanced male-to-female ratios, they were increasingly concerned by their slaves' natural "increase." In the 1645 lease of the Fresneda textile mill in nearby Atlixco, the (hypothetical) children born to an unnamed *mulata* were to become the property of the mill owner, Agustín de Sierra Vargas. Moreover, he would also come to possess "any of the children of other female slaves [*esclavas*] who might enter the *obraje*."[79] The lessee, by contrast, only held rights to these

---

75 AHJP, Exp. 1235, 22r–23r.

76 Only one enslaved *china*, Ana de la Cruz, appears in four *obraje* inventories for the early 1660s. Twenty-nine male Asian slaves appear in these inventories. See AGNP, Not. 3, Box 116, 1664 February, 64r.

77 Morgan, *Laboring Women*, 4.   78 Morgan, *Laboring Women*, 136–139.

79 AGNP, Not. 4, Box 170, 1645/10/20, 451r–458r. By the mid-1640s, Sierra Vargas was also deeply pessimistic about the state of *obraje* ownerhship. He agreed to lease his mill "in consideration that the affairs and ministries of the *haziendas de obrajes* are lost, and that neither in their administration nor in their body of goods is there enough of wealth to rescue them, [instead] one expects greater damages each day."

hypothetically enslaved children during the duration of the nine-year lease. Five years later, Jerónimo Tornes, the owner "of a hat-making workshop" (*obraje de hacer sombreros*) claimed dominion over "thirty-four pieces of slaves, journeymen and black [women] of my service and their small children."[80] Here, then, are local examples of "the web of expectations about child-birth" that informed a diasporic experience for women of African descent.[81] Within the confines of Puebla's increasingly racialized and slave-dependent mills, it was females of African descent who effectively transformed the composition of *obraje* demographics. For the slave owners of New Spain, the abrupt closing of the transatlantic slave trade in December of 1640 incentivized the natural reproduction of their coerced workforces. Ironically, enslaved African and Asian men found themselves working side-by-side with large numbers of enslaved black women only after the end of the Lusophone slave trade.

The presence of married couples in Puebla's *obrajes* may suggest that enslaved and free people held a modicum of authority over their bodies, emotions and desires. However, marital registers must also be studied from the cold, rational perspective of slave owners bent on augmenting the size of their coerced workforces at minimal cost. According to Richard Salvucci, *obrajeros* frequently exploited indigenous couples by "jointly indebting" husband and wives.[82] Thus, a couple's labor and their debts would be linked to a single mill. This spurious practice was directly tied to a worker's ability to enter and exit the mill and, thus, became known as *salir al trocado* (leaving in exchange for another).[83] Should one spouse fail in his or her obligations, fall sick, or perish, the other would pay the mill owner in labor. In this regard, manipulating slave matrimony became a crucial instrument of control among the *obrajero* class. This family-binding strategy was already well established since the 1580s, when indigenous women were listed in *obraje* inventories as "Joaquin's Sabina" or "Salvador's Juana."[84] By 1626, nine of the fifteen women who worked in Cristóbal de Carrera's mill were married to men in the *obraje*.[85] *Obrajeros* developed and intensified these labor-acquiring strategies in accordance with the increasing rights and protections afforded to Central Mexico's indigenous populations.

Despite the considerable obstacles inherent in *obraje* life, numerous enslaved laborers managed to formalize long-lasting relationships via the sacrament of matrimony. Of course, "parish books should not be viewed as

---

80 AGNP, Not. 4, Box 174, 1650 Testaments, 96r. Tornes would bequeath four of these enslaved women to the Santísima Trinidad convent as domestic servants for his daughters.

81 Morgan, *Laboring Women*, 4.

82 Richard Salvucci, *Textiles and Capitalism in Mexico* (Princeton, NJ: Princeton University Press, 1987), 116.

83 AGMP, Expedientes, Tomo 224, 3r.   84 AGMP, Expedientes, Tomo 221, 1v.

85 AHJP, Exp. 1355, 1626/02/10.

neutral or objective records" as measures of socialization, or as statistical indices of endogamous or exogamous unions.[86] This same concern should also apply to marriages among enslaved people in *obrajes*. Herman Bennett, for instance, has argued that "[t]hrough Christian marriages, Africans inaugurated and sustained the process of ethnogenesis, the creation of social networks inside the structures of domination."[87] Bennett's research proves that "most Angolans" in seventeenth-century Mexico City "established the most intimate associations with persons similarly identified."[88] Yet can one speak of ethnogenesis or marital agency within the confines of the textile mill? After all, these were spaces of coercion and punishment. Some *obrajes* even featured interior chapels to prevent slaves from leaving their confines to hear Mass.[89]

Thus, we must address the thorny issue of whether marriage between enslaved people in textile mills represented slave agency, slave-owner influence or perhaps both. Did indigenous women willingly enter formal unions with slaves of African or Asian descent within Puebla's *obrajes*? María Elena Cortés Jacome has demonstrated that free *obraje* wives of all backgrounds fled their confined husbands when conditions became intolerable.[90] Questions of willingness and coercion should also be extended to enslaved women in relation to their *obraje* spouses. Let us return to Alonso Gómez's textile mill. Between 1591 and 1605, eight of his enslaved male workers married in Puebla's cathedral chapter.[91] Yet only one of these men managed to marry a woman not employed or owned by Gómez.[92] The same pattern appears among the married workers of the *obrajeros* Francisco Ligero and Juan Barranco at the end of the sixteenth century.[93] Evidently, most enslaved people in Puebla were not subjected to this level of slaveholder

---

86 Douglas R. Cope, *The Limits of Racial Domination* (Madison: University of Wisconsin Press, 1994), 69.

87 Bennett, *Colonial Blackness*, 76. According to Bennett, from 1570 to 1640 African ethnicity remained the deciding factor in a slave's decision to marry in Mexico City. Patricia Seed notes that "two-thirds of all prenuptial conflicts brought before church officials in Mexico City between 1574 and 1689, couples and their advocates alleged excessive coercion." Patricia Seed, *To Love, Honor and Obey in Colonial Mexico: Conflicts over Marriage Choice, 1574–1821* (Stanford, CA: Stanford University Press, 1988), 42.

88 Bennett, *Colonial Blackness*, 78. Bennett notes that between 1595 and 1650, 72 percent of enslaved Angolans selected other Angolans as obs in Mexico City's Santa Veracruz and Salto del Agua parishes.

89 Salvucci, *Textiles and Capitalism*, 37; Jean-Pierre Tardieu, "Negros e indios en el *obraje* de San Ildefonso," *Revista de Indias* 77 no. 255 (2012), 537.

90 María Elena Cortés Jacome, "Los ardides de los amos: la manipulación y la interdependencia en la vida conyugal de sus esclavos," in *Del dicho al hecho... Transgresiones y pautas culturales en la Nueva España* (Mexico City: INAH, 1989), 47–49.

91 ASMP, *Libro de matrimonios de negros*, 1586–1606.   92 Ibid.

93 Ibid. Of the five brides employed or owned by Barranco between 1589 and 1593, four married men associated with the *obraje*.

influence with regard to their marital choices. Most non-*obraje* slaves had the right to conjugal visits at least once a week. Yet by promoting formal unions (endogamous and exogamous), *obrajeros* could guarantee the uncontested confinement of their laborers.[94] Why leave the textile mill if both husband and wife inhabited the same space? Within the *obraje* context, there are serious doubts that enslaved people exercised their will when choosing a spouse. Coercion was a defining element of *obraje* marriages.

During the early seventeenth century, practically any marriage between Africans would have proven beneficial to *obrajeros* as a binding union between unfree people. The same could be said for Asians were it not for the very reduced population of *chinas*. As a result, slave owners would often sponsor their unfree workers' marriages, cover their church fees or at least loan them cash advances for their religious expenses.[95] Sebastián Munguía, an enslaved Kongolese man, certainly understood his own *obraje* marriage to Isabel, an "Angola" slave, in relation to his master's motivations. Munguía alleged that the *obrajero* Luis de Mesquita had offered "them six pesos for the [marriage] rights" to formalize their union. Munguía understood this sponsorship as an attempt to keep him confined. Sebastián no longer had a legitimate reason to escape the textile mill, nor could the ecclesiastical authorities charge the *obrajero* with impeding a wedded Christian couple from engaging in conjugal life. Referring to himself as a financial investment, the Kongolese man suggested that by marrying another *obraje* slave Mesquita could successfully "secure his money."[96]

Based on *obraje*-by-*obraje* analysis of Puebla's surviving marital registers, Sebastián Munguía's perception of his master's motivations was absolutely correct. Seventeenth-century mill owners co-opted the sacrament of matrimony to increase their control over enslaved workers. This was certainly the case among Bartolomé de Tapia's forty-six slaves. Between 1629 and 1646, fifty-eight of his workers, free and unfree alike, married in Puebla's San José parish.[97] Twenty marriages took place between workers owned or employed by Tapia. In other words, more than 68 percent of Tapia's employees or slaves married people similarly defined. Of the twenty-eight black, mulatto and indigenous women affiliated to his *obraje* through slavery or debt, only six were able to marry men with no direct connection to the mill owner. Tapia incentivized marriage as long as potential grooms and brides married others under his control. In an urban setting defined by physical and financial control over spouses, marriage may have actually become a

94 Norma Angélica Castillo Palma, "Matrimonios mixtos y cruce de la barrera de color como vías para el *mestizaje* de la población negra y mulata (1674–1696)," *Signos Históricos* 2, no. 4 (June–Dec. 2000), 113.
95 AGN, Inquisición, Vol. 399, Exp. 2, 295v.   96 AGN, Inquisición, Vol. 399, Exp. 2, 307v.
97 APSJ, *Libro de matrimonios de morenos, 1629–1657*, 1v–31v.

Table 2.2 *Number of married slaves owned by* obrajeros *in seventeenth-century Puebla*

Obraje owner	Parish	Years	Male	Female	Total
Capt. Diego de Andrada Peralta	Sagrario	1664–1690	73	21	94
Bartolomé de Tapia	S. José	1629–1646	27	19	46
Juan Moreno	Sagrario	1663–1682	24	9	33
Capt. Don Domingo de Apressa	Sagrario	1687–1699	20	2	22
Capt. Don Pedro de Andrada Peralta	Sagrario	1690–1698	14	6	20
Capt. Gabriel Carrillo de Aranda	Sagrario	1678–1684	11	5	16
Capt. Don Juan de Guadalajara	Sagrario	1662–1682	7	7	14
Don Jerónimo Carrillo	Analco	1650–1656	9	2	11
Joseph de Tapia	S. José	1647–1654	5	5	10

Source: ASMP, APSJ & AHPA, *Libros de matrimonios de negros y mulatos*, 1629–1700. Table only includes *obrajeros* with ten or more slaves in the marital record.

liability for *obraje* slaves and their loved ones. These coercive practices continued well into the late seventeenth century and reached their apogee within Capt. Diego de Andrada Peralta's textile mill (see Table 2.2). Acknowledging these practices implies that some secular priests were simply indifferent or complicit with *obrajeros* in their influence over slave marriage.[98]

Obrajero interest in marriage and slave reproduction is especially notable in the two inventories produced for the Carrillo family's textile mill in 1655 and 1660. In 1655, Doña Francisca de Barrientos, widow and heir to Miguel Carrillo, leased the family's textile mill to her son, Don Jerónimo Carrillo Barrientos.[99] The lease included the rights to a large slave community of fifteen women and sixty-two men. It was a diverse, aging, sexually imbalanced group of laborers, with only a dozen laborers under the age of 30. In many ways, the *obraje* was representative of what one might expect from a slave-dependent enterprise in a city increasingly cut off from transatlantic slave trade. Enslaved creole and mulatto men and women outnumbered the twenty Africans labeled as *Angola, Benguela, Matamba* and *Anchico* people. These enslaved men represented the permanency that Puebla's mill owners had so desperately sought out at the beginning of the seventeenth century. On how many looms had the sixty-year old Manuel Mayayo worked? A cohort of fifteen Asian slaves, all men, and a few years younger than their African counterparts, also inhabited the *obraje*. For the handful of children living in enclosure, this group of people *was* the Carrillo

---

98 For a stunning image of the role of priests in coerced marriage in the Andean region during the early seventeenth century, see Guaman Poma de Ayala, *Nueva corónica y Buen gobierno* (1615), f. 573/587 (http://www.kb.dk/permalink/2006/poma/587/es/text/?open=idp468800) accessed 11/05/2017.

99 AGNP, Not. 3, Box 106, 1655 February, 1r–2v.

mill. Over the next five years, these youths would become an integral part of the workforce, their childhoods melding into the woolen textiles and looms.

By 1660, the proportion of women and children increased substantially within the Carrillo textile mill. Twenty-five women, ages four through seventy-four, now labored in enclosure.[100] That the number of children also rose during the same period was no coincidence. Ten children, who had not been accounted for in the 1655 lease, now appeared as property of the Carrillo family.[101] The administators of the mill understood that enslaved women and children were essential to its survival. The former acquired two enslaved mulatto mothers, Josefa de Aparicio and María de la Concepción. By 1660, María's 6- and 7-year-old daughters, Tomasa and Angela, belonged to the *obraje* community. For her part, Josefa gave birth to Lorenzo just two months before the last inventory was conducted. Along with Juan, age 8, Ignacia, 4, and Gabriel, 3, her progeny guaranteed the Carrillo family many more years of labor with little to no regard for the vicissitudes of the slave trade.

It is crucial to understand that the names of these women entered the notarial record as mothers and producers of slaves. No mention is made of the biological fathers of any of the above-mentioned children, a fact which should not diminish the possible affection, indifference and/or violence by which they were engendered. We simply do not know what circumstances led to their birth, but it is clear that these children benefited the Carrillos substantially. Another eight enslaved youths, aged 13 to 18, also labored in the textile mill as full-fledged workers.[102] Perhaps because of their status as working adolescents and human property, the names of their parents were not included in the inventory. In other words, Carrillo could count on his slaves to procreate between 13 and 23 percent of his workforce.

The Political Uses of Slavery

When *obrajeros* exploited enslaved women for sexual and reproductive purposes, they were not demonstrating a shifting preference for workers of African descent. The textile mills of Puebla became predominantly slave spaces during the mid-seventeenth century because *obrajeros* were politically motivated actors. Slavery allowed them to respond to labor reforms and ordinances that demanded a thorough restructuring of textile production. Ever since the days of the Marquis of Villamanrique (1585–1590), Puebla's

---

100 AGNP, Not. 4, Box 189, 1660 October, 1016r–1021r.
101 In a contemporary *obraje* in Quito, infants born to enslaved women were raised and breastfed by wage-earning indigenous women. See Tardieu, "Negros e indios en el *obraje* de San Ildefonso," 534–536.
102 Ibid.

obrajeros (read, immigrants from Brihuega) had been prohibited from hold-ing public office.[103] Only through different forms of subterfuge, such as leasing a mill to a close friend or relative, did mill owners like Alonso Gómez managed to serve on the Spanish municipal council (*cabildo*).[104] Well-connected men, however, learned to work the commercial and politi-cal spheres to their benefit. *Obrajeros* with sufficient political clout, such as Pedro Gómez and at least ten others, continued to exploit hundreds of con-fined indigenous laborers well into the 1620s.[105] The mill owner Cristobal de la Carrera recorded the debts of at least 108 indigenous workers, four free mulattos and one "chino mestizo" in 1626.[106]

By 1630, *obrajeros* were firmly entrenched in Puebla's municipal coun-cil. In late December of that year, Juan García del Castillo, who claimed the title of city regent as early as 1624,[107] agreed to sell his textile mill to Hernando de Chávez Tovar. In order to comply with the Crown's protec-tionist decrees, the former agreed to an inspection of his financial books and laborers. This was a gargantuan task, as García del Castillo owned what was undoubtedly one of the largest textile workforces in New Spain. A hundred slaves of African and Asian descent worked alongside another 150 indige-nous laborers.[108] Only indigenous workers would be given the chance to "liquidate" their debts. If unable to do so, their "willingness" to remain in the *obraje* would be recorded before a scribe and a Nahuatl interpreter.[109]

García del Castillo had ulterior motives in orchestrating the inspection and transfer of the *obraje*. Only a month after selling the mill, he would present city council with a petition in regard to his laborers' needs: "Being so many [workers] in number it is impossible that they be sustained with the little fresh water from a well that I have in [the *obraje*], and so that they might not suffer this need, I intend to ask your graces to grant me two *pajas* of water from the conduit that goes from the public plaza to the [church of] Our Lady of the Remedies."[110] He offered 300 pesos for the construction costs to sweeten the deal. The city council authorized the construction of water box to distribute the liquid that same day. Despite the notarized sale, the *obrajero* intended to retain ownership of the mill, otherwise there would

---

103 AGN, Gobierno Virreinal, Reales Cédulas Duplicadas, Vol. D20, Exp. 82, 52r–52v.
104 Altman, *Transatlantic Ties*, 91–92. Gómez had held the office of city regent (*regidor*) in 1593 and two years later, Pedro de Angulo, another successful migrant from Brihuega, held the same position. Also see ASMP, *Libro de matrimonios de negros*, 1586–1606, entries for 1593/01/31 and 1595/02/07.
105 Viqueira and Urquiola, *Los obrajes*, 140.   106 AHJP, Exp. 1355.
107 Gantes Tréllez, "Aspectos socioeconómicos," 259–263.
108 AGMP, Actas de Cabildo, Vol. 17, 255/246.
109 AGNP, Not. 4, Box 139, 1630 Diciembre, no folio, 1630/12/31.
110 AGMP, Actas de Cabildo, Vol. 17, 255/246. "Y por ser tanto numero no es posible se sustenten con agua dulze sino con la de un poço que tengo en el y Para que no padescan esta nesesidad Pretendo que Vuestra señoría se sirva de hacerme merced de dos Pajas de agua de la atarjea que ba de la Plaça publica a Nuestra Señora de los Remedios."

have been no point in investing in its infrastructure. Influential *obrajeros* in Puebla temporarily renounced their mills in order to curry political favors in city council.[111] Having expanded their properties or gained water rights, they then reacquired their *obrajes*. This was little more than subterfuge. Along with the continued exploitation of hundreds of indigenous workers, these corrupt practices justified a heavy-handed response from the Crown and its viceroys.

For Puebla's ambitious *obrajeros*, access to the influential offices of the municipal council hinged on ridding themselves of the indigenous work-forces that had provided them incredible wealth and labor for decades. Yet in contrast to the first years of the seventeenth century, by the 1630s replacing indigenous workers with black and mulatto captives was actually feasible. At least 10,000 men, women and children, mostly of African descent, were sold on the Puebla slave market between 1600 and 1639 (see Chapter 4). Enslaved laborers were readily available for mill owners able to finance the transition away from indigenous labor. Puebla's *obrajeros* simply did not want to.

In 1631, viceroy Rodrigo Pacheco de Osorio, the Marquis of Cerralvo, led a renewed royal backlash against Puebla's *obrajeros*. In 1633, he confirmed the Crown's stance by decreeing, "no regent may serve as an *obrajero* . . . likewise, the *obrajero* may not be elected into any office involving the administration of justice, and should he accept [such a post], he will suffer the loss of his textile mill."[112] In a show of force, the viceroy imposed a 44,000-peso fine on ten mill owners "for the liberation of their faults and the sentencing of their overseers, slaves and servants."[113] Shocked by this unprecedented punishment, Puebla's *obrajeros* offered a collective 50,000-peso payment to the Royal Treasury to placate Cerralvo, but the viceroy flatly refused.[114] In a letter to the king, Cerralvo noted that he would not relent in his campaign against Puebla's *obrajeros* for "less than 100,000 pesos." By early 1634, the same mill owners capitulated by submitting 103,550 pesos in *"composiciones."*[115] This stunning fine signaled that the Crown and viceroy would enforce the transition to non-indigenous textile labor or destroy Puebla's *obrajes* in the process.

Research in Puebla's notarial archives suggests that *obrajeros* purchased most of their slaves during the 1630s, when slave prices and purchases

---

111 AGMP, Actas de Cabildo, Vol. 15, 133/132. In 1616 García del Castillo sold his *obraje* to his mother, Doña Ana del Castillo. This was evidently a political measure that in no way kept him from controlling the *obraje*.

112 Zavala, *Ordenanzas*, 198.   113 Gantes Tréllez, "Aspectos socioeconómicos," 298.

114 AGI, México, 31, n. 14. Cerralvo's actions must also be contextualized within the royal initiative to put an end to the *repartimiento de indios*. The *repartimiento* for agricultural labor was abolished in 1632. For Cerralvo's restrictions on Puebla's regents, see AGI, México, 31, n. 1.

115 AGI, México, 31, n. 18.

reached record levels.[116] In 1630, for instance, Rodrigo García del Castillo purchased twelve slaves for 4,025 pesos. If we exclude the purchase of the 11-year-old Felipe, García del Castillo spent just under 348 pesos per slave.[117] Five years later, Bartolomé de Tapia spent 2,480 pesos on six enslaved workers, an average of 413 pesos per worker.[118] In fact, 54 percent of all *obrajero* slave purchases for the 1590–1639 period were made during the 1630s alone. The investment in slavery for textile production was evidently precipitated by Cerralvo's actions. In this respect, the traditional corpus of *obraje* leases, slave purchases and inventories must be read alongside the disputes between Puebla's *obrajero* class and Cerralvo's tenure as viceroy (1624–1635). García del Castillo eventually returned to the city council in 1637,[119] but most textile barons would be excluded from political office and its benefits until the early 1640s. The arrival of the Marquis de Villena (1640–1642) as viceroy signaled a fresh start for Puebla's *obrajeros*, as evidenced by Miguel Carrillo's admittance into the municipal government.[120] Shortly thereafter, Juan de Guadalajara, another textile baron, was allowed to serve in a number of official positions (*alcalde mayor* and *alcalde ordinario*).[121]

However, the clearest evidence of *obrajeros* using slavery politically is found in the case of Capt. Diego de Andrada Peralta. In 1655, he joined the ranks of the Carrillos and Guadalajaras by petitioning the viceroy for an exemption to anti-*obrajero* policies in order to serve as a constable (*alcalde ordinario*).[122] Judging from his notarial transactions, Andrada Peralta had been preparing the petition for some time. In 1650, he presented an inventory listing twenty *obraje* slaves and a fulling mill (*batán*) as collateral for his sister's admission fee to a prestigious convent.[123] That same year he purchased five slaves, four of whom had worked as journeymen in an *obraje* in Cholula.[124] In the months leading to his 1655 petition, Andrada Peralta would purchase another two slaves, including the rights to the convict

---

116 Proctor, "Afro-Mexican," 49. In his research on Querétaro and Mexico City *obrajes*, Frank Proctor finds "real growth in the demand for slaves in *obrajes*" from 1640 onward.

117 AGNP, Not. 4, Box 137, 1630 January-April, no folio; Box 138, 1630 July, no folio. García del Castillo purchased Felipe for 200 pesos, a reflection of his youth. The *obrajero* paid no less than 300 pesos for any other slave.

118 AGNP, Not. 3, Box 76, 2207r; Box 77, 1347r; Not. 4, Box 151, f. 1027r; Box 152, 1380r, 1512r.

119 Gantes Tréllez, "Aspectos socioeconómicos," 261.

120 AGN, Gobierno Virreinal, Reales Cédulas Duplicadas, Vol. D20, Exp. 82, 52r–52v.

121 Frances L. Ramos, *Identity, Ritual and Power in Colonial Puebla* (Tucson: University of Arizona Press, 2012), 2–11, 75–79. *Alcaldes ordinarios* served as annually elected constables. The *alcalde mayor* presided over the municipal council as its president. He held considerable influence over the *cabildo*'s participation in religious processions, receptions for incoming viceroys and numerous local disputes.

122 Ibid.   123 AGNP, Not. 4, Box 173, 1650 February, 173r.

124 AGNP, Not. 4, Box 174, transactions for 1650 June-August.

Diego de Santiago.[125] For this 18-year-old, entry into the *obraje* meant the inability to leave its confines for the next two years as stipulated by his sentence for an undisclosed crime. For the *obrajero*, the purchase merely reaffirmed his public commitment to investing in non-indigenous workforces.

In 1655, Andrada Peralta established himself as a member of Puebla's political elite. In the words of his counsel, "Captain Diego de Andrada Peralta at present holds an *obraje* in which cloths are produced with a great number of slaves of his own property, and in no situation has any Indian entered or exited."[126] Soon thereafter, a high Crown official approved Andrada Peralta's request on the grounds that "he did not work Indians in his *obraje*" and only "used the service of his slaves." By September of that same year, Andrada Peralta had entered a new petition to New Spain's highest authorities. The empowered mill owner now asked that the local inspecting judge refrain from interfering in his affairs, since he had proven "to have one hundred slaves in his mill" and a few "Spaniards and mestizos" in his service.[127] An examination of Puebla's baptismal registers indicates that, like the Carrillo family, Andrada Peralta had also purchased women of childbearing age to expand his slave workforce. At least fifteen Afro-Poblano infants were declared to be his slaves in their baptismal entries between 1655 and 1688.[128] For this particular *obrajero*, the political benefits of slaveholding were clear. Andrada Peralta was now free to rule his mill and influence the Puebla cabildo with no interference. By the end of the 1650s, true political power was accessible to textile barons willing to invest exclusively in enslaved laborers.

As could be expected, not many were able to do so. In February 1664, Juan Moreno asked for and received a 12,000-peso loan from a city regent in order to purchase "forty-nine pieces of slaves, wool, instruments, looms, *obraje* tools."[129] The *obrajero* already owned 51 slaves, which may indicate that ownership of 100 enslaved people served as the threshold for entry into the political elite. Moreno was unsuccessful in his bid to hold a lucrative public office. By June 1664, he had had sold twenty-eight of his enslaved workers to Melchor de Posadas, a notorious *obrajero* based in Coyoacán (presumably to pay off his considerable debt).[130] Despite Moreno's failure, it is

---

125 AGNP, Not. 4, Box 181, 1655 January, 52r; 1655 April, 330r.

126 AGN, Gobierno Virreinal, Reales Cédulas Duplicadas, Vol. D20, Exp. 82, 52r–52v.

127 Ibid., Exp. 93, 58r–58v.

128 ASMP, *Bautismos de negros y mulatos, 1654–1658*, 22r, 43v, 62r, 80v; *Bautismos de negros y mulatos, 1677–1688*, 3v, 16v, 60r, 105v, 2664, 290v, 317v, 335v, 358v, 378v. Undoubtedly, more references to baptized children owned by Andrada Peralta can be found in baptismal registers from 1658 to 1677.

129 AGNP, Not. 3, Box 116, 1664 February, f. 64r. The 100-slave hypothesis will need to be tested by studying the enslaved workforces of politically-active *obrajeros* in Querétaro and Coyoacán.

130 AGNP, Not. 3, Box 116, 1664 June, no folio.

clear that Puebla's mid-century *obrajeros* understood their slaves to be much more than laborers. The enslaved represented access to political power, even if they could not guarantee commercial success.

The Fall of Puebla's Textile Mills

During the mid-seventeenth century, Puebla's *obrajes* suffered a calamitous fall. If thirty-seven textile mills were active in the city during the 1620s, only twelve survived in the 1660s.[131] Historians have traditionally relied on three factors to explain this diminishment. First, continued restrictions on indigenous labor led to crippling sanctions, such as those launched by the Marqués de Cerralvo in the early 1630s. Second, the prohibition of the profitable inter-American trade route between Perú and New Spain dried up a valuable market for textiles in the Andes. Third, the textile mills of Mixcoac, Coyoacán, Querétaro and the greater Bajío region emerged as formidable competitors with lower transportation costs for wool.[132] With the notable exception of Frank Proctor, few scholars have sought to explain how slavery might have impacted this process.[133] It is clear that Puebla's textile barons invested substantial resources into purchasing enslaved people for a variety of reasons. Yet by the end of the seventeenth century, only a handful of *obrajes* were still operational. Was slavery not enough to save Puebla's textile mills?

Analysis of four *obraje* inventories from the early 1660s suggests that despite attempts to promote the natural reproduction of slaves, the workforces of most textile mills were not being replenished with young people. On average, *obraje* slaves were just over 37 years old and almost two-thirds of Puebla's textile workforce was over the age of 30.[134] Even the Carrillo family was unable to regenerate its enslaved population. Despite their strategic investment in enslaved women of childbearing age, the elderly outnumbered the young.[135] The aging of Puebla's textile slaves undoubtedly affected production. By the 1660s, if not a decade before, local *obrajeros*

---

131 Salvucci, *Textiles*, 137. A similar process took place in the greater Puebla-Tlaxcala Valley, as *obrajes* all but disappeared in Santa Ana Chiautempan and Tlaxcala.

132 John Super, "Querétaro *Obrajes*: Industry and Society in Provincial Mexico, 1600–1700," *Hispanic American Historical Review* 56, no. 2 (May 1976): 204. The cost of wool tripled from the seventeenth to the early eighteenth century. *Obrajes* located closer to sheep grazing areas, such as Querétaro and the greater Bajío, easily outcompeted the textile mills of Puebla.

133 Proctor, "Afro-Mexican Slave Labor."

134 Calculations based on 212 enslaved people held in the *obrajes* of Doña Ines de Ojeda Coronel, Juan Lozano de Soria, the Carrillo family, Juan Moreno and Diego de Andrada Peralta. See AGNP, Not. 3, Box 111, 1660 December & Box 116, 1664 February; Not. 4, Box 189, 1660 October.

135 Of the seventy-nine workers included in the Carrillo's inventory, thirty were over the age of 50. Eighteen infants and youths (aged 0–19) could not replace this aging population.

could no longer stay afloat. In 1664, Alonso Carrillo, the elder, and his sons Gabriel and Alonso, the younger, requested and received a 1,000-peso loan "for the support and benefit of their mill."[136] They were forced to mortgage six skilled slaves of African descent (all between 30 and 50 years of age) as collateral. Simply put, Puebla's enslaved textile workers were now concentrated in a dwindling number of *obrajes*.

Even Capt. Diego de Andrada Peralta's textile mill withered away. This was the largest *obraje* in late seventeenth-century Puebla, one that had been largely maintained by purchases of enslaved American-born youths and through slave marriage and reproduction. However, Capt. Don Pedro de Andrada Peralta was unable or unwilling to continue his father's line of work and reliance on slave labor. Instead, Don Pedro's aging workforce gradually became the property of Don Domingo de Apressa y Gandara, his brother-in-law and a powerful official in his own right.[137] The latter, perhaps thinking he could inject new life into the *obraje* by virtue of his mining connections and political influence, continued to purchase slaves, but ultimately failed in his bid to resurrect the *obraje*.

In 1700, an inspection of the Apressa's mill was carried out with the same purposes that these official visits had had since the late sixteenth century: indigenous workers were supposed to voice allegations of abuse at the hands of their overseers. However, there were no indigenous laborers in this particular mill. Thirty black slaves, all men, toiled instead. Only one enslaved worker, Francisco de la Cruz, was able to express the struggles of everyday life. He noted that that although he was a slave, he was not the property of Apressa and therefore asked to be "to be sold out of the *obraje*." For the rest of these men, voicelessness and confinement conditioned their everyday lives. Their exploitation did not save Puebla's textile mills. By the early eighteenth century, Puebla could no longer compete with the mills of the Bajío region.[138]

Conclusion

In this chapter, I have emphasized the importance of understanding specific spaces in relation to slavery and the Mexican city. For an enslaved person, the textile mills of Puebla were among the most oppressive spaces

136 AGNP, Not. 3, Box 116, 1664 April, 212v–213v. The creditors were Maria de San Miguel, a nun from the Catalina de Sena convent, and her father, Joseph Montero, a master surgeon.

137 Apressa, who hailed from a mining family from San Joseph del Parral, married Capt. Diego de Andrada Peralta's daughter, Doña María Teresa de Andrada Peralta. By 1693, Apressa operated his own *obraje* in Puebla. See AGNP, Not. 3, Box 158, 1693 July, 575v.

138 Super, "Querétaro *Obrajes*," 199–204. Between 1700 and 1710 only thirteen textile mills were still operational in the city, see Alberto Carabarín Gracia, *El trabajo y los trabajadores del obraje de la ciudad de Puebla, 1700–1710* (Puebla: Cuadernos de la Casa Presno, 1984), 61.

imaginable. Confined, threatened and abused, obraje slaves learned to expect no respite from royal officials during their inspections. Deploying blasphemy as a survival strategy within the obraje rarely paid off, as Inquisition officials contributed to the harrowing regimen of physical abuse. In effect, these perverse dynamics enabled textile mill owners to gain greater autonomy within New Spain's political landscape.

Through a close reading of *obraje* inventories, marital registers, Inquisition cases, bills of slave purchase and municipal petitions, I have demonstrated how textile production in Puebla transitioned from nominally free indigenous workforces to teams of African and Asian slaves by the mid-seventeenth century. Enslaved African and Asian males complemented the largely Nahua workforces up until the 1630s. These internal dynamics would change with the temporary closing of the transatlantic slave trade, but especially because of aggressive anti-*obrajero* decrees. Counter-intuitively, black, mulatto and *chino* textile workers would only outnumber their indigenous counterparts after 1640. The gradual transformation toward full-fledged slavery in the city's mills was not the result of massive purchases on the auction block. A small group of affluent *obrajeros* made strategic investments in enslaved women of African descent (and their children) through marriage, birthright and purchases during the second half of the seventeenth century. Indigenous-free workplaces meant that Crown officials could no longer interfere with *obrajero* activities. In the process, the men of the Carrillo, Guadalajara and Andrada Peralta families secured their political power as city regents, councilors and aldermen, even as their mills competed unsuccesfully with those of Coyoacán, Mixcoac and Querétaro.

By the early eighteenth century, there were virtually no *obraje* slaves to speak of in Puebla de los Ángeles because most of the mills had failed. This is not to say that enslaved people were no longer confined in large urban structures. As we shall see in the next chapter, the city's female convents presented similar physical limitations but radically different cultural expectations.

3

Captive Souls

Nuns and Slaves in the Convents of Puebla

My parents will also give and provide me with a black [woman] named Sebastiana, a creole [slave], whom I have already received. She will remain in my service as my personal property and I will be able to dispose of her at my will, and if I should desire to sell her I will be able to do so and commerce with her or any other [slaves] as I see fit.

— Josefa del Sacramento, 1675

On 9 September 1675, Josefa del Sacramento heeded the call to the religious life and dictated her testament in what was undoubtedly an emotional day for her and her parents. According to her will, she had been preparing for this moment since childhood and now looked forward to giving up the perils (and pleasures) of the secular world. Never again would she leave the confines of the Santa Clara convent. The cost of entering this sacred space and community of religious women was considerable. Only a 3,000-peso dowry would secure her admission as a nun of the black veil, the highest social category within the stratified world of the convent. Then again, there was also Sebastiana, the enslaved *criolla*. She would enter the cloister as a domestic servant, as human property, and as a cultural expectation. Sebastiana, however, had not vowed to become a bride of Christ, nor had she agreed to remain in enclosure for the rest of her days. Her bondage within a sacred space may shock our modern sensibilities, yet it should not. After all, slavery permeated every inch of the colonial city, convents included.

This chapter addresses the intersection of urban slave ownership and convent life in seventeenth-century Puebla. I focus on slave ownership within female convents to better understand slave-master relationships within a very specific urban niche — one defined by physical isolation from society at large, spiritual immersion into Baroque Catholicism, and female empowerment.[1] The following is by no means a comprehensive assessment

---

1 Although the Franciscans, Dominicans and other orders had "male convents" (*conventos de religiosos*), I use the term monastery in this chapter to avoid confusion. I will refer to female convents and nunneries interchangeably.

of everyday life in Puebla's nunneries, nor is it based on the kind of internal records that would be necessary for such a study.[2] Instead, I contextualize the actions of religious women and their kin in recreating the slaveholding culture of the city in the cloister. This chapter analyzes conventual slave-holding patterns, familial networks, and cultural expectations by drawing on external documentation: marital registers, baptismal entries, notarized testaments, donations, and bills of slave purchase.

Throughout this chapter, I borrow Kathryn Burns' concept of a "spiritual economy" to argue that among Puebla's elite nuns and convents, slavery constituted an important economic and cultural resource. In her seminal study of colonial Cuzco, Burns noted that religious authorities tolerated nuns' "control of other people as property" as long as it did not interfere with their monastic vows.[3] Based on more than 300 archival references to enslaved people in marital, baptismal, and notarial records, I argue that Puebla's highest-ranking nuns and their families were expert spiritual economists. Conventual slaveholding in seventeenth-century Puebla was not an isolated phenomenon; it was a recurrent practice among elite novices and nuns of the black veil.[4] Both groups entered enslaved women and children into convents because slaveholding was culturally ingrained in their families and residences and in their own expectations of servitude.

Buying, selling or transferring the rights to an enslaved person was a strategic, status-conscious decision. It required considerable paperwork and mobilized numerous actors in and outside of the convent. Cloistered women had to request permission from their abbess in order to sell a slave. On other occasions, abesses wrote the vicar or bishop informing them of a nun's request. Religious women drafted official paperwork in the convent *locutorio*, a liminal space divided by iron grilles where nuns interacted with notaries. Specifically appointed sisters policed these interactions, but otherwise nuns participated in Puebla's notarial culture like any other slave owner. Their ability to produce notarized documents also benefited their families, in that they could claim a slave's wages, progeny or both. By the late seventeenth century, nuns and their kin wrote increasingly restrictive clauses to specify their claims over enslaved people and protect their property rights from convent administrators.

In their demand for enslaved servants, Puebla's nuns replicated the socioracial hierarchy of the world outside the convent (*extramuros*), despite being hampered by the legal and spatial restrictions of cloistered life (*intramuros*).

---

2 For a Puebla-specific study based on internal records, see Rosalva Loreto López, *Los conventos femeninos y el mundo urbano de la Puebla de los Ángeles del siglo XVIII* (Mexico City: El Colegio de México, 2000).

3 Kathryn Burns, *Colonial Habits: Convents and the Spiritual Economy of Cuzco, Peru* (Durham, NC: Duke University Press, 1999), 115.

4 For an opposing perspective, see Loreto López, *Los conventos*, 89–90.

In many ways, the convent inverted the spatial and gender dynamics of slavery in the *obraje*. In this sacred urban setting, the captors were confined and female slaves outnumbered their male counterparts many times over. Nuns' limited mobility did not prevent them from owning enslaved children and adults, but their control over slaves was circumscribed by their vows of enclosure. This was especially true of relationships between nuns and male slaves. Of course, not all religious women owned slaves, and the latter often fared better in nunneries than in mines, plantations or textile mills. Nonetheless, slavery and servitude were inextricable elements of conventual life in seventeenth-century Puebla. This was true of the larger and wealthier calced convents, but also of the smaller, more austere discalced nunneries.[5] Wealthy novices and black-veiled nuns had no reason to shun the slave-owning practices that informed their everyday lives and those of their relatives.

Slavery in Male Religious Institutions

It is impossible to understand the pervasiveness of slavery within female convents without acknowledging the parallel practices of male religious institutions. As seen in Chapter 1, domestic slavery in Puebla can be traced back to the 1530s and was virtually coterminous with the city's foundation. Female convents, and slavery within them, could not emerge until a critical mass of Spanish women arrived from Iberia. By contrast, the presence of male religious orders since the military phase of the conquest guaranteed their early use of slave labor by the 1540s.[6] Puebla's bishops and the entire structure of the local cathedral's leadership operated along the same lines. Deacons, cantors and schoolmasters affiliated with the cathedral owned slaves because the latter signified social status and financial power. These men's religious vocations did not exempt them from the venial practice of owning and selling people. Thus, the Puebla cathedral and the numerous elite families associated with high office in the bishopric must also be considered male slaveholding institutions.

Puebla's bishops often purchased enslaved men, women and children by proxy, a practice that was well established by the late sixteenth century. In 1590, Gregorio Romano appeared before a local notary to state that Catalina, a "Lucumí" woman, and her son Diego did not belong to him, despite a 1589 bill of purchase in his name. Instead, mother and son belonged to "Don Diego Romano, bishop of Tlaxcala, who gave me

5 For a useful distinction between the two kinds of feminine orders, see Monica Díaz, *Indigenous Writings from the Convent: Negotiating Ethnic Autonomy in Colonial Mexico* (Tucson: University of Arizona Press, 2010), 7–9.

6 Peter Boyd-Bowman, "Negro Slaves in Early Colonial Mexico," *The Americas* 26, 2 (Oct. 1969), 145.

the money for the purchase, which amounted to 450 pesos."[7] In 1605, Bishop Romano authorized Juan de Ortega, the presbyter and administrator of the San Pedro Hospital, to sell María, a 32-year-old *ladina* woman.[8] The bishop netted 500 pesos in the transaction. Romano's successor, Don Alonso de la Mota y Escobar, also depended on men of the cloth to sign bills of slave purchase in his name.[9] In this sense, the bishops of Puebla truly operated as elite urban slave owners. Bishop Mota y Escobar singlehandedly owned forty-two domestic slaves in 1610.[10] Fifteen years later, he donated an entire enslaved family, the Mesas, to the Jesuit College of Puebla, reinforcing the link between the Cathedral and male religious orders as slaveholding institutions. The bishop intended the Company of Jesus "to sell the said seven pieces of slaves in the College's name and spend the proceeds" for its construction. Dehumanized into "pieces" or slave units, Gaspar Mesa and his wife, Ana, now ran the risk of permanent separation from their five children, María, Isabel, Gaspar, Domingo and Alonso.[11]

As male religious orders consolidated their hold on extensive urban and rural properties during the early seventeenth century, they also embraced slave ownership. By the mid 1620s, Puebla's Dominican order possessed 200 enslaved men, women and children in a nearby agricultural estate.[12] Even as relative latecomers to Puebla, the Jesuits distinguished themselves quickly as slaveholders. Marital registers are a useful, if indirect, measure of these practices. Between 1591 and 1605, the Company of Jesus claimed seven grooms of African descent as their slaves, but no women.[13] The Puebla Jesuits also facilitated wholesale slave purchases for their Mexico City brethren (see Chapter 4). Unfortunately, determining if and how the enslaved and their families remained in Puebla itself is difficult because of

7 Romano owned another two slaves between 1590 and 1605. AGNP, Not. 4, Box 36, 1590 January, 139r; Not. 3, Box 23, 1605 May, no folio; Not. 3, Box 15, 1605 November, 2362r.

8 AGNP, Not. 3, Box 15, 1605 November, 2362r.

9 AGNP, Not. 4, Box 98, 1620 February, 695r.

10 Biblioteca Nacional de España (BNE), "Papeles de Mota y Escobar," MS6877, 267r–267v.

11 AGNP, Not. 4, Box 124, 1625 March, 523r. In reality, the forced separation of this particular family had already begun since Isabel was working for the nuns of the Limpia Concepción convent.

12 J. Eric S. Thompson, ed., *Thomas Gage's Travels in the New World* (Norman: University of Oklahoma Press, 1958), 50–51; Blanca Lara Tenorio and Carlos Paredes Martínez, "La población negra en los valles centrales de Puebla: Orígenes y desarrollo hasta 1681," in *Presencia africana en México*, ed. Luz María Martínez Montiel (Mexico City: CONACULTA, 1994), 68.

13 ASMP, *Libro de matrimonios de negros, 1585–1607*, no folio, see entries for 1591/03/23, 1594/06/26, 1595/04/03, 1595/10/01, 1602/12/10, 1603/02/11, 1605/05/30. By 1607, they also owned Francisco, a black man who appears repeatedly as a godfather for incoming Africans. ASMP, *Libro de bautismos de negros, 1586–1606*, 2v, 17v, 32r. The Puebla Jesuits purchased no fewer than 41 black, mulatto and *chino* slaves between 1626 and 1652. Fondo Antiguo Jose María Lafragua (FAJML), Jesuitas, Escrituras Sueltas, Microfilm 4, Legajo 148, Cajón 24.

the Company's extensive rural properties and their need for mobile workers, especially shepherds and muleteers.[14]

By contrast, the presence of enslaved people in urban, religious corporations speaks to a continued reliance on coerced labor throughout the seventeenth century. Hospitals most resembled convents with respect to their use of slaves, their corporate nature, and a rotating administration by a distinguished merchant, lawyer or cleric.[15] The Hospital of Our Lady of San Juan Letrán held slaves as early as 1590, when its patron agreed to sell María, a 13-year-old girl, to the barber Antonio López. As corporations, hospitals exerted property rights like any individual slave owner. María, for instance, had been "branded on the face with letters that say 'ospital our our lady,'" in order to prevent her from fleeing the medical institution.[16] Hospitals and their administrators openly participated in the transatlantic slave trade. The prior of the San Bernardo hospital agreed to purchase Pablo, an 11-year-old African captive, from the notorious slaving agent Juan Fernández de Vergara in 1630.[17] Five years later, the same friar represented the hospital once more to purchase another new Angolan arrival, Simon, for 480 pesos.[18] As seen in this book's Introduction, enslaved families worked in the San Pedro hospital by the mid-seventeenth century.

Based on an extensive notarial and parochial sample, male religious institutions relied primarily on male slaves, while female convents mostly depended on the labor of enslaved female domestics.[19] The separation of the sexes allegedly reduced the risk of giving into venal sins. The religious authorities of New Spain instituted policies of female enclosure from the mid-1550s onward, while encouraging male mobility by way of missionary activities.[20] It is clear that Puebla's Dominicans, Franciscans, and

---

14 Ursula Ewald, *Estudios sobre la hacienda colonial en México. Las propiedades rurales del colegio Espíritu Santo en Puebla* (Wiesbaden: Franz Steiner, 1976), 29–32.

15 Ivan Escamilla González, "La Caridad Episcopal: El hospital de San Pedro de Puebla en el siglo XVII," in Monserrat Galí Boadella, ed., *El mundo de las catedrales novohispanas* (Puebla: BUAP/Instituto de Ciencias Sociales y Humanidades, 2002), 239–252; Nancy E. van Deusen, "The 'Alienated' Body: Slaves and Castas in the Hospital de San Bartolomé de Lima, 1680 to 1700," *The Americas* 56, no. 1 (July 1999), 1–30.

16 AGNP, Not. 4, Box 36, 1590 February, 22r–24r.

17 AGNP, Not. 4, Box 102bis, 1630 August, 1356r. The *encomendero* extended the hospital seven months to cover the 275 pesos owed for Pablo's purchase.

18 AGNP, Not. 4, Box 152, 1635 December, f. 2207r. For other slave-related documentation involving the San Bernardo hospital see AGNP, Not. 3, Box 101, 1650 March, 22r–24r.

19 This section is based on 300 notarial references found in Notarías 2, 3, 4, and 6. 135 enslaved females, in addition to 19 recently freed women, appear in this sample of Puebla's female convents during the seventeenth century. I have located 45 references to male slaves owned by nunneries, but only 8 enslaved women and 45 men in male convents.

20 Jacqueline Holler, *"Escogidas Plantas": Nuns and Beatas in Mexico City, 1531–1601* (New York: Columbia University Press, 2005), 237–241; Nancy E. van Deusen, *Between the Sacred and the*

Augustinians made use of enslaved people for a variety of tasks, but the friars' freedom of movement mitigated the perceived need for slaves.[21] By contrast, nuns' inability to leave the cloister helps explain why free and enslaved domestic servants played such an important part of life in female convents.

Female Convents: Wealth, Paper Trails and the Spiritual Economy

It is surprising that slave ownership in nunneries has not been previously studied for Puebla. Of the fifty-six convents erected in New Spain during the colonial period, eleven were established in Puebla alone.[22] By the late seventeenth century, the city "maintained the largest number of convents per capita" in Spanish America.[23] Moreover, scholars have demonstrated that slave ownership was widespread in female religious communities throughout Spanish America.[24] Lima's female convents concentrated anywhere from 300 to 1,000 inhabitants during the late seventeenth century, but nuns accounted for only one-fourth of that population.[25] For the case of New Spain, Asunción Lavrín notes that 500 servants attended 100 professed Clares in Querétaro during the 1660s. Incoming bishops unfamiliar with the scale of colonial slaveholding condemned the extravagant use of slaves and servants in Mexico City, Guadalajara and Querétaro convents.[26] Only convent-specific research will reveal if Puebla's nunneries concentrated similar ratios of veiled nuns and servant women, although it is certain that enslaved women formed a considerable portion of the latter.

In her analysis of Mexican nunneries, Nuria Salazar Simarro contends that the "cloisters reproduced what happened outside" and that therefore it "was quite logical for nuns to hold slave women." In her understanding,

Worldly: The Institutional and Cultural Practice of Recogimiento in Colonial Lima (Stanford, CA: Stanford University Press, 2002), 28–30.

21 Holler, *"Escogidas Plantas,"* 237–238.

22 Loreto López, *Los conventos*, 17. More than 70 religiously affiliated buildings were built in colonial Puebla.

23 Kathleen Ann Myers, *Neither Saints nor Sinners: Writing the Lives of Women in Spanish America* (Oxford: Oxford University Press, 2003), 51.

24 Rachel O'Toole, "Danger in the Convent: Colonial Demons, Idolatrous Indias, and Bewitching Negras in Santa Clara (Trujillo de Peru)," *Journal of Colonialism and Colonial History* 7, no. 1 (2006); Kris Lane, *Quito 1599: City and Colony in Transition* (Albuquerque: University of New Mexico Press, 2002), 59; Burns, *Colonial Habits*, 114–120; Frederick P. Bowser, *The African Slave in Colonial Peru, 1524–1650* (Stanford, CA: Stanford University Press, 1974), 104–105, 130–131, 267, 275; Nancy E. van Deusen, *The Souls of Purgatory: The Spiritual Diary of a Seventeenth-Century Afro-Peruvian Mystic, Úrsula de Jesús* (Albuquerque: University of New Mexico Press, 2004) 3–31, 51–61.

25 Bianca Premo, *Children of the Father King: Youth, Authority and Legal Minority in Colonial Lima* (Chapel Hill: University of North Carolina Press, 2005), 82.

26 Asunción Lavrín, *Brides of Christ: Conventual Life in Colonial Mexico*, (Stanford, CA: Stanford University Press, 2010), 161.

the relationship between slavery and conventual servitude was clear. Nuns, "like their fathers, judged servants and slaves as incompetent for religious life as the [latter's] worth was related to their ability to work."[27] Jessica Delgado also acknowledges these labor expectations, while considering "racialized relations of power and prestige" as integral elements of religious life in Mexico's female convents.[28] Indeed, concepts of race, gender, and religious purity were so intertwined that the viceroyalty's first convent for indigenous women was only established in 1724.[29] No comparable institutions were created for women of African descent. Convents, then, were a crucial battleground in the "exercise of Spanish superiority" and in the racialization of female honor in Puebla and other urban centers.

As old established families and immigrants vied for local brides during the mid- and late-sixteenth century, safeguarding the sexual purity and social repute of women of Spanish descent became a prime concern for elite Poblano families. The city's first convent, Santa Catalina de Sena, was founded in 1568 under the auspices of Dominican friars. At the time, Puebla was on its way to becoming an important textile center, but the number of Spanish women remained low. Most convent construction in the 1570s and 1580s took place in Mexico City, with other important nunneries built in Antequera (Oaxaca) and Mérida (Yucatán).[30] Thus, the foundation of two nunneries in the last decade of the sixteenth century marked a fundamental shift in Poblano attitudes toward female sexuality, reclusion, and religiosity. Clearly, "there were more eligible young women interested in entering the religious life than the one convent could accommodate" by the end of the sixteenth century.[31]

Convents were not built on novices' interest alone. Wealthy men of varied backgrounds played an essential role in the construction of these late-sixteenth-century convents. The curate Leandro Ruiz de Peña established a 14,000-peso trust in order to establish the Limpia Concepción nunnery in 1593.[32] Only four years later, Juan Barranco, a prominent textile

---

27 Nuria Salazar Simarro, "Niñas, viudas y esclavas en la clausura monjil," in *La "América abundante" de Sor Juana* (Mexico City: Instituto Nacional de Antropología e Historia/Museo Nacional del Virreinato, 1995), 181–183.

28 Jessica Lorraine Delgado, "Sacred Practice, Intimate Power: Laywomen and the Church in Colonial Mexico" (Ph.D. diss., University of California, Berkeley, 2009), 188.

29 Mónica Díaz, "The Indigenous Nuns of Corpus Christi: Race and Spirituality" in Susan Schroeder and Stafford Poole, eds., *Religion in New Spain* (Albuquerque: University of New Mexico Press, 2007), 179–180. Four convents for indigenous women were established during the late colonial period.

30 Nuria Salazar Simarro, "Los monasterios femeninos," in Antonio Garcia Rubial and Pilar Gonzalbo, eds., *Historia de la vida cotidiana en México: La ciudad barroca* (Mexico City: Fondo de Cultura Económica/Colegio de México, 2009), II, 249.

31 Julie Shean, "Models of Virtue: Images and Saint Making in Colonial Puebla (1640–1800)" (Ph.D. diss., New York University, 2007), 152–153.

32 Loreto López, *Los conventos*, 50; Shean, "Models of Virtue," 153.

mill owner, founded the San Jerónimo convent that would house several women of *briocense* descent. He formed part of an immigrant community that "retained its cohesiveness" through endogamous marriage and the use of various convents to advance the social repute of select families.[33] Four more nunneries were established in Puebla between 1604 and 1626 and another two in 1688 and 1695.[34] By the end of the seventeenth century, elite Poblano families relied on nine convents to educate and safeguard their daughters.

Poblanos took pride in this intense female religiosity. The 1604 foundation of the first Discalced Carmelite convent of the Americas was (and still is) a highlight of local history.[35] Seven nunneries were already fully operational before the much-celebrated completion of the cathedral in 1648.[36] Entrance into a reputable convent represented a considerable expense, but colonial families believed that they could capitalize on the veneer of morality and social status that nunneries guaranteed. As "symbols of religious perfection," nuns influenced local religiosity through acts of private piety that, when and if endorsed, became models of feminine behavior outside convent walls.[37] Along the same lines, prominent families heightened their own social standing by serving as benefactors for religious institutions. Only a handful of elite families earned the supreme distinction of being convent founders, but those that did cemented their belonging in the upper echelons of baroque society.[38]

The construction of physical spaces of sanctity was mirrored by the production of literary texts celebrating the virtues of *intramuros* devotion. By the late seventeenth century, Puebla had "published the largest number of biographical *vidas* of its local holy people in the Americas."[39] These hagiographic biographies presented a template to emulate for women outside the cloister by extolling the religious piety of "socially privileged white women" within it. The exclusion of women of other ethnic

---

33 Ida Altman, *Transatlantic Ties in the Spanish Empire: Brihuega, Spain & Puebla, Mexico 1560–1620* (Stanford, Stanford University Press, 2000), 110, 134–135. The timing of these foundations is suggestive of the constant competition between more established local families and *briocense* immigrants.

34 Simarro, "Monasterios femeninos" in García Rubial and Gonzalbo Aizpuru, eds., *Historia*, 249. No other Mexican city witnessed as many foundations during the seventeenth century.

35 Doris Bieñko de Peralta, "Voces del Claustro. Dos autobiografías de monjas novohispanas del siglo XVII," *Relaciones* 139 (verano 2014), 167.

36 Lavrín, *Brides of Christ*, 360.

37 Rosalva Loreto López, "The Devil, Women and the Body in Seventeenth-Century Puebla Convents," *The Americas* 59, no. 2 (Oct. 2002), 181–182.

38 Successful founder families included the Villanueva Guzmán (Santa Clara), Rodríguez Gallegos, Rivera Barrientos, and Hidalgo Avalos (Santísima Trinidad), and Barranco (San Jerónimo). Gonzalo Yanes Díaz, *Desarrollo urbano virreinal en la region Puebla-Tlaxcala* (Puebla: BUAP, 1994), 142–143. For the unsuccessful case of the Ravosso family, see Loreto López, *Los conventos*, 73–75.

39 Myers, *Neither Saints nor Sinners*, 51.

backgrounds was central to the establishment of many female convents. During the mid-1680s, Bishop Manuel Fernández de Santa Cruz lobbied for the construction of the Santa Mónica convent. The 130,000 pesos raised would pay for the building and dowries of women who were "virtuous, poor, and entirely Spanish, with no *mulata*, *mestiza*, or any other mixture of race."[40] For the same reason, colonial chroniclers and priests often excluded the experiences of enslaved women and other servants from texts that celebrated conventual life.

Hagiographic *vidas* occasionally fell into stereotypical depictions of slaves and servants as unreliable and conflictive actors that led nuns to sin. In his 1683 text, Diego de Lemus described an enslaved Asian woman as a "tyrant, who incessantly tormented" Sister María de Jesús Tomelín "with repeated actions of disgust and harsh words."[41] Mother María de San José's own writings reveal recurring visions of "the devil . . . in human form, like a naked mulatto."[42] Although San José did not own slaves of her own, these racialized and hypersexual associations are poignant reminders that nuns also played the role of colonizer and that they too "wished to control and to contain laborers, servants, and slaves on whom they depended, and yet, feared."[43] In other words, the architectural, financial, and literary investment in female honor, chastity, and religiosity must be situated alongside a parallel investment in servitude and slavery.

Despite the racial superiority embedded in conventual life, "women who were not permitted to take formal vows" because of their sociocial caste and ethnic backgrounds must have still found the certainty of regular meals, shelter, and medical care appealing.[44] In 1605, a free woman of African descent agreed to serve Puebla's Jeromite nuns over four years in exchange for meals and an annual salary of 50 pesos.[45] Moreover, many free and enslaved servants fostered genuine friendships based on mutual trust and considerable intimacy with nuns. When local hospitals refused to treat María de Barcena on account of her status as a slave, her Conceptionist owner freed her in order that she should receive medical care as a free woman.[46] At times, elite men even placed free girls into convents on the understanding that convents represented stability and relative safety. Based

40 Kathleen A. Myers and Amanda Powell, *A Wild Country Out in the Garden: The Spiritual Journals of a Colonial Mexican Nun* (Bloomington: Indiana University Press, 1999), 267.

41 Diego de Lemus, *Vida, virtudes, trabajos, fabores y Milagros de la Ven. M. sor María de Jesús Angelopolitana religiosa en el insigne Convento de la Limpia Concepción de la Ciudad de los Angeles, en la Nueva España y natural de ella* (Lyons: Anisson y Posuel, 1683), 361–365.

42 Myers and Powell, *Wild Country*, 15, 89, 145.

43 Rachel Sarah O'Toole, "Danger in the Convent," *Journal of Colonialims and Colonial History* 7, no. 1 (2006).

44 Ibid.   45 AGNP, Not. 3, Box 23, 1605 January, 220r.

46 AGNP, Not. 3, Box 147, 1685 April, 615r.

on the "love and good will" he had for Damiana de Valencia, a miner from Chiautla placed the free *mulata* (whom he had raised since her infancy) into the Catalina de Sena convent so that she might be "sheltered" and taken care of.[47] The record does not reveal how Damiana felt about this arrangement.

Throughout Spanish America, seventeenth-century nunneries reproduced the sociORacial structure of their respective cities (albeit with an inverted color scheme). Black-veiled nuns assumed the upper echelons of the social pyramid and were followed by white-veiled nuns, laywomen (*donadas*), free servants, and slaves. This internal stratification mirrored the financial capabilities of diverse groups of women and their families. Nuns of the black veil generally hailed from elite Spanish families (peninsular and American-born) that could prove their daughters' purity of blood and pay the 3,000-peso dowry for their admission to the convent.[48] After a year-long novitiate, aspiring girls spent the next two years completing a juniorate (*jovenada*) and lived together with their "peers in a separate part of the cloister, the novices' patio."[49] Elite novices typically entered the cloister at the age of 15, while those seeking the white veil entered three years later. This discrepancy was based on the expectation that white-veiled nuns (*legas*) needed physical "strength to serve" in the kitchen and other spaces of manual labor.[50] The latter paid 1,500 pesos for admission to the convent, but were still considered respectable women despite their more modest backgrounds.

As institutions designed to extol Spanish purity, Puebla's convents generally excluded women of African descent from entering lives of religious seclusion and honor as nuns. The accepted use of free and enslaved Afro-Poblana domestics and *donadas*, however, did not compromise the sanctity of these urban refuges. Most free women could aspire to serve as *donadas* if they could muster 500 pesos and agree to perform much of the manual labor required in the convent.[51] This required washing clothes, cleaning the chicken coop, tending to the infirm, and cooking for the entire cloistered community. In larger institutions, such as the Conceptionist convent, kitchen work meant preparing meals for more than 100 nuns, servants, and children at a time.[52] In 1714, for instance, the Santa Clara nunnery housed 110 religious women. The Santa Catalina de Sena and Limpia Concepción convents followed with 76 and 70 nuns, respectively. Of course, this was only a fraction of the convents' total population.

47 AGNP, Not. 4, Box 189, 1660 November, 1147v.
48 Loreto López, *Los conventos*, 90.   49 Myers and Powell, *Wild Country*, 270.
50 Loreto López, *Los conventos*, 92–93; Myers and Powell, *Wild Country*, 139.
51 Nancy van Deusen, "'The Lord walks among the pots and pans': Religious Servants of Colonial Lima" in Sherwin K. Bryant, Rachel Sarah O'Toole, and Ben Vinson III, eds., *Africans to Spanish America: Expanding the Diaspora* (Urbana: University of Illinois Press, 2014), 148.
52 Shean, "Models of Virtue," 148 n. 446.

According to Hugo Leicht, each nun in the Santa Catalina convent had "an excessive number of servants, 2 or 3 for each religious woman."[53]

Free and unfree servants made up the lowest strata of the internal hierarchy, although some *donadas* must have wielded less influence than certain convent slaves with powerful mistresses. Distinctions in a servant's legal status had important repercussions for spatial mobility. While free domestic servants were occasionally allowed to leave the convent,[54] slaves may have had to negotiate this right on an individual basis. Children formed the last category of people found in the convent. Scores of them were found in Puebla's cloisters as relatives of nuns, servants and slaves. According to the religious authorities, "boys and girls under the age of seven could enter and leave the Cloister" because they were incapable of sinning as children "before the age of reason."[55] This ability to navigate the *intra* and *extramuros* made children, free or enslaved, especially important to their mistresses. A separate category of female children were known as *niñas*: they often hailed from influential families and entered the convent to learn how to read, cook and sew. Not all orders accepted *niñas* into the cloister. In keeping with their austere ideals, the Discalced Carmelites rejected them entirely, but girls over the age of 10 could enter Puebla's Catalina de Sena convent.[56]

The Case of Magdalena de San Francisco

Despite their reputation as spaces for privileged nuns and less affluent laywomen, convents also had to accommodate the offspring of Afro-Poblano women and elite Spanish men. Where exactly did such women fit within the spiritual economy of Puebla's convents? On one hand, convents reproduced the social stratification of the colonial city. Whiteness, purity of blood, and economic might were all privileged within convent walls. On the other hand, children born out of wedlock to powerful Spanish patrons required deferential treatment of some variety or another. Acknowledging such children could certainly present problematic situations for nunneries. By mutual necessity, convents maintained close ties to high-ranking urban families for financial donations, political favors and potential recruits. Convents accordingly accommodated children depending on the social standing of their fathers.

---

53 Hugo Leicht, *Las calles de Puebla* (Puebla: Secretaría de Cultura / Gobierno del Estado de Puebla, 2007), 425–426. A total of 509 nuns lived in ten local convents in 1714.

54 Bieñko de Peralta, "Voces del Claustro," 175.

55 Andrés de Borda, *Práctica de confessores de monjas: En que se explican los quatro votos de obediencia, pobreza, casstidad y clausura, por modo de dialogo* (Mexico City: Francisco de Ribera Calderon, 1708), 57r–57v; Simarro, "Niñas," 169.

56 Loreto López, *Los conventos*, 94.

In 1625, Magdalena de San Francisco entered the *locutorio* from within the San Jerónimo convent. She intended to sign a power-of-attorney letter for her mother, Juana Barranco. As with any other transaction at the grille, a nun monitored her conversation with the local notary.[57] This, however, was no ordinary notarial transaction. San Francisco, who was identified as a *mulata*, had just turned over the rights to 1,500 pesos to her mother.[58] At the time, such an amount could secure a comfortable apartment for fifteen years or purchase a train of forty mule. It also amounted to half of the cost of the fee required to enter a convent as a black-veiled nun, or just enough to secure a position as a white-veiled sister. For her part, Juana Barranco was labeled as a *morena libre*, a deferential term for a free black woman. Curiously, the notary did not identify Magdalena de San Francisco as nun, laywoman or servant. In fact, her status within the social hierarchy of the convent is decidedly unclear. Whereas veiled nuns and novices explicitly specified their rank, San Francisco straddled the line as a free woman of African descent with enough resources to secure her permanence in a prestigious convent.

Both mother and daughter were clearly linked to the Barranco family and, more specifically, to Juan Barranco, the deceased founder of the San Jerónimo convent. Like many immigrants from Brihuega, Juan Barranco made a successful life for himself in Puebla as a textile mill owner. By 1593, he was wealthy enough to donate a building and establish a girls' school, the Colegio de Jesus María. On his death in 1594, he stipulated that the first generation of students should be Spanish, *mestizas* or *mulatas*, but generally "poor young women and orphans."[59] After eight years in the school, each of the students would receive 400 pesos as dowry, "which could be used to marry or enter a convent."[60] The San Jerónimo convent was founded in 1597, only three years after Juan Barranco's death. For the next eight years, it remained a small institution, with six nuns and eight students, which may have included the girl who would take the name Magdalena de San Francisco. San Francisco may have had an advantage, since "any students who were related to Juan Barranco would receive preference if they wished to profess in the convent."[61]

In the document drafted in 1615, Juan Barranco is never identified as Magdalena de San Francisco's father or as Juana Barranco's spouse or lover.[62] Perhaps there was simply no relationship between the three and San Francisco was merely a "poor young" Poblana who was admitted to his institution. Yet the details of the *obrajero*'s life suggest otherwise. Juan

57 Myers and Powell, *Wild Country*, 271. An *escucha* or listener was supposed to monitor these conversations.

58 AGNP, Not. 3, Box 49, 1625 June, 883r–883v.   59 Altman, *Transatlantic Ties*, 105–106.

60 Ibid., 106.   61 Ibid., 105–106.   62 AGNP, Not. 3, Box 49, 1625 June, 883r–883v.

Barranco owned four black women (Agustina, Victoria, María, and Isabel) whose marital records survive.[63] Barranco himself never married, which was a curious characteristic for a wealthy and devout immigrant who had spent his life in Puebla since the 1560s. Surely he could have secured a bride among Puebla's booming immigrant community. Yet he opted not to. Perhaps Juan held an unspoken relationship with Juana Barranco? The staggering sum of money awarded to Magdalena de San Francisco, in addition to her mother's free status, suggests this may have been the case.

Within her power of attorney, San Francisco explicitly states that Juan Barranco "bequeathed and sent her" (not her mother) the 1,500 pesos by a "clause in his testament and codicile."[64] In other words, the testator knew San Francisco personally. Moreover, it is clear that she had already spent time in the convent prior to the disbursement of such funds. Whether she entered the Colegio de Jesus María first and then the San Jerónimo convent remains a bit of mystery, but the fact that San Francisco was able to sign the document by her own hand indicates that she had been educated within the school or convent. However, we know nothing else about Magdalena de San Francisco, her mother, or her ancestors. Although San Francisco undoubtedly encountered Juan Barranco's nieces and other kin, the record does not reveal how they received her. The speculative nature of the discussion above points to the limitations that historians confront when addressing questions of affection, children born out of wedlock, and the slippery terrain of relationships. In the next section, we turn to the more concrete motivations and expectations of slave-owning nuns and their kin.

Nuns' Families and the Expectations of Servitude

By the 1620s, Puebla concentrated the wealth of much of south and central New Spain. A center of commerce and textile production and the headquarters of New Spain's wealthiest bishopric, newcomers (voluntary and coerced) soon made it the viceroyalty's "second city." Affluent religious officials, *obrajeros*, ranchers, merchants, and plantation owners sent their sisters, daughters, and nieces into its cloistered communities. Accordingly, the most important benefactors of female monastic institutions were often slave owners of the largest scale. Their daughters and nieces, future nuns and novices, were exposed to domestic slavery and servitude as children.[65] For instance, Mother María de Jesús grew up in the living quarters of her father's textile mill. According to one of her biographers, one night she noticed several slaves escaping the *obraje* and promptly notified her father

63 ASMP, *Matrimonios de negros 1585–1607*, no folio, entries for 1588/05/29, 1588/11/26, 1589/02/20 and 1593/10/10.
64 AGNP, Not. 3, Box 49, 1625 June, 883r–883v.   65 Myers and Powell, *Wild Country*, 30, 44.

"how many had escaped" and "where they were hiding."[66] The *obrajero* quickly recaptured his slaves (and, presumably, punished them severely).

Families associated with textile production and slavery loom large in the history of Puebla's convents. Diego de Andrada Peralta sent his sister, Juana de San Luis, into the Limpia Concepción convent by mortgaging his textile mill for the equivalent of 3,000 pesos.[67] Cristóbal de Guadalajara, another prominent *obrajero*, entered five of his daughters into the prestigious San Jerónimo convent,[68] where they joined the slaves and female relatives of Juan Barranco's family, as well as those of the Pastranas, owners of the San Joseph sugar plantation in Izúcar.[69] All this is to say that widespread evidence of slave ownership within colonial convents should not surprise us. Elite slaveholders and their female relatives simply informed the cultural expectations of the nunnery.

In a sense, understanding slavery within Puebla convents is also an exercise in studying the slaveholding families outside of them. For example, the Santísima Trinidad convent was linked to the fortunes of Manuel de Miranda Palomeque, an influential merchant involved in the Manila Galleon trade, and those of his extended family.[70] He would bequeath Manuela, Maria and Antonia, enslaved girls (all under the age of 12) to his three cousins, mothers Catalina de San Miguel, Maria de la Encarnación and Luisa de la Madre de Dios. The same convent was also home to the four daughters of Jerónimo Tornes, a milliner and owner of thirty-four enslaved workers.[71] Finally, the wealthy Pérez Delgado family, which also held slaves and plantations in Izúcar and Tehuacán, was closely associated with the Santa Inés Montepoliciano convent.[72]

Understanding these elite dynamics and cultural expectations helps explain how and why young women were often able to introduce large contingents of enslaved domestics into nunneries. In 1670, for instance, Isabel del Sacramento, a novice in the Santa Inés convent, entered the cloister with a retinue of five slaves for her exclusive service.[73] Such a high ratio of enslaved domestics per novice is surprising, until we consider del Sacramento's family history. Her brother, Jacinto Pérez Delgado, owned no fewer than ninety-seven enslaved workers on his sugar plantation in Tehuacán.[74] In sum, the slaveholding expectations of elite planters, politicians, and merchants crystallized within Puebla's nunneries.

---

66 Lemus, *Vida*, 20–21.   67 AGNP, Not. 4, Box 173, 1650 February, 173r-176v.

68 AGNP, Not. 4, Box 122, 1625 Testamentos, no folio (1625/08/07).

69 AGNP, Not. 4, Box 77, 1615 Testamentos, no folio (1615/03/23).

70 Manuel de Miranda Palomeque was bound to the Santísima Trinidad by affective and familial ties. He requested to be buried within the Santísima Trinidad convent at the foot of the altar he ordered constructed "at his expense." See AGNP, Not. 3, Box 129, 1675 Testamentos, 284r.

71 AGNP, Not. 4, Box 174, 1650 Testamentos, 96r.   72 AGNP, Not. 3, 1670 Testamentos, 104r.

73 Ibid.   74 AGNP, Not. 3, 1670 May, 339r.

Evidence of the elite's penchant for slavery in seventeenth-century convents is, thus, easily found amid bills of purchase, donations and letters of manumission. Just before professing, novitiates dictated testaments by which they symbolically declared their death to the world outside of the convent. These wills contain qualitative information on family histories, frictions with convent administrators, and personal interactions with free and enslaved domestics. Notarial documents drafted by nuns also merit an additional word of caution. Whereas most other groups in the colonial city merely had to visit the local notary to formalize a transaction, nuns were unable to leave the convent. Instead, notaries visited nuns in the convent *locutorio* at specific hours of the day. Typically these bureaucratic visits took place between 9 and 11 A.M. or 3 to 5 P.M.[75] Novices, nuns and their relatives often decide the fates of their enslaved servants in these sacred-secular "contact zones."[76] For instance, Mother Juana de la Encarnación agreed to sell her slave Josefa "while at one of the grills" of the Santa Catalina convent.[77]

Although all convents featured similar architectural elements (*locutorios*, choirs, and kitchens), the culture of slave ownership varied from convent to convent. The Discalced Carmelites were held in high esteem in Puebla for the severity of their religious devotion, which was heightened by their aversion toward unnecessary recreation, meals, slaves and servants.[78] This lore of austerity was celebrated outside convent walls.[79] By contrast, the Conceptionists were considered an ostentatious order due to their affiliated families' wealth, dowries and conspicuous slave cohorts. Based on the number of references to enslaved domestics during the seventeenth century, this same characterization should be extended to the San Jerónimo, Santa Clara, Santa Catalina and Santísima Trinidad convents (Table 3.1).

Although hundreds of enslaved women and children toiled in the convents of seventeenth-century Puebla, colonial chroniclers largely failed to record their experiences, with one notable exception. The life of Esperanza de San Alberto has survived in the historiography of New Spain because

---

75 Antonio Rubial García, *Monjas, cortesanos y plebeyos: La vida cotidiana en la época de Sor Juana* (Mexico City: Taurus, 2005), 226–234.

76 Promissory notes and rental contracts may yield much greater detail about the complex relationships between convents and Afro-Poblanos. As nunneries accumulated considerable urban real estate during the late seventeenth and early eighteenth centuries, property rentals became a major source of income. In these one- or two-year agreements, the interested party sought out the convent administrator to inquire about renting a living or working space. People of African descent increasingly appear in late seventeenth-century documents as renters – a trend that mirrors their gradual emancipation during the mature colonial period. There may be unexplored connections between former slaves and convents, especially if the former were able to secure preferential loans or leases because of their prior servitude.

77 AGNP, Not. 3, Box 106, 1655 June, 6v.　　　78 Lavrín, *Brides of Christ*, 190–196.

79 Bieñko de Peralta, "Voces del Claustro," 184.

Table 3.1 *Enslaved people in Puebla convents, 1597–1710*

Convent	Male	Female	Total
Santa Catalina de Sena	7	30	37
San Jerónimo	6	23	29
Limpia Concepción	7	22	29
Santa Clara	7	19	26
Santísima Trinidad	2	18	20
Santa Inés Montepoliciano	1	12	13
Santa Teresa (Discalced Carmelites)	7	4	11

Sources: ASMP, *Matrimonios de negros y mulatos*, 1585–1606, 1661–1699; APSJ, *Matrimonios de morenos*, 1629–1691, 1692–1739; ASMP, *Bautismos de negros y mulatos*, 1607–1609, 1654–1658, 1677–1680, 1686–1688; AGNP, Not. 2, Boxes 9, 26. AGNP, Not. 3, Boxes 16, 21–23, 36, 41, 49, 63, 75–76, 85–86 94–95, 101, 106, 111, 116, 122, 129, 139, 147–147bis, 153, 160, 164, 167, & 4, 1600–1700; AGNP, Not. 4, Boxes 48–49, 58, 66, 77, 98, 102–102bis, 122, 137–139, 150–152, 164–165, 170–170bis, 173–174, 181, 188–189, 196–197, 205, 208–209, 214, 216, 223, 229–230, 234, 240; AGNP, Not. 6, Boxes 6, 19–20, 29, 38–40; AHJP, Exp. 713, 823.

of her perceived holiness and humility. A "Bran" woman from Upper Guinea, San Alberto embodied the painful, austere ideal of the Discalced Carmelites. As a slave of the most devout religious women in Puebla, her indifference to her own suffering brought her a litany of notable admirers. After sixty-eight years of thankless service, she was permitted to profess as a Carmelite nun with the bishop's dispensation in 1678 (although she would pass away the following year).[80] Lionizing San Alberto, though, has rendered her an exceptional actor in a sanctified setting.[81] In reality, the story of the elderly enslaved woman was perpetuated because she behaved as the subservient subject that slaveholders expected her to be. Her humility and indifference to punishment and ridicule, as highlighted by her biographers, fell precisely within the prescribed behavior for enslaved convent workers. Indeed, José Gómez de la Parra framed the Carmelites' continued use of San Alberto as her own natural inclination toward spiritual withdrawal (*recogimiento*).[82] Her exceptional religious devotion enabled the Carmelites to retain her as a perpetual laborer, despite their fame as servantless nuns.

Whereas free women (*mozas libres*) attached to convents were periodically forced to leave these spaces, slaves and nuns remained. In 1675,

80 Joan Cameron Bristol, *Christians, Blasphemers and Witches: Afro-Mexican Ritual Practice in the Seventeenth Century* (Albuquerque: University of New Mexico Press, 2007), 23–24, 48–59.

81 For a similar case set in Mexico City, see Carlos de Sigüenza y Góngora, *Paraíso Occidental* (Mexico City: Cien de México, 1995), 214–215, 288–290.

82 Bristol, *Christians*, 55.

Agustina de San Francisco, an elderly mulatto woman, recalled her expulsion from the Santa Clara convent some twenty years before.[83] A high church official had determined that all free domestic workers (*mozas libres*) would have to leave the Clares' nunnery circa 1655. We do not know that motivated the expulsion decree, but the general consequences were quite clear. Wage-earning domestics could be transferred, fired, or expelled from a given convent, but slaves (like nuns) could not. Simply put, by the mid-seventeenth century, enslaved women and children had become fixtures of conventual life in Puebla de los Ángeles.

Hierarchies of Power and Privilege

Free and unfree laborers entered Puebla's convents on a piecemeal basis. Each institution's prominence, slave-owning culture, and the varying fortunes of its affiliated families affected the scale of these enslaved workforces. Individual nuns and convents generally received enslaved domestics as donations, as clauses in testaments, or as part of a novice's property upon entering the cloister. These documents, and not the internal records and inventories produced by convents themselves, form the basis for the following discussion. Convents that were established in the 1680s, such as Santa Mónica, are not well represented here because of their late formation. This technicality, however, does not discount their possible ownership of slaves as they accumulated wealth during the eighteenth century.

The high social standing of Poblano nuns and families involved in slave donations is evident in the earliest documents within the notarial sample. For instance, in February 1600, Doña Juana de Escobar and her husband, Don Jorge de Baeza Carbajal, agreed to donate an enslaved 8-year-old, Dominga, to the Limpia Concepción convent.[84] The child, born and raised in Puebla, would cook and clean in the convent while serving the couple's daughters, María de San Joseph and Isabel de San Jorge. In many ways, this case is illustrative of the social and power dynamics that defined urban slavery in colonial Puebla. Dominga was just old enough to become profitable for her former and new masters. In Puebla, slave children under the age of 6 were rarely sold separately from their mothers, suggesting that the Dominga's mother belonged to Doña Juana and Don Jorge.[85]

Young African women were commonly found in Puebla's nunneries during the early seventeenth century. For example, in 1605, the widow María

---

83 AGNP, Not. 3, Box 129, Testaments 1675, 112r. Agustina quickly found work and a permanent residence in the Jeromite convent.
84 AGNP, Not. 3, Box 16, February 1600, 317r.
85 AGNP, Not. 3–4, 1590–1710 database. Out of 143 bills of slave purchase that included children under the age of 5, on only ten occasions were they sold without their mother.

de Curiel, a neighbor of Tepeaca (a nearby town), donated an 18-year-old "Angola" slave, also named María, to her daughter, a nun in the Limpia Concepción convent.[86] In 1630, even the Discalced Carmelites made a profit of 620 pesos after selling two 15-year-old African girls who once belonged to Mother Margarita de Jesús María.[87] Although Angolan and Kongolese women predominate in this kind of record (in accordance with the general patterns of the slave trade to New Spain), African girls and women of all ethnicities entered Puebla's convents during the seventeenth century.

Novice wills offer a priceless window into conventual slaveholding through the analysis of a young woman's social milieu, her family's financial credentials, and the receiving institution's slaveholding culture. These variables impacted applicants on an individual level, rendering some more "suitable" for life in one convent or another. How enslaved and nominally free women felt about entering life in the cloister is an entirely different question. Consider the case of Doña Barbara de Polanco and her 10-year-old slave, María.[88] On 14 May 1650, Polanco ordered her executors to send María into the Limpia Concepción convent due to the "love she had for said mulata." Within the same document, Doña Barbara noted (in passing) that María was the daughter of Ana, her black slave.

The separation of mother and child did not seem to have overly concerned their mistress, who understood her donation as a pious act in favor of a reputable nunnery. It appears, however, that Ana and María protested this planned separation shortly after hearing about their owner's plan. The mutedness of the notarial record does not allow us to recover the angst and fear elicited by Doña Barbara's testament over the next ten days. All that remains of this case is a marginal annotation. On May 25, Doña Barbara revoked and amended her testament in order to allow Ana and María to remain together as the property of Doña Elvira Polanco, her daughter. The preceding case speaks to the strength and resilience of the enslaved and their social networks when threatened with separation. Many more children were likely unable to remain close to their mothers when confronted with a binding piece of paper and a notary's signature.

The age at which an enslaved person entered or exited the convent mattered a great deal. At the time of their entrance to a given nunnery, most enslaved people were just over 14 years old.[89] However, as previously discussed, some entered during their early childhood. On average, slaves

---

86 AGNP, Not. 3, Box 21, March 1605, 602r.
87 AGNP, Not. 4, Box 137, January 1630, no folio (1630/01/10).
88 AGNP, Not. 4, Box 175, 1650 Testamentos, 38r.
89 Based on fifty-three notarial references in which an enslaved person (whose age was specified) was sold or donated to a nun, novice, or convent.

were sold out of the convent at the age of 20.[90] From a slaveholding optic, these were rational decisions based on the expectation of higher sales prices. Nuns experiencing economic difficulties could resort to slave sales to secure financial stability for years to come. In 1660, one nun justified her sale of a young woman by noting, "I find myself with a few needs for my dress (*vestuario*) and to pay and satisfy a few debts that I owe."[91] Other, more affluent nuns engaged the language of the slave market in their transactions. Mother Juana de la Encarnación, the daughter of the governor of Tlaxcala, noted that she was selling Josefa, a 21-year-old *mulata criolla*, as a slave "who presently does not have any diseases, vices, or defects as I have raised her in the convent."[92] These types of claims were more common in bills of purchase for female slaves, since there were no restrictions on retaining them in the cloister.

Gender distinctions among enslaved convent youths mattered a great deal. In theory, boys were not supposed to remain in the cloister after the age of 7.[93] There restrictions would have been negotiated, of course, but they did influence the sales of some children. For example, mothers Teresa de San Gabriel, Micaela de San Joseph, and María de San Juan and vicar Fray Joseph de Tapia decided to sell Joseph, a 7-year-old boy, out of the Santa Clara convent. They justified their decision on the grounds that "said *negrito* was not necessary for the convent's service since it holds other servants who attend to what is necessary."[94] The nuns provided no information on Joseph or his kin, only noting that they had purchased him one year before. In other cases, nuns retained ownership over older boys (although it is unclear if they resided in the cloister). Mother Leonor de Santo Tomás agreed to sell a 14-year-old boy, Juan Alberto, for 300 pesos. The Conceptionist nun had received the youth as a donation from her mother several years before and was in no rush to collect payment. She awarded the new slave owner twelve months to satisfy his debt.[95]

Although notarial records do not provide systematic information on conventual slaveholding, they do allow us to understand broad trends. Most notarial references to enslaved people in Puebla nunneries come from the second half of the seventeenth century, specifically from the 1660s and 1670s.[96] In other words, nuns did not purchase or inherit most of their slaves at the height of the transatlantic slave trade during the 1620s and 1630s (see Chapter 4). What exactly motivated this intensifying practice of slave ownership in late-seventeenth-century convents is unclear.

90 AGNP, Not. 2, 3, 4, and 6, Bills of Purchase. Based on thirty-two bills of slave purchase in which the age of the slave was specified. The average slave was 20.2 years old when sold out of the convent.
91 AGNP, Not. 4, Box 189, 1660 September, 81or.
92 AGNP, Not. 3, Box 106, 1655 June, 6v.   93 Borda, *Práctica*, 57r-57v.
94 AGNP, Not. 3, Box 160, 1695 February, 117r.   95 AGNP, Not. 4, Box 1675 April, 383r.
96 I have located 149 references to enslaved people in convents for the period 1650–1699, but only 74 for 1600–1649. For specific notarial offices and box numbers, see the sources listed in Table 3.1.

The expulsion of the Clares' free servants circa 1655 may have set off unprecedented demand for enslaved domestics,[97] but this hypothesis needs to be extended to other convents and tested with internal documentation. What is certain is that although some enslaved Africans toiled in Puebla's nunneries, most convent-owned slaves were born in the Americas and secured from local families (see Chapter 4). Moreover, nuns who desired slaves-in-residence imposed a highly specific set of age- and gender-based demands on their benefactors and donors.

As members of the colonial elite, black-veiled nuns (*monjas de velo y coro*) owned the majority of convent slaves. The former simply possessed or could access the financial resources and external connections with which to sell, acquire, and replace enslaved laborers. In 1656, Mother Luisa de San Agustín, of the Santa Clara convent, sold Mariana, her 8-year-old slave, to Luisa López and Juan de la Portilla, husband and wife.[98] We do not know why the nun decided to part with the enslaved child. In many ways, this was a slave transaction between people of unequal classes. Mother Luisa self-identified as a *religiosa de velo y coro*, while the married couple claimed no honorific titles. Perhaps more revealing is that only four years after this transaction, Mariana was sold once again. Perhaps the 320 pesos they were offered for the 12-year-old slave were simply too enticing to refuse.

Another illustrative case from the Santa Clara convent establishes the association between upper echelon nuns and slave ownership. In 1680, the novice María del Costado de Cristo drafted her will and renounced her earthly possessions as she decided to enter the Clares' nunnery.[99] The fate of her four slaves (Salvador de Barrios, Serafina Josefa, and Jacinto and María de San Buenaventura), however, remained for her alone to decide. In the preamble to her discussion of heirs and executors, the novice made a revealing statement: "During the century, my name was Doña María de Vargas y Pliego, widowed wife of Sebastián Ponce de León." Widows, especially wealthy ones, could occasionally enter convents.[100] For Vargas y Pliego, abandoning the secular world for the cloister certainly marked a life-altering event in many ways, but not in the servitude she expected from her slaves.

Acknowledging seventeenth-century nuns as slaveholders is essential to understanding the late eighteenth-century reforms implemented by

---

97 AGNP, Not. 3, Box 129, Testaments 1675, 112r.

98 AGNP, Not. 3, Box 111, June 1660, 378r. In 1660, the couple sold Mariana to Capt. Diego de Barrios. The bill of sale indicates she was remitted to the countryside surrounding Cholula.

99 AGNP, Not. 3, Box 139, 1680 Testamentos, 208r, 284r.

100 Lavrín, *Brides of Christ*, 24–25. Lavrín highlights the "excruciating series of trials" that the widow María Núñez was forced to endure as a Carmelite novice in Puebla circa 1615. It seems unlikely that Vargas y Pliego, considering her financial credentials and Santa Clara's more relaxed culture, would have encountered such opposition by the late seventeenth century.

Puebla's bishop, Francisco Fabián y Fuero.[101] These reforms, known as *vida común*, had particularly disruptive effects in the city's calced convents in 1771 and 1772. The bishop ordered the expulsion of girls from the cloister, limited the number of servants, and prohibited the construction and sale of private cells for nuns.[102] The nuns of the Santa Inés convent deeply resented these impositions and "were especially grieved by the amount of labor imposed on them" under the new communal rules. Although they still managed to retain some servants, the nuns felt they were being treated like "*obraje* blacks."[103] This sentiment of racialized labor and confinement would have been shared in the city's other calced nunneries. Rosalva Loreto López notes that 378 nuns and 605 servants (*mozas*) and girls (*niñas*) lived in five Puebla convents in 1765. At the time, the Santa Catalina and San Jerónimo convents held the largest reported number of servants with ninety and seventy-six, respectively.[104] The same two nunneries were the female institutions most heavily linked to slave ownership among all Puebla convents during the seventeenth century (see Table 3.1).

"Returning to the Trunk": Slave Owning Families versus Convents

In early-seventeenth-century Puebla, elite families remained rather unconcerned over their slaves' eventual fate in the convent. During this period, donors specified that a slave was to be awarded to a religious woman for the remainder of the latter's days. Upon her death, the host convent generally acquired property rights over the slave.[105] In 1620, for instance, the widow Catalina de Aguilar donated a 6-year-old slave to her daughter, María de Santa Gertrudis, a nun in the Santa Catalina de Sena convent.[106] De Aguilar renounced "the rights and possession" she held over "said *negrita*, yielding, transferring and renouncing them to the aforementioned María

---

101　Several scholars have studied the difficult transition from the more relaxed, autonomous *vida privada* to the austerity of *vida común* during the 1760s and 1770s. Margaret Chowning, *Rebellious Nuns: The Troubled History of a Mexican Convent, 1752–1863* (Oxford: Oxford University Press, 2005); James M. Córdova, *The Art of Professing in Bourbon Mexico: Crowned-Nun Portraits and Reform in the Convent* (Austin: University of Texas Press, 2014), 122–144; Nuria Salazar Simarro, *La vida común en los conventos de monjas de la ciudad de Puebla* (Puebla: Gobierno del Estado, 1990); Lorenzo López, *Los conventos*, 87–98; Lavrín, *Brides of Christ*, 276–309.

102　Loreto López, *Los conventos*, 87; Ramos, *Identity, Ritual, and* Power), 88–89, 163–165.

103　Lavrín, *Brides of Christ*, 291–293. In the original Spanish, the phrase "negras de *obraje*" carries a gendered component.

104　Loreto López, *Los conventos*, 90. No information on servants was reported for the Limpia Concepción convent, however it likely matched or exceeded the average of 72.5 servants per convent reported for Santa Catalina, Santa Inés, Santísima Trinidad, and San Jerónimo.

105　AGNP, Not. 4, Box 165, 1640 Testamentos, 53r.

106　AGNP, Not. 3, Box 41, 1620 November, 1388r.

de Santa Gertrudis and to said convent." Fifteen years later, Capt. Sebastian de Trujillo and his son, Luis de Trujillo, donated Juana, an 11-year-old *china criolla*, to Mother Agustina de San Ambrosio.[107] The donors specified that upon the nun's death, Juana would serve the abbesses of the Santa Clara convent for the rest of her life. She would only leave if "on account of some event or accident [the nuns] threw her out of the convent." Through donations of this sort, Puebla's convents gradually came to be populated by enslaved women, who toiled alongside *donadas*, free servants, and school-age girls.

By the mid-seventeenth century, slaveholding nuns and their families began to exert greater control over the fate of convent slaves. This transformation is particularly evident from documents produced by nuns and novices. Enslaved women and children now saw their future predetermined by all types of clauses that their cloistered mistresses wrote into notarized wills and bills of slave purchase. In 1650, various actors within the San Jerónimo convent agreed to transfer the rights to María, an "Angola" slave, for the price of 350 pesos.[108] She had once belonged to Mother Juana de la Encarnación. At the latter's death, her executor agreed to sell the enslaved woman to Mariana de Jesús, a child who was living within the convent walls. Given Mariana's young age (she is described as a *niña* and the legitimate daughter of Joseph Vázquez de Gastelu), her status as a legal minor, and the considerable cost of the slave, the entire transaction seems to have been orchestrated by her four aunts, Sisters Jerónima de San Bernardo, Marina de San Jerónimo, Ana de San Lorenzo, and María de San Gabriel, who also lived within the convent.

According to the bill of purchase, María would serve young Mariana for the rest of her life, as long as the latter decided to profess her vows and formally enter the convent as a religious woman. However, should Mariana "perish before [her] slave did," the slave's property rights would pass to her surviving aunts.[109] Despite lacking a juridical persona as a minor, Mariana could still possess an adult African by virtue of her family's elevated social standing. Actual ownership of the 26-year-old María clearly resided in Mariana's aunts, who understood the dynamics of convent life to a much greater degree than their niece. More significantly, the Vázquez de Gastelu family (*intra-* and *extramuros*) managed to acquire the rights to a convent slave, who only a few decades before would have become part of the San Jerónimo convent's corporate property.

107 AGNP, Not. 3, Box 76, 1635 December, no folio (1635/12/15).
108 AGNP, Not. 4, Box 174, 1650 November, 941r. This is a valuable case study for tracing the reconstitution of an extended Spanish family, while simultaneously reproducing the socioracial hierarchy of the colonial city.
109 Ibid.

An emerging tension between nuns, novices, and convents (as slaveholding corporations) is especially evident in the novitiate wills of the 1660s and 1670s. In 1675, the novice Nicolasa de la Natividad drafted her testament in order to profess in the Santa Clara convent. In the event of her death, she bequeathed María Clara, her *mulata* slave, to Mother Antonia de San Joseph. The nun would "enjoy and possess" María Clara as her own, but the convent would "in no way acquire rights over said mulata."[110] Should the Clares' administrators attempt to claim the young Afro-Poblana as convent property, María Clara would become a free woman.[111] This willingness to manumit an enslaved servant rather than allow her legal incorporation to a convent was not specific to Puebla. A 1681 case from Querétaro features identical language, suggesting that Mexican novices, nuns, and their extended families were developing legal strategies to retain slaves during the second half of the seventeenth century.[112]

A qualitative reading of novitiate wills indicates that slaveholding operated both as a cultural expectation and as a financial resource for prospective nuns and the receiving convent. Consider the demands and expectations of the young woman in this chapter's opening vignette. In September 1675, Josefa del Sacramento, born and raised in Puebla to a high-ranking family, formally declared her desire to enter a life of religious devotion. According to the novice:

Ever since I had reason and discourse, and becoming aware of the perils of the century, I have contemplated retiring from [secular life], in order to begin a religious life through which to better serve God, our Lord, and in carrying out this decision, I chose this convent [of Santa Clara] where I was admitted as a veiled nun. I am now about to receive the sacred profession ... and I declare that at the moment I have no goods in property of which to dispose, other than my legitimate [rights] and inheritance. I declare that after my parents' days I will stake claim to all the goods that they may bequeath to my name. These include the three thousand pesos my father has paid to this convent for my dowry, and any other sums of money he may come to spend for my profession and entry costs. I declare that he has also purchased a cell [in the convent] for my use ... My parents will also give and provide me with a black [woman] named Sebastiana, a creole [slave], whom I have already

---

110 AGNP, Not. 3, Box 129, 1675 Testamentos, 230r.

111 Ibid., "Y mando a la madre Antonia de San Joseph religiosa de dho convento para que la tenga gosse y possea por suia propia disponga de ella a su voluntad sin que por parte de este convento se adquiera derecho a dicha mulata y si se yntentare esta manda a de ser ninguna y la dicha mulata quede libre de la sujezion y cautiverio en que estuviere."

112 Guillermina Ramírez Montes, *Niñas, doncellas, vírgenes eternas Santa Clara de Querétaro (1607–1864)* (Mexico City: UNAM/Instituto de Investigaciones Estéticas, 2005), 144. The case centered on the rights to a 12-year-old slave: "quede en este convento en mi servicio y compañía, por mi esclava, de la cual he de disponer en todo tiempo a mi voluntad y por fin de mis días, no habiendo dispuesto de ella, quede la dicha a mi hermana, sin que este convento tenga derecho alguno a ella."

received. She will remain in my service as my personal property and I will be able to dispense of her at my will, and if I should desire to sell her I will be able to do so and commerce with her or any other [slaves] as I see fit.[113]

For Josefa del Sacramento, ownership of Sebastiana represented one in a series of vital requirements for her proper installation into the Clares' convent. Here was a future nun of the black veil, as her 3,000-peso dowry established, who required the purchase of her private quarters and a personal attendant in order to begin a life of religious devotion. Sebastiana's bondage in no way contradicted the novice's quest for spiritual purity. Moreover, Josefa del Sacramento demonstrated a profound awareness of the limitations that nuns often encountered when it came to disposing of their personal property. Over the next ten years, she enacted the clause that allowed her to "commerce" with Sebastiana or other enslaved women at least twice.[114]

During the second half of the seventeenth century, novices drafted increasingly complex clauses into their wills specifying their enslaved servants' obligations to their estate. Whereas most elite adolescents reserved the right to sell their slaves, others preferred to detail which individuals would gain property rights over them. Francisca de la Concepción, a novice in the Santísima Trinidad convent, arranged complicated postmortem plans for her mulatto slave, María. In 1660, Francisca stipulated that at her death María would serve her "sisters in communion," Doña Isabel de Barros Galindo (in all likelihood, her aunt) and María de San Roque, another novice (and Francisca's biological sister), in the same convent. Listing two possible heirs and family members guaranteed Francisca that her slave would remain in the family, even in the event that one of them did "not feel called to religious life." And yet the clauses continued. The rights to the enslaved woman would pass to the convent infirmary "where she must serve and nowhere else," only if neither heir decided to remain in the convent.[115]

Poblano benefactors also demonstrated considerable concern over the fate of slaves assigned to convent labor. This was especially true of enslaved boys who, with the right training, could one day earn considerable wages for a slaveholding family. In early 1675, Dr. Bernabe Diez de Cordova Murillo, Chair of Theology in the San Juan and San Pedro Royal Colleges, bequeathed the labor of five enslaved black and mulatto youths to his sisters and nieces in the Limpia Concepción convent.[116] The three youngest

113 AGNP, Not. 3, Box 129, 1675 Testamentos, 223r.

114 AGNP, Not. 3, Box 147, 1685 March, 427r. In 1685, 10 years removed from her novitiate, Mother Josefa del Sacramento sold Luisa, an enslaved 13-year-old whose mother belonged to the nun's family. The buyer was Doña María del Castrillo, the nun's sister.

115 AGNP, Not. 3, Box 111, 1660 Testamentos, 56r.

116 AGNP, Not. 3, Box 129, 1675 Testamentos, 48r.

slaves, including a 2-year-old, would "serve and assist" mothers Ana de San Andrés, Francisca de San Felipe Neri, María de los Ángeles, Antonia de San Juan, and Josefa de Jesus María. In addition, Mother Josefa would receive an 11-year-old slave girl for her own personal service. For this enslaved child, an early exit from the convent was unlikely, as she would only become free after all the above-mentioned nuns died.

For Diez, the question of how to award the labor of Nicolás de la Cruz, an enslaved apprentice, was of paramount importance. The donor understood that male youths above the age of 7 could not physically remain within the nunnery, but their earned wages could. Accordingly, he bequeathed not de la Cruz himself, but "the use of [his] daily wages" to his sisters and nieces.[117] Diez strictly forbade his cloistered relatives from selling or alienating their rights over the youth in any way. Should the convent's administrators ever attempt to sell de la Cruz, he would become free that very day. For elite families, then, control over slaves also meant restricting nunneries' claims over their property rights.

Although owning enslaved boys and men presented logistical challenges to individual nuns, convents generally refused to relinquish their rights over them. Male slaves and their wage labor were valuable even though nuns could not personally supervise them. The former could always be sold during a time of need.[118] Based on Puebla's extant marital and baptismal registers, male slaves were more often retained as convent (corporate) property than as servants for individual nuns.[119] Although detailed information on their occupations and living arrangements are lacking, male slaves owned by nunneries enjoyed considerable autonomy in their everyday lives. Unable to live within the cloister, they likely rented rooms paid for by convent administrators or by their own wage labor. Male slaves owned by convents generally avoided formal unions with other free or enslaved convent domestics, a dynamic that was reciprocated by female convent workers.[120]

Establishing formal unions with people on the outside was of paramount importance to enslaved convent workers. Of fifty-two marriages, I have only identified one case in which a convent slave married another convent worker (in this case a free woman). As in *obrajes*, married slaves could not be lawfully separated from their spouses. However, two key differences emerge in this

---

117 Ibid.   118 AGNP, Not. 4, Box 234, 1695 Testamentos, 18r.

119 Within 104 marriages for convent-related brides and grooms, 13 men were owned by nunneries. By contrast, only one male slave was claimed as the property of an individual nun. Baptismal references for convent slaves are rare because most children were born to slaveholding families outside the convent. In only one of nine cases is an individual nun identified as a slaveholder within the baptismal record. The eight remaining references are for slaves owned by convents (as corporations).

120 ASMP, *Matrimonios de negros, 1661–1674,* 44v.

comparison. First, strict rules forbade adult males, especially non-clerics, from entering the convent.[121] Second, nuns exerted far less influence over the marital choices of their enslaved men than *obrajeros*. A perfect example of such a limitation on slaveholder power can be found in Don Melchor de Covarrubias's 1592 testament. The owner of four enslaved people, Covarrubias bequeathed Luisa and Juliana, mother and daughter, respectively, to the Santa Catalina de Sena nunnery. Juliana would serve Mother Mariana de Jesús and would be "unable to be sold or taken out of the convent" even after the nun's death. [122] Luisa, on the other hand, would be allowed to serve the nuns from outside the nunnery (*sirva de por fuera*) because she was married. She would only be compelled to serve within the convent if she attempted to escape her service.

In a sense, then, convent slaves could enter formal unions as a form of insurance against enclosure, but this strategy was largely restricted to enslaved men. The enclosure of enslaved women meant that they encountered greater difficulties in finding spouses. Women outnumbered men many times over as slaves in Puebla's nunneries, but within this specific population men married more often.[123] For instance, Miguel de los Santos, an enslaved mulatto owned by the Limpia Concepción convent, married Juana de San Diego in 1668.[124] The bride had been born and raised a free person in Puebla with no apparent connection to her husband's religious institution. The officiating priest listed the groom as the child of a Conceptionist slave, Nicolasa de la Concepción. By contrast, free mestizo, mulatto, and indigenous women appear repeatedly in marital documentation as servants for nunneries. Claiming the term *criada* allowed these brides to establish their servitude to a convent, but not their enslavement.[125] In 1673, Nicolasa de la Encarnación, a free *mulata*, made sure that she would not be mistaken for a convent slave. In her marital entry, she clarified that "it had been twelve days since she left the Limpia Concepción convent."[126] Many women would not be so fortunate.

By the early eighteenth century, the demand for conventual slaves was so institutionalized that slaveholding was openly justified within

121 Holler, *"Escogidas Plantas,"* 241–245.

122 Enrique Aguirre Carrasco, *Testimonio del patronazgo y testamento de Don Melchor de Covarrubias* (Puebla: BUAP, 2002), 97–99.

123 Four enslaved brides and eleven enslaved men owned by nunneries appear in fifty-one marriages with at least one convent-affiliated bride or groom.

124 ASMP, *Matrimonios de negros 1661–1674*, 92v.

125 Twenty-four free brides claimed to have been raised or served in a given nunnery, and all but two of them claimed the *criada* label to denote their affiliation and freedom.

126 ASMP, *Matrimonios de negros, 1661–1674*, 150v. For other cases in which brides specified they no longer resided in the convent; see folios 146v, 113r in the same register. Also see APSJ, *Matrimonios de morenos, 1629–1657*, 22r, and *Matrimonios de mulatos, 1658–1692*, 6v.

the literature of the period. For Fray Andrés de Borda, a Franciscan doctor of theology, the greatest threat to a nun's spiritual health was the dependence on superfluous practices and the corrupting influence of wealth. His *Práctica de confesores de monjas* (1708), an influential text framed as a series of questions and answers between a nun and her male confessor, addressed common debates regarding conventual life. According to Borda, nuns were supposed to abide by their vows of obedience, poverty, chastity, and enclosure. His *Práctica* critiqued nuns' vows of material poverty given the contemporary custom of eating and drinking from silver cups and plates, the ostentatious decoration of their private cells and the use of silk underskirts and embroidered blouses.[127] Yet on the issue of slaveholding, Borda adopted an acquiescent position in this fictional dialogue:

Father, in my will I left a little slave (*esclavilla*) for my service. After my death she will be freed. Do I sin mortally by having her? Señora, I say that you may make use of her, yet you must willingly allow her to serve the Prelate each time she might need her to service the Community, in addition to the necessary conditions for her rent, and the reason for that is that the service of the slave is appreciable in money, and peculium is nothing but money, or what money is worth, thereby being able to have peculium, not as one's own, you may have that slave, this is in reference to the Vow of Poverty, in the sense that the Religious may have young women of service (*mozas de servicio*)... Father, and if this young woman turns out to be perverse and I cannot suffer her [service], may I sell her?

It is true Señora, that you ask me a very pertinent thing, and one not addressed by the Authors, and therefore it is necessary that I answer with maturity. And therefore I say that you may sell her, but only for the days of your life, and it is understood that your grace may sell her with the explicit permission of the Abbess, which is proven according to the law; qui quadrag. ff. ad. legem falsid. The will of the testator must be understood according to the intention at the time the testament was drafted, and when your grace drafted your own, your [intention] was not to leave that slave [in your service] to inconvenience you, but to give you service and relief, which, if lacking, your grace is not required to have her in your company all of your life. Your grace may not sell her, other than for the duration of your life due to the law Contrabenda ff. de Regulis Iuris. The instructions given in testaments, are not made to expire, but to subsist, thereby having freed that slave after your days, she acquired the right to freely enjoy her liberty. Your grace must also understand that the money given for the temporal slavery of that slave must be placed as part of the Convent's goods, and may not be spent on your own use, except for necessary [expenses], and only then with the permission faltim presumpta of the Prelate.[128]

---

127 Borda, *Práctica*, 19–28. All translations of this text are my own.   128 Ibid., 24–26.

For Borda, slavery was a temporal matter that did not affect a nun's spiritual mission or endanger her vows of poverty.[129] As an advocate of the "spiritual economy," he defended a nun's right to slave-ownership. Borda only identified the money generated by the sale of a domestic servant as a potential stumbling block. Taking the side of convent administrators, he advocated the incorporation of a slave's monetary value to the coffers of a given nunnery.[130]

The early-eighteenth-century administrators of the Santísima Trinidad convent would have approved of Borda's take on slaveholding. Here was an institution with a long history of slave ownership by way of its affiliation with the Miranda Palomeque, Barros Galindo and Tornes families of the seventeenth century. As their representative nuns died, the Trinitarians encouraged the incorporation of those families' human property as part of the "Convent's goods."[131] When this did not occur, nunneries often sought the assistance of the courts. In 1715, the Trinitarians' administrator, José de Ledesma, presented a formal suit against the Pastrana family.[132] According to Ledesma, the Pastranas were illegally retaining Francisca de la Concepción, a 25-year-old *mulata* slave, who had belonged to Mother Rosa María de San Cayetano.[133]

At the nun's death, Concepción should have been formally incorporated as part of the body of goods belonging to the convent. Ledesma wanted Concepción immediately returned "with the children she has procreated" – a disturbing example of the web of expectations projected unto enslaved women.[134] Instead, the Trinitarians' administrator encountered a powerful planter family that was more than unwilling to return Concepción and her three children, Rosa, Pedro, and Tomasa. For the next four years, the Pastranas hid the enslaved family in their Tepeojuma sugar plantation, on a rural estate in Huexotzingo, and even in an *obraje* in nearby Cholula. The real losers in this legal dispute were Concepción, her children, and their father, an enslaved *mulato* by the name of Antonio de Cuellar. With every

---

129 Not all religious authorities shared this view. Bishop Manuel Fernández de Santa Cruz was adamantly opposed to the use of servants (free or enslaved) in New Spain's convents and advocated for their expulsion at the time of a nun's death or their reassignment to a servant-less nun. However, I contend that the bishop's rules and constitutions for Puebla's San Jérónimo convent refer to the accepted use of corporate slaves, especially when alluding to "criadas que son de la Comunidad." Manuel Fernández de Santa Cruz, *Regla del Glorioso Doct. de la Iglesia San Agustin que han de guardar las Religiosas del Convento del Maximo Doct. San Geronimo de la Puebla de los Angeles...* (Puebla: Imprenta de los Herederos del Capitan Juan de Villareal, 1701), 17v-18r, 24r-26r.

130 AHJP, Exp. 2783.   131 Borda, *Práctica*, 24–26.   132 AHJP, Exp. 2783, 13r.

133 The nun was none other than the daughter of Doña Isabel de Pastrana Esquivel, one of the wealthiest women in New Spain and owner of the San Joseph sugar plantation in Tepeojuma. Based on an extant inventory, 150 slaves toiled on the San Joseph plantation in 1680. See AGNP, Not. 4, Box 214, 1680 April, 1r.

134 AHJP, Exp. 2783, 10r.

relocation, Cuellar (who was owned by another slaveholder) struggled to keep in touch with his wife and children.

Enslaved Servants and Physical Resistance

When the burdens of convent life became too much to bear, slaves could and did manifest their displeasure. "Not infrequently," Michelle McKinley notes "enslaved girls and women in the cloisters protested their confinement by claiming lack of consent and duress, language that resonated with legal norms of limited autonomy regarding religious internment."[135] Quantifying the frequency of such events is impossible, but a few notarial transactions were the direct result of slaves' resistance to their mistresses and their cloistered lifestyle. In 1690, for example, Antonia Josefa, an enslaved creole, forced her owner, Mother Josefa de la Encarnación, to sell her out of the San Jerónimo convent.[136] Like many other enslaved women, Antonia had entered the nunnery by way of a donation her mistress's mother made six years before. At the time, Antonia was 18 years old. We will never know exactly what motivated her to leave, but according to her bill of sale, Antonia forced the transaction "on account of said *mulata* being displeased and not wanting to remain in the convent." The young woman exposed herself to great risk by entering a slave market that sent hundreds of Afro-Poblanos into sugar cane plantations infamous for their physical abuse.[137] She was first sold to her mistress's brother, Andrés Saenz de la Peña, an *obrajero*, but he decided to part ways with Antonia and sold her to a man in Tecamachalco.

A similar situation took in late July 1695, when Rosa Blanca Sentis, a 20-year-old slave in the Santa Clara convent, forced her mistress to sell her out of the convent.[138] In order to do so, mother Antonia de San Nicolás had to seek authorization from Fray Clemente de Ledesma, her superior in Mexico City. She described Sentis as "a slave . . . [who] lives in displeasure, in this our convent, and asks to be sold." Ledesma granted his approval quickly. Ten days after the petition was filed, Sentis succeeded in leaving the Clares' convent in her sale to Don Francisco de Leiba. Once more, the notarial record is silent on her specific grievances and motivations, although it does indicate considerable agency. We can only note that by the last two decades of the seventeenth century, most enslaved people in Puebla were

135 Michelle McKinley, *Fractional Freedoms: Slavery, Intimacy, and Legal Mobilization in Colonial Lima,* *1600–1700* (Cambridge: Cambridge University Press, 2016), 150.
136 AGNP, Not. 4, Box 230, 1690 Escrituras de Miguel Zerón Zapata, 849r.
137 Solango Alberro, "Juan de Morga and Gertrudis de Escobar: Rebellious Slaves" in Gary B. Nash and David G. Sweet, *Struggle and Survival in Colonial America* (Berkeley: University of California Press, 1981), 177–186.
138 AGNP, Not. 3, Box 164, August 1695, 653r.

members of resilient social networks that could and did influence sales (see Chapter 5).

Enslaved youths also rebelled against their male slaveholders in Puebla's monasteries. Understanding what specific actions and conditions led young people to resist their masters is difficult because of the impersonal nature of notarial documentation. Nuns and friars framed these alienating transactions as acts of moral rebellion. When Joseph, a 12-year-old slave, was sold out of the Redempción de Cautivos monastery in 1671, the transaction was justified by "said slave having a few defects in his service to the presbyter Priest as he does not serve him with the love and punctuality with which he should." The priest in question was Fray Joseph Suarez, but understanding what type of subordination he expected is impossible to ascertain. Joseph entered the monastery at the age of 7 and spent five years serving Suarez before his sale. In any case, male and female convents were often willing to part with enslaved youths who failed to properly contribute their labor and service. Occasional sales were tolerated as long as a nun, friar, or religious institution managed to retain the monetary value of the enslaved. After all, others, especially mulatto youths, could be easily purchased via the regional slave trade of the late seventeenth century (see Chapter 4).[139]

In the Santa Clara convent in Atlixco, another desperate slave decided to take matters into her own hands by attempting to physically escape the rigors of conventual life. Tomasa, at only 16 years of age, could not withstand her daily obligations to mothers Juana de la Encarnación and Micaela de San Joseph. Her owners were the daughters of the Jaimes Salas family. Tomasa's mother had been the family slave, and when her daughter was born, she also inherited the burden of the former's permanent servitude. By 1690, Tomasa had had enough of the Santa Clara nuns and "attempted to escape her service by climbing the walls [of the convent]."[140] Ultimately, her audacious plot failed, but only in the short term. A few days later, the sisters contacted a local trader and asked him to sell their slave. After a 335-peso payment from Lázaro López Berrueco, Tomasa was finally freed from the cloister. She would begin a life of uncertainty in a new city, at the hands of new owners, amidst the perils of the secular world.

Conclusion

Based on hundreds of notarial references, slavery was a recurring practice in the female convents of seventeenth-century Puebla. High-ranking novices and nuns depended on the physical labor of enslaved children and women

139 By 1675, the Redención de Cautivos convent had purchased another mulatto youth, this time an 11-year-old named Juan. See AGNP, Not. 4, Box 208, 1675 February, 145r.
140 AGNP, Not. 3, Box 153, June 1690, 327r.

in order to effectively retreat into lives of religious solitude and devotion. Clares, Conceptionists, Jeromites, and even Discalced Carmelites participated in this constant ebb-and-flow of enslaved workers. This should not imply that all nuns owned other human beings, as many certainly did not.

What I am suggesting is that it is impossible to disassociate black-veiled nuns from slaveholding during the seventeenth century. Ownership of enslaved domestics within convents was not occasional, accidental, or anecdotal. It was expected. Like any other colonizer, nuns and their extended families imposed spatial and gendered demands on the people sold on the Puebla slave market. In the following chapter, we turn to the specific spaces where the enslaved were sold and analyze the vagaries of the transatlantic and regional slave trade throughout the seventeenth century.

4

The Puebla Slave Market, 1600–1700

May all who see this letter know that I, Juan Fernandez de Vergara, vecino and encomendero of this City of the Angels [Puebla], truly sell, by means of this letter, to the College of the Company of Jesus, Advocation of the Holy Spirit, of this said city, and to the Rector, father Rodrigo de Vivero, four slaves named Antonio, another Antonio, Diego and Miguel, Angolas between thirteen and sixteen years of age, who belong to captains Pedro Jorge and Antonio Abreu and their slave ships. I sell them as captives subject to servitude.

– 1635 bill of slave purchase[1]

On 23 October 1635, Father Rodrigo Vivero, the rector of Puebla's Jesuit College, bought four "Angola" youths. Antonio, Diego, Miguel, and another Antonio no longer belonged to the Portuguese captains who purchased, branded, and transported them from Luanda to Nueva Veracruz and, finally, to Puebla. After months of maritime and overland travel, the captives – boys, really – would serve in Puebla as permanent laborers and status markers for the Company of Jesus. As slaves of the Jesuit College, they formed part of a larger group of enslaved men and women from Angola and Kongo and would be joined by many others in the following decades.[2] We know little else about the boys. Colonial notaries did not bother to record the individual circumstances of their enslavement or the specific occupations they would fulfill within the Jesuit complex. Without Spanish surnames (their African familial histories having been effaced), it is extremely difficult to track further references to them.[3]

The boys' relative anonymity in the archives, however, should not be equated with historical irrelevance. When studied collectively, their experiences are a powerful reminder that the transatlantic slave trade from West

---

1 AGNP, Not. 4, Box 152, 1720r.
2 Fondo Antiguo José María Lafragua (JASML), Jesuitas, Escrituras Sueltas, microfilm 4, leg. 148. The Puebla Jesuits purchased at least 22 slaves between 1626 and 1635, 14 of whom were labeled as "Angola." Another 19 slaves were purchased during the 1637–1652 period.
3 The marital records for people of African descent are missing from Puebla's Sagrario parish for the 1607–1660 period.

Central Africa thrived on children and youths.[4] These enslaved young people would spend their adolescence learning to navigate the Puebla slave market, its intermediaries, and the purchasing public that demanded their uncontested servitude. It was this young population that relieved many of the labor pressures leveled upon Mexico's native communities. These same captives enabled the Jesuits (and other religious orders) to expand their colleges, plantations, and chapels throughout the viceroyalty. For deracinated African (and Asian) people, the cost was social, familial, physical, and psychological. It was measured not in years, but in generations of servitude.

Poblano masters participated in the slave market in relation to what they could afford to pay in silver, textiles, soap, or even biscuits. Access to credit was essential. In this regard, Father Rodrigo de Vivero and the Puebla Jesuits were no different from other local slave owners. They purchased four African youths for a considerable amount of money (415 pesos for each), but eased their debt by agreeing to pay over twelve months. This financing of African captives on the promise of payment was only possible because a Lusophone intermediary, the *encomendero de negros*, streamlined the world of Atlantic slaving into Puebla and the central highlands. These slaving agents and their lines of credit had a disproportionate impact on the trade in African captives, but minimal influence on the sales of American-born youths and adults (*creoles*). Slaves born in the Americas did not experience the Atlantic crossing, but suffered the dismemberment of their families all the same. This creole experience is paramount to a comprehensive understanding of the local slave market, especially for the second half of the seventeenth century.

Altogether, no fewer than 20,000 people – African, Asian, and American-born – were sold in Puebla de los Ángeles between 1600 and 1700. This chapter provides the first systematic examination of the Puebla slave market for the entire seventeenth century. Although primarily based on bills of slave purchase, I complement my analysis with Inquisition documents, municipal minutes, contraband investigations and baptismal records in order to advance three main arguments. First, between 1616 and 1639, Puebla consolidated as a slave market and distribution center for Mexico by means of *encomenderos de negros*. These Portuguese intermediaries extended Atlantic and Caribbean slaving networks deep into the highlands of Central Mexico by offering African captives on credit up until Portuguese independence in 1640. Second, slave transactions in Puebla reached their highest levels in the 1630s, but this peak in slaving activity is only evident after accounting for sales of American-born people. Finally,

---

4 David Wheat, *Atlantic Africa and the Spanish Caribbean, 1570–1640* (Chapel Hill: University of North Carolina Press, 2016), 72, 95–100. For the 1663–1713 period, see David Eltis, *The Rise of African Slavery in the Americas* (Cambridge: Cambridge University Press, 2000), 106.

Poblanos did not renounce slave ownership during the second half of the seventeenth century. Despite the dysfunctional Grillo and Lomelín slaving monopoly (1663–1672), transactions on the local slave market rose once again between 1685 and 1695. This late surge in sales proves that for well over 100 years, Puebla was a crucial market and distribution center for the transatlantic and regional slave trade.

Puebla and the Slave Trade to Mexico

Establishing how many African captives entered the Mexican mainland during the colonial period remains an elusive problem for historians. Although some captives accompanied Spaniards as enslaved passengers throughout the colonial period,[5] most Africans arrived on slave ships (*armazones*) plying transatlantic and Caribbean routes during the late sixteenth and early seventeenth centuries.[6] Slaveholders in Puebla, Mexico City, Querétaro, and other highland cities depended on Veracruz to secure African captives. Moreover, Mexico's main Atlantic port often received slave ships that had already stopped illicitly in Jamaica, Cuba and Hispaniola. Enslaved people could also be purchased in Campeche, on the western edge of the Yucatan peninsula, or in Acapulco, along the Pacific shoreline. Nueva Veracruz, however, dwarfed these competing slave markets throughout the colonial period. Therefore, understanding the role played by the principal port of entry is essential to a proper understanding of the Puebla slave market.

Anywhere from 100,000 to 200,000 captives entered Mexico's principal port during the colonial period. Estimates vary widely depending on how scholars account for licensed slave entries vis-à-vis the contraband trade. The imprecision of these figures is the result of an indirect contract system, by which the Spanish Crown issued a set number of slaving licenses for the Spanish Indies. Powerful merchants and financiers in Iberian cities purchased the licenses, but subcontracted the actual slaving voyages to dozens of smaller slaving networks. By the end of the sixteenth century, the Portuguese were firmly in control of this licensing process.[7] However, slaving licenses and shipping records do not account for actual slave transactions and reveal little about sales in specific urban centers. For instance, Colin Palmer noted that between 1595 and 1622, Mexico received

---

5 Archivo General de Indias (AGI), Indiferente, 2077, N.367; AGI, Indiferente, 422, L.15, F.76V.

6 The term *armazón* did not specify the size or tonnage of a ship. In the slaving context, *armazón* was used as a collective term to describe a group of African captives taken to a port or mainland city.

7 Gonzalo Aguirre Beltrán, *La población negra de México: Estudio etnohistórico* (Mexico City: Fondo de Cultura Económica, 1972), 37–42; Germán Peralta, *El comercio negrero en América Latina (1595–1640)* (Lima: Universidad Nacional Federico Villareal, 2005), 47–68.

just over 50,000 African slaves.[8] He based his calculations on shipping records issued by Seville's *Casa de Contratación*, which kept track of "the number of slaves that each ship was registered to carry." Spanish record keepers, though, failed to mention the port of destination for America-bound captives during the next seventeen years of the Portuguese slaving contracts.[9]

Scholars' uncertainty about the organization of the slave trade to Mexico has led to the supposition that it declined between 1623 and 1640. Palmer noted that "the peak years were 1606, 1608, 1609, 1610, and 1616–1621, years when the slave trade was probably more effectively organized."[10] Herman Bennett builds on these claims by stating that "[a]fter 1622, the structure of the slave trade was less organized and Africans were shipped only sporadically until 1640, the year the universal Catholic monarchy was dissolved and the independence of the Portuguese Crown restored."[11] Bennett goes further, suggesting that 1622 "was the midpoint of the seventeenth-century slave trade."[12] My research on Puebla's slave market challenges this interpretation. Another scholar has noted how the "rapid rise and then decline of Vera Cruz as a rival for Cartagena in the first quarter of the seventeenth century" is still unexplained.[13] These observations run counter to Joseph Clark's claims that Nueva Veracruz saw two sustained peaks of slaving activity in the 1608–1625 and 1634–1639 periods.[14] In sum, a lamentable lack of studies on the transatlantic slave trade to Mexico as a whole has hampered our understanding of inland markets and slaves' experiences in them.[15]

Properly establishing Mexico's role in the transatlantic slave trade is all the more urgent due to Alex Borucki, David Eltis, and David Wheat's collaborative research. Based on their revision of the 2016 *Transatlantic Slave Trade Database* (*TSTD*), they find that previous scholarship underestimated the slave trade to Spanish America by 60 percent for the

---

8 Colin Palmer, *Slaves of the White God: Blacks in Mexico, 1570–1650* (Cambridge: Cambridge University Press, 1976), 13–17. Between 1623 and 1640, Iberian scribes did not record the final destination of slaves bound for the ports of the Indies; see Enriqueta Vila Vilar, *Hispanoamérica y el comercio de esclavos* (Seville: Escuela de Estudios Hispano-Americanos, 1977), 200–201.

9 Vila Vilar, *Hispanoamérica*, 200–201; Palmer, *Slaves*, 14–15.   10 Palmer, *Slaves*, 14.

11 Herman Bennett, *Colonial Blackness: A History of Afro-Mexico* (Bloomington: Indiana University Press, 2009), 18.

12 Ibid.

13 Antònio de Almeida Mendes, "The Foundations of the System: A Reassessment of the Slave Trade to the Spanish Americas in the Sixteenth and Seventeenth Centuries," in David Eltis and David Richardson, eds., *Extending the Frontiers: Essays on the New Transatlantic Slave Trade Database* (New Haven, CT: Yale University Press, 2008), 86–87.

14 Joseph M. H. Clark, "Veracruz and the Caribbean in the Seventeenth Century" (Ph.D. diss., Johns Hopkins University, 2016), 167.

15 Alex Borucki, David Eltis, and David Wheat, "Atlantic History and the Slave Trade to Spanish America," *American Historical Review*, 120, no. 2 (Apr. 2015), 460.

pre-1641 period.[16] Their research, which also accounts for intra-American slave voyages, indicates that approximately 529,000 African captives entered Spanish American domains during these years, with an additional 61,700 for the period between 1641 and 1700. Only Brazil received more African captives than Spanish America prior to the start of the eighteenth century.

This renewed attention on Spanish America has established two key parameters for a more accurate understanding of the slave trade to Mexico. First, Cartagena de Indias (in modern-day Colombia) clearly received more African captives than Veracruz.[17] Located along the Caribbean coast of the South American continent, Cartagena was better positioned as a transatlantic market than the Mexican port. For the very same reason, Cartagena often supplied Veracruz with captives by way of the intra-Caribbean trade. The Mexican port, however, did operate as a key slaving node during the first two centuries of colonial rule. After revising 2016 *TSTD* figures with unaccounted slaving voyages, Clark estimates that "approximately 155,000 slaves arrived in the port of Veracruz" between 1519 and 1700.[18]

By virtue of its strategic placement between the port of entry and Mexico City, Puebla factored significantly into this demand for African captives. Accordingly, Poblanos invested in and profited from a lucrative trade in enslaved Africans throughout the seventeenth century. No fewer than 2,500 black and mulatto slaves lived in Puebla in 1595.[19] These figures are significant and confirm that far more enslaved people inhabited the cities of the highlands than the silver mines of the north – despite the latter's centrality to the Iberian imperial project.[20] Indeed, the scale of urban slaveholding challenges the notion that African slaves were used primarily for mining. By the late sixteenth century, Poblanos held three times as many slaves as the miners of Zacatecas.[21] The African influx to Puebla would only accelerate during the next forty years.

16 Ibid., 440. Approximately 529,000 African captives entered Spanish American domains from 1500 to 1641, with an additional 61,700 for the next 60 years.

17 David Wheat, "The First Great Waves: African Provenance Zones for the Transatlantic Slave Trade to Cartagena de Indias," *Journal of African History* 52, no. 1 (Mar. 2011), 17.

18 Clark, "Veracruz and the Caribbean," 142.

19 Archivo Histórico Nacional (AHN), Inquisición, L. 1049, 54r–57v, cited in María Elena Martínez, *Genealogical Fictions: Limpieza de Sangre, Religion and Gender in Colonial Mexico* (Stanford, CA: Stanford University Press, 2008), 144. The city's total African-descended population was even larger in that 3,000 *obraje* workers (black, mulatto, mestizo and Spanish) were counted separately in the 1595 report. The same reported noted that 10,000 slaves lived in Mexico City.

20 Palmer, *Slaves*, 79–81. For an opposing view, see Nicolas Ngou-Mvé, *El África bantú en la colonización de México (1595–1640)*, (Madrid: Consejo Superior de Investigaciones Científicas/Agencia Española de Cooperación Internacional, 1994), 102–108.

21 Peter Bakewell, *Silver Mining and Society in Colonial Mexico* (Cambridge: Cambridge University Press, 1971), 122–124. Prior to becoming bishop of Puebla, Alonso de la Mota y Escobar estimated that 800 slaves of African descent lived in Zacatecas between 1602 and 1606.

Slaving Voyages to Mexico

African captives bound for Puebla departed from four principal slaving ports: Cacheu, Cape Verde, São Tomé, and São Paulo de Luanda.[22] Most captives from Upper Guinea embarked in Cacheu (in modern-day Guinea-Bissau) and Cape Verde.[23] Both ports concentrated slaves from the "Rivers of Guinea," an umbrella term used to encapsulate the vast region between the Senegal River and the mountains of Sierra Leone. Together, Cacheu and Cape Verde accounted for most of the captives sent to Mexico during the sixteenth century.[24] The island of São Tomé specialized as a slave factory for Lower Guinea, a broad expanse from the Windward Coast to the Bight of Biafra, but also exported captives from West Central Africa. As a result, ships that embarked in São Tomé often carried mixed populations of "Arara," "Caravalí," and "Kongo" captives.[25] Finally, West Central African captives were sent to Luanda for the arduous voyage across the Atlantic.[26] Most of the enslaved Africans sent to Mexico during the seventeenth century came from this last region.

During the late sixteenth century, the kingdoms of the West Central African region underwent severe political instability, suffering several major wars that continued well into the late eighteenth century. The Portuguese played a key role in this destabilization, first in the kingdom of Kongo and later in Ndongo. The establishment of São Paulo de Luanda in 1576 has particular importance to the history of Mexican slavery.[27] This Lusophone bastion guaranteed military access to inland provinces and allowed the slaving frontier to expand rapidly.[28] The young men and women shipped out from Luanda were mostly enslaved through two processes: capture in the regional wars waged between the political elites of various West Central African states or outright purchase through *pumbeiro* slaving networks. The former system largely depended on *pumbeiros*, black intermediaries employed by the merchants of Luanda.[29]

22 Alonso de Sandoval, *Un tratado sobre la esclavitud* (Madrid: Alianza Editorial, 1987), 136.

23 Linda Newson and Susie Minchin, *From Capture to Sale: The Portuguese Slave Trade to Spanish South America in the Early Seventeenth Century* (Leiden: Brill, 2007), 74–76.

24 Toby Green, *The Rise of the Trans-Atlantic Slave Trade in Western Africa, 1300–1589* (Cambridge: Cambridge University Press, 2012), 192–194; Aguirre Beltrán, *La población*, 114–123.

25 AGNP, Not. 4, Boxes 102bis and 138, 1630 June–August.   26 Sandoval, *Un tratado*, 136.

27 C. R. Boxer, *Portuguese Society in the Tropics: The Municipal Councils of Goa, Macao, Bahia, and Luanda, 1510–1800* (Madison: University of Wisconsin Press, 1965), 111–112.

28 For Luanda's development during the 1580s, see Ilídio do Amaral, O Consulado de Paulo Dias de Novais (Lisbon: Instituto de Investigação Científica Tropical, 2000), 93–105. The first references to Angolan slaves in Havana come from 1585. In Puebla they can be located in marital registers as early as February 1589. See Alejandro de la Fuente, *Havana and the Atlantic in the Sixteenth Century* (Chapel Hill: University of North Carolina Press, 2008), 105; ASMP, Matrimonios de negros, 1585–1606.

29 Roquinaldo Ferreira, *Cross-Cultural Exchange in the Atlantic World: Angola and Brazil during the Era of the Slave Trade* (Cambridge: Cambridge University Press, 2012), 60–66; Sandoval, *Un tratado*, 146; Amaral, *O Consulado*, 111.

Outfitted with teams of load-bearers, *pumbeiros* carried their commissioned merchandise, typically consisting of imported cloths and alcohol, 200 miles into the interior provinces of Angola, Matamba, and Malemba.[30] There they exchanged their products for slaves in several hinterland slave markets. *Pumbeiros* interacted with other African slave traders, who "came from over two hundred and three hundred leagues with many blacks from different Kingdoms."[31] Malemba, Monxiolo, and Anchico captives acquired in these inland markets received the homogeneous "Angola" label through the slave trade, obfuscating their own ethnic identities.[32] It was this influx of Angolan captives that composed the majority of new African arrivals sold in early seventeenth-century Puebla.

From 1600 to 1630, a series of shifting alliances between Lusophone actors and upstart Imbangala warrior groups exacerbated West Central Africa's instability. These alliances debilitated traditional political structures and created "a new set of European and African states founded on the export of slaves from Africa to the Americas."[33] The wars undertaken against Ndongo by Governor Luis Mendes de Vasconcelos (1617–1621) had direct consequences for the Puebla slave market.[34] The attacks had varying political and commercial objectives, but were driven by a single underlying principle: to produce as many captives as possible for the Americas. These military campaigns often consisted of raiding "baggage trains . . . composed of women, conscripts, and other noncombatants."[35] At least 30,000 African captives sent from Angola disembarked in the Spanish circum-Caribbean between 1617 and 1625. In this regard, most of the Middle Passage survivors who disembarked on Mexican shores during these years had been directly affected by warfare in West Central Africa.[36]

---

30 Newson and Minchin, *From Capture to Sale*, 73. Depopulation, shifting political alliances, and military campaigns affected the distances pumbeiros traveled in search of war captives. For a detailed analysis of the role of alcohol in slave trading, see José C. Curto, *Enslaving Spirits: The Portuguese-Brazilian Alcohol Trade at Luanda and Its Hinterland, c. 1550–1830* (Leiden: Brill, 2004), 53–65.

31 Sandoval, *Un tratado*, 141, 145.

32 West Central Africans claimed many "other Angolan eponyms of provenance." References to Ganguela, Masangano, Mondongo, Ambaca, Garangui, Songo, Mocondo, Cambonda, Casancha, Manguela, Camunda, Rebolo, Lubolo, Upolo, and Majumbe people can be found in eighteenth-century South American marital registers. See Alex Borucki, *From Shipmates to Soldiers: Emerging Black Identities in the Río de la Plata* (Albuquerque: University of New Mexico Press, 2015), 65–66.

33 Joseph C. Miller, *Kings and Kinsmen: Early Mbundu States in Angola* (Oxford: Clarendon Press, 1976), 176.

34 Linda Heywood and John K. Thornton, *Central Africans, Atlantic Creoles, and the Foundation of the Americas, 1585–1660* (Cambridge: Cambridge University Press, 2007), 116–129; Miller, *Kings and Kinsmen*, 196–199.

35 Wheat, *Atlantic Africa*, 80, 95–96.

36 Ferreira, *Cross-Cultural Exchange*, 15. The "everyday enslavement" of the eighteenth century, one produced by judicial punishment, kidnapping and witchcraft accusations in the Luanda hinterland, was not the main cause of enslavement among Central Africans sent to Mexico.

African youths, like the two Antonios, Diego and Miguel – in this chapter's opening vignette – were likely captured in one of these wartime raids. These adolescents were "between thirteen and sixteen years of age" at the time of their sale in 1635. The Portuguese captains Pedro Jorge and Antonio Abreu sold at least thirty youths (ages 10–15) from the same slave ship in Puebla. In fact, the vast majority of the youths' companions aboard the *San Jorge* were well under the age of 20.[37] In Portuguese-language documentation, these young captives were often called *muleques*. A 1611 letter written by a Luanda slave merchant confirms that African adolescents were especially sought out for American slave markets.[38] New Spain was no exception. In his detailed analysis of three slaving voyages, David Wheat found that *muleques* accounted for 16 to 23 percent of the "Angola" captives arriving in Nueva Veracruz.[39]

Slaving voyages from Angola to Mexico could theoretically be completed in two months, but most captives spent between three and four months aboard one or two slaving vessels after departing Luanda. Unfortunately, precise information on the duration of the transatlantic journey is difficult to obtain. Most ship captains merely recorded their date of departure from Seville or Lisbon and their arrival at a given American port. For instance, when sold and shipped from Luanda, captives spent between six and eight weeks within the confines of a slave ship before making landfall in Cartagena.[40] The sea voyage from the West African coast to Cartagena took between thirty-five and forty days, although the longer trip from Luanda could run up to fifty days.[41] Regardless of their original port of departure, the length of their trip would be unavoidably extended for another two to three weeks when the ship sailed from Cartagena to Nueva Veracruz.[42] Contraband stops in Campeche, Havana, Ocoa, or Santo Domingo further delayed the arrival of a slaving vessel to Nueva Veracruz, "the last port" of the Spanish Indies.[43] Although the evidence is fragmentary, captives en route to Mexico experienced especially high mortality rates (more than

---

37 *Transatlantic Slave Trade Database (TSTD)*, Voyage ID 29301. Of the *San Jorge*'s 302 survivors, 156 were sold in Puebla. Information on their names, ages and owners is found in AGNP, Not. 4, Box 152, 1635 Oct.–Dec, 1615r–2207r. The average captive from this shipment was 17.9 years old.

38 AHU, Conselho Ultramarino, Serie Angola, CU_001, Cx. 1, D. 18. Kara Schultz, "'The Kingdom of Angola Is Not Very Far from Here': The South Atlantic Slave Port of Buenos Aires, 1585–1640," *Slavery & Abolition* 36, no. 3 (2015), 434–437.

39 Wheat, *Atlantic Africa*, 97–99. The slaveships in question were the *San Francisco* (1622), *San Juan Bautista* (1619), and *La Trinidad y Concepción* (1638).

40 Sandoval, *Un tratado*, 152.   41 Vila Vilar, *Hispanoamérica*, 148–151.

42 Archivo General de la Nación (AGN), Real Fisco de la Inquisición, Vol. 10, Exp. 6, 207r–207v.

43 AGI, Escribanía, 295A, Leg. 1, no. 2, "Arribada de Jorge Nuñez de Andrada," 4v–7r; Wheat, *Atlantic Africa*, 87–99.

20 percent) due to the length of these voyages.[44] The captives that disembarked on Mexican soil, then, were the survivors of a seemingly interminable Atlantic and Caribbean voyage that dispersed hundreds of others into other ports. Emotionally, this meant that they recurrently witnessed the fragmentation of the shipmate communities formed above and below deck. Physically, the abuse was inhuman.

The Jesuit priest Alonso de Sandoval compiled dozens of letters and firsthand interviews from slave traders, ship captains, and clergymen that described the brutality of the slave trade during the early seventeenth century. Based in Cartagena, Sandoval visited several *armazones* and provides the most accurate description of the conditions found therein:

> The slaves are linked together at the neck with long chains in groups of six; at the same time, they are shackled two at a time by the feet in such a way that they are imprisoned from head to toe. They are kept below deck, and locked away from the outside, where they see neither the sun nor the moon. There is not a Spaniard who will dare stick his head below deck without sickening, nor will he persevere an hour below deck without risk of grave illness. Such is the stench, misery and tightness of this place.[45]

Under such conditions, slaving vessels were often little more than floating hospitals and cemeteries. Scurvy, or *mal de Luanda*, was particularly threatening to the captives.[46] The illness related to this acute vitamin C deficiency would develop upon boarding the slave ship on the Angolan coast and over time would cause extreme swelling and rotting of the gums. The humidity below deck exacerbated these symptoms and often led to sudden death.[47] The nudity of the slaves aboard the ship, compounded by extremely unsanitary conditions, high humidity, and poor diet, explains why many suffered from acute skin infections.[48]

Captives en route to Mexico disembarked on the San Juan de Ulúa fortress, a damp, windswept island a mile from the mainland. For many captives, the short passage aboard rowboats from the island-fortress to the mainland meant the end of a horrifying seabound ordeal.[49] For others, the viceroyalty's port of entry would simply be the place where they had come

---

44 Clark, "Veracruz and the Caribbean," 139 n. 214.

45 Sandoval, *Un tratado*, 152. All translations and interpretations of Sandoval's text are my own.

46 Ibid., 153.

47 Slave traders treated suffering captives with citric fruits, which could be acquired upon arrival in Veracruz by the early 1570s. Francisco del Paso y Troncoso, compil. *Papeles de Nueva* España, Segunda Serie, Tomo V (Madrid: Impresores de la Real Casa, 1905), 199; Newson and Minchin, *From Capture to Sale*, 99.

48 Sandoval, *Un tratado*, 153.

49 AGI, Escribanía, 295A, Leg. 1, no. 2, "Arivada de Jorje Nuñez de Andrada," 7r–9v; AGI, México, 74, R.2, N.30, "Sobre la visita de los oficiales Reales de la Veracruz y cosas tocantes a ella," no folio.

to die. But for most, an arduous land journey across the tropical coastlands and up the central highlands was about to begin.

The Trek to Puebla

On 23 September 1597, the *San Juan Bautista* slave ship arrived in San Juan de Ulúa carrying an unknown number of African slaves. For the captives aboard, this represented the end of a harrowing maritime journey that began several months before in Luanda aboard another slaving vessel, the *Santiago*.[50] No fewer than 455 captives had embarked in Luanda, but only 323 were officially accounted for in Cartagena in August 1597. We do not know what happened to the remaining 132 young African men and women. Despite high mortality rates, it is unlikely that they would all have perished during the Middle Passage. Perhaps some were sold or "gifted" to port officials in another Caribbean location. Once in Cartagena, Captain Enrique Méndez handed over a number of slaves to the captain of the *San Juan Bautista*, Francisco Rodríguez de Ledesma, for sale in Mexico.[51]

The itinerary of the *San Juan Bautista* and the experiences of the Africans aboard is essential to advancing our understanding of the transatlantic slave trade to Mexico. Many slave ships disembarked on Mexican shores before making one or more stops in other Caribbean ports. As a result, "it was not uncommon for Veracruz to be final port of call for crypto-Jewish [slave] merchants carrying cargos from Europe, Africa, South America and the Caribbean."[52] Between 1595 and 1640, almost one-fifth of the transatlantic slave ships destined for Mexico stopped in Jamaica first.[53] The same slave traders selling African captives in Jamaica from 1610 to 1630 were also active in the Puebla slave market.[54] Unfortunately, reconstructing the transfer of captives from a transatlantic slave ship to a Caribbean vessel is difficult. The Veracruz notarial archive no longer exists and inland Mexican archives rarely hold information to identify specific slave ships or their itineraries. The most detailed records, produced by

---

50 AGN, Real Fisco de la Inquisición, Vol. 10, Exp. 6. As an inter-American voyage, the arrival of these Angolan captives to Veracruz is not recorded within the *TSTD*. However, their survival aboard the *Santiago* is identified as Voyage 29034. The original data for the transatlantic passage is based on Vila Vilar, *Hispanoamérica*, Cuadro 2.

51 AGN, Real Fisco de la Inquisición, Vol. 10, Exp. 6, 61r–62r. Rodríguez de Ledesma traded European textiles (*ruan*) on the West African coast in exchange for captives since 1588, if not earlier.

52 Stanley Mark Hordes, "The Crypto-Jewish Community of New Spain, 1620–1649: A Collective Biography" (Ph.D. diss., Tulane University, 1980), 50.

53 David Wheat, "Garcia Mendes Castelo Branco, fidalgo de Angola y mercader de esclavos en Veracruz y el Caribe a principios del siglo XVII," in María Elisa Velázquez, ed. *Debates históricos contemporáneos: Africanos y afrodescendientes en México y Centroamérica* (Mexico City: INAH, 2011), 85–107.

54 See *TSTD*, Voyages 29196, 29197, 29253, 29282, 29283 and 29289. These are just a few instances in which the name of a Jamaica-bound captain coincides with Puebla transactions.

Inquisition officials targeting crypto-Jews and New Christian slave traders, offer valuable, but tangential, information on the slave trade. The 1597 voyage of the *San Juan Bautista* serves as a notable exception in its detailed reconstruction of the sea and land voyage from Cartagena to Puebla.

During the Caribbean portion of the voyage toward Veracruz, the *San Juan Bautista* made a strategic stop in Campeche on the southwestern edge of the Yucatan peninsula. The site of a flourishing contraband market in slaves, English products, and other prohibited goods, Campeche's location allowed slave traders to make indispensible stops for "water and food." In all likelihood, Ledesma also sold off a number of African captives there in order to avoid paying greater import duties in Veracruz.[55] Meals and medical care afforded to slaves improved considerably from Campeche onward. During the last leg of the sea voyage from Campeche to San Juan de Ulúa, Ledesma purchased meat, honey, and cider syrups.[56] As a veteran slave trader, he understood the importance of ameliorating his captives' diets and appearance for disembarkment in San Juan de Ulúa. Captives were supposed to be disembarked in broad daylight, mainly to avoid fraudulent entries (which were common).[57] Port officials and the factor for the slave trade would then conduct a head count and make a record of the captives' sex, age and apparent health.[58] Under Ledesma's orders, the resident medic at Ulúa was able to cure nine slaves before sending his captives on rowboats to the mainland. Potential purchasers in Veracruz would be immediately informed of the conditions and appearance of incoming slaves.

If disembarkment brought a brief period of relief for the captives, it marked the beginning of weeks of frenzied activity for incoming slave traders. Upon arrival in Veracruz, Ledesma was in debt, his slaves were naked, and he lacked funds to begin the ascent into the highlands. The slave trader quickly secured a loan of 495 pesos to pay his crew. He arranged for chickens to be purchased and cooked for those captives that remained ill from the sea voyage. He also entered a contract with a muleteer to transport his captives to Puebla. Underwriting most of these expenses was Gaspar Pérez, who was identified as a neighbor and the *encomendero* of the port

55 Slave traders traveled from Santo Domingo (Hispaniola) to Campeche in smaller slave ships (*barcas*). See AGNP, Not. 4, Box 124, 1625 March, 555r–559v. For the contraband slave trade to Campeche, see Matthew Restall, *The Black Middle: Africans, Mayas, and Spaniards in Colonial Yucatan* (Stanford, CA: Stanford, 2009), 13–14. For Hispaniola, see Marc Eagle, "Chasing the Avença: An Investigation of Illicit Slave Trading in Santo Domingo at the End of the Portuguese *Asiento* Period," *Slavery & Abolition* 35, no. 1 (2014), 99–120.

56 AGN, Real Fisco de la Inquisición, Vol. 10, Exp. 6, 513r–513v.

57 María Cristina Navarrete, *Génesis y desarrollo de la esclavitud en Colombia, siglos XVI y XVII* (Cali: Editorial Universidad del Valle, 2005), 121.

58 AGI, México, 74, R.2, N. 30, "Relación de los salarios, raciones y otras situaciones que se pagan de la Real Hazienda de la Veracruz y averia de ynpussicion de aquel puerto," 16 March 1621.

of Veracruz.[59] Slaving agents such as these were essential to expediting the trade, especially because incoming Africans often required medical care to reach the highlands. Four of Ledesma's captives were physically unable to continue the voyage and remained in Veracruz, where they were eventually sold at reduced prices.[60] In early October 1597, Ledesma finally left the port with a group of twenty-six Angolan slaves, thirteen men and thirteen women of all ages.[61] Altogether, they had spent sixteen days recovering in Veracruz before beginning the overland trip to Puebla.[62]

For slave traders en route to Puebla, the shifting terrain and climatological conditions represented threats to both captives and captors. The 170-mile trek required traversing the tropical lowlands of the coast, climbing through the dense, semi-temperate forests of the eastern Sierra Madre mountain range, and finally crossing the central plateau. The enslaved were susceptible to disease, especially during cool autumn nights. Depending on the route taken, slave trains rested in Acultzingo or Perote. According to Bishop Mota y Escobar, "New Spain's cold lands and temperatures begin [at Perote], reason for which the hospital was founded at this site. Since those from Spain and the fleet come up from the port and the hotlands, it is quite common that they fall ill in this place more than others."[63] Dense fog, frost, and sleet surprised incoming travelers, both free and enslaved, who were often unprepared for the weather at 7,000 feet above sea level.[64] A wintry ascent could prove especially dangerous for unacclimatized captives.[65] Ledesma understood the dangers of unnecessarily exposing his debilitated captives to such conditions. While still in Veracruz, he borrowed an additional 25 pesos from his associates to clothe his captives with rough sackcloths (*sayal*).[66]

A number of stops at travelers' inns were paramount to the survival of the slave train. These roadside inns provided relative safety from poor weather and respite for the enslaved and the mules that carried them.[67] From the

59 AGN, Real Fisco de la Inquisición, Vol. 10, Exp. 6, 129r–131v.

60 Ibid., 530v. In a tragic case, we learn of the death of Juan Ladino, who had emerged as a leader among the captives (*el negro capitanejo*) and learned some Spanish or Portuguese.

61 Ibid., 507r–510r.   62 Ibid., 513r–513v.

63 Alonso de la Mota y Escobar, *Memoriales del obispo de Tlaxcala* (Mexico City: Secretaría de Educación Pública, 1987), 36–37.

64 Juan de Palafox y Mendoza, *Relación de las visitas eclesiásticas de parte del Obispado de la Puebla de los Ángeles (1643–1646)*, (Mexico City: El Colegio de México, 2014), 77–78.

65 AGI, Escribanía, 297C, Leg. 3, No. 3, 4r–5v. In January 1687, a slave trader in Puebla noted that he "did not expect to sell more than twelve or thirteen [captives] because three of them are very sick. The cold has hurt them badly. In addition to those previously mentioned, ten [others] have died."

66 AGN, Real Fisco de la Inquisición, Vol. 10, Exp. 6, 129r.

67 Peter William Rees, "Route Inertia and Route Competition: An Historical Geography of Transportation between Mexico City and Vera Cruz" (Ph.D. diss., University of California, Berkeley, 1971), 71–92.

slave trader's perspective, innkeepers also provided information on run-away slaves, market conditions, and political developments further inland. Information of this nature was essential to traders unfamiliar with the sociopolitical terrain of Central Mexico. For traders leading slave trains along the northern trade route (via Xalapa and Perote), the stretch between the Rinconada and Río inns was an especially dangerous part of the land voyage.[68] The muleteers and guards assigned to the slave train had to be especially vigilant here, where the coastal plains gave way to brush at the foot of the sierra. Two other slave routes (via Acultzingo and the Venta de Cáceres) presented similar challenges to slave traders during the seventeenth century.[69] Once in the central highlands, the slave trains typically made their way to Puebla via the smaller settlements of Tepeaca and Amozoc.

After recovery at port and numerous stops at roadside inns, the enslaved reached Puebla approximately a month after arriving on the mainland. Ledesma's twenty-six captives finally arrived at their destination and were promptly housed in a single room of an inn on Puebla's outskirts in late October 1597. Suddenly, a group of local officials raided the inn, arrested Ledesma and embargoed his twenty-six "pieces of slaves, males and females."[70] The slave trader was promptly carried off to the secret dungeons of the Inquisition on charges of judaizing, an accusation often leveled against Portuguese slave traders.[71] His arrest did not result in the liberation of the Angolan captives, who would be eventually sold at auction. Over the next four decades, thousands of African captives encountered experiences similar to those of the twenty-six Angolans led by Ledesma in 1597 (although most would not see their captors imprisoned). Most slaves would endure a maritime voyage from Luanda to Cartagena or Jamaica before disembarking in San Juan de Ulúa and beginning the overland trek by mule.

Puebla, Atlantic Slaving, and the "Encomendero de Negros"

The coerced migration of African captives was integral to the creation of the Central Mexican economy at the end of the sixteenth century. Whether

---

68 AGNP, Not. 3, 1605 August, ff. 1629r–1631r. In 1605, seven of Capt. Baltazar Amat's captives escaped his control at la Rinconada and fled into the wilderness. In 1669, a group of incoming Africans rebelled in the same location, killing Don Agusto Lomelín, the factor for the slave trade to New Spain, and a handful of his guards. See AGN, Reales Cédulas Originales, Vol. 11, Exp. 99, 288r.

69 Pablo Miguel Sierra Silva, "The Slave Trade to Colonial Mexico: Revising from Puebla de los Ángeles (1590–1640)," in *From the Galleons to the Highlands* (Albuquerque: University of New Mexico Press, forthcoming 2018).

70 AGN, Real Fisco de la Inquisición, Vol. 10, Exp. 6, 98r–99r.

71 Ibid., 515r. Inquisition officials determined that the slaves were to be sent to Mexico City, where they were to be sold at public auction in December 1597.

masters bought into the slave trade with agricultural, textile, or domestic objectives, slavery stimulated regional markets throughout the colonial landscape. Slave-bearing mules bred in San Antonio Huatusco and the outskirts of Orizaba transported thousands of captives to and from the port during the following decades.[72] Many of those same mules would be used to transport sugar produced by slaves to the port or further inland for consumption in Puebla convents and residences.[73] With Philip III's restriction on the use of indigenous labor in textile mills and plantations (see Chapter 2), the ideological and physical infrastructure of the slave trade was now fully operational.[74]

By 1600, Puebla's influence on the viceroyalty's internal and Atlantic commerce was notable, and this influence was particularly felt at the port of entry. At the end of the sixteenth century, a group of Poblano merchants lobbied for the construction of a southern road that would connect Puebla directly to the port of entry by way of Orizaba.[75] The road lowered transportation expenses by allowing merchants (slave traders included) to bypass Mexico City entirely. It was also controversial in that it required moving the port a few miles south to the site known as the Ventas de Buitrón.[76] The proposed site had the undeniable advantage of being located directly across from the island-fortress of San Juan de Ulúa. Moreover, Poblano merchants and wheat farmers stood to gain considerably from the arrangement, especially since their wheat bread had supplied the site since the early 1580s. The intensification of the slave trade in the 1590s would only heighten the need for a direct access to the Orizaba and Puebla slave markets.[77] Despite considerable resistance from the residents of Veracruz, the port was officially moved in 1599. The old settlement became "La Antigua" or "Veracruz la Vieja," while the Ventas de Buitrón came to be known as "Nueva Veracruz."

The Puebla slave market grew rapidly with the establishment of the new port. In 1605, close to 140 slave purchases were registered in the city's notarial archive. Although Puebla residents conducted most slave transactions among themselves, Captain Justo Guzman, Hernan Juarez and Juan de Olivera sold forty-nine "Congo," "Angola," and "Anchico" captives from

72 Guillermina del Valle Pavón, "Desarrollo de la economía mercantil y construcción de los caminos México-Veracruz en el siglo XVI," *América Latina en la Historia Económica* 27 (Jan.–June 2007), 32.

73 Patrick Carroll, *Blacks in Colonial Veracruz: Race, Ethnicity and Regional Development* (Austin: University of Texas Press, 2001), 48–49.

74 Carmen Viqueira and José Urquiola, Los obrajes en la Nueva España, 1550–1630 (Mexico City: CONACULTA, 1990), 101.

75 Del Valle Pavón, "Desarrollo de la economía," *América Latina en la Historia Económica*, no. 27 (Jan–Jun. 2007), 38–42.

76 Rees, "Route Inertia," 105–119.

77 Approximately 5,396 African captives disembarked in Veracruz between 1592 and 1599. See *TSTD*, http://slavevoyages.org/voyages/jyBglprp (accessed May 22, 2017).

early September to late December 1605. At least two of the slave traders were Portuguese and, judging from their sales, rather unfamiliar with local demand for incoming Africans.[78] Their captives were all aged between 13 and 25, and collectively averaged 19 years of age. They were sold variously to a local official (*alcalde ordinario*), a blacksmith, a tilemaker, a widow, and the friars of the Dominican convent, to name but a few of their new owners.

By the second decade of the seventeenth century, slave traders en route to Puebla turned to local agents who understood the demands and limitations of Mexican slave owners. In 1610, Juan de Betancur fulfilled this role, although he only identified as a *vecino* of Puebla. By claiming citizenship (*vecindad*) in this way, Betancur established his obligations and rights as fiscally a responsible member of urban society but did not otherwise distinguish himself as a slaving agent. That year Betancur worked as an intermediary for seven slave ship captains, participating in the sales of at least ninety African captives.[79] Betancur allowed people of modest means to partake in the labor and prestige associated with the purchase of an African captive by offering payment plans and lines of credit. In December 1610, he agreed to sell nine "Angola" captives to the owner of a textile workshop and his business partner for 3,258 pesos to be paid over ten months.[80] In this regard, Betancur was not only responsible for selling and collecting payments for African captives, but he was also actively gauging the credit worthiness of diverse sectors of Mexican society. Between August and December of 1610, Betancur sold more than 31,000 pesos worth of African slaves.[81] Sometime around 1613, he relocated from Puebla to Nueva Veracruz, where he would serve as one of the key facilitators of the transatlantic slave trade.[82]

Betancur's move to the port of entry coincided with a moment of lower slaving activity which would not last long. Seville's merchant guild, ever resentful of Portuguese influence, held the slaving contract for Spanish America during this four-year period, but failed miserably in its attempt to replicate the Lusophones' trade. Palmer estimates that a total of 238

---

78 AGNP, Not. 3, Box 22 and Not. 4, Box 58, 1605 September–December. Juarez hailed from the village of Torres Novas in the Tejo region of Portugal, and Olivera betrayed his own Portuguese origins by signing numerous bills of purchase as João de Oliveira. Their voyage does not appear in the *TSTD*. The slave traders only managed to sell one captive for more than 400 pesos. In 34 other cases, masters more familiar with local demand sold captives for 400 pesos or more.

79 AHJP, Exps. 713 and 823; AGNP, Not. 4, Boxes 65–67, 1610 August, no folio.; Not. 3, Box 32, 1610 August, 1482r. Betancur held power-of-attorney for Captains Francisco López, Sebastián Rodriguez, Marcos Texeira, Andres Moreira, Alonso Rodriguez de Morales, Bartolomé Jorge, and Agustín de Vilasboas.

80 AGNP, Not. 3, Box 31, 1610 December, no folio (1610/12/12).   81 See note 81.

82 AGI, México, 74, R.2, N.30. In a 1621 investigation, visitor Pedro de Gaviria Vergara identified Juan de Betancur as a key culprit in several tax evasion schemes in Nueva Veracruz.

captives "sailed for Mexico" between 1611 and 1615.[83] If anything, the Sevilleans merely interrupted Portuguese slaving operations. In 1611, Dom Manoel Pereira Forjaz, the governor of Angola, and João de Argomedo, a merchant based in Lisbon, had already agreed to a three-year venture in wine, ivory, and slaves.[84] The contract specified the names of their factors in Bahia, Pernambuco, Cartagena, and New Spain. The governor and merchant stipulated that in the absence of Alvaro Ruiz de Acevedo or Garcia de Loadios, Andres de Acosta would represent their interests in New Spain. By 1618, Acosta served as prior of Mexico City's *consulado*, the powerful wholesale merchant guild, and described himself as the most influential "of the Portuguese slave merchants in New Spain."[85] Under the auspices of Betancur and Acosta, Mexico's slave markets were connected to those of Portugal, Angola, Cartagena, and northeastern Brazil.[86] In this regard, New Spain was merely one of many lucrative Atlantic markets.

The slave trade to early-seventeenth-century Mexico, however, had a distinguishing feature: the *encomenderos de negros*. These were Portuguese men who acted as agents on commission for incoming slave ship captains.[87] They were not factors for the slaving contracts, as they were not responsible for inspecting slave ships in Nueva Veracruz. Instead, the *encomendero de negros* was a municipally recognized slaving agent. As a taxpaying member of urban society, he was rooted in the social fabric and presented himself before city council with petitions or complaints. Claiming full citizenship as a *vecino* was an essential distinction for these men. Incoming traders, most of whom were also Portuguese but less familiar with local demand, could only claim to be temporary residents (*residentes*). *Encomenderos de negros*

---

83 Palmer, *Slaves*, 14.

84 Arquivo Histórico Ultramarino (AHU), Serie Angola, Conselho Ultramarino 001, Cx. 1, D. 19. The Sevillean interlude came at a fortuitous moment for the Lusophones. For the relative scarcity of captives in Luanda in 1611, see AHU, Conselho Ultramarino 001, Cx. 1, D. 18.

85 Louisa Schell Hoberman, *Mexico's Merchant Elite: Silver, State and Society* (Durham, NC: Duke University Press, 1991), 50. Acosta's family reflected the global reach of the Lusophone slaving networks of the early seventeenth century. His father was "based in Lisbon and his two brothers in Luanda and Goa." For his contested election as prior of the guild, see AGN, Real Hacienda, Vol. 218, "Litigio para que se declare nula la elección del consul Don Andrés de Acosta." For his 1606 appointment as *depositario* for the Audiencia of Mexico, see AGN, Reales Cédulas Duplicadas, Vol. D6, 24v.

86 AHU, Serie Angola, Conselho Ultramarino, 001, Cx. 1, D. 17. The slaving operations complemented what Antonio García de León has dubbed "la malla inconclusa," an overlapping network of Lusophone traders specializing in South American cacao, African captives, pearls, silver, and wheat. Antonio García de León, "La Malla Inconclusa. Veracruz y los circuitos comerciales lusitanos en la primera mitad del siglo XVII" in *Redes sociales e instituciones comerciales en el imperio español, siglos XVI y XVII* (Mexico City: Instituto Mora/UNAM, 2007), 41–45.

87 Pablo Miguel Sierra Silva, "Portuguese *Encomenderos de negros* and the Slave Trade within Colonial Mexico, 1600–1675," *Journal of Global Slavery* 2, no. 3 (special issue Fall 2017). These slaving intermediaries should not be confused with the other *encomenderos*, who received the tribute and labor of indigenous people.

streamlined the distribution of newly arrived Africans within Mexico through a superior understanding of local conditions.

In Puebla the *encomendero de negros* position was established between 1616 and 1620, an indication that slave trading networks were expanding. This development was tied to Antonio Fernão de Elvas securing the coveted slaving contract, which once more returned to the Portuguese in late 1615.[88] The contract included a special right, the *derecho de internación*, which allowed slave traders to travel inland and sell their captives, although in practice, Lusophone slave traders had done this for quite some time. The new *asiento* did pave the way for the formal recognition of the slaving agents who increasingly facilitated the trade within Mexico. Based on a later investigation into their activities, Betancur and Acosta intervened in several slave shipments in 1617.[89] By 1620, the entire system had come to rely on various recognized slaving agents distributed throughout the urban centers of New Spain.[90] In the case of Puebla, this man was Manuel González.

González began his career by helping slave ships captains sell contraband slaves. In November 1615, he worked as an agent for Captain Joseph Hurtado, alias Furtado, a Lisbonite temporarily residing in Puebla.[91] In a seemingly standard transaction, González helped Hurtado sell two young "Arara" women, Antonia and Ana, to one Nicolas Nuñez.[92] The purchaser, a resident of the heavily indigenous town of Calpan, was awarded five months to pay for both captives. The very next day, González assisted Hurtado with the sale of twenty-one "Arara" captives for a Poblano merchant.[93] The debt would only be paid off twelve months later. These transactions indicate that Puebla's slave market was increasingly dependent on intermediaries who (for a fee) allowed foreign ship captains into local society, while awarding credit to slave purchasers of all ranks and financial capabilities. Like

88 Aguirre Beltrán, *La población*, 45–47. During his term as *asiento* holder, "annual legal exports from the [West Central African] region ran around 9,000 captives and could be as high as 12,000, if estimates for smuggling are included." See Heywood and Thornton, *Central Africans*, 159–160.

89 AGI, México, 74, R.2, N.30.

90 More research on unofficial *encomenderos de negros* remains to be done. It is possible that other provincial cities, such as Antequera (Oaxaca), Xalapa, Santiago de Guatemala, and San Luis Potosí, had slaving intermediaries of their own. Juan Rodríguez, described as a *mercader de negros*, operated in Xalapa circa 1617; see Danielle Terrazas Williams, "Capitalizing Subjects: Free African-Descended Women of Means in Xalapa, Veracruz during the Long Seventeenth Century" (Ph.D. diss., Duke University, 2013), 328. For the activities of the slaving agent Juan de Alfaro in 1611–1612, see Ramón Alejandro Montoya, *El esclavo africano en San Luis Potosí durante los siglos XVII y XVIII* (San Luis Potosí: Universidad Autónoma de San Luis Potosí, 2016), 63–69.

91 AGNP, Not. 4, Box 78, 1615/11/06, no folio.

92 "Arara" or "Alara" was a corrupted Spanish spelling of Allada, a prominent kingdom in the Bight of Benin.

93 AGNP, Not. 4, Box 78, 1615/11/07, no folio.

Betancur, González formalized these transactions by having them nota-rized, a validating process in itself.

The *encomendero*'s recourse to local notaries is significant in that it protected ship captains and purchasers from prosecution. Captain Hurtado had illicitly introduced 340 captives to Nueva Veracruz by way of São Tomé in September 1615.[94] Yet after "donating" forty slaves to the port's customs officials, Hurtado was permitted to register 112 captives and enter the mainland with an additional 188 contraband slaves.[95] These arrangements, however, were meaningless should he not sell his captives. Thus, on 1 December 1615, Hurtado entered a bizarre notarial contract with Pedro García Palomino, the owner of a sugar plantation in Izúcar. With the assistance of González, the Portuguese captain agreed to sell fifty slaves, twenty-five men and twenty-five women of "Arara land," for a collective price of 18,750 pesos.[96]

With González's assistance, Hurtado sold fifty Lower Guinean slaves in a single transaction. According to the captain, "the twenty-five black men are all called Manueles and the twenty-five black women Marias, all of them are between twenty and thirty years old from Arara land." Undoubtedly, the members of this community already distinguished themselves by other names, relationships, and ritual scars.[97] Yet whereas most traders named individual slaves in order to differentiate them for sale, Hurtado sought to homogenize his captives to the greatest degree possible by assigning each one a generic name, age, skin color, and provenance (see Appendix A). This strategy is all the more evident in the buyer's admission that "I am satisfied of [the slaves'] worth, goodness, and quality because I myself chose them among many other pieces the captain had with him." Hurtado and González sold three more Arara captives in early December 1615.[98] Together, they had managed to sell no fewer than seventy-six captives in six weeks on the Puebla slave market. Clearly, González was an influential figure, but in 1615 he was still merely an intermediary with no official designation or title. This would soon change.

In August 1620, Manuel González protested before the local municipal council as a *vecino* of Puebla de los Ángeles. He prefaced his complaint by presenting himself as the commissioned agent for slave ship sales in the city (*encomendero de las armazones de negros que vienen a esta ciudad*). González claimed that local residents were mistreating the African men and women

---

94 Ngou-Mvé, *El África*, 165.   95 Ibid., 165.

96 AGNP, Not. 4, Box 78, 1615 December, no folio (1615/12/01).

97 The Portuguese had developed a "regular and substantial trade with Allada" by 1602. See Robin Law, *The Slave Coast of West Africa 1550–1750* (Oxford: Oxford University Press, 1991), 118–121. Arara captives were often described as scarred (*rayado*) in reference to the ritual marks on their temples. See Sandoval, *Un tratado*, 140.

98 AGNP, Not. 4, Box 78, no folio. See entries for 1615/12/02, 1615/12/10 and 1615/12/14.

he routinely sold. He argued that Poblanos "beat the slaves with sticks" and threw them out into the rain.[99] He asked the municipal council to prohibit such behavior, especially as His Majesty received "great quantities of pesos from the sales tax" derived from his activities.[100]

The timing of González's complaint matters. During the summer months of the rainy season (May–September), the *encomendero de negros* moved his captives from Puebla's central plaza to the portals underneath the municipal palace to keep them dry. Individual slaves were often exhibited "below the portals," where they would sold to the highest bidder by the towncrier.[101] However, González's slave lot would have been much larger and more difficult to accommodate during the wet summer months.[102] The year 1620 was exceptionally busy for González, for he would sell no fewer than 192 African captives. In early October, he was still responsible for seventy-eight of them. There was little room for such a large number of people, especially as the rains put the captives in competition for dry space with itinerant food vendors and other people. Ultimately, González's petition was approved and the regents ordered that no one impede the Africans from taking cover. In 1624, however, the same council banned González from selling slaves in the main plaza. The regents claimed that the captives stole bread and fruit from indigenous vendors, leading to numerous violent incidents. As a result, the *encomendero* would relocate his activities to a small plaza on the eastern edge of the city between the Franciscan convent's cemetery and the bridge leading to the downtown area (see Figure 0.1).[103]

Puebla emerged as a major slave market because the *encomendero de negros* increasingly extended credit to people of all walks of life. Since these merchants were permanent residents of the city, they could gauge with increasing certainty those who could and could not repay debts. Slave ship captains, ever on the move, signed power-of-attorney letters enabling *encomenderos* to collect outstanding debts in their name.[104] The security of payment allowed these slaving agents to sell three of every four new African arrivals on credit during the 1620s and 1630s.[105] Slave

---

99 AGMP, Actas de Cabildo, Vol. 16, 2r–3r.
100 Hoberman, *Mexico's Merchant Elite*, 50. Andrés de Acosta used similar language to highlight his own slave-based fiscal contributions, which suggests that *encomenderos de negros* understood that they held some leverage in local matters. He claimed to have paid 140,000 pesos in sales taxes over more than 12 years.
101 AGNP, Not. 4, Box 42, 1595 April, 166v.
102 AGNP, Not. 4, Box 101, 1620 October, 2947r–2957r.
103 Guillermo Alberto Rodríguez Ortiz, "El lado afro de la Puebla de los Ángeles. Un acercamiento al estudio sobre la presencia Africana, 1595–1710" (Ph.D. diss., Benemérita Universidad Autónoma de Puebla, 2015), 204–205.
104 AHJP, Exps. 1572, 1575, 1576, and 1648.
105 AGNP Database, Not. 3 and 4, slave purchases for 1620, 1625, 1630, and 1635. In this sample, *encomenderos de negros* sold 559 African captives on credit (74.1 percent) and 196 for cash

dealers gave their clients an average of nine months to pay off their debts. Typically this consisted of dividing the total purchase price evenly into two or three installments. The first installment was due upon drafting the bill of slave purchase, with the second or third to be collected months later. *Encomenderos* preferred payment in silver reales, but were willing to accept other forms that advanced their interests. For instance, Manuel González once agreed to sell Isabel, a 16-year-old "Angola" slave, for 320 pesos in biscuits and bread. The food would be delivered to his house every day and would presumably feed the slaves under his supervision.[106]

With credit easily extended in this form, middling Poblanos ventured into slave ownership during the 1620s and 1630s with the certainty that they could repay resident slave dealers the price of one or two Africans. For instance, for Pedro de León, a master carpenter, finding apprentices was a constant struggle. As unremunerated novices, apprentices often fled their employers, stole tools, and generally did not complete their stipulated training period. Concerned family members could also remove a young relative from a workshop if they found he was being overly exploited. Yet the local *encomendero* gave Pedro de León five months to pay off his purchase of a 15-year-old "Angola" slave. The carpenter now owned a permanent apprentice, who in due time could become a skilled artisan.[107] Even a lowly peanut vendor (*cacahuatero*) could access financing for slave purchases. In 1630, a *cacahuatero* was awarded six months to pay off his purchase of Juan, a 12-year-old captive.[108] Thousands of sales like these took place under the Lusophone system.

Between 1620 and 1639, the *encomendero de negros* dominated the Puebla slave market and exerted considerable financial power throughout the viceroyalty. In 1615, the first year in which we locate González in the notarial record, 134 slaves (Africans and creoles) were purchased in Puebla. By 1620, the year he formally appeared before Puebla's municipal council, that number had risen to 373. By 1630, another Poblano, Juan Fernández de Vergara, had taken over Manuel González's responsibilities as *encomendero de negros*.[109] Ironsmiths, clergymen, widows, plantation owners, nuns – all

(25.9 percent). When accounting for all sales, 50.2 percent (785) of slaves sold during *encomendero*-dominant years were bought on credit in Puebla and 45.5 percent (712) were paid for upfront in cash, while the remaining 4–5 percent were bought in account of previous debts or unspecified installments of textiles, sugar, wheat, and so on.

106 AGNP, Not. 4, Box 101, 1620 September, 2832r. Slave ship captains also accepted payment in ham, soap, and wheat. See AHJP, Exp. 713, 20r; AGNP, Not. 4, Box 100, 1620 July, no folio.

107 AGNP, Not. 4, Box 137, 1630 April, no folio.

108 AGNP, Not. 4, Box 138, 1630 June, no folio (1630/06/10).

109 A third *encomendero de negros*, Francisco Pérez de Albuquerque, was active in Puebla in the mid 1620s. We know little of his activities other than that he was arrested by the Inquisition in 1627. See AGN, Inquisición, Vol. 823, Exp. 2.

turned to Fernández de Vergara for African-born captives that represented wealth, status, and political power, but, especially, permanent, unremunerated labor.

As significant as these slaving agents were, it is also important to acknowledge the role played by non-specialized merchants, widows, priests, and *obraje* owners on the Puebla slave market. After all, potential slave owners seeking American-born (creole) slaves or Africans with experience in the colonies could also purchase from relatives, business partners and other individuals. Even at the height of the Lusophone period (1620–1639), more than 60 percent of all slave sales in Puebla were made by people who were not specialized slave merchants.[110] *Encomenderos de negros* were undoubtedly influential, but they held no claims over slaves that were not purchased from slave ship captains. As a result, they had little control over creole sales. And these transactions mattered. Puebla citizens, residents and foreigners sold an average of 395 slaves of all backgrounds per year between 1620 and 1639, leading to a projection of 7,900 individuals sold for that short period. Total sales peaked during 1630 and 1635, with 456 and 440 slaves being sold, respectively (Figure 4.1).

The scale of the Puebla slave market forces us to reconsider what we think we know about slavery in colonial Mexico. The local market evidently supplied African slave labor to a broad expanse of central and southern New Spain. Mexico City undoubtedly functioned as the primary slave market for the cities of Toluca, Guanajuato and Querétaro, and other settlements in the Bajío region. However, the capital's role in colonial slaving has been overstated. Puebla logically emerged as a competing market to Mexico City as the latter flooded time and again between 1629 and 1634.[111] The Mexico City Jesuits even purchased twenty-six "Angola" captives from Fernández de Vergara in a single transaction in 1635.[112] Puebla attracted buyers from Antequera (modern-day Oaxaca City), Atlixco, Córdoba, Cholula, Tepeaca, Tehuacán, Tlaxcala and Santiago de Guatemala. Sugar planters from Izúcar, Cuautla, and the greater Cuernavaca basin appear frequently in local sales. The reach of Puebla's *encomendero* even encompassed the silver mines of northern New Spain.[113] The expansion of this particular slave market is all the more remarkable given that the Portuguese holders of the slave

---

110 Based on 944 out of 1559 slave sales for 1620, 1625, 1630, and 1635.

111 Jonathan Israel, *Razas, clases sociales y vida política en el México colonial 1610–1670* (Mexico City: Fondo de Cultura Económica, 2005), 40. Members of Mexico's Audiencia considered moving the viceregal capital to Puebla during this five-year period.

112 AGNP, Not. 4, Box 152, 1635 October, 1720r.

113 AGNP, Not. 4, Box 98, 1620 January, 142r. In January 1620, González sent third parties to Zacatecas (some 440 miles to the north) to claim more than 9,000 pesos in promissory notes for slave sales. González sent an additional nine captives for sale in the mining center.

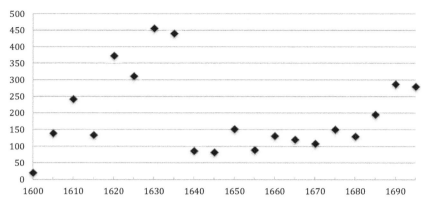

Figure 4.1 Number of enslaved people sold on Puebla slave market, 1600–1699. *Note:* Graph based on 4,331 references to enslaved people (for creoles, mulattos, chinos, and new African arrivals) in bills of slave purchase located within the Archivo General de Notarías de Puebla (AGNP). Puebla's third and fourth notarial offices contain the most complete and reliable documentary series, while information from the second and sixth offices is less consistent and fragmentary. The first and fifth offices were not consulted as they do not contain information for the seventeenth century. Due to the size of the archive and its lack of a catalogue or finding guide, the information recollected represents every fifth year of data starting with the year 1600, 1605, 1610, and so on. The graph depicts general trends in the Puebla slave market for a 100-year period based on observations for 21 points. Future research will correct for extreme fluctuations for periods of uncertainty, such as 1611–1614, 1636–1639, and 1686–1687. Additional bills of slave purchase may be found in the Archivo Histórico Judicial de Puebla (Exp. 713 & 823) and in the Puebla Notarial Collection at Tulane University.

trading contracts changed thrice during these years.[114] Despite the impact such administrative changes could have had, the Puebla slave market continually expanded until 1635 (and perhaps up to 1639).

Approximately 10,590 people were sold in the city of Puebla between 1590 and 1639. This is a conservative estimate since many enslaved people were purchased informally, leaving no paper trail. For instance, in 1640 the Jesuits purchased five slaves but only recorded the purchase of four. According to their internal records, when they bought Domingo, a black washer, "no bill of purchase was written in order to save the sales tax."[115] This type of admission is rare, although the practice of not notarizing a slave purchase must have been common. At other times, notarial information is missing for several months in a given year, resulting in a lower known number of transactions. Of course, many enslaved people were never sold at all, but

---

114 Antonio Fernández d'Elvas, alias Antonio Rodríguez de Elvas, held the slaving contract from 1615 to 1622. Manuel Rodríguez Lamego followed from 1623 to 1630, while Melchor Gómez Angel and Cristóbal Méndez de Sossa received the monopoly from 1631 to 1639. See Aguirre Beltrán, *La población*, 45–48.

115 JASML, Jesuitas, Escrituras Sueltas, microfilm 4, leg. 148.

remained in the service of a given individual or family for their entire life-time. Despite these limitations, studying bills of slave purchase allows us to imperfectly reconstruct the contours of the slave market. Overall, three of every four people sold during this fifty-year period were born on the African continent.[116]

West Central Africans formed the majority of the enslaved (Table 4.1), a reflection of Mexico's particular relationship with the slave merchants of Luanda. "Angola", "Congo," and "Anchico" captives accounted for 80 per-cent of all Africans sold in Puebla during these years (1590–1639).[117] By contrast, few Upper Guineans entered the city.[118] Even after combining captives from Cape Verde and the Canaries into this group, Upper Guineans accounted for no more than 6.4 percent of all Africans sold in Puebla. By contrast, Lower Guineans were slightly more numerous, although this fig-ure is distorted by Joseph Hurtado's 1615 slaving voyage from Alladah. In general, the Puebla slave market was extremely dependent on West Central Africa.[119]

Scholars of the slave trade have demonstrated that Spanish American slaveholders were willing to expend more money on Upper Guinean cap-tives than on West Central Africans. For instance, between 1626 and 1633, Angolan slaves in Cartagena sold for lower prices (268 pesos) than Upper Guineans (312 pesos).[120] In Puebla, a similar dynamic can be observed with two notable differences. First, the considerably longer sea and land voyage to Puebla raised slave prices considerably, but (in keeping with transportation expenses) not to the levels seen along Perú's Pacific coast.[121] Angolan captives between 14 and 30 years of age sold for an average of 433 pesos in Puebla during the 1630s, but individual sales could easily surpass 500 pesos.[122] It is clear that the merchants of Luanda understood

---

116 Africans were sold in 76.2 percent of purchases made in the period. See Table 4.1.

117 As a 20 percent sample of the Puebla notarial archives, these figures project the sales of approxi-mately 6,000 "Angolans," in addition to 500 Kongolese and 100 Anchicos. These figures offer a slight downward revision of Vila Vilar's estimate that 84.14 percent of all slaving vessels in Ver-acruz embarked captives in Angola, but otherwise confirm the provenance data in her study. Vila Vilar, *Hispanoamérica*, 153.

118 This data differentiate the Mexican case from the purchasing preferences seen in Cartagena de Indias. For instance, between 1593 and 1601 Cartagena received more captives from Upper Guinea than from any other region. See Wheat, "The First Great Waves," 17. Also, Newson and Minchin, *From Capture to Sale*, 68.

119 Outside of Mexico, only Buenos Aires had a comparable reliance on Luanda for the transatlantic trade. Schultz, "The Kingdom of Angola," 426–432; Borucki, Eltis, and Wheat, "Atlantic His-tory," 447.

120 Newson and Minchin, *From Capture to Sale*, 152.

121 Borucki, Eltis, and Wheat, "Atlantic History," 456; Vila Vilar, *Hispanoamérica*, 218–220.

122 AGNP. Bills of slave purchase for 1630 and 1635. This calculation is based on the prices of 230 working-age, newly arrived Angolan slaves sold in Puebla by Portuguese slave ship captains or the local *encomendero de negros*.

Table 4.1 *Sample of slaves in Puebla bills of purchase by region of provenance, 1590–1639*

Region	No. (Share)	Ethnonym/Location	No.
West Central Africa	1293 (61.0%)	Anchico/Teke	18
		Angola	1169
		Congo	100
		Others (2 groups)	6
Lower Guinea	154 (7.3%)	Arara/Allada	107
		Caravali/Calabar	25
		Terranova/Lucumí	17
		Others (2 groups)	5
Upper Guinea	91 (4.3%)	Bañon/Bañun	7
		Biafara/Biafada	13
		Bran	41
		Jalofe/Wolof	6
		Rios	6
		Others (5 groups)	18
African Entrepôts	32 (1.5%)	Cabo Verde	5
		Canarias	9
		São Tomé	18
East Africa	21 (1.0%)	Cafre	3
		Mozambique	18
Africa (unknown)	23 (1.1%)	"Bozal" (no info.)	23
Americas (creoles, include black, chino and mulatto)	306 (14.4%)	Cartagena	6
		Guatemala	19
		Habana	7
		Hispaniola	8
		New Spain	126
		"Creole" (no info.)	130
		Others (5 locations)	10
South Asia	35 (1.6%)	Bengal	5
		Filipinas	5
		Malabar	5
		India de Portugal/Goa	10
		Others (6 groups)	10
Europe	36 (1.7%)	Spain & Portugal	36
No information	127 (6.0%)	No information	127
Total	2118 (100%)		2118

Source: AGNP, Quinquennial sample from bills of slave purchase for 1590–1640, Not. 3 & 4.

that the urban centers of Central Mexico represented an invaluable market, especially in light of Cartagena's preference for Upper Guinean captives.[123] The latter sold for 482 pesos on average in Puebla, but very few captives from that region could be found after 1615.[124] Finally, sales for Lower Guineans averaged some of the lowest prices among African-born captives during the 1630s. On average, Poblanos paid 354 pesos for people with "Arara," "Terranova," "Benin," and "Mina" ethnonyms.

A modest, but important, number of creoles were also sold in Puebla during the first half of the seventeenth century. In a society that privileged African captives over their American counterparts, the latter sold for 347 pesos on average during the 1630s. At least 14 percent of all people sold in Puebla by 1639 had been born in the Americas.[125] This is a conservative estimate in that the provenance of children under 4 years of age was rarely listed in bills of sale.[126] Those born in New Spain formed the majority of creole slaves sold in Puebla. The evidence points to the rather logical presence of slaves from Nueva Veracruz, Mexico City, and Tlaxcala (see Table 4.1). A smaller creole component hailed from the southern limits of New Spain, with places like Campeche, Oaxaca, Chiapas, and even Santiago de Guatemala appearing repeatedly in slave purchases.

When combining sales for all slaves sold in Puebla by gender, an important price differential emerges during the first forty years of the seventeenth century. Enslaved women (ages 14–35 and listed with individual prices) were valued at an average of 352 pesos at the time of their sale, although sales for female *bozales* frequently surpassed the 420-peso mark.[127] In general, male slaves in Puebla sold for 364 pesos, with correspondingly higher prices for recent African arrivals.[128] Although the notarial sample for pregnant women is too small to speak of any definitive trend, it does suggest that masters valued slaves for their reproductive abilities. Pregnant slaves

---

123 Wheat, "The First Great Waves," 17.

124 AGNP. Bills of slave purchase for 1630 and 1635. Slave transactions for new African arrivals in the 1630s show 11 Upper Guineans, 101 Lower Guineans, and 657 Central Africans.

125 AGNP. Bills of slave purchase, 1595–1635. Of the 1,984 people whose sales were recorded in the Puebla notarial sample, 235 were identified as creoles.

126 Of 62 children aged 4 or younger in the sample, only 4 were assigned the *bozal* label. Notaries more often recorded the mother's ascribed ethnonym or birthplace, but at times did note that children were creoles. American origins can be inferred for almost half of these children by studying their mothers' ages and caste categories. By contrast, African-born children ages 10 and older were often sold in Puebla and labeled as *bozales*.

127 AGNP. Bills of slave purchase, 1595–1635. Calculations based on 409 individual women listed from a total 565 transactions.

128 *Ibid.* Calculations for enslaved men are based on 584 individual transactions. Additional information on 371 enslaved men was excluded because of collective sale prices.

sold for an average of 406 pesos.[129] When the widow Leonor de Linares sold Antonia, an African woman in the eighth month of her pregnancy, the former declared that the buyer assumed all risk in the event of Antonia's death. Linares would receive 400 pesos in this exchange.[130] Antonia's new mistress likely accepted this arrangement under the premise that her slave could be hired out as a wet nurse or that Antonia's unborn child would one day be worth a considerable return on her investment.

Despite the growth of local creole populations, the slave market data indicates that Poblanos were willing to pay elevated premiums for Africans throughout the first forty years of the seventeenth century. Counterintuitively, locals purchased people unfamiliar with the Castilian language and Mexican setting over those that had been born immersed in their culture. Why? After all, African-born slaves carried a heavy price tag that did not even factor the costs of providing them with the linguistic and cultural skills required for their daily lives. Again, we must look past sheer financial figures to understand the cultural aspects of urban demand for slave labor. Purchasing new African arrivals signified financial power, but especially status.[131] Slave owners understood the social significance of their actions in the slave market.

"Chinos" and the Transpacific Slave Trade

During the period of *encomendero* influence (1616–1639), hundreds of Asian captives were also sold on the Puebla slave market. By the early seventeenth century, Spain had consolidated the transpacific route pioneered by Miguel López de Legazpi in 1565 by way of the Manila Galleon trade. The galleons linked the Spanish American demand for slaves with Asian markets laden with silk, porcelain and captives of their own. Quite incorrectly assigned the label of *chinos*, the majority of these men and women actually came from diverse Asian kingdoms that interacted with Lusophone merchants in Goa, Macao and Cochin during the early seventeenth century. Some captives hailed from Malabar and the Bay of Bengal. Others received vague descriptors, such as "de la India de Portugal," that merely established an undefined provenance from territories with Portuguese contacts. Many Asians were captured in regional wars (such as those of the Arakan) or sold into slavery by their parents during periods of extreme drought or famine.[132] After several months or even years of sailing the Indian Ocean,

---

129 *Ibid.* I have identified nine bills of purchase for pregnant slaves, but only six transactions feature individual prices.

130 AGNP, Not. 4, Box 67, 1610 January, no folio.   131 Bryant, *Rivers of Gold*, 16, 19.

132 Tatiana Seijas, *Asian Slaves in Colonial Mexico: From Chinos to Indians* (Cambridge: Cambridge University Press, 2014), 36–38.

they reached the Philippine Islands and the capital of Manila to serve a growing mass of colonizers. By the 1620s, approximately 10,000 slaves of extremely diverse origin resided in Manila alone.[133] Spaniards en route to New Spain drew from this enslaved population to introduce Asian captives to Puebla by way of Acapulco.

Slaveholders did not view Asians as a substitute population for people of African descent. In fact, most Asian captives entered the Puebla slave market at the peak of the transatlantic slave trade.[134] More than half of all seventeenth-century *chino* slave sales took place in the 1630s. They constituted up to 2 percent of all slave sales in early seventeenth-century Puebla.[135] Slaveholders associated Asian captives with specialized textile production, which explains their disproportionate numbers in *obrajes* and milliner workshops. For example, Marcos de Arellano and Jerónimo Tornes, two milliners, each bought two *chino* captives in 1635 from Juan García del Brocal and Juan Campos, Poblano merchants with apparent connections to Acapulco and the transpacific slave trade. These merchants sold another six *chino* captives (with "Corumbi," "Bengala," and "India de Portugal" ethnonyms) that year.[136] Like their *encomenderos de negros* contemporaries, both merchants were willing to extend four to eight months of credit to their clients and accepted payment in kind.[137]

Poblanos paid an average of 348 pesos for working-age Asians during the early seventeenth century, practically the same price as creole slaves.[138] The relative affordability of *chino* slaves is perplexing because Spaniards generally perceived them as skilled textile workers (see Chapter 3).[139] Moreover, Asian slaves should have been more expensive because their transportation costs to Mexico were much more elevated.[140] Just the transpacific voyage from Manila to Acapulco could take up to six months. After arrival in Acapulco, slaves were forced to follow a series of rugged trails up the sierras

133 Ibid., 35.
134 Among the 84 South Asian slaves sold within the Puebla notarial sample, 52 were sold during the 1620s and 1630s.
135 This number rises slightly to 2.5 percent of all sales for the 1590–1644 period if accounting for creole *chinos*.
136 AGNP, Not. 3, Box 76, 676r, 680r. AGNP, Not. 4, Box 150, 199r, 683v and Box 151, 1002r, 1223r. At least two of these captives, Juan Morgado and another Juan, completed the transpacific voyage aboard the *San Luis* galleon.
137 Ibid. García del Brocal sold Felipe and Salvador, "Columbi" and "Bengala" captives respectively, for 460 pesos each. Marcos de Arellano, a Puebla milliner, paid for them in "fine hats" (*cascos de sombreros finos*) due by late 1635.
138 This observation is based on 58 bills of slave purchase for South Asians aged 15 to 35.
139 Ngou-Mvé, *El África*, 116. As early as 1600, Spaniards esteemed Asian captives "as people more domestic than blacks and skilled in all kinds of work," but refused to match the latters' prices.
140 Seijas, *Asian Slaves*, 73. In 1635, recently disembarked *chinos* could be purchased for 200 pesos in Acapulco.

of modern-day Guerrero and Oaxaca in order to reach the urban centers of Central Mexico.[141]

The transpacific slave trade to Puebla was also distinct from its transatlantic counterpart in that it largely consisted of captive men. This may have been the result of an early-seventeenth-century petition that called for an end to "the small harems" of enslaved Asian women that routinely traveled on the Manila Galleon.[142] With only sixteen *chinas* surfacing in the Puebla sample, the enslaved chino population held a severely unbalanced 4.25:1 male-to-female sex ratio.[143] This suggests that travel restrictions on *chinas* were stringent enough that only the most influential merchants and officials could afford to import them. Given the scarcity of *chinas*, Poblanos demonstrated little to no concern for the natural growth of an enslaved Asian population.

In this regard, the story of Catarina de San Juan, alias "la china poblana," is remarkable. While the memory and folklore surrounding this remarkable holy woman have made her an iconic figure in Puebla, her experiences as an enslaved person have not been properly contextualized.[144] Captured by pirates in India as a child, San Juan sailed through the Indian Ocean as a captive before being sold in Cochin and Manila. In 1619, at the age of 12 or 13, she disembarked in Acapulco and soon thereafter became the property of Captain Miguel de Sosa, a prominent Portuguese merchant and *vecino* of Puebla.[145] In effect, San Juan arrived in Puebla at the height of the slave trade. Captain Sosa was well acquainted with the value and demand for captives of all backgrounds.[146] Upon entering his household, San Juan joined a community of enslaved domestics, most of whom were of African descent. Juan, an "Arara" man, had been a part of the Sosa household in 1610.[147] Gracia, a black woman from Lisbon, worked in the same residence until 1620, when she was sold to Puebla's municipal scribe.[148] By 1623, San Juan would have also briefly interacted with three Angolan boys,

141 Ibid., 96–97.   142 Ibid., 15–16, 79. In 1608, Philip III ratified the petition.

143 Ibid. Seijas proposes a 3:1 male-to-female ratio for New Spain's chino population.

144 The historiography on Catarina de San Juan is extensive. The most accurate contextualization for her life is found in Seijas, *Asian Slaves*, 8–31. For other recent studies, see Kathleen Ann Meyers, *Neither Saints Nor Sinners: Writing the Lives of Women in Spanish America* (Oxford: Oxford University Press, 2003), 44–68; Roshni Rustomji-Kerns, "Las raíces olvidadas de Mirrah-Catarina," *Artes de México* 66 (2003), 20–33; Kate Risse, "Catarina de San Juan and the China Poblana: From Spiritual Humility to Civil Obedience," *Confluencia* 18, no. 1 (Fall 2002), 70–80.

145 BNE, MSS 6877, "Papeles de Mota y Escobar," 293v. In 1619, Puebla's bishop, Alonso de la Mota y Escobar, asked Sosa to personally deliver 200 pesos to Vieja Veracruz for the refurbishment of the parish church.

146 In 1615, Sosa helped Capt. Alonso de Mojica sell Esperanza, a 20-year-old *china*, to Doña Maria Landeras. See AGNP, Not. 3, Box 36, 1615 December, no folio.

147 AHJP, Exp. 713, 21r.   148 AGNP, Not. 4, Box 102, 1620 December, 3602r.

Diego, Domingo, and Ignacio, who were held in deposit at the Sosa residence before being sold off to a third party.[149]

Catarina de San Juan's early experiences in Puebla were informed by the inhumanity of the slave market and the ever-present possibility of being sold to an unknown master. Her purchase by Captain Sosa also speaks to the domestic (and sexual) expectations that Spanish masters held over enslaved women. Sometime before her purchase in 1619, Sosa asked a fellow merchant to buy "a modest and attractive Chinita to serve as a comfort to him and his spouse."[150] Sales of this type were common as relatives, friends, and business associates inspected and prodded potential domestic slaves for acquaintances. Yet, we must be explicitly clear on one point. Women of African descent outnumbered *chinas* sixty-four times over in Puebla's notarial records.[151] The distinctiveness of Catarina de San Juan lies in the fact that she was an enslaved Asian woman in a city where few could be found. Thus, it is troubling that the modern memory of slavery in Puebla is often exclusively remitted to her exceptional circumstances. In doing so, colonial chroniclers, hagiographers, and modern-day scholars have effaced the experiences of a much larger demographic of African descent.

The Puebla Slave Market after 1640

The rebellion of the Portuguese nobility against the Spanish monarch on 1 December 1640 had a tremendous impact on the transatlantic slave trade to Spanish America. The sudden loss of the Lusophone slaving networks meant that the primary mechanism for purchasing African captives was no longer operant. Moreover, in August 1641, Dutch forces seized the port of Luanda and would occupy it for the next seven years.[152] Aware of the acute need and profitability of the Mexican market, the Dutch offered the Spanish Crown to serve as suppliers of the slaving contract, but were rebuffed in 1650.[153] A year later, the Audiencia of Mexico requested that the Crown authorize a shipment of "one thousand *piezas* of black slaves from Angola, Cape Verde or the Rivers [of Guinea], which this kingdom so badly needs."[154] Petitions of this nature were unsuccessful in restarting

149 AHJP, Exp. 1350, 1r. Sosa had agreed to sell off the three youths in the name of Andres Luis Guerrero, a temporary resident of Puebla.

150 Tatiana Seijas, Tatiana Seijas, "Transpacific Servitude: The Asian Slaves of Colonial Mexico, 1580–1700," Doctoral dissertation (Yale, 2008), 3–4.

151 My sample from Puebla's third and fourth notarial office (including sales, wills, inventories, loans, etc.) contains 2,824 references to women of African descent and 44 references to *chinas*.

152 For a detailed discussion of the Kongolese response to the Dutch occupation, see Heywood and Thornton, *Central Africans*, 145–148.

153 Aguirre Beltrán, *La población*, 53–54. In 1655, the Crown rejected two other Dutch proposals.

154 AGI, México, 36, n. 57, 1651.

the transatlantic slave trade to Mexico. In the local context, the end of the Portuguese slaving contracts meant that Puebla's *encomendero de negros* would no longer distribute new African captives to the city and its hinterland. Tens of thousands of creoles, mulattos, *chinos*, and older Africans were still available for sale, but the certainty that they could be replaced with shiploads of new African captives was gone.

Political and religious events within Mexico played a crucial role in the interruption of the transatlantic slave trade. Anti-Portuguese sentiment was especially acute between 1641 and 1649, in large part due to Puebla's bishop, Juan de Palafox y Mendoza, and his successful campaign to overthrow the Duke of Escalona as viceroy.[155] The new ruler of independent Portugal, King Jõao IV, was Escalona's brother-in-law. In order to undermine confidence in Escalona in the Madrid court, "Palafox deliberately exaggerated the Portuguese menace in order to lend force to his reports that the duke's government was jeopardizing the security of New Spain."[156] Key to these allegations was the insinuation that the Lusophones "owned many black slaves who would gladly support them should they choose to rebel." In 1642, Palafox ordered the Portuguese community of Nueva Veracruz to move twenty leagues inland.[157] The Lusophone traders – many of whom were accused of secretly practicing the Jewish faith – left Mexico, went into hiding, or were imprisoned by the officers of the Inquisition during the 1640s. Ultimately, the auto-da-fé of 1649 destroyed the viceroyalty's Portuguese community. By targeting the wealthiest Lusophone merchants, the Inquisitors disarticulated the slaving infrastructure and credit that underpinned the slave trade within Mexico.[158]

The transatlantic slave trade to New Spain took a precipitous fall between 1640 and 1664. African captives continued to enter New Spain during the second half of the seventeenth century, albeit in irregular shipments. Based on Puebla sales, this diminution in slave transactions mirrors the contraction of Spanish America's Atlantic trade during the second third of the seventeenth century.[159] In Puebla, just over 100 slaves were sold on average each year between 1640 and 1659.[160] Few slave ships docked

155 Israel, *Razas*, 131–136, 212–219, 246–249.

156 Cayetana Álvarez de Toledo, *Politics and Reform in Spain and Viceregal Mexico: The Life and Thought of Juan de Palafox 1600–1659* (Oxford: Oxford University Press, 2004), 125, 130.

157 Israel, *Razas*, 127–135; Antonio García de León, *Tierra adentro, mar en fuera: El puerto de Veracruz y su litoral a Sotavento, 1519–1821* (Mexico City: Fondo de Cultura Económica, 2011), 528.

158 Quiroz Norris, "La expropriación inquisitorial de cristianos nuevos portugueses en los Reyes, Cartagena y México, 1635–1649" *Histórica* 10, no. 2 (December 1986), 244–248, 254–256, 295–303; Hordes, "Crypto-Jewish Community," 42, 50, 107–109, 126–146, 153. The Mexican Inquisition collected more than 3 million pesos in confiscated goods from the 1646, 1647, and 1649 *autos*.

159 Hoberman, *Mexico's Merchant Elite*, 13–17; Mervyn Francis Lang, *Las flotas de Nueva España (1630–1710): Despacho, azogue, comercio* (Seville: Muñoz Moya Editor, 1998), 23–26.

160 AGNP, sales database, 1640, 1645, 1650, 1655. See Figure 4.1.

at Nueva Veracruz during this period.[161] It is likely that some arrived in clandestine operations, while others made port as part of the fleets (*flotas*) sent from Spain.[162] Whatever the case, these slaving voyages left little to no record in the Puebla archives. Curiously, in his *Istorica Descrizione*, compiled circa 1662, Giovanni Antonio Cavazzi noted that in Portuguese Angola slaves obeyed "not only the word but even the signal of their masters, since they are afraid of being carried to New Spain."[163] This threat, however, represented the fears of young Central African captives one to two generations before. At the time Cavazzi was gathering his historical notes on Queen Jinga and her court, most "Angolans" were being shipped to the Caribbean and Brazil, not Mexico.

Between 1645 and 1699, enslaved creoles formed the overwhelming majority of those bought in Puebla. Approximately 8,615 people were sold in the city during this period, and American-born people accounted for three of every four slaves in these transactions.[164] These observations challenge the notion that in New Spain "slaves became more difficult to obtain" after 1650.[165] In fact, Poblano slaveholders could draw on thousands of creole slaves during the second half of the seventeenth century. Acquiring new African arrivals, however, was difficult. The Puebla slave market stabilized in the 1660s and 1670s, when an average of 127 slaves were sold annually. Poblano slaveholders adapted to the loss of Lusophone slaving networks by redirecting their demands onto enslaved creole populations.[166]

---

161 Only two slave ships on transatlantic voyages disembarked in New Spain between 1640 and 1649. *TSTD*, http://www.slavevoyages.org/voyages/xZiGnzIL (accessed 05/25/2017).

162 The *TSTD* reports eleven slave ships disembarking at Veracruz between 1647 and 1659, but all come from one single source: AGI Contratación 2896. I have been unable to identify any sales for new African arrivals within Puebla transactions for 1650, 1655 or 1660; see *TSTD* http://www.slavevoyages.org/voyages/DEuJO7Zq (accessed 05/25/2017). Slave ships arriving in 1647, 1650, 1653, 1654 and 1656 may have arrived with the fleets that departed Spain via Cape Verde or the Canaries, although this hypothesis requires further research. This was not possible for the voyages listed for 1652 and 1659 because the fleet was not dispatched those years. See Lang, *Las flotas*, 31–32, 128–174, 325–326.

163 Heywood and Thornton, *Central Africans*, 186.

164 The projection of 8,615 slaves sold is based on purchase records from 1,723 individuals in AGNP, Notarial offices 2, 3, 4, and 6 for the 1645–1699 period. Sales for 1,381 people were recorded in Puebla's third and fourth notarial offices, and that data was used to determine American provenance. Of those individuals, 756 (54.7 percent) were labeled as black, mulatto and chino "creoles" in their bills of purchase. American origins can be inferred for another 264 enslaved people (19.1 percent) by taking into account their family histories. Only 242 African-born individuals (17.5 percent) appear in the sample. I am unable to classify the provenance of 114 people (8.2 percent).

165 Douglas Cope, *The Limits of Racial Domination: Plebeian Society in Colonial Mexico City, 1660–1720* (Madison: University of Wisconsin Press, 1994), 96.

166 This is similar to the manner in which Jalapa's merchant-planters adjusted to the mid-century decline in Atlantic trade by turning to Puebla for creditors and clients. See Carroll, *Blacks in Colonial Veracruz*, 46–48.

The consolidation of this creole-dependent slave market hinged on the understanding that enslaved females would serve as the primary purveyors of slave labor. This is not to say that these ideas were new. Elite Spaniards had relied on generations of enslaved domestic workers since the mid-sixteenth century and, as seen in Chapter 2, politically savvy *obrajeros* used similar tactics since the 1630s. However, because of the intermittent closing of the transatlantic trade, reproduction among enslaved creoles became a greater concern for masters in the years after Portuguese independence. Accordingly, enslaved women (14–35) sold for slightly higher prices in Puebla than their male counterparts from 1640 to 1699.[167] For instance, a Poblano slaveholder sold Sebastiana, a 15-year-old *mulata* from the town of Tepeaca, to Joseph Moncayo. In the seller's words, "if during the next fifteen months . . . I should return and deliver the said 290 pesos, [Moncayo] will return and deliver the said Sebastiana mulatta with the fruits she procreated, in case she has any, without any excuse or delay."[168] These childbearing expectations were firmly entrenched by the time the intra-Caribbean slave trade resumed in the early 1660s.

In 1662, the Spanish Crown entered an exclusive slaving contract (*asiento*) with the Genoese merchants Domenico Grillo and Ambrosio Lomelín, and within a few years African captives made their way to Puebla once again. The *asiento*, however, did not result in a mass influx of slaves. Of the 18,134 enslaved men, women and children introduced to Spanish America by this *asiento* (1662–1674), only 2,100 arrived in Nueva Veracruz.[169] The contract was polemic from the start in that English and Dutch merchants served as Grillo and Lomelín's providers. Moreover, the *San Juan Bautista*, the *asiento*'s first vessel to Mexico, only arrived in 1664. Many of its captives were so debilitated by their time in the Barbados slave dêpots that they were labeled as "refuse" slaves (*del desecho*) upon arrival in Nueva Veracruz.[170] Despite their physical condition, Captain Santiago Daza Villalobos sold 266 captives in the port between August 1664 and March 1665.[171] At least another twenty were sold in Puebla, but

---

167 AGNP, Not. 3 & 4, Bills of slave purchase for 1640–1699. Based on 269 observations with individual prices, enslaved women (ages 14–35) sold for an average of 335 pesos. This calculation excludes extraordinary purchases for women that surpassed 800 pesos. Working-age males, by contrast, sold for 331 pesos. This calculation was based on 377 transactions. For the pre-1640 period, see notes 130 and 131.

168 AGNP, Not. 3, Box 129, 1675 January, 10r.

169 Marisa Vega Franco, *El tráfico de esclavos con América (Asientos de Grillo y Lomelín, 1663–1674)* (Seville: Escuela de Estudios Hispanoamericanos/Consejo Superior de Investigaciones Científicas, 1984), 186.

170 AGI, Escribanía, 292A, Segundo legajo, 9v–28v.

171 Ibid. Based on a rare register for slave sales in Nueva Veracruz, the *San Juan Bautista* carried nearly equal numbers of male and female captives. Daza sold 126 females and 127 males of all ages at port. I cannot determine the gender of 13 captives, who were sold in collective transactions.

unfortunately local records are incomplete for late 1664.[172] Nonetheless, a comparison between the sites reveals an 86-peso differential between both markets.[173] This was the extra cost that Poblano slaveholders were willing to pay incoming slave ship captains rather than go to Nueva Veracruz themselves.

Despite the evident demand for African captives, the Grillo and Lomelín monopoly was controversial because it threatened the tax-farming interests of local elites. Whereas *encomenderos de negros* of the pre-1640 period traditionally paid thousands of pesos each year in sales tax (*alcabala*), the *asiento* exempted incoming slave traders from making such payments to municipal councils.[174] Undeterred, Puebla's regents attempted to charge Daza Villalobos the sales tax in November 1664.[175] The situation deteriorated because the *asiento* holders were supposed to have appointed a local arbitrator to resolve these types of conflicts.[176] In practice, that person was nowhere to be found. Eventually, Daza Villalobos returned to the port with no fewer than 50,000 pesos in silver and fled in the spring of 1665.

During the 1670s, a modest influx of African captives did impact the Puebla slave market. From January to March 1670, two Nueva Veracruz-based merchants, Francisco Arias de Viveros and Sebastian de Velasco, sold sixteen "Arara" captives in Puebla at an average price of 428 pesos.[177] All of them had been purchased from the slave dêpots of Barbados, a reflection of the growing influence of English slave traders on Spanish American markets. Only one of the sixteen – Francisco, an 18-year-old "Mina" captive – was baptized, and only three had been given Christian names.[178] The Africans sold in Puebla in early 1670 were the survivors of an

---

Once in Puebla, he at least sold 8 females and 12 males, who had been given names but were listed as unbaptized. Unfortunately, notarial records for the last months of 1664 are incomplete, and those that do survive do not provide ethnonyms or African ports of provenance. Two isolated bills of slave purchase from 1665 indicate that some of the captives were labeled "Arara" and "Quimi." See AGNP, Not. 4, Box 196, 1665 October, 1047r; Not. 4, Box 197, 1665 February, 225r.

172 AGNP, Not. 4, Box 194, 1664 November, 1166r–1169r.

173 Based on 288 observations for both sites, Daza's captives sold for an average of 311.4 pesos in Nueva Veracruz and 398 pesos in Puebla.

174 Pablo Miguel Sierra Silva, "Portuguese *Encomenderos*," *Journal of Global Slavery* 2, no. 3 (Fall 2017 special issue), 238–239.

175 AGMP, Actas de Cabildo, Vol. 26, 77r–79v, 113r–117v.

176 Alejandro García Montón, "Corona, hombres de negocios y jueces conservadores. Un acercamiento en escala trasatlántica (S. XVII)," *Jerónimo Zurita* 90 (2015), 88–89, 110–111.

177 AGNP, Not. 4, Box 205, 1670 January–March, 104r, 113r, 120v, 122r, 123r, 123v, 187r, 190r, 192r, 213r, 214r, 268r, 328r, 368v.

178 By contrast, it is rare to locate a notarial transaction for a nameless slave in Puebla archives prior to 1640.

October 1669 slave rebellion that took place and was suppressed en route to the highlands.[179] Two other slave ships docked in Nueva Veracruz in 1672 and 1673 from Curaçao, but more research is needed to reconstruct the Puebla slave market for those two years.[180] Despite the deficiencies of the *asiento*, small groups of African captives continued to arrive in the highlands throughout the 1670s.

The Puebla market slowly recovered as 150 slaves were sold in 1675, but incoming Africans accounted for only 4 percent of those sales. If anything, the Grillo and Lomelín *asiento* accentuated the importance of owning enslaved women of childbearing age. On 23 December 1672, the expectations of slave reproduction fell squarely, if symbolically, on the shoulders of women of African descent. That day Queen Mariana of Spain issued a general decree abolishing the enslavement of all Asians and Native Americans (under the premise they were all *indios*).[181] Slaveholders in Acapulco, Puebla and Mexico City were disproportionately impacted by the decree. In response, many Poblanos attempted to reclassify their Asian slaves as *negros* and *cafres*, and thus legitimate slaves.[182] Others simply did not care and continued selling *chino* slaves openly.[183] One might argue that the decree had limited ramifications since Asians constituted a small minority of those sold on the Puebla slave market. Still, Afro-Poblanos surely grasped the racial implications of the decree. Slavery was now exclusively equated with people of African descent.

The association between enslavement and African descent was reinforced by the *asientos* of the 1680s, which were virtually awarded to the Dutch under the *asiento* holders Juan Barroso del Pozo (1682–1685) and Baltazar Coymans (1685–1689).[184] Unfortunately, the notarial sample used for this study does not capture most *asiento* transactions from the 1680s, but Puebla's baptismal registers provide useful, if indirect, evidence for these years. From early 1686 to mid-1688, more than 56 adult

179 AGI, México, 45, N.57, 2r–4v, 9v–12v, 29r–32r. The captives-turned-rebels murdered the incoming factor, Agustín Lomelín, at the Rinconada rest stop, before falling to a motley crew of muleteers, merchants, and sugar planters from Xalapa and La Antigua. See Sierra Silva, "Portuguese Encomenderos."

180 Clark, "Veracruz and the Caribbean," 182–183.

181 Seijas, *Asian Slaves*, 229–234; Reséndez, The Other Slavery, 131–148. The decree targeted indigenous slavery in New Mexico, Chile, Argentina, coastal Colombia and Venezuela and the Philippines.

182 AGNP, Not. 3, Box 139, 1680 November, 1554r; Not. 4, Box 209, 1675 December, 1144v; Not. 4, Box 230, 1690 May, 826r; Not. 4, Box 230, 1690 September, 29r.

183 AGNP, Not. 4, Box 214, 1680 June, 58v. In 1680, Don Nicolasa de Sosa Victoria, a lawyer, and his family brazenly sold Clemente, a 38-year-old creole *chino*, for 200 pesos to an *obrajero*. Baptismal data from Puebla's central parish indicates that slaveholders continued to own slaves of South Asian descent well past 1675. See *ASMP*, "Bautismos de negros, mulatos y chinos, 1677–1687," f. 15r, 57r, 333r.

184 Aguirre Beltrán, *La población*, 62–66.

Africans (all recent arrivals) were baptized in the Sagrario parish.[185] An extant investigation into Dutch contraband networks revealed that in 1686 Captain Juan Cavero delivered 134 captives to Martin de Aranguti, who acted as a local slaving agent in Puebla.[186] These captives were but a fraction of the 1,800 who arrived aboard three slave ships, the *Santa Rosa Americana*, *Santa Alida* and *Santísima Trinidad y San Antonio Abad*, in a twelve-month period.[187] Poblano militia captains, wealthy *doñas*, and other high-ranking members of society claimed most of the "Arara," "Mina," and "Loango" captives listed in Puebla' baptismal books. Many other Africans would be sent to the sugar plantations of Izúcar, Chietla, and Córdoba. Although further research is required for this brief period, Cavero, Aranguti, and Captain Juan de la Carra were especially active in the Puebla, Orizaba, and Mexico City slave markets.[188]

The ethnonyms attached to the African captives entering Puebla during the late seventeenth century reveal the growing influence of Dutch and English slave trading on the greater Spanish American region. Multiple references to "Arara" people indicate that most of the enslaved were drawn from the Bight of Benin. From a quantitative perspective, the transatlantic slave trade to late-seventeenth-century Puebla was modest. Culturally, however, the influx of these Lower Guinean captives complicates the "Angolan" identity that is often projected onto turn-of-the-century African populations in Central Mexico.[189] Linguistically, politically, and religiously, the incoming Africans sold on the Puebla slave market during the 1670s and 1680s did not embody a cultural continuum with the Central African populations of the past.[190] Regardless of their regions of provenance, one point must be very clear: African-born people were vastly outnumbered by creoles in urban and rural spaces during the second half of the seventeenth century.

---

185 ASMP, "Bautismos de negros, mulatos y chinos, 1677–1688," 334r–376r.

186 AGI, Escribanía, 297C, Leg. 3, Núm. 3, 4v–20r.

187 AGI, Escribanía, 297C, "Testimonios y Zertificaçiones que se an sacado de los Rexistros de embarcaçiones," 4r–12v. In June 1686, the *Santa Rosa Americana* disembarked 300 African slaves in Nueva Veracruz, only to be followed by *Santa Alida* with 927 enslaved Africans. In May 1687, the *Santísima Trinidad y San Antonio Abad* disembarked another 580 captives. Clark provides different slave ship names for the two years in question raising the possibility of many more 1680s slaving voyages than previously acknowledged. See Clark, "Veracruz and the Caribbean," 182–183.

188 Tatiana Seijas and Pablo Miguel Sierra Silva, "The Persistence of the Slave Market in Seventeenth-Century Central Mexico," *Slavery & Abolition* 37, no. 2 (Jan. 2016), 313; AGI, Escribanía, 297C, Leg. 4, 2r–5v.

189 Bennett, *Colonial Blackness*, 18–19; Bryant, *Rivers of Gold*, 65.

190 For a discussion of Arará diviners in another late-seventeenth-century setting, see Russell Lohse, *Africans into Creoles: Slavery, Ethnicity and Identity in Colonial Costa Rica* (Albuquerque: University of New Mexico Press, 2014), 113–114. For a later time and Brazilian setting, see James H. Sweet, *Domingos Álvares, African healing, and the Intellectual History of the Atlantic World* (Chapel Hill: University of North Carolina Press, 2011).

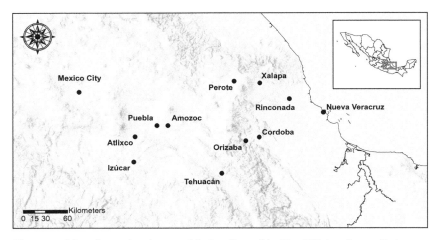

Figure 4.2 Map of central and eastern Mexico. Created by Tim O'Brien. *Sources:* Esri, USGS, NGA, NASA, CGIAR, N Robinson, NCEAS, NLS, OS, NMA, Geodatastyrelsen, Riijkswaterstaat, GSA, FEMA, Intermap and the GIS user community.

Elite urban-dwellers continued to purchase slaves, but the greater trend suggests an exodus toward the sugar plantations to the southwest and east.[191] During the second half of the seventeenth century, powerful Poblano families, such as the Ravosso de la Plaza, Pérez Delgado and Colón, bought hundreds of slaves for hard labor in sugar-producing estates (*ingenios*) to the southwest of the city. Some of these *ingenios* concentrated considerable enslaved populations: the San Joseph plantation in Izúcar held 220 slaves in 1643,[192] in 1680 the San Joseph *ingenio* in Tepeojuma held 150 enslaved workers; 156 captives labored in the *ingenio* San Cosme y San Damian outside of Chietla in 1691 (Figure 4.2).[193] By the 1690s, the Puebla market was also impacted by demand from Córdoba and continued to redistribute urban slaves toward that area.[194] Between 1685 and 1695, slave sales in Puebla reached levels unseen since the days of the *encomenderos de negros.* More than 280 enslaved people were sold in 1690 and the same number again in 1695 (see Figure 4.1). Once more, this unacknowledged

---

191 I have collected information for the destination of 748 slaves (of a total of 1498) sold in my sample for the period 1640–1700. The very large proportion of missing destinations complicates further analysis. Many purchasers from surrounding agricultural settlements lived in Puebla year round, thereby making a slave owner's residency an unreliable measure of his or her slave's ultimate destination.

192 Hoberman, *Mexico's Merchant Elite*, 108.

193 AGNP, Not. 4, Box 214, f. 1r; Not. 3, Box 166, f. 606r.

194 The slave trade to Córdoba intensified during the early eighteenth century, as planters concentrated enslaved populations in central Veracruz; see Adriana Naveda Chávez-Hita, *Esclavos negros en las haciendas azucareras de Córdoba, Veracruz, 1690–1830* (Xalapa: Universidad Veracruzana/Centro de Investigaciones Históricas, 1987), 35–37.

surge in slave purchases alters our understanding of the history of slavery in colonial Mexico. It is now evident that local slave markets adapted and, in fact, rebounded during the late seventeenth century.

Conclusion

The preceding characterization of the Puebla slave market aligns well with Louise Hoberman's understanding of the Mexican economy as a whole: "contracted growth from the 1590s to 1630s, a contraction from the 1640s until the 1660s or 1670s; and an erratic recovery until the end of the century."[195] In slaving terms, the period of Lusophone dominance (1590–1639) was only briefly interrupted by a failed Sevillean initiative. In the decades after 1640, Mexican slaveholders adapted to a systemic change in transatlantic slaving by resorting to enslaved creole populations for hard labor, domestic servitude, and social status. Three of every four slaves sold in Puebla during the second half of the seventeenth century were born in the Americas. The logistically deficient Grillo and Lomelín *asiento* did not resolve the demands of slaveholding Poblanos in the 1660s and 1670s. Instead, the recovery of the Puebla slave market in the 1680s and 1690s was primarily due to the steady growth of the enslaved creole population.

Throughout this chapter, I have suggested that local archives have been underused in the development of a more precise history of the slave trade to and within colonial Mexico. The links between incoming African youths, Poblano slaveholders, and Lusophone ship captains only come into relief by situating *encomenderos de negros* in the notarial and municipal records of the early seventeenth century. Studying these local records for the second half of the seventeenth century also proves that while enslaved people were plentiful, African-born captives were not. The crux of the matter lies in acknowledging the experiences of enslaved creoles.

Finally, this study of a Mexican slave market should serve as a cautionary tale. Although I have presented figures on prices, ages, and terms of repayment, the notarial record rarely reveals motivations or emotions. It does not speak to despair, nor does it acknowledge the separation of enslaved families. For the most part, these are records for and by slaveholders. The debasement of a captive's physical inspection in a public plaza did not concern the local notary. If anything, this chapter documents one city's enduring commitment to the inhumanity of slavery. Poblanos demanded and paid for the uncontested servitude of people of African descent for the entirety of the seventeenth century and well into the eighteenth. In the following chapter, I turn to the experiences of the enslaved and their families in the streets, churches and residences of Puebla.

195 Hoberman, *Mexico's Merchant Elite*, 17.

5

Life in the Big City

Mobility, Social Networks and Family

Doña Juana Melendez, legitimate wife of the Contador Juan de Burboa Guevara, and a neighbor of this city, I say that . . . we have become so needy and poor that in no manner are we able to sustain ourselves, were it not for six black journeymen stonemasons, who have worked for over ten years constructing the Cathedral church of the city of the Angels, and as four of them are the best journeymen in this kingdom they would earn an additional four reales [anywhere else] than what is paid for their labor there [at the Cathedral], yet in order to keep them and their pay secure, we have left them there.[1]

Doña Juana Melendez, 1610

For well over a decade, six black stonemasons toiled atop the Puebla cathedral as enslaved men, wage earners, and skilled laborers. None of these descriptors capture the experiences or friendships that these men had with one another. We do not know their names, those of their spouses, partners, siblings, or children. We do not know if and how the famed indigenous stonecutters of Calpan interacted with this black crew. All we can state with certainty is that six enslaved men of African descent helped construct Puebla's most important religious center and its greatest colonial edifice. Their owner was Doña Juana de Melendez, the wife of a disgraced and infirm public official. In 1610, the cathedral's head architect, Joseph de Bañuelos, intended to fire three of Melendez's slaves, alleging that they were not properly trained. Perhaps the architect resented being charged 9 pesos per week, a considerable wage, for the crew.[2] Yet their salaries were the financial backbone of a once prominent family. Meléndez's husband had come to New Spain in the service of Viceroy Don Luis de Velasco (the younger). The Meléndez Bañuelos family was gradually reduced to poverty through the husband's descent into mental instability. Only slavery kept them afloat.

---

1 Archivo General de la Nación (AGN), Indiferente Virreinal, Box 6610, Exp. 1.
2 Ibid. The architect intended to reduce this sum to just over 5 pesos per week for the most skilled stonemasons.

For this Spanish family, slavery represented a financial necessity. But what did it represent to the enslaved stonemasons?

In the following pages, I focus on how mobile slaves negotiated their enslavement in a variety of settings in the seventeenth-century city. Unlike those confined in convents and *obrajes*, most urban slaves were not restricted to a singular space, such as the elite household, or to domestic labor in that space. Instead, each slave-owning household and its attendant families must be understood as an expansive social network – one whose influence reached artisan workshops, parish churches, public fountains, and other urban centers. Slaves enjoyed considerable spatial mobility within the Puebla city limits, which in turn allowed for remunerated labor and constant communication with free and enslaved individuals of varied backgrounds. While many women remained in the elite household as unfree servants, others were sent out to work as laundresses, food vendors, and wet nurses. Their male counterparts entered apprenticeships with master artisans or were retained as coachmen or armed bodyguards. These blurred boundaries between the domestic, artisanal and political were integral to urban slave-ownership. Most masters trusted their slaves and depended on their mobility to profit from their subjection.

Why, then, did Spaniards fear their slaves? Moreover, how did the fear and imagined threat of black rebellion affect the lives of Poblano slaves during the 1610s and 1620s? What about the remaining decades of the seventeenth century? In this chapter, I argue that Spaniards' paradoxical fear of their own slaves was incompatible with the reality of urban slave ownership. Colonizers certainly had reason to fear the African maroons who disrupted commerce and raided rural estates, but not the domestic communities that were intimately enmeshed in their everyday lives during the seventeenth century. Enslaved families, sometimes three generations at a time, lived within the households of the political elite and contributed to their economic well-being. As parents, nephews, nieces, grandchildren and fictive kin, enslaved people simply had too many options and too many allies at their disposal to need to resort to outright violence against their masters. By mid-century, urban slaves in Puebla were far more likely to join religious brotherhoods than maroon communities. Conspicuous participation in local religiosity further rooted enslaved people in the social fabric.

Drawing on baptismal and marital records, criminal cases, apprenticeship contracts, and inventories, this and the following chapter focus on enslaved individuals and families to understand slavery outside of the convent and *obraje*. Both chapters use testaments dictated by Afro-Poblanos to unravel the social networks that bound former slaves to free and enslaved counterparts. In using these materials, I engage an African Diaspora scholarship intent on understanding the diverse strategies by which people of African descent constructed community in colonial Spanish

America.[3] Slaves and their kin exploited political differences, neighborhood rifts and jurisdictional boundaries in order to better their lives. Enslaved families made use of wage labor, urban mobility and expanding social networks (intra- and inter-racial) to erode the foundations of slaveholder power. Most enslaved people did not secure their freedom by running away, since this would sever the social ties that bound them to their urban community. Whenever possible, they pooled together resources to buy freedom papers for enslaved relatives, but this was not the primary avenue for ending bondage. Freedom in Puebla was largely attained through birthright in the last three decades of the seventeenth century. By engaging the local parish and religious leadership, enslaved Afro-Poblanos upheld their social bonds and the rights of their free children one baptismal entry at a time.

Mobility, Space and Social Networks

Scholars of slavery and the African Diaspora have often highlighted the mobility that characterized urban slave labor in Latin America.[4] Unlike their rural counterparts, city-dwelling masters depended on their captives' ability to freely navigate the streets, churches, and markets of the city. Doña Juana Melendez's enslaved stonemasons could support her family because their labor was mobile and valuable as long as there were construction projects in the city. The same could be said about any number of occupations filled by enslaved laborers who were allowed to retain a fraction of their daily earnings (*jornal*). As water carriers, muleteers, cantors, coachmen, bodyguards, and domestic servants, the slaves of Puebla quickly learned to use such freedom of movement to their advantage.

During the early seventeenth century, Poblanos became increasingly dependent on slaves for their domestic necessities, perhaps none more pressing than securing potable water. Fresh springwater was not readily available throughout the city. During the 1550s, only three prominent families had

---

3 Alex Borucki, *From Shipmates to Soldiers: Emerging Black Identities in the Río de la Plata* (Albuquerque: University of New Mexico Press, 2015); Michelle McKinley, *Fractional Freedoms: Slavery, Intimacy, and Legal Mobilization in Colonial Lima, 1600–1700* (Cambridge: Cambridge University Press, 2016); Herman Bennett, *Colonial Blackness: A History of Afro-Mexico* (Bloomington: Indiana University Press, 2009); Rachel Sarah O'Toole, *Africans, Indians and the Making of Race in Colonial Peru* (Pittsburgh: University of Pittsburgh Press, 2012).

4 The literature on slavery and urban mobility is daunting. For a few examples, see Frederick P. Bowser, *The African Slave in Colonial Peru, 1524–1650* (Stanford, CA: Stanford University Press, 1974), 100–106; Colin A. Palmer, *Slaves of the White God: Blacks in Mexico, 1570–1650* (Cambridge, MA: Harvard University Press, 1976), 45–46; Mary Karasch, *Slave Life in Rio de Janeiro, 1808–1850* (Princeton, NJ: Princeton University Press, 1987), 185–213; O'Toole, *Africans, Indians*, 122–156; Pablo F. Gómez, *The Experiential Caribbean: Creating Knowledge and Healing in the Early Modern Atlantic* (Chapel Hill: University of North Carolina Press, 2017), 70–94; Borucki, *Shipmates to Soldiers*, 84–114. Also, see the excellent essays in Jorge Cañizares Esguerra, Matt D. Childs, and James Sidbury, eds., *The Black Urban Atlantic in the Age of the Slave Trade* (Philadelphia: University of Pennsylvania Press, 2013).

been awarded the rights to build private conduits.[5] Convents and monasteries secured exclusive rights to fountains, but common people could only obtain fresh water from a few public fountains or by searching for springs outside of the city.[6] The arduous work of fetching potable water fell therefore to free and enslaved domestics in most urban households. As the urban population grew, black water carriers (*negros aguadores*) came to occupy an increasingly important role. In February of 1608, they even were accused of "breaking and closing the central plaza's water conduits" in order to secure a monopoly (of sorts) on their precious resource.[7] Alleging that they brought their barrels from a great distance, carriers charged two reales for their services.[8] These men represented an extreme urban specialization, but their mobility as enslaved people was otherwise normative.

Two Inquisition cases from 1606 exemplify the type of spatial mobility that urban slaves routinely enjoyed even while subjected to unreasonable cultural and linguistic obstacles. In the first case, a Spanish carpenter voluntarily appeared before the local comissary of the Inquisition to denounce Lucía, an enslaved black woman whom he described as "more bozal than ladina."[9] The carpenter qualified his slave's unfamiliarity with Catholicism by noting that he had only purchased her six months prior to her religious offense. On Easter Sunday, he sent Lucía to hear mass at the (unfinished) cathedral at around 8:00 A.M. Lucía did just as she was told and entered the sanctuary unescorted, where she heard what must have been a rather unintelligible sermon in Latin. Then she "saw that many people were taking communion, so she did the same and received the Holy Sacrament and brought a communion certificate to her master." Her crime consisted of having eaten breakfast that morning before attending mass and receiving the consecrated host. A similar case involved Pedro, an enslaved black man who had been brought to Puebla from "the land of Angola" in 1605.[10] Pedro had also been sent to hear mass, in his case at the Augustinian church. Unaccompanied, he heard mass and received communion, but failed to confess himself beforehand. Upon hearing of this transgression from a third party, Pedro's owner denounced his slave to the Inquisition. In his defense, Pedro explained that he had already confessed during the feast of San Juan and merely received communion as others were doing.

In both cases, recently arrived Africans were able to visit public spaces with considerable freedom of movement while being simultaneously

---

5 Alberto Carabarín Gracia, *Agua y confort en la vida de la antigua Puebla* (Puebla: BUAP, 2000), 69.

6 Ibid., 53–70.

7 AGMP, Actas de Cabildo, Vol. 14, 65/64 v. City council considered the situation sufficiently severe to order a punishment of 100 lashes and a six-peso fine for the carriers.

8 This was a considerable fee. A daily barrel of water would amount to 91.25 pesos per year.

9 AGN, Inquisición, Vol. 471, Exp. 40, 140r.

10 AGN, Inquisición, Vol. 471, Exp. 66, 249–250r.

subjected to religious technicalities that constituted crimes in the eyes of the Holy Office and especially devout masters. As Bennett aptly states, "Christianity played the dominant role in controlling slaves and free blacks in the early seventeenth century."[11] For Pedro and Lucía the experience of slavery included a series of cultural constraints and proscriptions, but minimal control over their physical movements. On the contrary, both were expected to attend mass regularly, which, more than simply a religious ceremony, represented an ordinary opportunity to speak with friends, seek legal counsel, visit a lover, or even perhaps purchase a pastry.

Highly skilled enslaved people could expect even greater freedom of movement. Consider the case of Juan de Vera, the Puebla Cathedral's slave cantor. A remarkable singer, composer, and teacher of religious music, Vera had free passage in and out of the massive cathedral complex and downtown area. At one point in the 1590s, Vera was even reprimanded for removing a harp – at the time an extremely rare instrument in the Americas – from the cathedral. At the time of his owner's death in 1610, Juan de Vera had spent thirty-four years working in the cathedral and lived in his own apartment.[12] This relaxed attitude about the movements of urban slaves continued throughout the colonial period.[13]

Gender affected the type and scale of mobility an enslaved person in Puebla could expect. This is most evident in the use of male slaves in commercial transportation. Within the first two decades of the city's foundation, enslaved men served as muleteers in the city and surrounding region.[14] In the early 1570s, Pedro and Francisco served in this capacity for Martín Asturiano along the old Veracruz-Puebla road. Both were expected to control a train of twenty-eight mules, and, more importantly, protect the valuable merchandise en route to the port.[15] Hundreds of enslaved men based in Puebla crisscrossed the viceroyalty in this manner.[16] The continued

---

11 Bennett, *Colonial Blackness*, 50.

12 Omar Morales Abril, "El esclavo negro de Juan de Vera: Cantor, arpista y compositor de la catedral de Puebla *(florevit* 1575–1617)" in *Historia de la Música en Puebla* (Puebla: Secretaría de Cultura del Estado de Puebla, 2010), 51–54, 59. He was also responsible for annotating and mending missals and other books.

13 AHJP, Exp. 5034. As late as 1786, enslaved domestic servants could be seen freely riding on horseback in Puebla. The slave youth Miguel José Meza, for instance, regularly took his master's horses out from the stables unannounced. A witness claimed that Meza would take the horses "to bathe, to brand, or to do anything he felt like".

14 Peter Boyd-Bowman, "Negro Slaves in Early Colonial Mexico," *The Americas* 26, no. 2 (Oct. 1969), 146.

15 AHJP, Exp. 22.

16 Searching for enslaved men specifically identified as muleteers (*arrieros*) only produced five references among bills of sale for the period 1590–1699. Within a 20 percent sample of bills of slave purchase found in Notarías 3 and 4, men identified as *arrieros* or mule train owners (*dueños de recua*) bought 116 slaves during the period. This leads to a minimum projection of 580 enslaved muleteers bought by men involved in transportation.

decimation of the indigenous population in Central Mexico accentuated the intermediary role played by black, mulatto, and *chino* men by the end of the sixteenth century.[17]

The concentration of religious and political offices in Puebla guaranteed that the demand for slave coachmen (*cocheros*) was also high. High-ranking religious officials relied on enslaved youths and adults to transport them in the city or deliver sensitive packages throughout the highlands. For instance, Bishop Alonso de la Mota y Escobar sent Pascual, his mulatto slave, to deliver 1,000 pesos to Father Antonio Perez de las Casas in Atlixco.[18] Such trust, however, should not be mistaken for goodwill. The bishop had previously ordered Pascual's face branded with his name, presumably for running away on two separate occasions.[19] In 1610, Tomás, a 13-year-old slave, was charged with driving the coach belonging to Dr. Don Agustín de Salazar, the cathedral's cantor.[20] A gendered demand for men in transportation allowed male slaves to frequent different cities, towns and plantations within the viceroyalty.

Enslaved women enjoyed considerable mobility within the city, but their movements were more circumscribed. They were generally allowed to purchase foodstuffs at market, deliver messages and attend mass. Like many other women throughout the Americas, their most profitable activity was selling food in the marketplace (*tianguis*).[21] Free and enslaved domestic servants were expected to wash clothes in public spaces even if such activities irritated nearby residents. During their time off, enslaved women could also frequent *temazcales*, native steam baths, in the San Sebastián neighborhood or take a stroll up San Juan hill.[22]

Most enslaved women were described in relation to the expectations of the household: cooking, washing, and breastfeeding. Domestic slaves were expected to make chocolate beverages first thing in the morning. They prepared three labor-intensive meals during the course of the day – at noon (*almuerzo*), 5:00 P.M. (*merienda*), and 9:00 P.M. (*cena*) – and then needed to clean the kitchen and prepare for the next day.[23] At 1 to 2 pesos per month,

17 AGNP, Not. 4, Box 137, 1630 February, no folio and Box 123, 1625 October, 2424r.

18 Biblioteca Nacional de España, Mss. 6877, Papeles de Mota y Escobar, 248r.

19 Ibid. "Un esclabo mulato blanco de color llamado Pasqual herrado en el rostro de mi nombre el qual vendio al Sr. Arzobispo de Mexico en qui[nient]os p[es]os en rr[eale]s, era cochero." For Pascual's two escapes, see Fray Alonso de la Mota y Escobar, *Memoriales del Obispo de Tlaxcala: Un recorrido por el centro de México a principios del siglo XVII* (Mexico City: Secretaría de Educación Pública, 1987), 98–99, 116.

20 AGNP, Not. 4, Box 65, 1610 December, no folio; AGNP, Not. 4, Box 100, 1620 August, 2498r.

21 Pilar Gonzalbo Aizpuru, *Familia y orden colonial* (Mexico City: Colegio de México, 1998), 219.

22 AGN, Inquisición, Vol. 536, Exp. 17, 142r, 195r.

23 María Elisa Velázquez, *Mujeres de origen africano en la capital novohispana, siglos XVII y XVIII* (Mexico City: UNAM/INAH, 2006), 197–201.

domestic service itself was poorly remunerated in Puebla,[24] but slaveholders esteemed the cultural power and intimacy embedded in mistress-slave interactions. In 1626, the widow Mariana de Montemayor valued Isabel, her 20-year-old *mulata* slave, at a staggering 600 pesos due to her superb cooking and washing.[25] By contrast, wet nurses fulfilled a more urgent need in elite households, even if references to *chichiguas* or *nodrizas* are rare in mundane documentation.[26] An indicator of this demand can be found in dozens of bills of slave purchase for pregnant women or mothers with breastfeeding infants (*de pecho*).[27]

In many respects, enslaved wet nurses were exceptionally mobile in that they were valued for the breast milk produced by their own bodies. As mothers, they were interested in securing a stable environment for their children. As enslaved women, they negotiated their bondage and sought to find better patrons or owners whenever possible. A densely populated city presented considerable opportunities for breastfeeding women. When Nicolasa fled a sugar-producing estate in Teutitlan with her infant daughter, she quickly found employment in Puebla by working as a wet nurse for Don Antonio Guerrero's family. When her owner eventually heard of her whereabouts and demanded her return, Guerrero argued that he could not allow this to happen since Nicolasa "was raising Don Joseph Guerrero, his fourteen-month-old legitimate child, and if said black woman stopped feeding him, he would die as he did not want to admit any other person's breast." Don Antonio agreed to compensate Nicolasa's owner with a monthly wage of 3 pesos.[28] Meanwhile, Nicolasa had successfully escaped her master's physical control and established herself as an indispensable servant in an elite urban household. Mobile, enslaved, and trusted, she was one of thousands of similarly defined women in Puebla.

This mobility, however, was not without its dangers, especially for enslaved girls. On 1 August 1628, Luis de Aguiar, a Spaniard and the owner

---

24 AGNP, Not. 4, Box 67, 1610 May, no folio, 1610/05/08 and Box 78, 1615 July, no folio, 1615/07/01.

25 Úrsula Camba Ludlow, *Imaginarios ambiguos, realidades contradictorias: Conductas y representaciones de los negros y mulatos novohispanos, Siglos XVI y XVII* (Mexico City: Colegio de México, 2008), 129.

26 By the eighteenth century, the image of black and mulatto women breastfeeding Spanish infants was firmly established in the Mexican imaginary. The satirical *Ordenanzas del Baratillo* noted Spanish mothers "would seek black or mulata wetnurses . . . to excuse themselves from raising their children at their breasts." UCLA Young Research Library, Special Collections, Mss. 170/513, *Ordenanzas del Baratillo de Mexico dada per via de exortazion o consejo a sus dotores* (circa 1735), 47r–47v. Also, see Francisco de Ajofrín, *Diario del viaje a la Nueva España* (Mexico City: Secretaría de Educación Pública, 1986), 67.

27 AGNP, Not. 3 and 4 bills of slave purchase, 1600–1695. I have located 93 transactions in which enslaved infants (aged 2 and under) were sold with their mother.

28 AGNP, Not. 3, Box 116, 137v–139v. The same monthly wage was assigned to a wet nurse working in 1730, see AHJP, Exp. 3108, 256r–260r.

of a corner store, raped Agustina, a 7-year-old child. Her mistress had sent her to purchase a bit of chocolate at 6:30 A.M. Agustina had been to the store, which was located just in front of the cathedral, before and knew the owner. On that morning, Aguiar grabbed Agustina by the arm, covered her mouth to keep her from screaming, and carried her to the top floor of the building, where he raped her. He then promised to give the child 1 peso if she promised to not tell anyone what happened. When she finally returned home, visibly bloodied and limping, her owners summoned a local justice. Two midwives were also brought along and immediately confirmed Agustina's version of the events.[29]

Later that same day, Aguiar was arrested and sent to the Puebla jail on charges of *violación*, "non-consensual sex achieved through physical force."[30] These types of incidents must have been common in the city, but extant documentation on rape is extremely limited.[31] Agustina's case survived not due to the brutality of the attack but because she belonged to the household of Puebla's *alcalde mayor*, Alonso Ordoñez. As "master and lord of Agustina, his black slave," Ordoñez's reputation as an elite man had been tarnished by Aguiar's aggression. Dozens (perhaps hundreds) of similar cases were never recorded in Puebla because they took place *within* elite households and would have threatened the socioracial hierarchy. Enslaved women were especially disadvantaged in presenting rape cases against elite Spaniards.[32] Even the resolution of this particular case speaks to the pressures against charging Spanish men (of any social stratum). On 8 August 1628, Ordoñez dropped all charges against Aguiar due to "the pleas of a few honorable people."[33]

Agustina's case speaks to the entanglement of paternalism, slavery, sexual aggression, and childhood in Puebla. Her rape is a reminder of "the ways enslaved and black women's seemingly unfettered mobility often made them more vulnerable" in urban society.[34] But what happened when enslaved adult women made explicit use of their mobility to challenge the orders of a common slaveholder? What options did they have in how, where, and for whom they labored? For an illustrative case, we turn to María, an

---

29 AHJP, Exp. 1475, 1r–10r.

30 Jessica Lorraine Delgado, "Sacred Practice, Intimate Power: Laywomen and the Church in Colonial Mexico" (Ph.D. diss., University of California, Berkeley, 2009), 7, 21.

31 The only other similar case took place in a rural setting in the early eighteenth century. See AHJP, Exp. 2804, "Proceso criminal promovido por Juan Melchor, pardo libre, contra un hijo de Juan Gonzalez."

32 Ramón Alejandro Montoya, *El esclavo africano en San Luis Potosí durante los siglos XVII y XVIII* (San Luis Potosí: Universidad Autónoma de San Luis Potosí, 2016), 169–172.

33 AHJP, Exp. 1475, 8r–10r.

34 Marisa J. Fuentes, *Dispossessed Lives: Enslaved Women, Violence and the Archive* (Philadelphia: University of Pennsylvania Press, 2016), 97.

enslaved woman from São Tomé, who in the fall of 1603 moved through multiple residences in Puebla in a quest to secure a less abusive master. María's judicial case begins with an unusually flattering statement from her owner, Hernando Díaz.[35] He described her as a *"ladina,* of very good manners, loyal, humble, servicial, diligent, withdrawn, and of much trust." According to Díaz, all of María's positive attributes changed suddenly when she came under the influence of Miguel Hernández de Ñagas, an *obraje* owner. Under the latter's influence, María had become careless and argumentative in her service to Díaz (or so he claimed). Moreover, from August to September 1603, María evaded her master by hiding in different houses in the city and negotiating her own sale to Hernández de Ñagas. She had an extensive knowledge of the city, its churches, *obrajes,* and even the residences of her master's relatives.

María had already suffered two years of conflict with Díaz and his wife. In 1601, threatened with a flogging after breaking some of her mistress's china plates, María fled to the house of Díaz's brother, a presbyter, where she spent the night before returning to her owner.[36] By seeking recourse with her master's sibling (and a cleric, no less), María exposed the type of personal relationships that the enslaved could exploit to their own advantage. We do not know much more about María's experiences for the next two years, but it is clear that her relationship with Díaz was tempestous. In mid-1603, Díaz placed María in the city jail and then confined her to the *obraje* of Hernández de Ñagas for nine days.[37] It was there that María overheard the dreaded news that "her master wanted to sell her out of the city."[38]

Throughout the Spanish Americas, enslaved people feared banishment from their cities of residence more than the threat of lashings or hard labor in an *obraje.* While physical punishment could cripple, the loss of friends, godmothers, relatives, and friendly patrons was far more devastating. María's reaction to the news that she was to be sold far from her social circle parallels that of Sebastiana Paramos's legal battle to secure the intra-urban sale of her son in the opening vignette of this book.[39] Fortunately for her, María had developed a reliable network of friends, specifically women, whom she trusted greatly. Catalyzed by the fear of expulsion, María sought out Hernández de Ñagas's wife and asked to be purchased. During her time with Díaz, the African woman had managed to save up 147 pesos for her

---

35 AHJP, Exp. 575, 2r–2v.   36 Ibid., 25v–27r.

37 Depositing slaves in *obrajes* was a common and profitable punishment. Masters received a daily wage for the time their slaves were kept in a textile workshop. See AGNP, Not. 4, Box 152, 1635 Testamentos, no folio (1635/07/21).

38 AHJP, Exp. 575, 25v–27r. "Estubo en el [*obraje*] esta declarante como nueve dias durante los cuales entreoyo dezir quel d[ic]ho su amo la queria vender fuera desta ciudad."

39 For an eighteenth-century case in which an enslaved woman (deposited in an *obraje*) refused to be sold out of the city for fear of being separated from her daughter, see AHJP, Exp. 2952/530.

freedom. María was even willing to provide this money to her potential new owners in order to expedite her transfer. Hernández de Ñagas and his wife agreed to assist in plotting her escape, which led to a lengthy legal dispute between Hernando Díaz and the mill owner.[40]

In negotiating her purchase to the *obrajero*, María relied on the testimony and mobility of several black and indigenous women. Three free *ladina* black women, Gracia María, Esperanza de Molina and Antonia, testified that María had turned 147 pesos over to Hernández de Ñagas.[41] All three lived in the predominantly indigenous neighborhoods of San Pablo and Santa Ana. Another of María's acquaintances, Barbola Ruíz, identified herself as an *india ladina* and a native of Puebla's San José neighborhood. More importantly, Barbola claimed to be María's *comadre*, an intimate term for a godmother, a neighbor, or a close friend. Finally, a female indigenous cook from the Hernández de Ñagas textile mill also agreed to help María recover the money she had saved for an eventual letter of manumission. In other words, enslaved women could rely not only on their own resources and mobility, but also on the testimony of Spanish women, free Afro-Poblanas, and female indigenous actors in the colonial city. These social networks enabled enslaved people to negotiate or, at the very least, mitigate slave-holder power. Most slaves, like María, preferred to exert pressure within the urban slaveholding system rather than flee it outright.

However, some enslaved people preferred to take their chances on country roads and rural settings. This was certainly the case for Anton, a 20-year-old "Angola" slave living just outside of Puebla, who decided to flee his master for the coastal lowlands of Veracruz in 1605.[42] The direction is puzzling, since Anton would have certainly found anonymity in Mexico City and its massive slave community, but he was recaptured in a much smaller space: the coastal town of San Cristóbal de Alvarado (220 miles southeast of Puebla). Yet rather than claim his slave and pay the mounting jail fees, Anton's frustrated owner decided to sell the young man by proxy to a resident of the neighboring town of Tlalixcoyan.[43]

Poblano slaveholders awarded powers of attorney to third parties or bounty hunters to recover their captives. Whoever held such a document

---

40 AHJP, Exp. 575, 3r–7r.   41 Ibid.   42 AGNP, Not. 3, Box 22, 1681r–1682v.

43 In late 1609, the bishop of Puebla described a community of Greek fishermen (*de nación Griegos*) from the "Tlalixcoya doctrine" who were married to black and mulatto women; see Mota y Escobar, *Memoriales*, 53. This strip of tropical coastline just to the south of the Nueva Veracruz was a hotbed for runaway slave communities during the early seventeenth century. In 1609, maroons from "old and new Veracruz, Río Blanco, and Punta de Antón Lizardo" entered Tlalixcoyan "to rob and loot houses, seize black domestics and remove them from their master's houses and threatening the Spaniards by setting their houses on fire"; see Guadalupe Castañon González, "Yanga y cimarronaje en la Nueva España" in Javier Laviña, ed., *Esclavos rebeldes y cimarrones* (Madrid: Fundación Hernando de Larramendi), 78.

(and a recaptured slave) could formally transfer the captive's property rights to another master.[44] In October 1600, another Anton, labeled with the "Anchico" ethnonym, ran away from Puebla for coastal Veracruz.[45] Two weeks into his escape, Anton was captured in the town of Cotaxtla, located along the southern route to the port. We do not know what happened to Anton after his arrest. The man responsible for recovering him may have found it more convenient to sell him in Cotaxtla rather than risk another escape by bringing him back to Puebla. In fleeing their owners, both Antons ultimately failed in securing their freedom. Flight, recapture and relocation seem to have been the usual outcome for runaway slaves in New Spain.

The archival silence surrounding escaped slaves presents a number of challenges to historians attempting to understand runaways' motivations, successes and failures. Slaves who absented themselves for a day or two within Puebla's city limits rarely generated any kind of paper trail, but they were subjected to various forms of punishment.[46] Based on subsequent sales, recaptured slaves were often branded on the face.[47] Masters mostly produced powers of attorney after hearing news of a runaway's whereabouts in a distant location, or they might note a slave's absence when giving bed-side testaments. The case of Domingo, an escaped 26-year-old *chino*, combines both scenarios. In June 1626, Bachelor Juan de Diosdado awarded power of attorney to another well-educated man, Felipe de Santiago, the priest of the Apango district.[48] Typically the drafting of such a document was suggestive of a runaway's refuge in the vicinity of the empowered party and an impending recapture. However, after a year on his own, Domingo remained elusive.

In this particular case, it was not Domingo himself that Diosdado valued, but rather the monetary value that his permanent servitude represented. Diosdado empowered Santiago "to sell said *chino* slave for cash, credit or by trading and exchanging him for another black man or woman." Note the apparent interchangeability of slaves despite their different racial backgrounds. Yet nearly two months later, Domingo, who bore the brand "Diosdado" on his forehead, was still on the run.[49] In the interim, his master had died, so it was now the widow, Elvira Zambrano de Bolaños, who pursued the matter. She tasked Antonio Domínguez, the parish priest

44 For a few examples of this slaveholding strategy, see AGNP, Not. 3, Box 16, 1496r and Box 11, 1590/03/16, no folio; Not. 4, Box 98, 1620 February, 464r and Box 99, 1620 March, 893r.

45 AGNP, Not. 3, Box 16, 1600 October, 1165r.

46 In 1605, the blacksmith Francisco Montiel sold Diego, his 30-year-old "Congo" slave, but noted that the latter "has absented himself from my house on two occasions, but had not left the city. Due to this [behavior], I have a chain on him." AGNP, Not. 4, Box 59, 1605 April, 457r.

47 For a few illustrative examples, see AHJP, Exp. 713, 10v; AGNP, Not. 4, Box 59, 1605 March, 408r; AGNP, Not. 4, Box 98, 1620 February, 464r; AGNP, Not. 4, Box 121, 1625 May, 1120r.

48 AGNP, Not. 4, Box 100, 1620 June, 1750r.	49 AGNP, Not. 4, Box 100, 1620 July, 2276r.

of Piastla, with capturing the runaway, so that now two priests and a widow were searching for the escaped Asian man.

Enslaved men in and outside of Puebla had greater mobility than women, which examining documentation on runaways confirms. Based on a notarial sample of eighty runaway slaves, men were seven times more likely to escape than women during the seventeenth century.[50] This notable difference is consistent with the extra-urban mobility that male slaves, as muleteers and coachmen, enjoyed throughout New Spain. It also helps explain the gendered and hypersexual fears of slave uprisings led by male agressors.

Puebla and the Repression of 1612

If unencumbered mobility defined slavery in Puebla and other Mexican cities, slaveholders still exhibited a profound fear of violent uprisings and racial vengeance. But urban masters' fear of slave rebellion should be contextualized more precisely. Given the general brutality of their textile mills and the gradual shift to all-slave workforces, *obrajeros* certainly had reason to fear slave uprisings. So did slaveholding muleteers, because their jobs required them to constantly travel through rural areas under maroon control. However, it is not clear that nuns, municipal officials and other urban slaveholders felt the same anxieties. Thanks to María Elena Martínez's analysis of the events of 1608 through 1612, we have a remarkable understanding of what Gaspar Yanga's maroons came to mean to elite Spaniards in Mexico City.[51] But what did Yanga represent to slaveholders outside the viceregal capital? What did his community signify to the thousands of enslaved people living in elite residences in Puebla?

During the early seventeenth century, Gaspar Yanga and his men became infamous for their raids on passing mule trains and coaches loaded with merchandise along the Puebla-Veracruz road. Nestled in the mountains separating Puebla from the port, Yanga's maroon community (*palenque*) posed a real threat to colonial commerce.[52] By 1608, Viceroy Luis Velasco, the younger, had appointed Manuel Carrillo, a Portuguese man and the administrator of the slaving contract, to negotiate the pacification of the maroon community.[53] That Carrillo was tasked with this mission indicates

---

50 AGNP, Notarial database, 1600–1695. By combing through powers of attorney, bills of purchase, and inventories I have located references to eighty runaways. Only nine of these cases refer to women.

51 Martínez, "The Black Blood of New Spain: Limpieza de Sangre, Racial Violence and Gendered Power in Early Colonial Mexico," *The William and Mary Quarterly* 61, no. 3 (July 2004), 479–520.

52 Palmer, *Slaves of the White God*, 124–131. Jane Landers, "Cimarrón and Citizen: African Ethnicity, Corporate Identity, and the Evolution of Free Black Towns in the Spanish Circum-Caribbean," in Jane G. Landers and Barry M. Robinson, eds., *Slaves, Subjects, and Subversives: Blacks in Colonial Latin America* (Albuquerque: University of New Mexico Press, 2006), 133–135.

53 AGN, Inquisición, Vol. 283, Exp. 26, 186r–187v.

that the slave trade was being affected directly by the runaways' raids.[54] Incoming African captives had no reason to aid their slave traders when attacked by Yanga's followers.[55] The intensification of the transatlantic slave trade to Puebla coincided with the perception that maroons were increasingly threatening to the colonial project.

In 1609, Viceroy Velasco sent a punitive expedition to destroy Yanga's redoubt.[56] Pedro González de Herrera, a wealthy Spaniard established in Puebla,[57] would lead the raid. He was joined by Juan Laurencio, one-time rector of Puebla's Jesuit College, who witnessed the Spanish attack on the palenque firsthand. Bishop Mota y Escobar, another elite Puebla resident, wrote of the expedition's failure. On 3 December 1609, the bishop received news that "a troop of blacks, of the insurgents" had attacked two Poblano merchants en route to Nueva Veracruz.[58] The maroons also stole 100 pesos from a safebox, abducted two married indigenous women and a newborn, and murdered the 12-year-old brother of one of the merchants. The bishop himself visited the site of the raid and found "the dead boy with his intestines out and throat slit." Mota y Escobar sent out a messenger to report the raid to the viceroy, which exacerbated fears of the maroons' prowess. These fears intensified over the next three years. According to Jonathan Israel, 1612 was the most racially tense year in the history of colonial Mexico.[59]

Scholars have reassessed the slave uprising and repression of 1612 due to the recovery, transcription and translation of Domingo de San Antón Chimalpahin's writings.[60] Written from an urban indigenous perspective, Chimalpahin's text sheds light on how Spaniards, Nahuas and people of African descent imagined and experienced the tense months leading up to Holy Week of 1612 in Mexico City. In January 1609, Chimalpahin recorded that "the blacks were going to rebel and make war here" and that they had gone as far as naming a king and queen who would distribute "all the various

54 AGI, Contratación, Leg. 5282, No. 7.

55 Andres Pérez de Ribas, *Corónica y historia religiosa de la provincia de la Compañía de Jesús de México* (Mexico City: Imprenta del Sagrado Corazón de Jesús, 1896), 285–292. Francisco Javier Alegre, *Historia de la Compañía de Jesús en Nueva España*, Tomo II, Libro V (Mexico City: Imprenta de J. M. Lara, 1842), 11–12. Incoming African captives would have a found a ready ally in Francisco de la Matosa, an Angolan maroon who served as Yanga's field marshal (*maeste de campo*)

56 Palmer, *Slaves of the White God*, 128–130.

57 Landers, "Cimarrón and Citizen," 142 n. 21.   58 Mota y Escobar, *Memoriales*, 46.

59 Jonathan Israel, *Razas, clases sociales y vida política en el México colonial 1610–1670* (Mexico City: Fondo de Cultura Económica, 2005), 78.

60 Don Domingo de San Antón Muñón Chimalpahin, *Annals of His Time*, edited and translated by James Lockhart, Susan Schroeder, and Doris Namala (Stanford, CA: Stanford University Press, 2006); Don Domingo Chimalpahin, *Diario*, edited and translated by Rafael Tena (Mexico City: Cien de México, 2011); Susan Schroeder, *Chimalpahin and the Kingdoms of Chalco* (Tucson: University of Arizona Press, 1991); Martínez, "Black Blood"; Landers, "Cimarrón and Citizen."

altepetl here to the blacks who would rule there."[61] The organizers of the plot were arrested, preventing bloodshed, which was a positive outcome in the chronicler's view, especially since it was rumored that indigenous people would have been forced to serve these new dark-skinned rulers.

In the years leading up to the 1612 repression, Puebla's municipal council tried to stave off the perceived insecurity outside the city. In 1609, the regents established a municipally funded local militia that would give chase and apprehend the "Spanish and black and Indian" assailants in rural areas.[62] Wealthy Poblanos had much to gain by backing such initiatives because so many of them owned vast rural estates to the south and east of the city. Don Juan López Mellado, a *vecino* of Puebla, appealed directly to the viceroy for permission to arm the men on his estate in Amatlán and allow them to secure the pass of Coapa.[63] In early December 1609, his cattle ranches had been repeatedly attacked by fifteen to twenty maroons "armed with their bows and arrows" and machetes. Three of López Mellado's men had been killed in these raids and a number of their women abducted, a common practice among maroons throughout the Americas.[64] Though these events took place in a rural setting, the stories they generated were circulated and consumed in Puebla's municipal palace, elite residences and marketplaces.

Many Spaniards certainly feared a mass slave attack on their urban dwellings, but these racial and gendered anxieties need to be localized and contextualized. The imagined threat of a vengeful, male maroon force loomed large in Chimalpahin's reconstruction of the events of 1612.[65] But by his own admission, Spanish religious men did not share these fears, and the Mexican indigenous population was likely unimpressed.[66] In an entry for the same year, the anonymous chronicler of Puebla's indigenous annals

---

61 Chimalpahin, *Annals of His Time*, 155.   62 AGMP, Actas de Cabildo, Vol. 14, 97/96.

63 AGN, Indiferente Virreinal, Box 4156, Exp. 38.

64 Landers, "Cimarrón and Citizen," 121–125; Palmer, *Slaves of the White God*, 126; Bowser, *African Slave*, 189.

65 Martínez, *Black Blood*, 507–508. In the original Nahuatl, Chimalpahin uses the term *cimalonti tliltique* for "black renegades," incorporating and combining the Spanish term for a runaway slave, *cimarrón*, with a Nahuatl form and color description, *tliltique*, literally, "blacks," see Chimalpahin, *Annals of His Time*, 216–217.

66 Chimalpahin, *Annals of His Time*, 217–219. "And all the different groups of ecclesiastics who live in Mexico were just laughing; they were not frightened by what they were hearing about all the different kinds of news of war concerning the blacks, what they supposedly wanted to do. And we Mexica commoners were not at all frightened ... but were just looking and listening, just marveling at how the Spaniards were being destroyed by their fear." The Spanish chronicler Fray Agustín Vetancur was also skeptical of the maroon threat. In his account, a herd of swine entering through one of Mexico City's causeways led to rumors that the black rebels had arrived. See Fray Agustín de Vetancur, Theatro Mexicano. Descripción breve de los sucesos ejemplares históricos y religiosos del nuevo mundo de las Indias (Mexico City: Editorial Porrúa, 1982), 13.

simply declared, "at this same time some blacks were about to make war (*quichihua yaoyotl*) in Mexico City on Holy Thursday."[67] No further reference is made to the slave rebellion.

Even though absolutely nothing happened in Puebla, local councilmen decreed a series of bans on black and mulatto gatherings on 7 April 1612. "Blacks and free mulattos and slaves are not to carry swords, daggers, knives, nor other public weapons, nor are they to hold cofradía meetings, or song gatherings, or dances," read the local municipal decree.[68] The movement of free and enslaved people of African descent, both *vecinos* and outsiders (*forasteros*), was to be curtailed. This was also an inconvenient order for Poblano masters, because they were so reliant on their slaves' wage labor. All festivities for Holy Week 1612 were canceled. Although there is no record of an uprising or of mass hangings in Puebla, it is clear that a tense atmosphere prevailed in the following weeks.[69]

On April 15, "when all the Spaniards who live in Mexico [City] became very agitated and fearful," the capital's regents wrote letters to their counterparts in other cities warning them of the impending threat.[70] The Puebla municipal council received one that urged its members to take all necessary precautions. The exchange of letters among elite Spaniards in both cities was intended to counteract the letters that black messengers (*negros correos*), some dressed "in the habits of friars," had been carrying in and out of Mexico City for quite some time.[71] Elite residents of the capital urged their Poblano counterparts to follow their lead in banning black religious brotherhoods. The imagined terror of raped Spanish women that catalyzed the repression in the capital was now relayed to other urban populations.[72] Puebla's *obrajes* and their black and mulatto populations soon became targets. The regent Melchor de Cuellar notified all mill owners to "lock in, every day and night, their people, blacks and mulattos, not allowing them to leave and imposing the punishment they might find necessary and convenient for this matter."[73] In other words, the daily regimen of scarce

---

67 Camilla Townsend, ed. and transl., *Here in This Year: Seventeenth-Century Nahuatl Annals of the Tlaxcala-Puebla Valley* (Stanford, CA: Stanford University Press, 2010), 88 n. 3. In the postconquest period, *quichihua yaoyotl* could be used to describe "fights, disturbances, riots, anything involving group violence." For variations of *quichihua yaoyotl* in relation to the rebellion, see Lidia Gómez García et al., eds., Anales del barrio de San Juan del Rio. Crónica indígena de la ciudad de Puebla, siglo XVII (Puebla: BUAP/ICSyH, 2000), 42, 78.

68 AGMP, Actas de Cabildo, Vol. 14, 220/219.

69 On 2 May 1612, the civil and criminal judges of Mexico's Audiencia oversaw the execution of thirty-five black men and women by hanging. See Chimalpahin, *Annals of His Time*, 219–225.

70 Ibid., 215.

71 Pedro López de Villaseñor, *Cartilla vieja de la nobilísima ciudad de Puebla* (Puebla: Secretaría de Cultura, 2001), 98.

72 Martínez, "Black Blood," 481–483.   73 López de Villaseñor, *Cartilla vieja*, 100.

food, insomnia, and physical abuse within the mills would now be heightened by the punitive reign allowed to textile masters and overseers.

From the vantage point of free and enslaved Afro-Poblanos, April 1612 must have represented a profoundly oppressive time. In a city under martial law, two militia companies were stationed in front of the municipal palace to prevent "any occasion or discourtesy of the blacks and mulattos."[74] Men on horseback patrolled the city with their lances, while others armed with harquebuses guaranteed the safety of Puebla's convents and hospitals. Fray Agustín de Vetancur noted that guards were placed in the churches.[75] Regents watching over the San José and San Francisco neighborhoods were tasked with controlling areas that had large numbers of people of African descent. Municipally funded purchases of gunpowder and bullets suggest that the regents would spare no expense to keep the peace. And yet, one must wonder, what happened to the enslaved families that lived with these Spaniards? Who patrolled the streets of Puebla with the regents and local officials if not their own enslaved men?

Local Contexts

On the night of 18 April 1612, Dr. Don Juan de Arboleda "and the people he might have" were instructed to guard the cathedral, the central plaza, and the immediate vicinity.[76] Arguably, these "people" were his slaves. A lawyer by profession, Arboleda was also *alcalde mayor*, the highest-ranking official in Puebla's municipal council. It was now his reponsibility to enforce the decrees that targeted the Afro-Poblano population in the wake of the Mexico City repression.[77] Arboleda certainly experienced a conflict of interest that night and many others. He and his wife, Doña Francisca de Silva y Santiago, owned nineteen people of African descent, who cooked, cleaned, washed, drove, and otherwise accompanied them every minute of the day.[78]

Jerónima, an elderly black woman and mother of five, was the matriarch of this enslaved community. Her children, Sebastián Gómez, Juan "the coachman," Joseph de Arboleda, Damiana "mulata," and the curiously named Bartolomé de la Casas were all born enslaved. By 1620, Jerónima had six mulatto grandchildren, the youngest a mere six months old and the eldest fifteen years old. This tri-generational family also shared the lawyer's

74 Ibid.   75 Vetancur, *Theatro Mexicano*, 13.

76 López de Villaseñor, *Cartilla vieja*, 100.   77 AGMP, Actas de Cabildo, Vol. 14, ff. 220/219.

78 J. Eric S. Thompson, ed., *Thomas Gage's Travels in the New World* (Norman: University of Oklahoma Press, 1958), 73. Gage's description of Mexico City elites with "their train of blackamoor slaves, some a dozen, some half a dozen, waiting on them . . . with silk stockings on their black legs, and roses on their feet, and swords by their sides" immediately comes to mind, although we have no proof that Arboleda's enslaved retinue dressed in this manner.

residence with Juana and her 15-year-old daughter, Ana, who were also both enslaved. Four more slave children with no apparent familial ties to Jerónima or Juana lived there too. This enslaved domestic community was large, but not exceptional, among the city's political elite. By the same measure, the interaction between enslaved grandchildren and their parents, aunts, uncles and a grandmother was also quite common. Many affluent masters retained similar slave communities for generations, without having to frequent the slave market.[79]

What was everyday life like for enslaved urban families such as Jerónima's? Based on Arboleda's inventory, this particular slave community inhabited a set of houses facing the cathedral, one of the most valuable properties in the bishopric and, presumably, the viceroyalty. Given the location of the residence, the enslaved women attended mass regularly, as waiting ladies for Doña Francisca de Silva y Santiago, the lawyer's wife. The marketplace was located some 200 yards from their residence, so purchasing chile peppers, fish, and other perishables was an easy, everyday chore. The youngest children ran similar errands and served as pages during social functions. We know with certainty that Juan, a coachman, drove his owner to private residences and estates on the outskirts of the city. Establishing the day-to-day activities for Arboleda's three other male adult slaves is more difficult. Were they day laborers, rented journeymen, or bodyguards for an influential man with plenty of enemies in the city?[80] Likely, all three.

Yet the members of Jeronima's family were far more than enslaved workers. They were parents, siblings and godparents. Excluding the matriarch, three enslaved adults in the Arboleda household had children of their own to raise. In 1607 and 1608, Sebastián Gómez and his wife, Magdalena, had their sons Jacinto and Andrés baptized in the cathedral.[81] They went on to raise three more children who grew up alongside their Aunt Damiana's three children. As deeply rooted urban actors, Sebastián and Magdalena sought out godparents for their children and in turn served as *compadres* and *comadres* for other enslaved individuals and families. Jerónima and her sons Sebastián Gómez and Juan served as godparents on nine occasions between 1607 and 1609. By assuming this socioreligious commitment, Jeronima's kin brought seven Afro-Poblano children and two recently arrived Africans

---

79 AGNP, Not. 4, Box 122, 1625 Testamentos, no folio (1625/03/20). Arboleda does not appear as a buyer or seller in any of the thousands of slave purchases studied in Chapter 4. Thus, the notarized inventories of the elite are a necessary complement to studies exclusively based on bills of slave purchase.

80 AGN, Indiferente Virreinal, Box 5775, Exp. 6.

81 ASMP, *Bautizos de negros, 1607–1616*, 3r, 27v. The boys, however, do not appear in the 1620 listing along with the rest of their family. They may have died young, like many colonial children, or been sold to another master before they reached puberty. The couple's three other children, Inés, Juan, and Sebastián, did live with their parents through the heady 1610s.

Table 5.1 *Brotherhoods for people of African and Asian descent in seventeenth-century Puebla*

Confraternity	Membership	Host Institution	Foundation	Reference
Congregation of Saint Michael	*Indios, pardos, morenos*	Espíritu Santo College (Jesuits)	1583	Torres Domínguez, "Los colegios regulares y seculares de Puebla," 46
Saint Benedict of Palermo	*Pardos, morenos*	San Francisco Church	Prior to 1611	Castañeda García, "Santos negros," 149
The Piety of Our Lady	*Morenos*	Santo Domingo Church	Unknown	Alcalá y Mendiola, *Descripción en bosquejo*, 130
The Expiration of Christ	*Pardos, morenos*	Limpia Concepción Hospital	Prior to 1631	AHJP, Exp. 1622, Will of Marta Rodríguez
Our Lady of Consolation	*Pardos, morenos*	Santa Veracruz Church	Prior to 1633	AHJP, Exp. 1617, Will of Francisco de Carmona and Catalina Bran
Our Lady of Guadalupe	*Chinos*	Santa Veracruz Church	1655	AGNP, Not. 4, Box 181, 1655 June, 555–560v
Congregation and Slavery of the Annunciata	*Pardos, morenos*	Espíritu Santo College (Jesuits)	1663	Von Germeten, *Black Blood Brothers*, 227–229

captives into their social circle.[82] Despite the family's enslavement, their social network was rapidly expanding and would continue to grow before, during and after the terrible events of 1612.

In the aftermath of the Mexico City repression, local officials implemented various restrictions against black and mulatto socialization in Puebla. For instance, the municipal council prohibited people of African descent, both free and enslaved, from holding dances, meetings and other forms of recreation.[83] These measures would have been particularly injurious to Afro-Poblanos, who took pride in the relative autonomy of their religious brotherhoods. The members of the San Benito de Palermo confraternity, housed at the Franciscan convent, would have certainly resented the insinuation that they represented a threat to the social order (see Table 5.1).[84] It is worth noting that, despite their enslavement, Asians were not targeted in the same manner. The municipal ordinances restricting slave socialization were specific to people of African descent. Blacks and

---

82 ASMP, *Bautizos de negros, 1606–1617*, 4v, 12r, 13v, 22r, 23v, 25r, 26v, 32v, 36v.
83 AGMP, Actas de Cabildo, Vol. 15, 190/189.
84 Rafael Castañeda García, "Santos negros, devotos de color. Las cofradías de San Benito de Palermo en Nueva España. Identidades étnicas y religiosas, siglos XVII–XVIII," in *Devoción paisanaje e identidad* (Bilbao: Universidad del País Vasco, 2014), 149–155.

mulattos in Puebla were once more paying the price for developments outside of their immediate sphere of action.

In March 1618, the Marquis of Guadalcázar launched a new series of punitive raids on the maroons of the Veracruz highlands.[85] Once more the campaign failed. Only with the foundation of Córdoba, a decidedly Spanish town, in October of that year would this maroon zone begin the transition "from a runaway-slave haven to slave-worked, white-controlled plantation center."[86] Implicit in the pacification was the submission of African-derived cultural expressions and socialization in surrounding settlements and urban centers, Puebla included. The perceived need to control a growing non-Spanish population could border on the ridiculous. Just before the feast of *Carnestolendas* (Mardi Gras), the Puebla *cabildo* decreed that blacks, mulattos and indigenous people caught throwing limes and oranges at one another would suffer one hundred lashes.[87]

During the tenure of Viceroys Guadalcázar (1612–1621) and Gelves (1622–1624), free people of African descent were ordered to abandon their independent households and move into Spanish residences where they would work as domestic servants.[88] In theory, middling Spaniards might have benefited from such legislation, but the nature of patron-client relationships and the economic opportunities available to freed people in the city largely trumped the decrees (see Chapter 6). Moreover, many recently freed people maintained close ties to elite patrons, whose self-interest and protection extended to former household servants and slaves. The slaves of the elite already lived with their masters, gathered in large numbers (because the household consisted of numerous slaves), and were largely immune to legal prosecution because of their proximity to men with considerable political power. These connections mitigated the enforcement of racially specific ordinances and also prevented the collection of tribute among free people.[89]

85 AGI, México, Leg. 29, no. 4.

86 Patrick Carroll, *Blacks in Colonial Veracruz: Race, Ethnicity and Regional Development* (Austin: University of Texas Press, 2001), 92.

87 AGMP, Actas de Cabildo, Vol. 15, 56/55. Spaniards would receive a fine of 6 pesos and three days in jail, while mestizos would pay half that amount but endure ten days in the city prison.

88 Palmer, *Slaves of the White God*, 141; AGMP, Actas de Cabildo, Vol. 16, 107/106. In 1624, the *cabildo* ordered a cave that was being used as a gathering place and hideout for blacks and mulattos to be closed off. "Many offenses against our lord God" were being committed there, an unclear reference to practices that somehow offended elite morality. The ban could have referred to drumming and dancing, but I have not located additional information specific to this petition. If destroying the cave was intended as a measure to halt male-male sexual relationships, the municipal council failed miserably. See Serge Gruzinski, "The Ashes of Desire: Homosexuality in Seventeenth-Century New Spain," in Pete Sigal, ed., *Infamous Desire: Male Homosexuality in Colonial Latin America* (Chicago: University of Chicago Press, 2003), 202–207; Townsend, *Here in This Year*, 151.

89 Douglas Cope, *The Limits of Racial Domination: Plebeian Society in Colonial Mexico City, 1660–1720* (Madison: University of Wisconsin Press, 1994), 92.

Gelves' decrees were ultimately unenforceable and counterproductive. Elite Spaniards already owned the domestic workers they needed and would buy many more as the local slave market expanded between 1616 and 1639. Neither the 1612 slave repression nor the subsquent discriminatory campaigns altered the Poblano penchant for slave ownership. In fact, slave transactions reached their highest levels in the 1630s because slave ownership simply symbolized power (economic, political, and cultural). The patrimonial declarations of Puebla's councilmen confirmed this reality in 1622 and 1623.[90] In a listing of sixteen council members, fifteen certified owning slaves. These elite men (and their wives) declared their mastery over 203 enslaved people, an average of thirteen or fourteen slaves per household. Moreover, patrimonial declarations of this sort consistently undercounted the enslaved.[91]

The enslaved communities owned by Dr. Arboleda and other elite Poblanos were largely immune to the discriminatory ordinances of the 1610s and 1620s. Members of the political, merchant, and religious elite had invested far too heavily in their human property and the cultural power projected by the ownership of slave retinues to follow through with restrictions on slave mobility and socialization. Throughout Spanish America, affluent masters dressed their enslaved pages, chambermaids, coachmen, and wet nurses in fine, imported silks and other textiles to publicly demonstrate their families' fortunes.[92]

Moreover, Jerónima's family had other concerns and these centered on the possible fragmentation of their community. Dr. Arboleda fell ill in the summer of 1620, and in July he drafted an inventory of all his possessions and made final preparations for his estate. He designated his sister, Doña Barbola de Pineda, as his heir. Pineda was the wife of a high-ranking Spanish council member in Yanhuitlan, a Mixtec community 170 miles to the southwest (in what is today the state of Oaxaca). Relocation to Yanhuitlan would have represented a profound cultural shock for an urban family unfamiliar with this most indigenous of spaces. Few people of African descent inhabited the Mixteca region – a demographic reality that would have also inhibited participating in black or mulatto confraternities.[93] The social ties

90 José F. de la Peña, *Oligarquía y propiedad en Nueva España, 1550–1624* (Mexico City: Fondo de Cultura Económica, 1983), 177.

91 De la Peña, *Oligarquía*, 178. Notably absent from these inventories were the slave workforces owned by Puebla's dominant *obrajero* families as they ascended into the political elite. These patrimonial declarations do not contain information on free black, mulatto, *chino*, indigenous, or mestizo servants either. These omissions matter. The free children of enslaved domestics usually lived with their parents in these same residences and contributed their labor.

92 Tamara Walker, "'He outfitted his family in notable decency': Slavery, Honour and Dress in Eighteenth-Century Lima, Peru," *Slavery & Abolition*, 30 no. 3 (Sept. 2009), 391.

93 Kevin Terraciano, *The Mixtecs of Colonial Oaxaca: Ñudzahui History, Sixteenth through Eighteenth Centuries* (Stanford, CA: Stanford University Press, 2001), 225–228, 339.

that bound Jeronima's family to Puebla would be severely strained or severed by this potential relocation.

There were more than a few reasons for Jerónima to fret over her master's looming demise. True, her son Sebastián Gómez would secure his freedom in the event of Arboleda's death. But what of the remaining members of her extended family? As a 40-year-old freed man, Gómez likely spent the remainder of the year trying to keep the family intact, but these efforts fall outside of the written record. His younger brother, Bartolomé de las Casas, received a conditional freedom letter from Doña Francisca de Silva y Santiago in late 1621.[94] Las Casas would serve his master's widow for an entire year by bringing her one real each day and then become a free man.[95] We do not know what happened to the women of Jerónima's family or to the remaining members of her extended family in the following years. The historical record has only left traces of Magdalena de Arboleda, Gómez's wife. In 1630, Gómez appeared before the Puebla municipal council to request a plot of land on which to build a house. The council readily granted him a plot in the Analco neighborhood.[96] Twenty-three years later, his widow still claimed the land. Like many other free Afro-Poblanas, she was able to establish her family and lay roots in what had once been an indigenous barrio.

Families in a Time of Slavery

Despite any number of municipal restrictions, evidence of the social and economic empowerment of ex-slaves and their families in Puebla can be traced back to the 1620s and 1630s. Of course, references to free people that expose deep familial relations can be found well before then. In 1602, a free 15-year-old presented genealogical information on his background before a local justice to clarify his legal status. In his own words, "Jeronimo de Vargas, of *loro* color, native of this city [Puebla], I say that it in my right it is convenient to prove . . . that I am the legitimate son of Andres de Vargas, of *moreno* color, and Magdalena Sánchez, of *mulata* color, my parents, free people and natives of this city." The youth then presented three witnesses who proved that his parents were married, economically self-sufficient "and not subject to any captivity."[97] The timing of Vargas's statement suggests that at the time most youths of African descent were assumed to be born

---

94 AGNP, Not. 4, Box 100, 1620 July, 2278r. One real a day would amount to 45.6 pesos over the course of the year.

95 Tulane University, Puebla Notarial Collection, Box 4, Folder 21, no folio (1621/10/25).

96 AGMP, Actas de Cabildo, Vol. 17, 208/199 and Vol. 23, 278/276.

97 AHJP, Exp. 553, 2r–5r. For other cases in which *loro* was used to denote freedom, see AHJP, Exp. 386; AGNP, Not. 4, Box 56, 1590 November, 556r–557r and Box 36, 1590 July, 402r–403r.

enslaved and out of wedlock. Vargas countered these assumptions and further established his roots and privileges as a Poblano by noting that he and his parents were born in the city (*naturales*).[98]

Africans could not claim nativity in Puebla, but they could and did stake claims to family and freedom. In 1615, Francisco Carmona, who identified as a free, dark-skinned man (*moreno libre*), freed María, his 2-year-old *mulata* granddaughter.[99] He and the child's father (who remained unnamed) had gathered 130 pesos to purchase María's freedom. Carmona offered a monetary incentive for her liberty, but also "pleaded with the owner as the child's grandfather" and succeeded. In essence, Carmona exempted his granddaughter from the experiences of his own enslaved daughter, Antonia de Jesus. He also protected the child from his own trajectory as the slave of an affluent Spaniard – Carmona had once been the human property of Bishop Mota y Escobar. He and his wife, Catalina Bran, had only managed to experience freedom as adults at a combined price of 600 pesos.[100] Manumissions of any kind were rare before 1620,[101] but when used to purchase the freedom of young girls they were effective in preventing the birth of future generations of enslaved children.

In 1633, Francisco Carmona prepared his will, and in doing so unveiled a fascinating social network that helps us understand how he was able to intercede in his granddaughter's freedom eighteen years earlier.[102] Carmona identified as a free black man, a *vecino* of Puebla and the husband of Catalina Bran. He also identified by the "Bran" ethnonym, making him part of an aging Upper Guinean community at a time when thousands of West Central African youths were arriving in Mexico. Carmona was a shoemaker, an occupation which apparently earned him enough money to purchase a house in the Analco neighborhood. Carmona's testament serves as proof that Africans contributed significantly to the development of Puebla's peripheral barrios. At his death, he contributed alms to the local Santo Angel Custodio parish, which had just been finished in March 1632.[103] He also served as an intermediary for other enslaved people seeking letters of

---

98 AHJP, Exp. 553, 2r. One of Vargas's witnesses noted that they knew his parents for more than thirty years. That would place the parents in Puebla in the early 1570s at the latest.

99 AGNP, Not. 4, Box 78, 1615 July, no folio (1615/07/13).

100 AGNP, Not. 4, Box 78, no folio (1615/11/09).

101 I have only located four other *cartas de libertad* for the years 1600, 1605, and 1615. Based on 166 freedom papers, these documents became more numerous from the 1620s onward.

102 AHJP, Exp. 1617, 1r–3r. I have located 18 wills written by people of African descent for the period 1588–1699.

103 Camilla Townsend, ed. and transl., *Here in This Year: Seventeenth-Century Nahuatl Annals of the Tlaxcala-Puebla Valley* (Stanford, CA: Stanford University Press, 2010), 95; Miguel Ángel Cuenya Mateos, "La evolución demográfica de una parroquia de Puebla de los Ángeles, 1660–1880,"*Historia Mexicana* 36, no. 3 (Jan.–Mar. 1972), 447.

manumission: in 1627, he helped María de Terranova, an African woman, purchase her freedom papers (see Chapter 6).[104] In his will, Carmona also urged his executors to recover the 111 pesos he loaned "the wife of black Roque" for her manumission (Appendix B).[105]

Francisco de Carmona was a community leader and, as a freedman, a particularly influential figure among Puebla's Upper Guinean community. He asked to be buried in the Santa Veracruz church, where a black confraternity (Our Lady of Consolation) gathered for their services. His death in July 1633 would have been mourned by many. In September of that year, his widow, Catalina Bran, also drafted her will. She named her stepdaughter Antonia de Jesus, now a free married woman, as her heir.[106] In other words, between 1615 and 1633, an African couple secured the freedom of their granddaughter and daughter, while simultaneously establishing themselves in a neighborhood that was transitioning from an indigenous settlement to a mixed-race barrio. By late 1633, only their son, Juan Blas, remained enslaved. Similar family histories repeated themselves throughout the city during the mid-seventeenth century, but few are as well documented as the Carmona Bran family.

Of course, the colonial "family" was not restricted to the nuclear, two-parent household. In her 1631 testament, Marta Rodríguez, a free black woman and the owner of an inn, claimed affective ties to a predeceased son, a daughter-in-law, and a niece. We do not know if she or her son, Jerónimo Miguel, had ever been enslaved. Instead, Rodríguez owned an enslaved family of her own, demonstrating that slave ownership was accessible to people of all racial backgrounds.[107] Magdalena was the enslaved mother of Diego, aged 4, and Ana, just fourteen months old. This too was a female-led family unit. Rodríguez's slaves likely assisted her in running both the inn (*mesón*) and the house, which were located in the Analco neighborhood. Their mistress's 1631 testament was cause for grave concern. Rodríguez intended to separate the family by sending the infant Ana to a free woman, Juana Bautista. Diego would serve the friars of the Mercedarian convent "for all the days of his life," and the cleric Juan Díaz de Estalaya would receive Magdalena and the inn.

Most people of African descent remained enslaved in the mid-seventeenth century even as an Afro-Poblano minority increasingly made their way into the middle stratum of society. Those that did secure their freedom mostly did so by birthright. However, some did receive their freedom papers through self-purchase, manumission, or by some clause in a

---

104 AHJP, Exp. 1260, 1r–2r.   105 AHJP, Exp. 1617, 1r–3r.

106 Ibid., 6r–6v. De Jesus married Lucas de Carmona, a free man.

107 The indigenous woman Francisca Juana and her free *pardo* husband were also slave owners. AGNP, Not. 4, Box 220, 1683 Testaments, no folio (1683/03/01).

master's will. I have located 340 such references in my 20 percent sample of Puebla's notarial archives for the seventeenth century.[108] At best, this would suggest that some 1,700 people received notarized freedoms in Puebla. However, the figure overstates the actual number of people freed in this manner. Masters often agreed to manumit their slaves, but only after specifying additional months or years of service to a relative, convent, or some other institution.[109] For instance, in 1660, Doña Beatriz Dávila "freed" Juana and María, but they would not enjoy their freedom for another six years.[110] Dávila's son, the regent Luis de Carrera, was their new master. Other cases speak to an additional ten or fifteen years of labor after the drafting of a manumission clause.[111] Bernarda, a 36-year-old *mulata* woman, was given her freedom 30 years after it had been promised in 1615. These binding strategies further blurred the line between slavery and freedom, especially since the enslaved often remained in the service of the master's family or associates.

As in other Spanish American cities, women accounted for most of the people freed by notarial means. In his comparative essay on free people of color in Mexico City and Lima, Frederick Bowser indicated that "freedom was a goal obtained for the most part by women and small children."[112] In Puebla, six of every ten freed people were females (adults and girls). Generationally, enslaved boys and girls (ages 0–10) accounted for 39.6 percent of all manumissions, while freed slaves (male and female) over the age of 40 accounted for 14.4 percent. This age distribution largely mirrors Frank Proctor's findings for Mexico City and Guanajuato for the late seventeenth and early eighteenth centuries.[113]

Establishing why manumission documents were drafted, however, is exceedingly difficult. In the case of Francisco Carmona's granddaughter, the slaveholder was willing to relinquish his dominion for multiple reasons. From the latter's perspective, "the child is not old enough to be of service and the laws favor the liberty of slaves." Second, Carmona and the unnamed father offered an incentive of 130 pesos. Finally, the master claimed that

---

108 This sample recovered 271 references to freeing transactions in Puebla's third and fourth notarial office. Another 69 references were found in the second and sixth office. The monetary contingencies in many of these documents are further grounds for skepticism.

109 AGNP, Not. 3, Box 111, 1660 Testaments, 29r, 66r; Box 122, 1670 June, 407r; Box 139, 1680 June, 26r; AGNP, Not. 4, Box 152, 1635 October, 1682r; Box 209, 1675 October, 858.

110 AGNP, Not. 3, Box 111, 1660 Testaments, 66r.

111 AGNP, Not. 4, Box 152, 1635 Testaments, no folio (1635/03/14) and 1635 October, 1682r; Box 170b, 1645 April, 209r.

112 Bowser, "The Free Person of Color in Mexico City and Lima," in Stanley Engerman and Eugene D. Genovese, eds., *Race and Slavery in the Western Hemisphere: Quantitative Studies* (Princeton, NJ: Princeton University Press, 1975), 350–351.

113 Frank Proctor, *Damned Notions of Liberty: Slavery, Culture and Power in Colonial Mexico, 1640–1769* (Albuquerque: University of New Mexico Press, 2010), 161–162.

granting freedom was also done "for service to God our Lord." Undoubtedly, many slaveholders held intimate ties with their slaves and felt true appreciation for their work and companionship. This would have been especially true of slaveholders raised or breastfed by their enslaved servants. In sum, a combination of guilt, gratitude, economic expediency and pressure led slaveholders to grant manumission documents.

Considering the actions of blood-related and fictive kin in these liberating documents is essential to a greater appreciation of the enslaved's social networks. Spouses, parents, and godparents claimed social bonds to 109 of the 173 freed people found in the manumission records of Puebla's third and fourth notarial office. For example, in 1635, Manuel, a black "Angola" man, was freed by his *comadre* Isabel, a free black woman. That same year, the merchant Gaspar de Sosa freed Jacinto, his four-month-old godson, for 70 pesos. Juan Rincón, an enslaved confectioner, was freed by his wife Madgalena and his brother Juan Ponce, who amassed 520 pesos to purchase his freedom.[114]

These intermediaries served as representatives for larger groups of people, whose names were infrequently preserved in the notarial record. Dominga, for instance, a 40-year-old woman, was freed "because other blacks, her relatives, and Gabriel, the black slave of Esteban Alonso, her husband" promised 460 pesos for her manumission in 1650.[115] Acknowledging families, then, allows us to look past academic debates on the nature of seventeenth-century "personal liberty" or "piecemeal freedoms."[116] Slaves understood freedom from a familial, collective perspective and often endured decades during which a sister, nephew or father remained enslaved. This did not make the quest for liberty any less real or unreasonably idealistic. In fact, significantly more manumissions were produced in the second half of the seventeenth century precisely because slaves constructed more resilient social networks.[117]

The baptismal records of Puebla's largest parish, the Sagrario, serve as a useful indicator of how slavery persisted among people increasingly rooted in the fabric of urban society. These parish-level records hold invaluable clues to understanding how urban people transcended their enslavement. Although formulaic, baptismal entries offer an important counterpoint to the freedom papers drafted in the 1650s.[118] Between 1655 and 1657, more

114 AGNP, Not. 4, Box 150, 1635 February, 270r and Box 152, 1635 December 2080r.

115 AGNP, Not. 4, Box 121, 1625 July, 1641r.

116 Proctor, *Damned Notions*, 152–158, 184–185.

117 AGNP, Not. 3 and 4. Approximately 75 percent of the former slaves in this sample were identified as spouses, mothers, fathers, sons, grandchildren, or godparents in testaments and *cartas de libertad* produced between 1650 and 1695.

118 Some 38 freeing testaments and manumission were found for 1650 and 1655, but as previously seen only some of these would be honored.

than half of all infants of African descent in Sagrario baptismal entries were labeled as slaves.[119] The 21 January 1657 entry for baby Victoria is representative of this dynamic. Victoria was the daughter of Clara del Puerto, an enslaved black woman and a single mother. In keeping with standard baptismal practices, no mention was made of Victoria's ascribed caste or skin color.[120] Likewise, no information was entered for her father. Mother and daughter were both owned by Juan García, who likely did not care if the name of the father was included or not. Whether Victoria's father was enslaved or free did not influence "the law of the womb." Juan de Sabano and Josefa del Puerto, two members of the Sagrario parish (*feligreses*), served as the child's godparents.

Despite their enslavement, children in Puebla were increasingly born to families with relatives, friends, and acquaintances firmly embedded in society. As seen in the preceding sections, social networks mattered immensely. During the first decade of the seventeenth century, parish priests failed to record the name of a baptism recipient's parents 79 percent of the time.[121] In the case of recent African arrivals, local clerics simply chose not to recognize their genealogies and in the process effaced their families, names, and lineages from the historical record. This was less common in the 1655 to 1657 period, when 55 percent of baptism recipients were entered without familial ties.[122] By the late 1670s, the erasure of African-descended families had been effectively reversed. Local priests only failed to record the names of mothers or fathers in 3 percent of Afro-Poblano baptisms.[123]

The increasing recognition of African-descended lineages in Puebla's Sagrario signaled a crucial, yet gradual, shift in urban slave ownership. Afro-Poblano infants were now discernable members of families whose bonds were validated by the local religious establishment. During the mid-1650s, parish priests identified only 15 legitimate children in their baptismal books, but produced entries for 150 *hijos legítimos* between 1677 and 1680. There was an evident tension in the 1679 baptismal entry for baby Micaela. She was the "legitimate daughter of Joseph de Espina, mulatto slave of Capt. Juan de Valera, and Inés la Cruz, [a] free [woman]."[124] As lawfully wedded people, Espina and de la Cruz could claim respect, and this was respect was based on their claims as Catholic parents. If "the concept of *hijo legítimo* was not widely manifested among enslaved Africans and the initial generations of creoles," this was no longer the case by the

---

119 ASMP, *Bautismos de negros, 1654–1658*. Based on 336 cases out of a total of 652 baptisms. Future research should explain if similar ratios were present in the San José and Santo Angel Custodio (Analco) parishes. These were spaces with lower Spanish populations and greater numbers of indigenous, mestizo, and Afro-Poblano inhabitants.

120 Cope, *The Limits*, 55.

121 ASMP, *Bautismos de negros, 1607–1610*.   122 ASMP, *Bautismos de negros, 1654–1658*.

123 ASMP, *Bautismos de negros, 1677–1680*.   124 Ibid., 54r.

mid-1680s.[125] In the baptismal entries of 1685 through 1688, the Sagrario's priests recorded 245 Afro-Poblano infants of legitimate birth.[126] Their parents' active participation in Catholic sacraments, especially marriage, forced slaveholders into recognizing Afro-Poblanos as people worthy of honor during the late seventeenth century.

There was no singular moment of freedom in Puebla, or any other Mexican city for people of African descent. Queen Mariana of Spain did emancipate slaves of Native American and Asian descent in 1673, but she did not issue a comparable decree freeing those of African heritage.[127] Instead, Afro-Poblano families earned their freedom generationally through birthright. By the late 1670s, two of every three infants of African descent were born to free mothers in the Sagrario. No fewer than 638 free children were baptized between 1677 and 1680, and they would be followed by another 700 between 1685 and 1688.[128] At this rate, some 5,760 children of African descent were baptized in the Sagrario during the 1670s and 1680s – more than 3,800 would have been born free.[129] By resorting to the local parish, Afro-Poblano families, nuclear and extended, matrilineal and patrilineal, achieved a gradual but irreversible victory over slaveholders.[130]

Conflict versus Confraternities

The mundane lives of Jerónima, Francisco Carmona and Catalina Bran are not the stuff of epics. These were common people rooted in specific parishes, barrios and religious societies. Enslaved people constructed expansive social networks and familial structures that were validated at the parish

---

125 Bennett, *Colonial Blackness*, 149–150. Moreover, only twenty-three "hijos legitimos" were registered as slaves in this last set of baptismal books.

126 ASMP, *Bautismos de negros 1654–1658* and *1685–1688*. This last baptismal book also registered an average of 295 Afro-Poblano baptisms per year.

127 Tatiana Seijas, *Asian Slaves in Colonial Mexico: From Chinos to Indians* (Cambridge: Cambridge University Press, 2014), 229–235. The official abolishment of slavery only came in 1829 under President Vicente Guerrero, himself a man of partial African descent.

128 These are minimum figures – the baptismal book for 1677 starts in September. The 1688 register ends in May.

129 I have calculated an average of 288 Afro-Poblano baptisms per annum based on the complete yearly entries for 1678, 1679, 1680, 1685, 1686, and 1687. These figures exclude children baptized in the Santo Angel Custodio (Analco), San José, and other urban parishes. They do not include infants of African descent who were registered in Spanish baptismal books. At the very least, these figures suggest that Puebla was far more than a city of Spaniards. In fact, the Sagrario baptismal books for Afro-Poblanos help explain why 33,800 of Puebla's 63,650 inhabitants were of mixed or African descent. See Peter Gerhard, "Un censo de la diócesis de Puebla en 1681," *Historia Mexicana* 30, no. 4 (Apr.–Jun. 1981), 534–536.

130 For the erosion of slaveholding in New Spain in the eighteenth century, see Dennis N. Valdés, "The Decline of Slavery in Mexico" *The Americas* 44, no. 2 (Oct. 1987): 167–194.

level. This, in turn, meant that slaves cultivated favorable relationships with local priests, friars and high-ranking religious men over the course of the seventeenth century. Yet these relationships and the spaces they generated have rarely been studied for Puebla. The construction of La Soledad Church, for instance, was the direct result of the alms-raising of Manuel de los Dolores, a *mulato* servant of the Count of Casa Alegre.[131] An especially devout Catholic, Manuel spent fourteen years raising funds to build the chapel that would house a miraculous statue of Our Lady of Solitude. The most important Afro-Poblano religious confraternity of the seventeenth century occupied a chapel in the Limpia Concepción Hospital, on the same street (see Chapter 6).[132] Mid-seventeenth-century Spaniards, mestizos and indigenous people understood these Afro-Poblano spatial and religious linkages, even if historians have failed to acknowledge them. By the 1640s, even Puebla's bishops, once infamous for their enslaved retinues, had come to recognize that people of African descent contributed to local religiosity.

We turn to a polemic figure, the bishop, viceroy and royal reformer Juan de Palafox y Mendoza, to study this transformation. Between 1643 and 1646, Palafox set out on three separate inspections (*visitas*) of the religious communities under his vast and wealthy bishopric. He was bent on establishing whether the secular clergy were adequately fulfilling their religious obligations to their assigned communities. For the purposes of his study, his inspections are valuable in that they provide information on the free and enslaved people in the bishopric from the perspective of a powerful official based in Puebla.

The *visitas* of the 1640s generally contradict historians' ideas regarding Palafox and his thoughts on New Spain's population of African descent. Cayetana Álvarez de Toledo, for instance, understands black and mulatto people as a "force of potential instability" in Palafox's writings.[133] This prejudice, she argues, was based on their lack of "political or social responsibilities within the community."[134] The bishop's memoirs, however, contradict,

131 Mariano Joseph Antonio Fernández de Echeverría y Veytia, *Historia de la Fundación de la Ciudad de la Puebla de los Ángeles en la Nueva España, su Descripción y Presente Estado* (Puebla: Ediciones Altiplano, 1962), 480–482; Padre Francisco de Florencia, *Zodiaco mariano, en que el sol de justicia Christo con la salud en las alas visita como Signos y Casas proprias . . .* (Mexico City: Antiguo Colegio de San Ildeonso, 1755), 180–188.

132 AGNP, Not. 4, Box 218, Testaments 1682, 15r–17v; Box 219, 1682 October, 925r–926r.

133 Cayetana Álvarez de Toledo, *Politics and Reform in Spain and Viceregal Mexico: The Life and Thought of Juan de Palafox 1600–1659* (Oxford: Oxford University Press, 2004), 91, 130. Palafox's persecution of the resident Portuguese community and its alleged black allies in the wake of Portugal's independence also contributes to such a narrative.

134 Álvarez de Toledo, *Politics*, 92.

or at the very least complicate, the idea that blacks were consistently perceived as an internal enemy. Consider the following entry from Palafox's 1643 ecclesiastical visit:

San Lorenzo, a town that was established by fugitive blacks with permission from the Señor Marquis of Cerralbo, to whom they asked for forgiveness and freedom in order to excuse the damages they caused. [In return] they took on the obligation of capturing and turning in other [fugitives] that found their way into the highlands. They have their own form of republic, and justices among themselves, and a company of soldiers for the occassions and prisons that others might need.

The setting of this town is hot and bad, with a few mosquitos and venomous animals, although it is fertile in rice and maize. It is composed of 40 families and within them 125 people. The church is reasonable, with a few good ornaments and little silver. Around this town [one may] find cedar and valuable lumber. All these people turned out to receive and celebrate His Excellency [Palafox] with great love.[135]

In this remarkable passage, Palafox describes the town of San Lorenzo de los Negros, Gaspar Yanga's former maroon community. The bishop depicts a town of peaceful, evangelized people. Palafox presents an autonomously governed community with its own "justices" and "republic,"[136] instead of a *palenque* once imagined as the scourge of Mexico. The transformation from military threat to Catholic settlement over a thirty-year period must be reassessed as a profound ideological transformation. Other Afro-descended communities in towns and cities within the Puebla bishopric received similar praise or neutral observations. In Tepeaca, Palafox noted that nine religious confraternities regularly held meetings and processions. One of the nine was the brotherhood "of the blacks," who venerated the Virgen de la Caridad.[137] These references suggest that the fear of slave rebellion had dissipated by the mid-seventeenth century, at least in the minds of elite Poblanos.[138]

---

135 Juan de Palafox y Mendoza, Relación de las visitas eclesiásticas de parte del Obispado de la *Puebla de los Ángeles* (Mexico City: El Colegio de México, 2014), 66–67.

136 In 1683, the residents of San Lorenzo even attempted to rid the port of Veracruz of the buccaneer forces of Laurens de Graaf and Nicolas van Horn. See Camba Ludlow, *Imaginarios*, 113–114.

137 Palafox y Mendoza, *Relación*, 49–50.

138 The study of seventeenth-century religious music also suggests that Spanish fears of black rebellion had diminished by mid-century. In particular, Juan Gutiérrez de Padilla's 1652 Christmas *villancico* "To the most joyful manger" ("Al establo más dichoso") features Africans and angels singing together in a Nativity scene. The piece, featuring a stereotyped Angolan character, would have been performed in the recently inaugurated Cathedral. See Andrew Cashner, ed. *Villancicos about Music from Seventeenth-Century Spain and New Spain* (WLSCM, no. 32, 2017), 26–28, 42–46.

This is not to say that Puebla was free of violent, racially tinged incidents. María de las Mercedes Gantes Tréllez describes violent incidents (*revueltas*) involving free black men in 1635 and 1647, but does not elaborate on the roots or consequences of these disturbances.[139] In 1659, an indigenous chronicler mentioned a skirmish between "blacks and Spaniards . . . in the place where the tortilla makers sell their wares [in the marketplace]" on Holy Thursday.[140] Yet there are no further references to this event, suggesting its relative unimportance to this elite Nahua man and his community. Instead, racial conflict appears to have been increasingly individualized and rooted in barrio politics and family disputes.[141] I contend that the Afro-Poblano investment in Baroque Catholicism increasingly discredited blanket assessments of blacks and mulattos as rabble-rousers and potential insurrectionists.

The emergence of racially defined brotherhoods from the early to mid seventeenth century allowed free and slave blacks, mulattos and *chinos* to project themselves as devout, honorable Catholics in a city steeped in Baroque religion. Identifying as a *cofrade*, a confraternity member, rather than as a third party's human property, played a crucial role in redefining the social and political roles assigned to enslaved people.[142] Between 1611 and 1663, people of African and Asian descent participated in no fewer than six religious brotherhoods in Puebla (Table 5.1). These confraternities allowed members to pool resources, celebrate religous processions, pay for funeral costs and purchase letters of manumission. In sum, brotherhoods allowed enslaved people to engage urban society as full-fledged Catholics, and not merely as slaves.

The brotherhoods also opened up spaces and opportunities for interracial interaction. In 1648, a *chino* confraternity housed in Puebla's Santa Veracruz Church sought to build its own chapel for the burial of its members and veneration of its distinctly Mexican patroness, Our Lady of Guadalupe. Bishop Palafox received the original petition, which was then passed along to Dr. Alonso de Salazar y Verona, the governor of the Puebla bishopric. The Asian brothers had already gathered 150 pesos to purchase the grounds and were committed to pooling further resources in order to build the actual

---

139 María de las Mercedes Gantes Tréllez, "Aspectos socio-económicos de Puebla de los Ángeles (1624–1650)," in Carlos Contreras Cruz and Miguel Ángel Cuenya Mateos, eds., *Ángeles y constructores. Mitos y realided en la historia colonial de Puebla, siglos XVI y XVII* (Puebla: BUAP/Fomento Editorial), 240–241.

140 Townsend, *Here in This Year*, 101–105. In an alternate, bilingual version of the annals, an image of a black hand and a white hand crossing swords was drawn just above the entry. See Gómez García *et al.*, eds., *Anales del barrio*, 88–89.

141 AHJP, Exp. 2329, 2355; AGN, Inquisición, Vol. 536, Exp. 18, 108r–116v.

142 Nicole von Germeten, *Black Blood Brothers, Confraternities and Social Mobility for Afro-Mexicans* (Gainesville: University of Florida Press, 2005), 2–10.

chapel. Joseph Roberto and Juan Gómez Bueno, who self-identified as *chinos* and the confraternity's leaders (*mayordomos*), turned to a black brotherhood housed in the same church for a model to follow. In their own words, "all the *chino* brothers and those of any other color that might be buried in the chapel or in the church will pay for the [chapel's] construction just as is done by the black brothers of the confraternity of Our Lady of Consolation, also founded in said church."[143] By appropriating the language of religious service and piety, members of black and *chino* religious communities transcended their juridical status as free or enslaved people.[144] They instead presented themselves as members of honorable religious corporations.

By the mid-seventeenth century, enslaved people in Puebla were more likely to be members of religious confraternities than potential insurrectionists. This situation benefited the city's religious orders and secular priests as well. Puebla's Franciscans, Dominicans, and Jesuits could count on vibrant and lucrative Afro-Poblano brotherhoods to extol their own patron saints and advance their respective interests. The same could be said for the nuns of the Immaculate Conception and the secular priests of Santa Veracruz Church. In the early eighteenth century, the chronicler Miguel de Alcalá y Mendiola reminisced on the orderly, splendorous religious processions of Puebla's *morenos*, *pardos*, and *chinos* of the previous century. For Alcalá, their Maundy Thursday and Good Friday processions were inextricably linked to devout urban populations. Their prior enslavement of the *cofrades* did not factor into his understanding of their activities.[145]

Slavery, Freedom and Economic Contraction

The consolidation of Puebla's confraternities and the remarkable growth of the free population have been largely forgotten in the focus on the city's economic struggles during the early eighteenth century. The fall of the textile mills, the closing of the inter-American trade with Perú and the growing importance of the Bajío region are all cited as causes for the city's gradual deterioration. The excessive taxation imposed on Puebla in order to fund the Armada de Barlovento and the militia companies for the

---

143 AGNP, Not. 4, Box 181, 556r.

144 Chino confraternities were rare and limited to spaces that concentrated large numbers of free and enslaved Asians. For a *chino* brotherhood in Mexico City, see von Germeten, *Black Blood Brothers*, 101.

145 Miguel de Alcalá y Mendiola, *Descripción en bosquejo de la imperial cesárea muy noble y muy leal ciudad de Puebla de los Ángeles* (Puebla: BUAP/Fomento Editorial, 1997), 127, 130, 140, 145, 150–152. Alcalá extended his positive depiction of Afro-Poblanos to their service in the city's eighteenth-century militias.

Philippines also weighed on this development.[146] The economic historians Garavaglia and Grosso have highlighted an economic depression that characterized all but five years from 1640 to 1670. A period of vigorous growth followed between 1670 and 1695, only to be dismantled by a severe decade-long depression that would leave Puebla an impoverished city well into the eighteenth century.[147] An alternative interpretation of Poblano history, however, must acknowledge that for many families the transition from slavery to freedom was achieved during a time of economic depression. The city's defeatist, economically based narrative must be reassessed and repackaged to include the social experiences of black, mulatto and *chino* families.

For young enslaved men, dozens of workshops afforded the opportunity to serve as apprentices and journeymen during the second half of the seventeenth century. Some would even attain the skill and status of master artisans.[148] By mid-century, Afro-Poblano families began to assert their own notarial privileges by negotiating their children's contracts. The bond between father and son was especially significant at this moment, because both free and unfree men could present themselves before a public notary to ratify their sons' apprenticeship papers. Within my sample, Afro-Poblano fathers approved of seventeen apprenticeship contracts, sixteen of which took place between 1630 and 1700.[149]

For families with one or two enslaved parents, a son's apprenticeship represented the promise of future financial stability and perhaps even the genealogical end to their bondage. In 1660, for example, Cristóbal de Santa Ana allowed Pascual de la Cruz, his 16-year-old son, to learn the shoe-making trade.[150] De la Cruz was a free person, a reflection of his mother's legal status. For the next two and a half years, he would toil for a master shoemaker even though his father belonged to an elite Spanish woman. A similar case from 1675 points to the social and cultural capital that enslaved parents cultivated by way of their sons' training. That year, Joseph

---

146 Yolanda Celaya Nández, *Alcabalas y situados: Puebla en el sistema fiscal imperial 1638–1742* (Mexico City: El Colegio de México, 2010), 56–59, 116–119.

147 Juan Carlos Garavaglia and Juan Carlos Grosso, *La región de Puebla-Tlaxcala y la economía novohispana* (Mexico City: Instituto Mora/BUAP, 1996), 161–163.

148 AGNP, Not. 3 & 4, 1590–1700 apprentice database. During the early seventeenth century, Spanish masters placed their slaves under the tutelage of master artisans with the expectation that this investment would produce a reliable monthly salary. I have located eighty-three apprenticeship contracts for young men of African descent – although many more informal agreements would have taken place, especially among illiterate master artisans. Typically, a Spanish administrator (*curador ad litem*) was assigned to these minors: a formality intended to prevent the latter's exploitation.

149 Enslaved fathers appear in five apprentice contracts. These examples are valuable as they speak to the undeniable bias in favor of male figures (even enslaved ones) inherent in Spanish law, business and society.

150 AGNP, Not. 4, Box 188, 1660 March, 238r.

de Pantoja allowed his son and namesake to begin a four-year apprenticeship with a master milliner. The elder Pantoja belonged to a cloistered nun from the Santa Clara convent. By contrast, Joseph de Pantoja the younger presented himself as a free 17-year-old and the "legitimate child" of his father and Juana Ibañez. The young Joseph was not the only Pantoja Ibañez to complete an apprenticeship. Between 1681 and 1685, his three brothers (Miguel, Antonio and Baltazar) also appear in Puebla's parish registers as free mulattos, certified journeymen (milliners and tailors), and married men.[151] All four siblings married free women. No convent or widow would claim their children as human property.

Conclusion

At the dawn of the eighteenth century, thousands of slaves still toiled in Puebla. Still, most enslaved people established themselves firmly in the urban sphere and devised manifold strategies to withstand and, eventually, transcend slavery. This was a generational process that involved African-born grandparents, free wives, Spanish, mestizo, indigenous and free-colored allies. Its success must be measured in relation to the terror unleashed against people of African descent during the spring of 1612. And yet, we must recognize that a normative slave experience did not exist in Puebla de los Ángeles. Jerónima, the enslaved matriarch of the Arboleda residence, did not experience the city as her son Sebastián Gómez did. Only by acknowledging the diversity of the enslaved's lives and the breadth of their social networks are we able to understand the dynamics that gradually eroded the foundations of slavery in Puebla. By appealing to a freedman minority, numerous Afro-Poblano families were able to safeguard their life earnings in trusted hands. However, the baptismal font represented the single most important avenue for Afro-Poblano freedom. Enslaved and free families defended their social bonds at the local parish and increasingly claimed the language of legitimacy. These men, women and children were people of trust, not internal enemies. Rationalizing their continued enslavement became increasingly difficult as the seventeenth century progressed. By then, the former slaves of Puebla had begun to exert real influence over everyday commerce. We now turn to their experiences.

---

151 ASMP, *Matrimonios de negros y mulatos, 1675–1686*, 88r, 109v, 133r, 179v.

6

The Other Market

Commerce and Opportunity

Let it be known that I, Felipe de Mojica, free mulato of this city of [Puebla] de los Angeles, owe and am committed to paying Ignacio de Orrega, merchant and *vecino* of this city, and to anyone who might hold his power [of attorney] 3844 pesos of common gold. He has lent and supplied me this money in reales to purchase chile peppers, beans, and other things to sell in the stand that I have in this city's public plaza.[1]

– Felipe Monsón y Mojica, 1664

Tortillas, beans, chocolate and chile peppers were the mainstays of the Poblano diet of the seventeenth century. Whether in convents, elite residences or artisan workshops, free and enslaved Poblanos consumed these products in massive quantities. The marketplace and its diverse actors responded to this demand in the city's central square, the *plaza pública*. Among the vendors there were Felipe Monsón y Mojica, a former slave, and his wife, the indigenous woman Juana María de la Cruz, who offered chiles for sale. When Monsón entered a debt contract for 3,844 pesos with Ignacio de Orrega in 1664, he underscored his public reputation as a man of credit and trust.[2] He committed to paying his creditor "fifty pesos at the end of each week," until his debt was satisfied. For almost a year and a half, Monsón and de la Cruz made these weekly payments on time. They were more than motivated because their house in the San José barrio was subject to repossession if they failed to make two consecutive payments. Fortunately, they satisfied their debts with Orrega and with many other creditors. In fact, Monsón and de la Cruz became creditors in their own right. The couple's chile business thrived over the next twenty years. For this Afro-indigenous couple, the marketplace allowed them to navigate colonial society, expose its fractures and ultimately emerge as urban patrons.

---

1 This chapter is based on two previous publications, see Pablo Miguel Sierra Silva, "From Chains to Chiles: An Elite Afro-Indigenous Couple in Colonial Mexico, 1641–1688," *Ethnohistory* 62, no. 2 (April 2015), 361–384 and "María de Terranova: A West African Woman and the Quest for Freedom in Colonial Mexico," *Journal of Pan African Studies* 6, no. 1 (July 2013): 45–63.

2 AGNP, Not. 4, Box 194, 1664 February, 183r–183v.

In the midst of stalls stacked with chiles, fish and indigenous garments, the slaves of Puebla and their associates crafted a superior understanding of supply, demand, honor and family. Historians of colonial Mexico have often understood the colonial marketplace as a contested space for the urban underclass.[3] In Puebla, Mexico City and other urban centers, a "plebian subculture" emerged in the public plaza and the stands of the *baratillo*, the infamous secondhand market. The *baratillo* served as a site for "escaped slaves, mulattos, mestizos, Indians and even Spaniards" to gamble, drink and gossip.[4] Whereas "[e]lite Spaniards had little sympathy for, or understanding of, the social benefits of the marketplace," common folk established personal bonds within it as vendors, suppliers, debtors and friends. In Puebla, this was especially true for enslaved people and their kin, who found economic opportunity and an accepting culture in the plaza. Slaves and freedmen extended their social networks in the market and *baratillo*.

Historians of the Iberian Atlantic have used social networks to study merchants and their long-distance communications with associates and kin.[5] More recently, Alex Borucki has studied black social networks in the Río de la Plata region by analyzing Africans' interactions and relationships across the Atlantic, in various Brazilian ports, and in Montevideo and Buenos Aires.[6] By contrast, in this section, I use the networking concept to analyze the interactions of enslaved and free people within a single city. According to Eric van Young, as "relationships of trust," social networks were founded on "interest and economic exchange" and "another form of social relation, be it friendship, kinship, micropatriotism (*paisanaje*), religious affiliation, or common membership in an organization without immediate and overt economic importance, such as a *cofradía* or a political

3 Douglas Cope, *The Limits of Racial Domination: Plebeian Society in Colonial Mexico City, 1660–1720* (Madison: University of Wisconsin Press, 1994), 37–38; Magali M. Carrera, *Imagining Identity in New Spain: Race, Lineage and the Colonial Body in Portraiture and Casta Paintings* (Austin: University of Texas Press, 2003); Jorge Olvera Ramos, *Los mercados de la Plaza Mayor en la Ciudad de México* (Mexico City: Centro de estudios mexicanos y centroamerianos, 2013); Andrew Konove, "On the Cheap: The Baratillo Marketplace and the Shadow Economy of Eighteenth-Century Mexico City," *The Americas* 72, no. 2 (April 2015), 249–278.

4 Cope, *The Limits*, 37–38.

5 Daviken Studnicki-Gizbert, *A Nation upon the Ocean Sea: Portugal's Atlantic Diaspora and the Crisis of the Spanish Empire, 1492–1640* (Oxford: Oxford University Press, 2007), 66–95; Nikolaus Bötcher, Bernd Hausberger, and Antonio Ibarra, eds., *Redes y negocios globales en el mundo ibérico, siglos XVI–XVIII* (Vervuert: Instituto Ibero-Americano, 2011); Xabier Lamikiz "Flotistas en la Nueva España: diseminación espacial y negocios de los intermediarios del comercio trasatlántico, 1670–1702," *Colonial Latin American Review* 20, no. 1 (April 2011), 9–33; Guillermina del Valle Pavón and Antonio Ibarra, "Redes sociales e instituciones: una nueva mirada sobre viejas incógnitas," *Historia Mexicana* 56, no. 3 (Jan.–Mar. 2007), 717–723.

6 Borucki, *From Shipmates to Soldiers: Emerging Black Identities in the Río de la Plata* (Albuquerque: University of New Mexico Press, 2015), 1–5, 57–114.

entity (e.g., an *ayuntamiento*)."[7] He notes that social networks also required "powerful nodes – points of high traffic or concentration of power," with central actors mediating social and economic exchanges.

In the following pages, I argue that slaves and freedmen established resilient social networks throughout the course of the seventeenth century and that these social, economic and familial bonds are especially evident in the marketplace. Through a qualitative reading of testaments, debt contracts, indigenous annals and parochial information, I frame the marketplace and its free and enslaved actors as the "node," while their associates around and outside the plaza serve as "satellites."[8] The distances covered by these linkages could vary from a few hundred feet to hundreds of miles but are not the focus of this study. I am more interested in exploring the socio-commercial context of a marketplace that connects Afro-Poblanos and their spouses to debtors, creditors and suppliers. This framework also sheds light on family formation and on the differing ways in which free and enslaved men and women negotiated slavery in the colonial city.

We begin with María de Terranova, an enslaved African woman and fish vendor, who purchased her own freedom and became her former master's principal competitor in the 1620s. We then turn to the Monsón de la Cruz household to study Afro-indigenous interactions through the sale of chiles, beans, and other agricultural products. The final case study, that of the Pardave Cabrera family, focuses on the social networks found in the *baratillo* at the end of the seventeenth century. It also sheds light on how men of African descent made strategic use of matrimony with free women. These, then, are the stories of enslaved people who mastered the colonial marketplace in order to secure their own freedoms and those of their relatives. At one point or another, María de Terranova, Felipe Monsón, and the Cabrera siblings had all been considered human property. Their stories as successful free people are remarkable, but not exceptional, as many other former slaves carved niches for themselves in the markets of the colonial city.

María de Terranova

Entering the world of commerce perhaps represented the best possiblility of acquiring long-term stability and security for families descended from slaves. In a competitive urban marketplace that cared little for racial background, enslaved men and women found an arena of possibility by selling fish, clothes, chiles and pastries. On any given evening, black women fried

---

7 Eric van Young, "Social Networks: A Final Comment," in Bötcher, Hausberger, and Ibarra, eds., *Redes negocios globales*, 298–308.
8 Studnicki-Gizbert, *Nation upon the Sea*, 9–10, 81, 99.

sweet *buñuelos* in the main plaza for hungry folks heading home from the cathedral.[9] In a city addicted to chocolate and *pulque* (the fermented alcohol of the maguey plant), both beverages could produce handsome profits for female vendors,[10] although the continuing restrictions on alcohol sales made the latter a risky venture. Puebla's judicial archive is littered with references to free women, mostly *mestizas* and *mulatas*, selling *tepache*, a yellow variant of *pulque*, in the city's peripheral barrios.[11] It is likely that occasional brushes with the law did not affect these women significantly, which perhaps explains why unfree people do not surface in similar documentation. But what of enslaved women selling licit products?

The case of María, "the black woman from Terranova," speaks to the creation of specific ethnic identities, the preservation of family, and the commercial competition that characterized the colonial marketplace. The information we have on María is drawn from a lengthy 1627 judicial case in which she defended her right to freedom by arguing that a manumitted slave could not be restricted when freed by her own financial resources.[12] Her case reveals a complex sociocommercial network that included lawyers, merchants and self-sufficient ex-slaves.

Based on her reported age in the lawsuit, María was born in Lower Guinea circa 1594, placing her entry to New Spain somewhere around 1612. During her first years in the colony, she endured the difficult period of "seasoning," as she acclimatized to the new social, cultural and biological environment of Central Mexico. An acquaintance noted that she had been economically active in Puebla's central market as a fishmonger since 1613. These were difficult years for people of African descent as the viceregal and municipal government clamped down on black socialization and religious associations and recreation in the wake of the 1612 Mexico City conspiracy (see Chapter 5). We know little about her life between her arrival and the 1627 lawsuit, except that in her early twenties she gave birth to two girls who were born into slavery. In 1626, María was already 32 years old, and her daughters, Gertrudis and Teresa, were 11 and 7, respectively. During these crucial years in Puebla, María had also worked for two Spanish men who had profited greatly from her bondage. A third was interested in her services. [13]

In November 1626, Julián Bautista, a *vecino* of Puebla, purchased María along with her two daughters and an infirm slave, Lucrecia, for the

9 AHJP, Exp. 643, 17r.

10 In 1637, Isabel Ruíz made her living and owned a house thanks to her work as a chocolate vendor (*chocolatera*). See APSJ, *Matrimonios de morenos, 1629–1657*, 14v.

11 For *tepache*-related suits, see AHJP, Exps. 1538, 1741, 2063.   12 AHJP, Exp. 1260,11–46r.

13 AGNP, Notarías 3 y 4. Based on 273 observations taken for the period 1600–1700 for enslaved mothers of African descent, the normal age to begin motherhood in Puebla fell somewhere between 18 and 26. Adolescent mothers, 18 and younger, generally do not appear in the historical record.

exorbitant price of 2,000 pesos. In the bill of sale, the notary identified María as an "Angola [woman] from the land of San Tomé," in reference to the sugar-producing island and slave dêpot in the Gulf of Guinea.[14] However, during her legal battle, María time and again self-identified as "María, the black woman from Terranova."[15] What exactly did this mean? In redefining herself as woman from Terranova, María challenged the idea that she was from Angola or São Tomé. Her decision to identify as a person from Terranova is fascinating because the term itself does not refer to an African location or polity. After all, *Terranova*, literally meaning "new land," was a Portuguese label for the coastline west of Benin. María's parents would not have claimed such an ethnic marker in their home society.

For María, the concept of "Terranova" linked her to a distinct linguistic community during her years in Puebla. Perhaps her identification as a non-Angolan woman was associated to her time aboard a slave ship in São Tomé or its barracks. Slave traders sailing from the island usually carried captives from West Central Africa and Lower Guinea on the same ship. Henry Lovejoy and Olatunji Ojo note that the term "Terranova" generally identified Yoruba speakers in the late sixteenth and early seventeenth centuries, but was otherwise malleable.[16] Africans in Spanish America who identified as "Lucumí" were often equated with "Terranova" people.[17] In any case, a small Terranova community, consisting of a few dozen enslaved men and women, implanted itself in Puebla during the early seventeenth century.[18] They were outnumbered hundreds of times over by Kikongo and Kimundu-speaking West Central Africans, which perhaps explains why their identification as Yoruba speakers mattered a great deal. Very few members of this distinctive community managed to secure their freedom prior to mid-century, making María's case all the more significant.[19]

---

14 AHJP, Exp. 1260, 27r.   15 AHJP, Exp. 1260, 6r, 15r, 46r.

16 Henry Lovejoy and Olatunji Ojo, "'Lucumí,' 'Terranova,' and the Origins of the Yoruba Nation," *Journal of African History* 56, no. 3 (Nov. 2015), 358–359, 364–368. People from Yoruba-speaking communities received "Lucumí" or "Terranova" designations depending on the viccissitudes of state expansion and the transatlantic slave trade. Captives labeled as "Terranova" were acquired between the Volta River and Lagos channel, but could also include "other non-Yoruba groups such as Popo, Whyday, Allada and beyond."

17 For one such Lucumí community, see Rachel Sarah O'Toole, "To Be Free and Lucumí: Ana de la Calle and Making African Diaspora Identities in Colonial Peru," in Sherwin K. Bryant, Rachel Sarah O'Toole, and Ben Vinson III, eds., *Africans to Spanish America: Expanding the Diaspora* (Urbana: University of Illinois Press, 2012), 73–94.

18 I have located thirty-six references to "Terranova" people in Puebla's notarial and parish archives. Of those references, twenty-six are found in the period 1610–1650. For Terranova communities in early colonial Cuba, see Alejandro de la Fuente, *Havana and the Atlantic in the Sixteenth Century* (Chapel Hill: University of North Carolina Press, 2008), 106.

19 AGNP, Not. 4, Box 174, 1650 Testaments, 83r–84v.

Table 6.1 *Manumission of María de Terranova compared to other prices*

Category	Price (Pesos)	Year	Observations
Total price for Terranova's sale (includes two children, sick adult slave, storefront)	2,000	1626	1
Price of Terranova's letter of manumission	600	1627	1
Avg. price of manumission for Africans	309	1620–1665	14
Avg. price of manumission, all slaves	221	1600–1690	65
House (stone and adobe walls)	420	1633	1
Purchase of African slave (new arrival)	411	1630, 1635	509
Purchase of American-born slave (creole)	311	1630, 1635	101
Textile mill overseer (annual salary)	500	1622	1
Storefront lease with storage (annual price)	60	1610–1650	4

Source: AGNP Notarial Database, 1600–1690. AHJP, Exp. 1260. AHJP, Exp. 1235.

In his 1627 lawsuit against his former slave, Julian Bautista bitterly noted that he had been forced to purchase a three-member family (in addition to a sick slave and a decrepit storefront) simply to secure María's commercial services. Bautista's complaint highlights his own middling position in Puebla society. Unlike his aristocratic contemporaries in the Spanish municipal council, Bautista was a seafood vendor. Expending 2,000 pesos to purchase an enslaved family represented a monumental purchase at the time (see Table 6.1). He would have certainly preferred to purchase María alone. Thus, the sale of the latter's family can be read from two vantage points. Either María convinced Bautista to maintain her family intact in return for her commercial abilities, or Cristóbal de Malla, her previous owner, forced an inconvenient slave purchase on a naïve fish vendor.

María's success in retaining her family was likely a combination of both. In Bautista's own words, María had proven to be quite "adept in the ministry of fish, which she always sold for Manuel de Rojas, her first owner, and for the mentioned Cristobal de Malla."[20] Both of her former masters had "gathered and acquired such a large sum of pesos" from her sales that they were able to return to Spain as wealthy, successful men. A glorious return to the motherland was the dream of most Spaniards, but the reality of only a handful. Under the expectation that María would produce similar profits for him, Bautista purchased the enslaved fish vendor along with her two daughters.

---

20 AHJP, Exp. 1260, 9r–10r. "La dicha Maria negra por ser diestra en el ministerio del pescado que siempre bendio a Manuel de Rojas su primer amo y al dicho Xpoval de Malla se les avia seguido dello mucho interes y aprovechamyento en gran suma de pesos de modo que fue parte para que los dichos dos sus amos aquiriesen y Juntasen caudal con que se fueron a España."

A mere six months later, María managed to secure her freedom. According to Bautista, María had pleaded her case by "offering to work better and more willingly [as a free woman] than as a slave."[21] In May 1627, she received her freedom papers from a reluctant Bautista. In the *carta de libertad*, Bautista noted that he was freeing her for 600 pesos.[22] In order to secure her freedom papers, María sought the assistance of a freed African named Francisco Carmona. This was a wise decision. Carmona had already purchased his own freedom, in addition to that of his wife and his granddaughter in 1615 (see Chapter 5). He was exceptionally well prepared when it came to negotiating letters of manumission. Together, María and Carmona paid Bautista 500 pesos in cash. This money presumably constituted her life savings. She also agreed to complement that sum with an additional 100 pesos to be paid over six months.[23] María committed to paying off the remaining amount by selling fish for Bautista in the marketplace. As seen in Chapter 5, labor-extending clauses such as these were quite common in seventeenth-century manumission documents.

In addition, Bautista imposed a very specific restriction on María's freedom: "Never and in no manner, is she to sell fish of her own, nor a third party's, even free of charge. Instead, she is to continue selling only my product as she has done up to now," he stated.[24] After fulfilling her debt to Bautista, María would receive the respectable salary of 6 pesos per month in addition to her daily meals, but only if she remained under her former master's nominal authority. Judging from the ensuing judicial case, it is clear that María had no intention of following these restrictions. Instead, she quickly began a commercial relationship with Domingo de Olivera, a 26-year-old Spanish merchant, who supplied her with the fish she so expediently sold in Puebla's central plaza. María and her new supplier had known each other for three years (prior to her manumission), raising further questions about her intent to abide by Bautista's restrictive clause. Feeling betrayed, Bautista presented a criminal complaint against María only two weeks after having freed her.[25] The former owner claimed that he had explicitly outlined María's post-manumission obligations and she had failed to follow them. Therefore, her freedom papers were to be declared void.

As a non-elite slave owner, Julian Bautista de Cabrera attempted to profit from the xenophobic climate that the viceroys and governing bodies of New Spain had instilled since the slave repression of 1612. To curtail María's autonomy, he specifically cited the 1623 ordinance promulgated by the

21 Ibid., 3r–3v.   22 Ibid., 1r–2r.   23 AHJP, Exp. 1260, 1r–2r.   24 Ibid.
25 Ibid., 1r–3v. María was formally awarded her freedom on 31 May 1627. Bautista entered his first
   formal complaint against his ex-slave on June 12 that same year.

Marqués de Gelves.[26] "In conformity with this kingdom's ordinance for good government as stipulated by the lord viceroys, the aforementioned [slave] cannot live or negotiate on her own, instead she should be precisely compelled to serve a Spaniard for her daily wage," Bautista noted.[27] From his perspective, if María were to remain free, then he alone should be the recipient of her labor. Puebla's local justice agreed. Elite Spaniards rarely needed to resort to such strategies, since their wealth enabled them to easily purchase slaves at a moment's notice. However, Bautista was little more than a supplier of seafood, and his former slave's competition was threatening his very own livelihood.

In response to her former owners' threats, María hired the attorney Cristóbal Guillén to represent her before the city's courts and justices. In the ninety-six pages of litigation that ensued, they never took more than a day to respond to Bautista's accusations. The case opens a fascinating window into the complex relationships between ex-slaves and their legal representatives in colonial Spanish America.[28] Since the privilege "of making contracts and sworn statements" was typically the domain of free people, Poblano slaves rarely surface in judicial disputes of this nature. An enslaved person could appeal to the authorities for the right to seek a new owner or to be reunited with a spouse, but this was not the case with María.[29] As a recently liberated person, María managed to secure competent legal counsel. Rather than submit to her former owner's demands, she and her attorney presented the following response:

The act of liberty . . . is so pure in its nature and so perfect that it admits no conditions, nor has any doubts, and those that have been placed on me should be removed and taken away since Julian Bautista did not offer a liberal manumission [for me]. Instead, I executed the rescue of my person, satisfying and giving far more . . . than was necessary.

By emphasizing that she had purchased her freedom outright, María argued that her manumission could not be conditioned by her former master's demands. She specifically targeted the "conditions" that Bautista attempted

26 Cope, *The Limits*, 21; Colin A. Palmer, *Slaves of the White God: Blacks in Colonial Mexico: 1570–1650* (Cambridge, MA: Harvard University Press, 1976), 135–141.

27 AHJP, Exp. 1260, 9r–10r.

28 Michelle McKinley, *Fractional Freedoms: Slavery, Intimacy, and Legal Mobilization in Colonial Lima, 1600–1700* (Cambridge: Cambridge University Press, 2016); Brian Owensby, "How Juan and Leonor Won Their Freedom: Litigation and Liberty in Seventeenth-Century Mexico," *Hispanic American Historical Review* 85, no. 1 (2005), 39–79; Frank Proctor, *Damned Notions of Liberty: Slavery, Culture and Power in Colonial Mexico, 1640–1769* (Albuquerque: University of New Mexico Press, 2010), 166–185.

29 AGNP, Not. 4, Box 152, August 1635, 1355r–1356r; AHJP, Exp. 4840; AGN, Bienes Nacionales, Box 131, Exp. 1.

to impose on her freedom as unnatural limitations that corrupted the very concept of liberty. This strategy had a more practical objective: to allow María to continue selling fish in Puebla's central market during the summer of 1627.

Bautista understood that the very foundation of María's growing independence rested on the profits she was able to generate as a fish vendor. Ever since receiving her *carta de libertad* on 31 May 1627, María had continued plying her trade in the public plaza, but she was clearly no longer in the employ of Bautista. Instead, she had become her ex-owner's competitor. María excused this behavior by noting that she had done so since attaining her freedom only "in order to sustain herself with it and pay His Majesty's royal tribute."[30] This last reference to her fiscal obligations was a tactic commonly used by free individuals of African descent, who were continually portrayed as tax evaders.[31] María was well aware of these stereotypes and aggressively countered any insinuation that they might apply to her situation. In mid-July 1627, she and Guillén stated that even the viceroys' ordinances could limit neither "human actions nor the commerce [undertaken] by those of my color."[32] And so, María continued selling her fish well into the rainy months of the Puebla summer.

If Julian Bautista's intentions were to limit his former slave's "human actions" and interactions, then his strategy was simply deficient. María countered with too many allies. Her social network included Spanish merchants, mestizo fish vendors, African freedmen, her own daughters, and the dozens of clients who purchased from her stall, to say nothing of her legal counsel. Among the witnesses called forth to testify about María's activities was Alonso Pérez, a Spaniard who claimed to have known her for fourteen years.[33] Joseph de Arauz, a *mestizo* fish vendor, confirmed that he had known María for more than eight years, while the shoemaker Gonzalo del Puerto also admitted their acquaintance for the same span. All the witnesses acknowledged that María sold fish for Domingo de Olivera, but noted that this had only taken place after she secured her freedom.

In September 1627, Bautista made a final, desperate appeal to limit María's activities. His commercial interests had been negatively affected by María's competition during the entire summer. Unable to put up with the situation any longer, Bautista suggested that she should sustain herself in a different branch of commerce. "She can occupy herself in selling cooked meat, or honey, or fruit, and have other sources of revenue as other black women do," he protested.[34] Bautista touched on an important point.

---

30 AHJP, Exp. 1260, 22v.

31 Ben Vinson III, *Bearing Arms for His Majesty: The Free-Colored Militia in Colonial Mexico* (Stanford, CA: Stanford University Press, 2001), 132–134.

32 AHJP, Exp. 1260, 11r–12r.   33 Ibid., 27r–46v.   34 Ibid., 25–26r.

By the late 1620s and early 1630s, itinerant slaves and freedmen reaped considerable profits by selling tax-free "sugar, cacao and other species" on the street.[35] In any case, it is quite clear that María had succeeded in continuing her profitable trade in Puebla's central plaza. The city's justices tired of the case and remitted Bautista's claims to the Real Audiencia, New Spain's supreme governing council. The last surviving piece of evidence for the lawsuit is dated 1 October 1627. By this point, the case had reached the office of Don Cristóbal de la Mota y Osorio, Secretary of the King's Chamber.[36] Both parties were instructed to present themselves before the Secretary in Mexico City. Frustratingly, the documentary record does not reveal Mota y Osorio's final determination. All we are left with is the defendant's presence among the most powerful men of the viceroyalty of New Spain, along with her former master. Only four months before, María had been Bautista's human property. Now, she was his foremost foe and competition.

Chiles and Afro-Indigenous Interactions

Not all enslaved people encountered such determined resistance to their freedom. Most, however, did require extensive social networks in order to carve a place for themselves in the colonial economy. Only recently have historians begun to consider Afro-indigenous interactions in Mexico as avenues toward family formation, financial stability, and commercial success.[37] Commercial interactions of this sort dated back to Puebla's early days. Maria Elena Martínez notes that, in the mid-1550s, Afro-Poblanos "discovered that they could buy maize, wheat, chickens, salt, fish and various other products from the native population and then sell them to

---

35 Yovana Celaya Nández, *Alcabalas y situados: Puebla en el sistema fiscal imperial 1638–1742* (Mexico City: El Colegio de México, 2010), 90 n. 45. In 1632, the merchant Francisco Gómez complained that these *alcabala*-free sales were illicit and hurting his business. "[N]egros, negras, mulatos y chinos" and even a few Spaniards participated in this operation. Gómez even accused priests (who were exempt from paying the sales tax) of partaking in these commercial activities by way of their slaves.

36 AHJP, Exp. 1260, 46r.

37 Robert Schwaller, "'Mulata, hija de negro y india': Afro-Indigenous *Mulatos* in Early Colonial Mexico," *Journal of Social History* 44, no. 3 (Spring 2011), 889–914; Matthew Restall, *The Black Middle: Africans, Mayas and Spaniards in Colonial Yucatan* (Stanford, CA: Stanford University Press, 2009), 112–152; Paul Lokken, "Marriage as Slave Emancipation in Seventeenth-Century Rural Guatemala," *The Americas* 58, no. 2 (Oct. 2001), 175–200; Norma Angélica Castillo Palma, *Cholula: Sociedad mestiza en ciudad india* (Mexico City: Universidad Autónoma de Metropolitana/Plaza y Valdés, 2008), 358–380, 400–415; Patrick Carroll, "Black-Native Relations and the Historical Record in Colonial Mexico" in Matthew Restall, ed., *Beyond Black and Red: African Native Relations in Colonial Latin America* (Albuquerque: University of New Mexico Press, 2005), 252.

Spaniards for a decent profit."[38] These transactions for chickens or fish were worth fractions of a peso and certainly were not notarized, but their low monetary value does not mean that they were socially insignificant.

In a city of 100,000 people, even the smallest exchange could amount to thousands of pesos over time. Approximately 34,095 *castas* (black and racially mixed) adult parishioners and 14,500 indigenous counterparts lived in Puebla in 1681. Parish priests calculated the number of Spanish parishoners at 19,178.[39] The potential for Afro-indigenous commercial interactions, therefore, was immense. These demographic considerations are central to explaining how and why successful enslaved and free people constructed commercial alliances in the marketplace. Of course, these interactions also extended to Spanish councilmen, clergy and wholesale merchants. Perhaps no case illustrates this market dynamic better than that of Felipe Monsón y Mojica and his indigenous wife, Juana María de la Cruz.[40]

Like most freedmen, slavery had played a destructive role in Felipe Monsón's upbringing – one that he was loath to recall. As an elderly man drafting his final will in 1682, Monsón was unable or unwilling to name his parents or relatives. Instead, he repeatedly claimed to be a native son of Puebla and a member of the San José parish.[41] Monsón defined himself as a *vecino*, a free man, and less consistently as a *mulato*. At times, he claimed to be a *pardo*, a term of respect generally associated with free people of partial African descent. He also identified as "a vendor of chile peppers and other legumes in this city's public plaza," and it was this by this *chilero* identity that he was most commonly known in the marketplace. Yet in framing his testament, Monsón focused on his relationship with his wife and her role in his liberation:

As ordered by our Holy Mother Church, I am legitimately married and veiled with Juana María de la Cruz, with whom I am making married life.

And when we contracted matrimony the aforementioned did not bring a dowry, nor did I have any capital as I was a slave of Joseph de Higueras at the time ... furthermore my wife earned the amount of money with which I was freed.

---

38 Martínez, *Genealogical Fictions: Limpieza de Sangre, Religion and Gender in Colonial Mexico* (Stanford, CA: Stanford University Press, 2008), 147. The municipal council sought to eradicate these interactions.

39 Peter Gerhard, "Un censo de la diócesis de Puebla en 1681," *Historia Mexicana* 30, no. 4 (Apr.–Jun. 1981), 534–536. These figures are for *comulgantes*, individuals over the age of 12 or 14 who could receive communion. The city's total population in the 1680s would have been close to 100,000 people. Based on the baptismal data seen in Chapter 5, I tentatively estimate that 5,000 to 10,000 slaves lived in Puebla in 1681. Further demographic work is needed to corroborate this rough approximation.

40 For an in-depth examination of this couple, see Sierra Silva, "From Chains to Chiles."

41 AGNP, Not. 4, Box 218, Testaments 1682, 15r–17v.

Monsón would never again allude to his enslavement, nor would his wife. Even when both produced a joint testament in September 1682, this single reference to his past as a slave would be omitted.[42] Six years later, when dictating her own testament de la Cruz once again opted to not recall her husband's bondage. These were deliberate and empowering decisions.

As with most family histories of enslaved people, the silences of the archival record conceal a lifetime of labor and abuse, but they also conceal love, companionship and friendship. Precise details on how Monsón and de la Cruz met or when she freed him have eluded this investigation. The baptismal records for the Sagrario parish indicate that in 1657, the couple served as godparents for Nicolás, the freeborn son of a *mestiza* woman and an enslaved man.[43] Monsón may still have been a slave at this point, but the baptismal entry does not elaborate on this. All we can state with certainty is that he and his spouse chose to shoulder the responsibility of godparenthood for baby Nicolás. Monsón and de la Cruz never had biological children of their own, so their appearance in baptismal registers is limited to their participation as godparents.[44] During the 1670s, however, they adopted and raised two orphan boys, Felipe and Matías Monsón.[45]

By her own account, Juana María de la Cruz had been raised in the Santa Ana neighborhood, a peripheral, indigenous area of the city.[46] She claimed to be an indigenous woman, a *vecina* of Puebla, and the "legitimate daughter" of Juan de la Cruz and Pascuala de la Cruz. Her upbringing in the Santa Ana barrio mattered a great deal. During the mid-seventeenth century, the Santa Ana barrio had been incorporated into the San José parish, perhaps providing a meeting point for the couple. Local records show that Afro-indigenous interactions were quite common in San José. Urban indigenous leaders known as *fiscales* served as witness in dozens of Afro-Poblano weddings.[47] According to Lidia Gómez García, the Nahuatl-language "Anales de fiscales de San José" indicate that during the 1640s "a new set of relationships began, first and foremost with the Spanish, mestizo and mulatto parishoners of San José" who embarked on the construction of a chapel for the parish's indigenous population (*capilla de indios*) during the 1640s.[48] This neighborhood on the city's northern limits was

---

42 AHJP, Exp. 2463/1935, 221r–229v.   43 ASMP, *Bautizos de negros y mulatos, 1654–1658*, 73v.

44 ASMP, *Bautizos de negros y mulatos, 1677–1688*, 73v, 95v.

45 AHJP, Exp. 2463, 75v, 216r. The boys were the designated heirs for the Monsón de la Cruz estate.

46 AHJP, Exp. 2463, 221r.

47 APSJ, *Libro de matrimonios de morenos, 1629–1657*, 21r–46v; APSJ, *Libro de matrimonios de mulatos, negros y chinos, 1658–1692*, 12v–17v. One particularly active *fiscal*, Marcos Juan, served as a witness to at least twenty marriages involving Afro-Poblanos in San José between 1641 and 1649. Numerous other indigenous officials consistently participated as witnesses in Afro-Poblano formal unions throughout the 1650s and 1660s, thereby strengthening parish and barrio affiliations.

48 Lidia E. Gómez García, "El impacto de la secularización de las parroquias en los pueblos indios del obispado de Puebla, siglos XVII–XVIII," in *Palafox, Obra y Legado: Memorias del ciclo de conferencias*

a site of intensive interaction between free and enslaved people of varied backgrounds, who increasingly identified as members of a highly localized religious community. In turn, Juana María de la Cruz and Felipe Monsón's identities as San José parishioners overlapped with their commercial activities in the marketplace downtown.

By purchasing her husband's freedom, de la Cruz enabled him to formalize their business contracts before any notary. Other indigenous women in Puebla helped secure their husbands' freedom after their marriages.[49] This was the case of Francisca Juana, another indigenous woman with deep ties to the Santa Ana church and San José barrio. In her 1683 testament, she noted her marriage to Juan Martín, a free *pardo*, whom she had married while he was still enslaved.[50] As his legitimate wife, "she could not enter into contractual dealings without the permission of her husband."[51] However, Martín would have struggled to enter contracts of any kind as an enslaved person. Upon securing his freedom, however, he could represent the family's interests, secure loans for their mule pack business and inherit property. Identifying trustworthy men to carry the family business was an important notarial strategy among women in Puebla.

Other free women also sought male representatives to vouch for their interests. For instance, in 1664, Juana de Aguilar, a free *parda* and the owner of bakery, presented a statement in which she recognized a 130-peso debt in favor of Francisco López Osorio, the owner of a peanut shop.[52] This was the cost of renting a house, which López Osorio had done in Aguilar's name. There is no indication that Aguilar had to resort to a male figure to run her business. As a notarial strategy, she may have simply found it convenient to send a man to whom she was not married to represent her at a notarial office.

In the case of Monsón and de la Cruz, the freedman soon became the public (read, notarial) persona for his wife. Between 1660 and 1671, he entered at least four debt contracts worth over 5,000 pesos to invest in agricultural products for his stall in the public plaza.[53] On Wednesdays, Monsón and his wife could also take some of their wares to a smaller market (*mercado y tianguiz*), which was located in front of the San José parish

---

sobre la vida y obra de Juan de Palafox y Mendoza (Puebla: Instituto Municipal de Arte y Cultura de Puebla, 2011), 224–225. This is my translation of Gómez's work, and I am responsible for any errors or misinterpretations of the original.

49 For instance, Magdalena Luisa, a noblewoman from Tlaxcala (*india principal de la provincia de Tlaxcala*), spent 600 pesos to free her husband, Antonio, an enslaved man from Bengal. AGNP, Not. 4, Box 138, 1630 June, no folio (1630/06/10).

50 AGNP, Not. 4, Box 220, 1683 Testaments, no folio (1683/03/01).

51 Kathryn Burns, *Into the Archive: Writing and Power in Colonial Peru* (Durham, NC: Duke University Press, 2010), 116.

52 AGNP, Not. 4, Box 194, 1664 December, 1246r.

53 AGNP, Not. 4, Box 188, 1660 May, 506v, 518r; Box 194, 1664 February, 183r; Box 205, 1671 May, 190r.

church.[54] For most of the 1660s and up until the 1680s, the couple specialized in procuring and selling chile peppers, a crucial staple of the Poblano
diet. They competed with male and female *chileros* of all racial backgrounds
who secured their product from Huexotzingo, Acatzingo, Calpan, Cholula,
and Atlixco.[55] The sheer number of references to chile cultivation in the
1660s and 1670s counters the suggestion that its consumption declined
during the colonial period.[56] In Jesuit haciendas, chile was the most labor-
intensive and expensive crop to cultivate after sugar cane.[57] During the dry
season (November–March), agricultural estates in nearby Atlixco sent dried
and packaged peppers in reed mats (*petates*) for sale by specialized vendors
in the Puebla marketplace.[58] Monsón and de la Cruz stored their wares just
off the central plaza, in a room sheltered by the city portals.[59] Based on
the inventories produced in 1682 and 1688, they did rather well for themselves. So well, in fact, that they operated as urban creditors for several rural
associates.

When Monsón died in 1684, several parish priests had outstanding
debts in his favor. Father Sebastián Sánchez, the curate of San Juan Agua-
catlán, regularly supplied Monsón with crates of eggs, in addition to
orange blossom water (presumably for confectionery purposes). Upon her
husband's death, de la Cruz requested that Sánchez satisfy his financial
obligations to the estate. In his response to "Señora Juana Moxica," Sánchez
asked the widow to accept his pawned set of silver plates (which the couple
already held) as payment for his debt. In addition, Dr. Juan González
of Tlatlauquitepeque, Father Joseph Zurita of Suchipango, and Father
Diego de Mirón of Ayutla, were also indebted to Monsón's widow. These
clergymen had supplied the Monsón de la Cruz household with essential
products from Puebla's hinterland. Once more, these rural-urban networks
are suggestive of the commercial potential that slaves, freedmen and their
kin could tap under the right circumstances.

In colloquial terms, Monsón and de la Cruz became Puebla's premier
chileros. In 1683, the city's indigenous chronicler identified him as "a

---

54 Carlos Montero Pantoja, *El Barrio de San José* (Puebla: BUAP/Instituto de Ciencias Sociales y
   Humanidades, 2007), 20. "Spaniards, Indians, and other people [came by] to sell different merchandise" in the San José market.
55 AGNP, Not. 4, Box 197, 1665 January, 115r; Box 194, 1664 November, 1180v; Box 1689, 1660
   October, 1091r; AGNP, Not. 3, Box 111, 1660 Testaments, 113v. Juan Crisostomo identified as a
   free mulatto chile vendor (*mulato libre tratante en chile*). The indigenous woman, Francisca, worked
   as "chilera in the Santa Ana barrio." Juan Gacho, likely a Spaniard, also identified as a chile vendor.
56 Janet Long-Solís, "El abastecimiento de chile en el mercado de la ciudad México-Tenochtitlán en el
   siglo XVI," *Historia Mexicana* 34, no. 4 (Apr.–Jun. 1985), 713–714.
57 Ursula Ewald, *Estudios sobre la hacienda colonial en México. Las propiedades rurales del colegio Espíritu Santo
   en Puebla* (Wiesbaden: Franz Steiner Verlag, 1976), 16–19. Chiles eroded soil nutrients rapidly, so
   that a given plot could only be cultivated once every 10–12 years. This necessarily raised their price.
58 Ibid.; Long-Solís, "El abastacimiento," 713–714.   59 AHJP, Exp. 2463, 170r.

mulatto named Felipe Monso[n] y Mojica, the chilero" (*se mulato ytoca felipe monso y mojica chilero*). A few years after Monsón's passing, de la Cruz became "la chilera." The 1688 inventory of the latter's goods helps explain why the couple earned their monikers. In what turned out to be a massive listing, the executors found no fewer than 9,250 pounds of chile ancho, chile jamanqui, and chile pasilla in addition to fifteen crates of copal, ninety-four salt petates, and various measures of ayacote and chichimeco beans, shrimp, tobacco, and achiote. In an earlier will, Monsón and de la Cruz stipulated that they held more than 2,000 pesos in produce alone.[60]

For this merchant couple, success in the marketplace was directly tied to their creditworthiness, which, in turn, was correlated to the real estate they owned. Monsón and de la Cruz owned a large private residence in the San José neighborhood. Time and again, Monsón assured his creditors that he could put up a 12,000-peso house as collateral for his obligations. The house, complete with fruit orchards, stables, and a private well, would have also served as the focal point for the racially diverse barrio. The couple further owned a semi-private *temazcal*, a prehispanic steamhouse "in which people continually bathed."[61] Such an edifice is suggestive of the Afro-indigenous cultural fusion that defined their household and social circle. Moreover, it is likely that they also earned a significant side income by charging for access to the *temazcal*.[62]

Success in the marketplace enabled Monsón and de la Cruz to become urban patrons. Douglas Cope understands urban patron-client networks as relationships of dependency in which Spaniards typically operated as employers, protectors, and holders of financial resources for a broad, multiracial population.[63] The Monsón de la Cruz case suggests that people of African descent, even ex-slaves, could rise to such economic and social prominence within a single generation. By the early 1680s, Monsón was wealthy enough to commission the work of two indigenous master artisans for the Expiración confraternity. This was a singular achievement. The brotherhood was esteemed among people of African descent by 1631, when Marta Rodríguez bequeathed four paintings to "the confraternity of the *mulatos*."[64] It was housed in the chapel of the Limpia Concepción Hospital, an institution with ties to the convent of the same name. The leading members of the confraternity (*cofrades*) committed to leading religious

---

60 AGNP, Not. 4, Box 218, 1682 Testaments, 76r. To compare the opulence of the urban colonial context versus that of the rural, see the case of Capt. Lázaro del Canto in Restall, *Black Middle*, 153–156.

61 AHJP, Exp. 2463, 103r.

62 Patricio Hidalgo Nuchera, "Los 'malos usos' y la reglamentación de los temascales públicos mexicanos (1686–1691)," *Anuario de Estudios Americanos* 69, no. 1 (Jan.–Jun. 2012), 95–97. Men and women of African descent also owned *temazcales* in Mexico City.

63 Cope, *The Limits*, 91–93. 64 AHJP, Exp. 1622, 1r–4v.

processions and outfitting their members with tunics and candles at their own expense. Not all succeeded, however. Monsón, by contrast, worked his way up the brotherhood's ranks, despite not appearing in the Expiración leadership positions in 1658 or 1664.[65]

In October 1682, Felipe Monsón and Bartolomé de Santander appeared before a local notary as free men, *vecinos* of Puebla, and head administrators of the Expiración confraternity.[66] They intended to press Diego Lázaro and Juan Lázaro, an Indian father-and-son team of woodworkers, to complete a "white side altar for an image of Our Lord Christ of the Expiration." As *mayordomos* (administrators), they had commissioned and paid the artisans 424 pesos for the altar earlier that year. Now, wielding a binding notarized document, they expected the artisans to fulfill their obligations to the confraternity.

Commercial success enabled Afro-Poblano freedmen to participate in a number of parallel communities (militias, confraternities, merchant groups) that were not defined by slavery. In 1683, only a year before his death, Monsón was charged with organizing Puebla's free-colored militia to rescue Nueva Veracruz from Laurens de Graaf's terrible raid. Monsón became captain of the *pardo* militia, and Lorenzo de Tapia led the *moreno* unit.[67] Ben Vinson has demonstrated that the May 1683 sack led to a sweeping reorganization of New Spain's free-colored militias.[68] Although the campaign to save the port was unsuccesful, Monsón's rise to military captain speaks to the trust he enjoyed among elite and common Poblanos. In subsequent years, other men of African descent would claim similar leadership positions.[69]

By the time of his death in 1684, Monsón had risen to become one of the most prestigious men of African descent in Puebla. Born enslaved, he died a rich man, a beloved spouse, the leader of a religious confraternity, and the captain of the city's *pardo* militia. Unlike many of his Afro-Poblano contemporaries, Monsón never owned slaves of his own.[70] For this man

---

65 AGNP, Not. 3, Box 116, 1664 March, 126v. Juan Zerón, Joseph de los Reyes, and Joseph de Córdova were removed from their leadership positions in 1664.

66 AGNP, Not. 4, Box 219, 925r–926r.

67 Camilla Townsend, ed. and transl., *Here in This Year: Seventeenth-Century Nahuatl Annals of the Tlaxcala-Puebla Valley* (Stanford, CA: Stanford University Press, 2010), 124–127.

68 Vinson, *Bearing Arms*, 29–31, 246 n. 84.

69 The ideological implications of this Afro-Poblano military service are considerable. In 1612, Spanish militiamen armed themselves against the threat of black rebellion. By the early eighteenth century, Afro-Poblano militiamen "were asked to protect the cathedral, jails, hospitals, and administrative structures." Vinson, *Bearing Arms*, 29–31.

70 For Afro-Poblanos as slave owners, see the following cases for Antonia de Jesus, María de Jesús, Juana de Aguilar, Ana de Santiago, Juan Martin and Diego de Cobos. The cases are all located in AGNP, Notaría 4. See Box 165, 1640 Testamentos, 1r–2v; Box 174, Testamentos 1650, 83v–84r; Box 194, 1664 December, 1246r–1246; Box 209, 1675 Testamentos, 85r–86r; Box 220, no folio

and his wife, status, power, and influence were intimately tied to the marketplace and parish. Monsón and de la Cruz agreed that upon one's death, the other would fund a chaplaincy and an annual mass in their memory. She honored his request.[71] Ultimately, this case study proves that enslaved and free people successfully operated "across different arenas of social experience" in colonial Puebla.[72] By weaving resilient social networks in the public market, San José parish, and Limpia Concepción Hospital, the couple successfully navigated the city within the parameters of colonial rule. Many others would do the same.

Men, Commerce and Marriage

In 1694, the freedman Marcos Pardave presented himself before a public notary to dictate his testament. Although bound by the formulaic narrative of Spanish Catholicism, Pardave crafted a narrative of his life that accentuated his success in commerce, his children's inalienable rights to his material rewards, and others' obligations to his estate. He appropriated terms of honor as a free *pardo*, a Puebla-born man, and a *vecino* when referring to himself. When referring to his sons and daughters, he used no caste label of any sort. Instead, Marcos de Pardave described them as the "legitimate children" of a "legitimate husband and wife."[73] Pardave could claim honor as a lawfully wedded man, but also because he earned the social respect of his contemporaries as a merchant in Puebla's *baratillo*.

Paradoxically, the *baratillo* was not a space traditionally associated with notions of honor and legitimacy. Stolen or damaged goods were often sold there. Within the urban colonial economy, these markets were also important points of interaction for less affluent members of society. However, their poor reputation should not discount the profits or opportunities found within them. Andrew Konove finds that Mexico City's *baratillo* "offered an outlet for the import merchants of the Mexico City Consulado – the exclusive merchant guild – to sell damaged or subpar goods, and members of the elite themselves bought and sold clothing and household furnishing in the Baratillo."[74]

In Puebla, the *baratillo* was also the site to acquire indigenous clothing from the viceroyalty's southern limits. Pardave's inventory of hundreds of

---

(1683/03/01); Box 223, 1685 January, 17r. For a nuanced discussion slave ownership among people of African descent, see Danielle Terrazas Williams, "Capitalizing Subjects: Free African-Descended Women of Means in Xalapa, Veracruz during the Long Seventeenth Century" (Ph.D. diss., Duke University, 2013), 273–339.

71 AHJP, Exp. 2463, 72v; AGN, Bienes Nacionales, Vol. 1592, Exp. 13. The chaplaincy was still operant in 1851.

72 Borucki, *Shipmates to Soldiers*, 3–4, 85–98.

73 AHJP, Exp. 2551, 1v.   74 Konove, "On the Cheap," 251.

pesos worth of silk and cotton *huipiles*, *chapaneco* cloths and Chinese "ruan" indicates that he had tapped into Mixtec, Zapotec and Maya trade routes that intersected with the imports brought by the Manila Galleon.[75] Pardave catered to a broad, multiracial urban population that demanded indigenous and foreign items of clothing at competitive prices. This unacknowledged dynamic between indigenous producers and Afro-Poblano vendors (*tratantes*) suggests that the roles of people of African descent in colonial commerce must be reevaluated from the *baratillo* and not merely from the slave market.

In his testament, Pardave asked his executors to recover several debts in his favor, and these reveal fascinating glimpses into the life of a *baratillo* merchant. Miguel Limón, who was described as a vendor (*tratante en el baratillo*), owed him 100 pesos.[76] Pardave had given him this amount to purchase goods, whose profits they would split equally. The freedman had a similar 100-peso investment with Joseph Vazquez, for the "goods and merchandise I gave him." Antonio Camacho, an itinerant mestizo merchant, owed Pardave another 400 pesos. The latter provided other *baratillo* vendors with hundreds of pesos of merchandise at a time. His debtors ranged from the humble owner of a small portable stand (*mesilla*) to more established merchants such as Joseph de las Casas.[77]

If Pardave behaved like a successful merchant, he was never far removed from his obligations as a free Afro-Poblano of means. Like many other free(d) people, he operated as an intermediary for slaves saving money for their own manumissions. At the time of his death, Pardave held 100 pesos for Magdalena de Salazar, an enslaved woman who trusted him with her life earnings. He ordered his executors to return the money with an additional five percent interest. Pardave also declared that a free *pardo* milliner only owed him "sixty pesos which I lent him in [silver] reales to help with his freedom." Pardave was careful to note that although the original loan amounted to 109 pesos, the milliner had repaid him 49 pesos. He extended loans to other free men of African descent who did not work in the *baratillo* but evidently depended on his financial support.[78] More than financial obligations, these ties speak to a sense of social responsibility. They are also suggestive of Pardave's own experiences as a former slave.

Pardave formed part of an enslaved family that had once belonged to Captain don Alonso de Cordova Bocanegra and Doña María de Cabrera.

75 AHJP, Exp. 2551, 14r–15v.   76 Ibid., 2r–3v.

77 AGI, México, 319, 1r–1v. In 1697, the Puebla municipal council proposed removing "the portable tables" and their attendant vendors for "permanent stands" (*cajones*).

78 AHJP, Exp. 2551, 3r. Pardave loaned different sums of money to three free men of African descent (*pardos libres*): Joseph de Cuellar, a weaver; Antonio Vicente, a tailor; and Pedro de Salazar, the aforementioned milliner.

In fact, Pardave was Cordova's son and slave. Only once did he indirectly acknowledge this conflicted relationship when he claimed to be the "natural son of Captain Don Alonso de Cordova Bocanegra and Maria de Pardave, *morena* slave of Doña María de Cabrera, and later free."[79] By framing his mother as a free *morena*, Marcos distanced his mother, himself, and their lineage from the cultural baggage of slavery. Like Felipe Monsón, he consciously excluded references to his siblings' and his own prior enslavement. However, as we shall see, his older sister, Juana de Cabrera, and his younger brother, Lorenzo de Pardave, also experienced slavery in an elite residence. Fragments of the Pardave Cabrera family history are scattered in at least four Puebla archives, and presumably many more. As isolated references, they present the story of enslaved, atomized individuals. However, when cross-referenced through thousands of notarial, judicial and parochial documents, they paint the story of one family's partial path to freedom.

In December 1675, Doña María de Cabrera listed three mixed-race siblings as her property. Their mother, a black creole woman in her forties, had escaped her mistress's service some time before. Her physical absence as a runaway (*esclava huida*) was not enough to escape the binding paper trail. According to the testament, Juana de Cabrera, Marcos de Pardave, Lorenzo de Pardave and their mother were all destined to become the property of Captain Ignacio de Acosta. Or so they thought. Four years later, the siblings remained together. Their mistress had overcome the disease that had earlier threatened her life. For a fleeting instant, Doña María's impending death had presented an alluring but uncertain future. As she drafted her testament in 1675, she promised freedom to the slave family that resided in her house. Juana de Cabrera would (in theory) have received a manumission letter at her mistress's passing. All these possibilities, fears and uncertainties dissipated with Doña María's restored health.

For better or worse, the Pardave Cabreras would remain enslaved, but united. This relative stability allowed the family to extend its social networks during the following years. In 1679, Marcos de Pardave married María de Jesús, a *castiza* woman.[80] At the altar, de Jesús would have been asked if she was certain she wished to enter a formal union with an enslaved man.[81] She was. Shortly thereafter the couple witnessed the birth of Manuel

---

79 AHJP, Exp. 2551, 1r.

80 ASMP, *Matrimonios de Negros y Mulatos, 1675–1686*, 55r. In seventeenth-century Puebla, *castizas* were understood to be people of mostly Spanish descent, but likely with one mestizo parent. If socially prominent, *castizo* people were at times considered "españoles."

81 APSJ, *Matrimonios de Negros y Mulatos 1629–1657*, 49r–49v. For decades, parish priests were explicitly instructed to ask potential brides if they understood the implication of marrying enslaved men. Priests were to explain that an enslaved groom "was not the owner of his own work, and as such, could not sustain her." The same was true of enslaved brides and free grooms, but greater emphasis was placed on free women entering formal unions.

de Pardave, the first of the couple's six "legitimate children."[82] This label signaled a shifting social and cultural terrain, as enslaved and racially mixed people succesfully claimed honor through familial responsibility.[83] Four years later, Marcos's brother, Lorenzo, followed suit. A trained chairmaker (*sillero*), Lorenzo de Pardave professed his vows to Micaela Gámez, a *mestiza* domestic servant. She, too, agreed to marry an enslaved man.

These were fruitful years for the Pardave Cabrera family. In 1680, the arrival of baby Manuel, the first freeborn member of the family, signaled the beginning of a ten-year process through which almost all of the Pardave Cabreras would attain their liberty. Micaela Gámez and María de Jesús gave birth to eight free infants between 1680 and 1692.[84] As seen in Chapter 5, these children were part of a remarkable transition to a majority freeborn population during the last quarter of the seventeenth century. When Doña María de Cabrera finally passed away in early 1690, the male adults in the family joined their children, nephews and nieces as free people. On April 21, Lorenzo and Marcos each paid 50 pesos for the freedom they had been promised fifteen years before.

For the men of the Pardave Cabrera family, marriage and procreation with free women guaranteed the proliferation of free children. They were not alone. Between 1661 and 1700, enslaved grooms in Puebla's Sagrario parish married free women more than 63 percent of the time.[85] By contrast, enslaved brides married free men only 20 percent of the time. Even fewer slave women married free grooms in the San José parish.[86] The same pattern has been observed for Mexico City.[87] Men of all backgrounds in Puebla

---

82 AHJP, Exp. 2551/2023, 1r–1v. Manuel was the eldest; he was followed by Joseph Esteban, Sebastián de la Cruz, another Joseph, Gertrudis de San Antonio, and Ana María. Their father highlighted that these were his "legitimate children" time and again throughout his will.

83 Sandra Lauderhale Graham, "Honor among Slaves" in *Sex, Shame and Violence: The Faces of Honor in Colonial Latin America* (Albuquerque: University of New Mexico Press, 1998), 206–207. I agree with Graham's suggestion that by looking "for the rules by which slaves and freed persons governed relations among themselves, we discover that the sources (however fragmented) are many and rich."

84 In addition to Marcos and María's six children, I have located references to Joseph Joaquín and Francisca de Pardave, two children born to Lorenzo and Micaela. ASMP, *Bautizos de negros y mulatos, 1677–1688,* 305v; ASAC, *Informaciones de castas y españolas, 1687–1698,* 191v.

85 The following analysis is based on 2,783 marriages involving people of African or Asian descent in Puebla's Sagrario parish for the years 1661 to 1700. ASMP, *Matrimonios de negros y mulatos, 1661–1674, 1675–1686, 1687–1699; Matrimonios de españoles, 1660–1669, 1669–1674, 1674–1679, 1679–1688, 1688–1696, 1696–1702.*

86 AHJP, *Matrimonios de morenos, 1629–1657, Matrimonios de mulatos negros y chinos, 1658–1692, Matrimonios de negros y mulatos, 1692–1739; Matrimonios de españoles, 1629–1655, 1662–1672, 1672–1681.* In the San José parish, more than 50 percent of enslaved grooms managed to marry free brides during the period 1629–1700. By contrast, only 13.5 percent of enslaved brides were able to marry free grooms. Observations based on 650 marriages.

87 Edgar F. Love, "Marriage Patterns of Persons of African Descent in a Colonial Mexico City Parish," *Hispanic American Historical Review* 51, no. 1 (Feb., 1971), 85–87; Cope, *The Limits,* 81–82.

discriminated against enslaved brides, especially if the parish scribes identified them as *negras*. Black women's much higher probability of being enslaved negatively impacted their marital options. Out of the 338 women labeled as *negras* in Sagrario marriages, 296 (88 percent) were slaves. By contrast, 1,262 *mulatas* married in the same parish, but only 239 (19 percent) were enslaved. Among the 30 *pardas* who married in the Sagrario, not a single one was listed as a slave, reinforcing the notion that to claim the *parda* label in Puebla was to claim status as a free person.

Despite being raised in the same household and born to the same mother, Juana de Cabrera confronted a very different marriage pool than her younger siblings, Marcos and Lorenzo. The stigma of bearing enslaved children impacted her directly. In 1675, she was already an enslaved mother. That same year, Juana de Cabrera learned that her mistress intended to donate her daughter, Rosa de Santa Gertrudis, which would ensure that this 2-year-old "white mulata with blonde hair" would serve Doña Ana de Pardave for all the days of her life.[88] Thousands of others enslaved mothers and daughters confronted the same situation throughout the seventeenth century and well into the eighteenth.

I contend that the men of the Pardave Cabrera family made instrumental choices based on their own enslavement and their brides' freedom when it came to selecting their spouses. Of course, these choices were also determined by the trust, affection, convenience, reputation and financial position of the women they married. I acknowledge that it is impossible to state what "combination of affection, sexual desire, family considerations and economic calculation went into this [marital] decision."[89] However, it is clear that matrimony mattered, perhaps especially to enslaved men, because it served as a public, certifying act that validated the freedom of their freeborn children. There was no such incentive for enslaved women. In this regard, men and women experienced significantly different slaveries at the altar.

The men of the Cabrera Pardave family wielded matrimony and free birth against the notarial claims and cultural expectations of their slaveholding mistress and did so effectively. This was not a question of "passing" into a lighter-skinned caste category.[90] Marcos and Lorenzo did not "marry

88 AGNP, Not. 3, Box 129, 1675 December, no folio. AGNP, Not. 4, Box 229, 1690 April, 259r. I have been unable to locate any further archival references to Juana de Cabrera or Rosa de Santa Gertrudis.

89 Cope, *The Limits*, 6–7.

90 Vinson, *Bearing Arms*, 96. Vinson has proven that Afro-Mexican men in *pardo* and *moreno* militias and confraternities generally did not benefit from "passing." Degler's concept of "the mulatto escape hatch" is not operant here because marital choices were made based on the enslavement or freedom of a given woman, not her ascribed race. Degler, *Neither Black nor White: Slavery and Race Relations in Brazil and the United States* (Madison: University of Wisconsin Press, 1971), 224–225.

up" by entering formal unions with *mestiza* and *castiza* women; they married free. As previously discussed, Marcos de Pardave did not shun Afro-Poblanos, free or enslaved, in his daily interactions. In 1687, while still enslaved, he and his wife served as godparents for Francisco Javier, an enslaved child.[91] These social ties with other Afro-Poblanos continued into the next generation as when Marcos's son, Manuel de Pardave, took a free *mulata* woman as his wife in 1698.[92] Based on these family histories, it might be worth interpreting interracial marriage among enslaved people as a liberation strategy rather than the rejection of a given racial or cultural group.

In sum, Marcos de Pardave's life speaks to the everyday experiences of slaves and freedmen in late-seventeenth-century Puebla. The father of six free children, he remained a slave for most of his life. Like most married enslaved men of his time, he was able to marry a free woman. Upon securing his freedom, he quickly became an intermediary for other enslaved people. His stand in the *baratillo* brought him into contact with *pardo* weavers, Spanish ironsmiths, mestizo peddlers and high religious officials. Despite being surrounded by churches, chapels and convents, he did not care to specify in which church he wanted to be buried, nor did he offer donations to any of the numerous religious confraternities in the city. He did, however, own eleven religious paintings, including a large image of the Virgin of Guadalupe. He also donated 1 peso to the "beatification or canonization of Father Gregorio López," whose local cult had attracted a large following since the early seventeenth century. In other words, Marcos de Pardave was deeply rooted in the cultural, social and economic fabric of Puebla de los Ángeles.

Conclusion

Felipe Monsón and Marcos Pardave's commercial interactions in the colonial marketplace are typical of what one would expect to find among vendors and merchants in a bustling Mexican city. However, their success contradicts the image of poverty that historians of Puebla have often projected on the late-seventeenth-century city. One could even argue that a vibrant Afro-indigenous dynamic briefly revitalized the commerce of New Spain's second city. Free and enslaved residents of Puebla respected Monsón and Pardave despite their prior enslavement. Their testaments prove their intimate familiarity with the appropriate forms of respect afforded to many of their contemporaries. Their expansive social networks

---

91 ASMP, *Bautizos de negros y mulatos, 1677–1688*, 360v.
92 ASMP, *Matrimonios de negros y mulatos, 1687–1699*, 178v.

are proof of how free and enslaved men constructed social, commercial and religious ties to improve their lives in any and every manner.

We know much less about commercially active women such as María de Terranova and Juana María de la Cruz. Despite their uncontestable presence in the marketplace and *baratillo* and in the streets of Puebla, the archive has not preserved their credit, debt or other business transactions. María's story survives because she actively contested her enslavement, and that decision disrupted her former owner's livelihood over the course of one summer. We still do not know what kind of fish she sold, how she prepared it or to whom she sold it in the marketplace. We do not know whom she loved. These archival silences limit our understanding of her life, but they cannot negate her affective ties for her daughters or for a small Yoruba-speaking community in the seventeenth-century city.

Epilogue

This study ends in 1706, when thirty-six *obraje* slaves were sent from Don Domingo de Apressa's mill in Puebla to Mixcoac, a small town south of Mexico City.[1] The sale of this male community (only one woman was included in the bill of sale) is extremely significant to the history of slavery in Puebla. The workers represented the city's last enslaved textile workforce. At the time, most of Puebla's remaining *obrajes* were small enterprises, run by nominally free, indebted workers.[2] Yet in 1700 an official had stopped by Apressa's *obraje* to inspect the workforce. He found four free mulattos and twenty-eight enslaved black men, who allegedly had no complaints "because they are treated well and are given food and clothing and the work is not too much." Such a rosy assessment of the *obraje* is not at all surprising, as Apressa was an influential regent with ample power. The inspector made no record of the slaves' ages or specific occupations. Not a single woman was listed in the report. The inspector only noted the separation of Juan Pedro de la Cruz from his wife, who had been sold to a man in Nueva Veracruz. No other mention was made of a married worker, giving the impression that this enslaved workforce was almost entirely composed of enslaved and unattached black men.[3]

In fact, seventeen of Apressa's men married between 1687 and 1699. They were not all black: many of them were labeled as light-skinned men of African descent (*mulatos blancos*) in their marital entries.[4] Most of their wives hailed from Puebla and Tlaxcala and claimed to be *mestizas, mulatas* and *indias*. These women were parishioners of the Sagrario parish and

---

1 Archivo General de Notarías de la Ciudad de México (AGNCM), Not. 692, Vol. 4700, 323r–325v cited in Frank Proctor, *Damned Notions of Liberty: Slavery, Culture and Power in Colonial Mexico, 1640–1769* (Albuquerque: University of New Mexico Press, 2010), 170.

2 Alberto Carabarín Gracia, *El trabajo y los trabajadores del obraje de la ciudad de Puebla, 1700–1710* (Puebla: Cuadernos de la Casa Presno, 1984), 61.

3 AGNP, Not. 4, Box 224, 176r.

4 ASMP, Matrimonios de negros y mulatos, 1687–1699, ff. 18v, 75v, 122v, 126v, 135v, 136v, 139v, 140v, 144v, 169v, 175r, 181r, 187r, 188v, 191r.

mostly free people. At the time of their marriage, the wives named their parents, living and deceased, to the local priest. Notably, their husbands did not. If they did, the priest chose or was persuaded not to record this information. All of Apressa's slaves were listed as single or widowed men, but their family histories were not considered. It was as if confinement in Apressa's mill erased their genealogies from the historical record, much like a transatlantic slaving voyage. What happened to these couples in 1706? Did the men's wives set out for Mixcoac to preserve their marital rights? Did they leave behind their barrios, churches, friends and kin to follow their confined husbands? What of their children? We simply do not know.[5]

We do know that space and family mattered immensely to enslaved people in colonial Puebla. Slaves understood that *obrajes* and convents represented confinement, which limited their ability to raise families, earn wages and establish friendships with a variety of urban actors. Confined people still loved, fought, married and worked as social beings in their own right. However, they were generally unable to construct the resilient social networks that defined the lives of their more mobile counterparts. Specifying the impact of these varying constrictions within the city is of paramount importance. Slaves working for elite families, middling merchants, priests and artisans encountered other challenges, promises and concerns. How to prevent the fragmentation of one's family? How to keep a loved one close? People with more established networks and greater autonomy over their everyday movements were increasingly able to resolve these questions in the late seventeenth century.

The gradual empowerment of Puebla slaves is evident in the baptismal books of the 1670s and 1680s. Enslaved people asserted familial responsibilities as spouses, parents and fictive kin, thereby destabilizing the notion that others could disregard these social ties with a bill of purchase. Cultivating ties at the local parish was essential to this development. When Afro-Poblanos claimed "legitimate children" in the 1680s, they signaled a decisive shift in the nature of slavery in the city. They and their families were worthy of honor and possessed the social relations to defend those claims. This does not mean that slaves were freed upon entering formal unions or receiving baptism. Many *hijos* and *hijas legítimas* were born into slavery. It certainly does not mean that Poblanos renounced slave ownership by 1700. Yet by constructing competing social identities, slaves prevented masters from doing as they pleased with them and their families.

---

5 Only one family unit is found among the enslaved community sent to Mixcoac: Miguel de Sempertigui and his three sons, Antonio de la Cruz, Francisco and Isidro. Archivo General de Notarías de la Ciudad de México (AGNCM), Not. 692, Vol. 4700, 323r–325v. Many thanks to Philip Ninomiya for sharing this document.

As people increasingly rooted in their owners' neighborhoods, parishes and markets, the enslaved staked claims as *vecinos*, parishioners (*feligreses*), vendors (*tratantes*) and so on. Their expansive social networks mitigated the resurgence of the Puebla slave market in the late seventeenth century.

Throughout this book, I have demonstrated that slaving transactions in Puebla peaked in the 1620s and 1630s because Lusophone agents and slave traders extended credit to people of all walks of life. Middling and elite urbanites did not renounce the inherent power of slave ownership in 1640 or thereafter. Whether as a cultural expectation or as a political need, Poblanos continued to demand enslaved people throughout the second half of the seventeenth century. This demand was especially evident in the city's convents and textile mills. From the local perspective, Portuguese independence meant that purchasing African-born captives became increasingly difficult. Potential slaveholders turned to enslaved women of African descent to procure American-born slaves. Enslaved Asian women were never brought to colonial Mexico in enough numbers to impact the slave market in a similar capacity. The impulse to redirect slaving efforts unto local populations was only heightened by the failures of the Grillo and Lomelín *asiento*. The slave market surged once more in the 1680s, mostly on the sales of enslaved creoles and a smaller group of Lower Guinean captives. By that point, however, slaves had far more resources at their disposal to negotiate their bondage.

As the enslaved accumulated wages, friendships, spouses and patrons over the course of the seventeenth century, masters held less and less control over their subjects' lives. By mid-century, a growing free population meant that slaves could turn to an emergent group of urban actors to mediate in their favor. In the 1610s and 1620s, men like Francisco de Carmona were early exponents of this type of intermediary. Whether we assess his influence in Analco real estate, silver pesos or manumitted relatives, Carmona served as a leading figure among "Bran" people in the early seventeenth century. Other Africans and their American-born children also turned to him for trust and support to resolve the most delicate situations.

Freed intermediaries, such as Felipe Monsón y Mojica and Marcos de Pardave, followed in Carmona's footsteps in the following decades. Monsón tapped into Afro-indigenous social networks by virtue of his marriage to Juana María de la Cruz in order to develop a successful business downtown and construct a respectable residence in the San José barrio. His participation in religious confraternities and militia service further distinguished him and his wife as urban patrons at a time of Afro-Poblano empowerment. Pardave experienced a generational shift toward free birth through his children, the result of enslaved men's considerable access to free spouses in the city. The confluence of free birth, expanding familial ties and patronage enabled freedmen and their descendants to formalize their participation in the urban economy.

Afro-Poblano men and women had differing experiences in the workplace and local parish. By the late seventeenth century, free men and their male children were increasingly part of a skilled community of apprentices and journeymen, some of whom would attain master artisan status.[6] In the eighteenth century, free-colored militias would present men of African descent yet another community through which to consolidate their ascending status. The exclusion of women from formal apprenticeships and the male bias in notarial documentation means that we know less about female social networks. In exceptional cases we learn about Marta Rodríguez, Juana de Aguilar and their businesses, but most Afro-Poblana women appear in indirect references to their work as domestic servants, wet nurses or food vendors. María de Terranova's case is exceptional for its detailed discussion of her commercial success and contested manumission, but her work itself was common.

There is no doubt that enslaved women were indispensable members of the city's urban economy. However, more precise work in Inquisition and judicial records is needed to contextualize enslaved women's participation in Puebla's overlapping communities of labor, recreation and religion. This study has attempted to situate enslaved and freed women as wives, sisters, aunts and as biological and fictive mothers. Unfortunately, we still know too little about how enslaved women interacted with one another outside the nuclear and extended family. These voids matter, especially in light of the female-headed households and businesses that have been discussed throughout this book. More spatially focused studies on enslaved and free women in inns, taverns, *temazcales* and other urban spaces should bring further female socialization into relief.

Studying the chapels and churches that housed specific confraternities in Puebla should resolve many doubts regarding female leadership among free and enslaved people. "African women led and were the founding members of confraternities" in Mexico during the seventeenth century,[7] yet we know next to nothing about these organizations or their founders in Puebla. Did specific groups of "Bran" or "Terranova" women lead these religious

---

6 The free *pardo* Lázaro Rodríguez de la Torre, for instance, worked as a master printer and typesetter in Puebla from the 1660s to the 1680s. In 1662, Rodríguez printed Fray Bartolomé de Letona's *La perfecta religiosa*, which would become a seminal text for female monastic life. AGNP, Not. 4, Box 209, 1675/12/30; Mercedes Isabel Salomón Salazar, "Los Borja: Una dinastía de libreros e impresores en la Puebla de los Ángeles del siglo XVII. Un primer acercamiento," in *Miradas a la cultura del libro en Puebla* (Puebla: UNAM/Gobierno del Estado de Puebla, 2012), 233.

7 Nicole von Germeten, *Black Blood Brothers, Confraternities and Social Mobility for Afro-Mexicans* (Gainesville: University of Florida Press, 2005), 8.

societies in the 1610s? Did the thousands of West Central African captives participate in a similar process at a later date? Finally, what to make of the *chino* confraternity modeled after its black counterpart in the Santa Veracruz church? Did the holy woman Catarina de San Juan ever frequent the former's services? Much work remains to be done.

Indeed, the study of slavery in Puebla is an open invitation to consider the complex interplay between religion, social networks and bondage in urban spaces. How common or exceptional were slaves in securing free birth at the baptismal font in other Mexican and Spanish American cities? The Poblano case seems to indicate that enslaved people had greater recourse to Church-sanctioned rights because of the high concentration of parishes and priests within the city. Was this also the case in inland cities like Antequera, Santiago de Guatemala and Quito? If so, the preceding chapters may serve as a baseline for discussions about family formation within slavery, the attainment of generational freedoms and the fall of urban slaveholding in the very heart of Spain's American empire.

Ultimately, however, this is a study of slavery in one Mexican city. In privileging specific settings and the actors within them, it traces urban slaveholders' varied and shifting objectives during the seventeenth century. More importantly, this book recovers the motivations, constraints and opportunities that enslaved people encountered in and outside of convents, *obrajes*, elite residences and markets in Puebla. By the end of the seventeenth century, enslaved people increasingly transcended the spaces and relations of slavery that bound thousands of others before them. Their stories and those of their families have, for the most part, never been told. Precisely because of this historical silence, it is important to know their struggle. It is important to know where and how they lived. It is important to say their names: Sebastiana de Paramos, Alonso Valiente, Sebastián Munguía, Esperanza de San Alberto, Antonio, Antonio, Diego, Miguel, Catarina de San Juan, Sebastián Goméz, María de Terranova, Felipe Monsón y Mojica.

Appendix A

Bill of purchase for Arara captives on the Puebla slave market, 1615

May all who see this letter know that I, Capt. Joseph Hurtado *vecino* of the city of Lisbona [sic] present in this [city] of the Angels of New Spain, truly sell to Pedro García Palomino, *vecino* of the Izucar jurisdiction, who is present, fifty pieces of slaves, the twenty-five of them male and the [other] twenty-five female. The twenty-five black men are all named Manueles and the twenty-five black women are named Marías, all of them between twenty and thirty years of age from Arara land. I sell them as my own, free of lien, mortgage or any obligation, which they do not have on them. [I sell them] as *bozales* recently brought from their land and as bones-in-a-sack without insuring them, as I do not insure them against any flaw, defect or disease and sell them with any that they might have. [I sell them] at the price and sum of 375 pesos of common gold each, which amounts to 18,750 pesos, which will be payed to me in installments, as shall be declared below . . .

And I, the aforementioned, Pedro García Palomino, who am present, accept this written contract as it is drafted and I confess to have in my possession the said fifty pieces of slaves, twenty-five males and twenty-five females . . . and of their worth, value and quality I am satisfied, because I chose them myself among many other pieces said captain had. At 375 pesos each, they amount to 18750 pesos, which I am obligated to pay Captain Joseph Hurtado and Manuel Gonzalez, *vecino* of this city. [I will pay this amount] in his name and to whomever might have their power-of-attorney in this city or wherever I might be asked in the following manner, 6300 pesos by the end of April of this coming year, 1616, and the remaining 12450 pesos by the end of March of the following year, 1617, in order to fulfill said amount . . . all [the slaves] are marked on the chest with the mark [as seen] on the outside [margin, an interwined BR] and are not to be sold or in any way relinquished until I have finished paying them . . .

This letter is awarded in the City of the Angels on the first day of the month of December of 1615 and I, the scribe, know the parties who signed it. Witnesses: Sebastian Rodriguez, Joseph Ortiz de Aviles and Juan Bautista Marin, vecinos and residents of this said city.

Pedro Garcia Palomino [rubric]
Josef Hurtado [rubric]

before me, Juan de Zamora, public scribe
Source: AGNP, Notaría 4, Box 78, 1615 December, no folio.

[Spanish transcription]
Sepan quantos esta carta vieren como yo el capitan Joseph Hurtado [vecino de la] ciudad de Lisbona [sic] y estante en esta de los Angeles de la Nueva España otorgo que vendo en venta real a Pedro Garcia Palomino, vezino de la jurisdiçion de Ysucar, que esta presente, cinquenta piesas de esclavos los veynte y çinco de ellos varones y las veynte y çinco hembras. Los veynte y çinco negros llamados todos Manueles y las veynte y cinco negras llamadas Marias, de hedad todos ellos de veynte a treinta años de tierra Arara. Las quales les vendo por mios propios libres de empeño hipoteca y otra enagenaçion que no la tienen y por bossales reçien benidos de su tierra y por huessos en costal sin los asegurar como no los aseguro de tacha defecto ni enfermedad, porque con las que tuvieren se los vendo y en precio y contia de trescientos y setenta y çinco pesos de oro comun cada uno que montan diez y ocho mill y sieteçientos y cinquenta pessos que me a de pagar a los plaços que iran declarados...

E yo el dicho Pedro Garcia Palomino que presente soy açepto esta escriptura según y como en ella se contiene y confieso tener en mi poder las dhas cinquenta piessas de esclavos veynte y çinco machos y veinte y çinco hembras... de cuyo balor y bondad y calidad estoy satisfecho porque yo propio las escogi entre otras muchas piesas que tenia el dicho capitan que a los dichos presçios de tresçientos y setenta y cinco pesos cada una montan los dichos diez y ocho mill y sieteçientos cinquenta pesos los quales me obligo de se los pagar al dicho capitan Joseph Hurtado y a Manuel Gonzalez, vezino desta ciudad, en su nombre y a quien poder de qualquier dellos ubiere en esta manera seis mill y tresçientos pesos para en fin del mes de abrill del año que viene de mill y seiscientos y diez y seis y los doze mill quatroçientos y cinquenta pesos restantes cumplimiento a toda la dicha cantidad para en fin del mes de março del año proximo venidero de mill y seiscientos y diez y siete en esta ciudad u en la parte que se me pidieren... todos [los esclavos] estan marcados en el pecho con la marca de fuera [carimbo BR conjunta] para no los poder vender ni en manera alguna enagenar hasta aberle acavado de pagar...

Es fecha la carta en la çiudad de los angeles en primero dia del mes de dizienbre de mill y seiscientos y quinze años e yo el escrivano conozco a los otorgantes que lo firmaron. Testigos, Sebastian Rodriguez, y Joseph Ortiz de Aviles y Juan Bautista Marin, vezinos y estantes en esta dicha ciudad =

>   Pedro Garcia Palomino
>   Josef Hurtado
>   ante mi Juan de Zamora, escribano publico
>   *Fuente: AGNP, Notaría 4, Caja 78, 1615 December, sin folio.*

Appendix B

Testament of Francisco Carmona, 1633

In the name of God the almighty, amen.

May all who see this letter know that I, Francisco de Carmona, a free black [man] from the land of Bran and a neighbor of this city [Puebla], am sick in bed and in my free judgment and understanding, which God our Lord has been well served to grant me.

I believe, as I well and truly believe, in the mystery of the Holy Trinity and in everything that our Holy Mother Church believes. I profess the Catholic faith and belief and have lived and died in it. And now, as I am fearful of death and eager to put my soul en route to salvation, I choose our Lady, the Holy Virgin Mary, as my counsel and intercessor, so that she might intercede before her precious son in my favor.

I award this letter that I am making and order my will in the following manner.

First, I trust my soul to God our Lord, who raised and redeemed it by his precious blood, death and passion. When God sees it to take me, I wish to be buried in the church of the Santa Veracruz with the accompaniment and burial that my executors decide and agree on. The day of my burial, a Mass shall be sung for me with my body present at a decent hour, and if that is not possible, the following day.

I order that one hundred masses be prayed for my soul in the parts [and churches] that my executors prefer.

I send six pesos of common gold as alms to the hermitage of the Santo Angel Custodio.

I send four *reales* to the customary and obligatory [charities], these I separate from my belongings.

I own as my property the houses of my residence, which are in the Analco neighborhood of this city. An inventory will be made of the furniture and jewelry boxes from my house.

Gaspar de Arano, a free black man and *vecino* of this city, owes me 73 pesos which is the remainder of what I have loaned him.

The wife of Roque, the black man, who was a female slave of Don Luis de Cordova, owes me 111 pesos, which I loaned her for her freedom.

Luis Moreno, a free black man and *vecino* of this city owes me 5 pesos and 1 tomin, which I loaned him.

I declare Antonia de Jesus and Juan Blas de Carmona, black *vecinos* of this city, as my natural children, whom I had with a single [unmarried] woman as I was also single at the time. I have no others.

I declared that I am married with Catalina, a black woman with whom I am making married life. At the time that we married we had no capital whatsoever. We have not had children from our marriage and the goods that we own were acquired during our marriage. And so that I may satisfy and pay this will and the orders contained in it, I name Catalina, my wife, and the said Antonia de Jesus, my daughter, and Gaspar de Arano, the black man, as my executors. . . .

And having satisfied and paid the remainder of my rights, actions, and goods, I leave and name the said Antonia de Jesus and the said Juan Blas de Carmona, my son, as my heirs, so that one and the other may inherit as equals . . . this is done in the city of [Puebla] de los Angeles on the fifteenth day of the month of July of 1633, and I, the scribe, attest to the fact that [Francisco de Carmona] did not sign, because he said he did not know how. A witness signed at his request. Witnesses, Diego Cortes de Brito, his Majesty's scribe, Pedro Mexia de Leon and Francisco Ruiz Paladin, *vecinos* of this city . . .

I signed in testimony of truth

> Alonso Corona [rubric]
> public scribe

[Spanish transcription]
En el nombre de dios todo poderoso amen sepan quantos esta carta bieren como yo Francisco de Carmona negro libre de tierra bran vezino desta ciudad Estando enfermo en cama y en mi libre Juicio y entendimiento al qual dios nuestro señor a sido se avido darme creyendo como bien y berdaderamente creo en el misterio de la santisima trinidad y en todo aquello que cree nuestra santa madre yglesia en cuya fee y catholica creençia me huelgo aber bivido y protesto vivir y morir y temiendome de la muerte deseando poner mi alma en carrera de salbaçion y eligiendo por mi abogada e ynterzesora a nuestra señora la birgen Santa Maria para que ynterçeda por mi a su preçioso hijo otorgo por esta carta que hago y ordeno mi testamento en la manera siguiente.

Lo primero encomiendo mi alma a dios nuestro señor que la crio y rredimo por su preçiosa sangre muerte y pasion y quando dios fuere servido de llebarme quiero ser Enterrado en la yglesia de la Santa Veracruz con el acompañamiento y en la sepoltura que a mis albaçeas pareçiere y señalaren y el dia de mi entierro siendo ora deçente y no la siendo El siguiente se me diga En la dicha yglesia misa cantada de cuerpo presente y se pague la limosna de mis bienes.

Mando se digan por mi alma çien misas rreçadas en las partes que pareçiere a mis albaceas.

Mando en limosna a la hermita del Santo Angel de la Guarda [Analco] desta çiudad seis pesos de oro comun.

Mando a las mandas forçosas y acostumbradas a todas quatro rreales con que las aparto de mis bienes.

Tengo por mis bienes las casas de mi morada que son en el barrio de analco desta çiudad y los muebles y alajas de mi casa que que se hara ynventario.

Debeme Gaspar de Arano negro libre veçino desta çiudad setenta y tres pesos de rresto de los que le E prestado.

Debeme la muger de Roque negro que fue esclava de don Luis de Cordova çiento y once pesos que le di para su libertad prestados.

Debeme Luis Moreno negro libre veçino desta çiudad çinco pesos y un tomin que le preste.

Declaro por mis hijos naturales avidos En muger soltera siendo lo yo tanbien a Antonia de Jesus y a Juan Blas de Carmona negros veçinos desta çiudad y no tener otros.

Declaro estoy casado con Catalina negra con quien Estoy haçiendo vida maridable y al tiempo que nos casamos no teniamos capital alguno ni emos tenido hijos del dicho matrimonio y los vienes que tenemos son adqueridos durante el dicho matrimonio y para cumplir y pagar Este mi testamento y las mandas en el contenidas dejo y nombro por mis albaçeas a la dicha Catalina mi muger y a la dicha Antoña de Jesus mi hija y a Gaspar de Arano negro a los quales y a cada uno ynsolidun doy poder en bastante forma para el uso del dicho albaçeazgo y para que Entre En mis bienes y los vendan y rrematen en almoneda o fuera della como les pareçiere y lo cumplan como dicho es.

Y cumplido y pagado en el rremaniente que quedare de todos mis bienes derechos y acçiones dejo y nombro por mis herederos a la dicha Antonia de Jesus y al dicho Joan Blas de Carmona mi hijo los quales los ayan hereden por yguales partes tanto El uno como el otro . . . ques fecho en la çiudad de los angeles en quinçe dias del mes de Jullio de mill y seisçientos E treinta y tres años y el otorgante a quien yo el escrivano doy fee que conozco no firmo porque dixo no saver a su rruego lo firmo un testigo siendo testigos Diego Cortes de Brito escrivano de su mag.d Pedro Mexia de Leon y Francisco Ruiz Paladin veçinos desta çiudad . . .

Fize mi signo En testimonyo de Verdad

    Alonso Corona
    scrivano publico

Bibliography

Aguirre Beltrán, Gonzalo. *La población negra de México, 1519–1810: Estudio etnohistórico.* Mexico City: Fondo de Cultura Económica, 1972.

Aguirre Carrasco, Enrique. *Testimonio del patronazgo y testamento de Don Melchor de Covarrubias.* Puebla: BUAP, 2002.

Alberro, Solange. "Juan de Morga and Gertrudis de Escobar: Rebellious Slaves." In *Struggle and Survival in Colonial America*, 165–188. Edited by David G. Sweet and Gary B. Nash. Berkeley: University of California Press, 1981.

Alcalá y Mendiola, Miguel. *Descripción en bosquejo de la imperial cesárea muy noble y muy leal ciudad de Puebla de los Ángeles.* Puebla: BUAP/Fomento Editorial, 1997.

Alegre, Francisco Javier. *Historia de la Compañía de Jesús en Nueva España.* Tomo II, Libro V. Mexico City: Imprenta de J. M. Lara, 1842.

Altman, Ida. *Transatlantic Ties in the Spanish Empire: Brihuega, Spain, & Puebla, Mexico, 1560–1620.* Stanford, CA: Stanford University Press, 2000.

Álvarez de Toledo, Cayetana. *Politics and Reform in Spain and Viceregal Mexico: The Life and Thought of Juan de Palafox 1600–1659.* Oxford: Oxford University Press, 2004.

Amaral, Ilídio do. *O Consulado de Paulo Dias de Novais.* Lisbon: Instituto de Investigação Científica Tropical, 2000.

Anderson, Arthur J.O., Frances Berdan and James Lockhart. *The Tlaxcalan Actas: A Compendium of the Records of the Cabildo of Tlaxcala, 1545–1627.* Salt Lake City, UT: University of Utah Press, 1986.

Bakewell, Peter. *Silver Mining and Society in Colonial Mexico.* Cambridge: Cambridge University Press, 1971.

Bazant, Jan. "Evolución de la industria textil poblana." *Historia Mexicana* 13, no. 4 (Apr.-Jun. 1964): 473–516.

Beatty-Medina, Charles. "Between the Cross and the Sword: Religious Conquest and Maroon Legitimacy in Colonial Esmeraldas." In *Africans to Spanish America: Expanding the Diaspora*, 95–113. Edited by Sherwin K. Bryant, Rachel Sarah O'Toole and Ben Vinson III. Urbana: University of Illinois Press, 2012.

Beazley, C. Raymond, ed. *An English Garner: Voyages and Travels Mainly during the 16th and 17th Centuries.* Vol. I. New York: E. P. Dutton and Co., 1902.

Bennett, Herman L. *Africans in Colonial Mexico: Absolutism, Christianity and Afro-Creole Consciousness, 1570–1640.* Bloomington: Indiana University Press, 2003.

Colonial Blackness: A History of Afro-Mexico. Bloomington: Indiana University Press, 2009.

Bieñko de Peralta, Doris. "Voces del Claustro. Dos autobiografías de monjas novohispanas del siglo XVII." *Relaciones* 139 (verano 2014): 157–194.

Boornazian Diel, Lori. "Manuscrito del aperreamiento (Manuscript of the Dogging): A 'Dogging' and Its Implications for Early Colonial Cholula." *Ethnohistory* 58, no. 4 (Fall 2011): 585–611.

Borah, Woodrow and Sherburne Cook, "Conquest and Population: A Demographic Approach to Mexican History," *Proceedings of the American Philosophical Society* 113, no. 2 (April 1969): 177–183.

Borda, Andrés de. *Práctica de confessores de monjas: En que se explican los quatro votos de obediencia, pobreza, casstidad y clausura, por modo de dialogo.* Mexico City: Francisco de Ribera Calderon, 1708.

Borucki, Alex, David Eltis, and David Wheat. "Atlantic History and the Slave Trade to Spanish America." *American Historical Review* 120, no. 2 (Apr. 2015): 433–461.

Borucki, Alex. *From Shipmates to Soldiers: Emerging Black Identities in the Río de la Plata.* Albuquerque: University of New Mexico Press, 2015.

Bötcher, Nikolaus, Bernd Hausberger, and Antonio Ibarra, eds. *Redes y negocios globales en el mundo ibérico, siglos XVI–XVIII.* Vervuert: Instituto Ibero-Americano, 2011.

Bouhrass, Asmáa, "El intervencionismo en el desarrollo de los *obrajes* mexicanos." *Estudios sobre América, siglos XVI–XX*, 993–1012. Edited by Antonio Gutiérrez Escuero and María Luisa Laviana Cuetos. Seville: Asociación Española de Americanistas, 2005.

Boxer, C.R. *Portuguese Society in the Tropics: The Municipal Councils of Goa, Macao, Bahia, and Luanda, 1510–1800.* Madison: University of Wisconsin Press, 1965.

Bowser, Frederick P. *The African Slave in Colonial Peru, 1524–1650.* Stanford, CA: Stanford University Press, 1974.

"The Free Person of Color in Mexico City and Lima." In *Race and Slavery in the Western Hemisphere: Quantitative Studies*, 331–368. Edited by Stanley Engerman and Eugene D. Genovese. Princeton, NJ: Princeton University Press, 1975.

Boyd-Bowman, Peter. "Negro Slaves in Colonial Mexico." *The Americas* 26, No. 2 (Oct. 1969): 134–151.

Bristol, Joan Cameron. *Christians, Blasphemers and Witches: Afro-Mexican Ritual Practice in the Seventeenth Century.* Albuquerque: University of New Mexico Press, 2007.

Brown, Vincent. "Mapping a Slave Revolt: Visualizing Spatial History through the Archives of Slavery." *Social Text* 125 (2005): 134–141.

Bryant, Sherwin K. *Rivers of Gold, Lives of Bondage: Governing through Slavery in Colonial Quito.* Chapel Hill: University of North Carolina Press, 2014.

Burns, Kathryn. *Colonial Habits: Convents and the Spiritual Economy of Cuzco, Peru.* Durham, NC: Duke University Press, 1999.

Into the Archive: Writing and Power in Colonial Peru. Durham, NC: Duke University Press, 2010.

Camba Ludlow, Úrsula. *Imaginarios ambiguos, realidades contradictorias: Conductas y representaciones de los negros y mulatos novohispanos, Siglos XVI y XVII.* Mexico City: Colegio de México, 2008.

Cañizares Esguerra, Jorge, Matt D. Childs, and James Sidbury, eds. *The Black Urban Atlantic in the Age of the Slave Trade.* Philadelphia: University of Pennsylvania Press, 2013.

Carabarín Gracia, Alberto. *El trabajo y los trabajadores del obraje de la ciudad de Puebla, 1700–1710.* Puebla: Cuadernos de la Casa Presno, 1984.

Carrera, Magali M. *Imagining Identity in New Spain: Race, Lineage and the Colonial Body in Portraiture and Casta Paintings.* Austin: University of Texas Press, 2003.

Carroll, Patrick. *Blacks in Colonial Veracruz: Race, Ethnicity and Regional Development.* Austin: University of Texas Press, 2001.

"Black-Native Relations and the Historical Record in Colonial Mexico." In *Beyond Black and Red: African Native Relations in Colonial Latin America*, 245–267. Edited by Matthew Restall. Albuquerque: University of New Mexico Press, 2005.

Cashner, Andrew, ed. *Villancicos about Music from Seventeenth-Century Spain and New Spain.* Web Library of Seventeenth-Century Music (No. 32), 2017. www.sscm-wlscm.org.

Castañeda García, Rafael. "Santos negros, devotos de color. Las cofradías de San Benito de Palermo en Nueva España. Identidades étnicas y religiosas, siglos XVII–XVIII." In *Devoción paisanaje e identidad. Las cofradías y congregaciones de naturales en España y en América (siglos XVI–XIX)*, 145–164. Edited by Oscar Álvarez Gila, Alberto Angulo Morales and Jon Ander Ramos Martínez. Bilbao: Universidad del País Vasco, 2014.

Castañon González, Guadalupe. "Yanga y cimarronaje en la Nueva España." In *Esclavos rebeldes y cimarrones*, 69–96. Edited by Javier Laviña. Madrid: Fundación Hernando de Larramendi.

Castillo Palma, Norma Angélica. "Matrimonios mixtos y cruce de la barrera de color como vías para el *mestizaje* de la población negra y mulata (1674–1696)." *Signos Históricos* 2, no. 4 (Jun.-Dec. 2000): 107–137.

Cholula: Sociedad mestiza en ciudad india. Mexico City: Universidad Autónoma Metropolitana/Plaza y Valdés, 2008.

Castro Morales, Efrain, ed., *Suplemento de el Libro Número Primero de la Fundación y Establecimiento de la Muy Noble y Muy Leal Ciudad de los Ángeles*. Puebla: Ayuntamiento del Municipio de Puebla, 2009.

Suplemento de el Libro Número dos de el Mismo Establecimiento y Dilatación de la Ciudad. Puebla: H. Ayuntamiento del Municipio de Puebla, 2010.

Celaya Nández, Yolanda. *Alcabalas y situados: Puebla en el sistema fiscal imperial 1638–1742*. Mexico City: El Colegio de México, 2010.

Chevalier, François. "Signification sociale de la fondation de Puebla de los Angeles" *Revista de Historia de América* 23 (1947 Jun.): 109–110.

Chimalpahin, Don Domingo de San Antón Muñón. *Annals of His Time*. Edited and translated by James Lockhart, Susan Schroeder, and Doris Namala. Stanford, CA: Stanford University Press, 2006.

Diario, edited and translated by Rafael Tena. Mexico City: Cien de México, 2011.

Chowning, Margaret. *Rebellious Nuns: The Troubled History of a Mexican Convent, 1752–1863*. Oxford: Oxford University Press, 2005.

Clark, Joseph M. H. "Veracruz and the Caribbean in the Seventeenth Century." Ph.D dissertation, Johns Hopkins University, 2016.

Cook, Karoline P. *Forbidden Passages: Muslims and Moriscos in Colonial Spanish America*. Philadelphia, PA: University of Pennsylvania Press, 2016.

Coote, Jeremy. "A Textile Text-Book at the Pitt Rivers Museum." *African Arts* 48, no. 1 (Spring 2015): 66–77.

Cope, Douglas R. *The Limits of Racial Domination*. Madison: University of Wisconsin Press, 1994.

Córdova, James M. *The Art of Professing in Bourbon Mexico: Crowned-Nun Portraits and Reform in the Convent*. Austin: University of Texas Press, 2014.

Cortés Jacome, María Elena. "Los ardides de los amos: la manipulación y la interdependencia en la vida conyugal de sus esclavos." In *Del dicho al hecho ... Transgresiones y pautas culturales en la Nueva España*, 43–57. Mexico City: INAH, 1989.

Cruz, Salvador. *Alonso Valiente: Conquistador de Nueva España y poblador de la Ciudad de Puebla de los Ángeles*. Mexico City: H. Ayuntamiento del Municipio de Puebla, 1992.

Cuenya, Miguel Ángel and Carlos Contreras Cruz, *Puebla de los Ángeles: Una ciudad en la historia*. Puebla: Océano/BUAP, 2012.

Curtin, Philip D. *The Atlantic Slave Trade: A Census*. Madison: University of Wisconsin Press, 1969.

Curto, José C. *Enslaving Spirits: The Portuguese-Brazilian Alcohol Trade at Luanda and Its Hinterland, c. 1550–1830*. Leiden: Brill, 2004.

Davidson, David. "Negro Slave Control and Resistance in Colonial Mexico, 1519–1650." *Hispanic American Historical Review* 46, no. 3 (August 1966): 235–253.

de la Fuente, Alejandro. *Havana and the Atlantic in the Sixteenth Century*. Chapel Hill: University of North Carolina Press, 2008.

de la Mota y Escobar, Fray Alonso. *Memoriales del obispo de Tlaxcala*. Mexico City: Secretaría de Educación Pública, 1987.

de la Peña, José F. *Oligarquía y propiedad en Nueva España, 1550–1624*. Mexico City: Fondo de Cultura Económica, 1983.

Degler, Carl N. *Neither Black nor White: Slavery and Race Relations in Brazil and the United States*. Madison: University of Wisconsin Press, 1971.

del Paso y Troncoso, Francisco, ed., *Epistolario de Nueva España*. Mexico City: Antigua Librería Robledo de J. Porrúa, 1939. Vol. 3.

Papeles de Nueva España, Segunda Serie, Tomo V. Madrid: Impresores de la Real Casa, 1905.

del Valle Pavón, Guillermina. "Desarrollo de la economía mercantil y construcción de los caminos México-Veracruz en el siglo XVI." *América Latina en la Historia Económica* no. 27 (Jan.–June 2007): 7–49.

del Valle Pavón, Guillermina and Antonio Ibarra. "Redes sociales e instituciones: una nueva mirada sobre viejas incógnitas." *Historia Mexicana* 56, no. 3 (Jan.–Mar. 2007): 717–723.

Delgado, Jessica Lorraine. "Sacred Practice, Intimate Power: Laywomen and the Church in Colonial Mexico." Ph.D dissertation, University of California-Berkeley, 2009.

Díaz, Mónica. "The Indigenous Nuns of Corpus Christi: Race and Spirituality." In *Religion in New Spain*, 179–192. Edited by Susan Schroeder and Stafford Poole, eds. Albuquerque: University of New Mexico Press, 2007.

Indigenous Writings from the Convent: Negotiating Ethnic Autonomy in Colonial Mexico. Tucson: University of Arizona Press, 2010.

Dufendach, Rebecca. "Epidemic Contact: Nahua and Spanish Concepts of Disease, 1519–1615." Ph.D. diss., University of California-Los Angeles, 2016.

Eagle, Marc. "Chasing the Avença: An Investigation of Illicit Slave Trading in Santo Domingo at the End of the Portuguese *Asiento* Period." *Slavery & Abolition* 35, no. 1 (2014): 99–120.

Echeverría y Veytia, Mariano Joseph Antonio Fernández de. *Historia de la fundación de la ciudad de la Puebla de los Ángeles en la Nueva España, su descripción y presente estado*. Puebla: Ediciones Altiplano, 1962.

Escamilla González, Iván. "La Caridad Episcopal: El hospital de San Pedro de Puebla en el siglo XVII." In *El mundo de las catedrales novohispanas*, 239–252. Edited by Monserrat Galí Boadella. Puebla: BUAP/Instituto de Ciencias Sociales y Humanidades, 2002.

Ewald, Ursula. *Estudios sobre la hacienda colonial en México. Las propiedades rurales del colegio Espíritu Santo en Puebla*. Wiesbaden: Franz Steiner, 1976.

Fernández de Santa Cruz, Manuel. *Regla del Glorioso Doctor de la Iglesia de San Agustín que han de guardar las Religiosas del Convento del Máximo Doctor San Geronimo de la Puebla de los Angeles, y los demas que se fundaren en el mismo instituto*. Puebla: Imprenta de los Herederos del Capitan Juan de Villareal, 1701.

Florencia, Padre Francisco de. *Zodiaco mariano, en que el sol de justicia Christo con la salud en las alas visita como Signos y Casas proprias para beneficio de los hombres, los templos, y lugares dedicados a los cultos de su SS. madre por medio de loas mas celebres, y milagrosas imagenes de la misma señora que se veneran en esta America septentrional, y reynos de la Nueva España*. Mexico City: Antiguo Colegio de San Ildeonso, 1755.

Fromont, Cécile. *The Art of Conversion: Christian Visual Culture in the Kingdom of Kongo*. Williamsburg: Omohundro Institute, 2014.

Fuentes, Marisa J. *Dispossessed Lives: Enslaved Women, Violence and the Archive*. Philadelphia: University of Pennsylvania Press, 2016.

Gantes Tréllez, María de las Mercedes. "Aspectos socio-económicos de Puebla de los Ángeles (1624–1650)." In *Ángeles y constructores. Mitos y realidades en la historia colonial de Puebla, siglos XVI y XVII*, 207–318. Edited by Carlos Contreras Cruz and Miguel Ángel Cuenya Mateos. Puebla: BUAP/Fomento Editorial.

Garavaglia, Juan Carlos and Juan Carlos Grosso, *La región de Puebla-Tlaxcala y la economía novohispana*. Mexico City: Instituto Mora/BUAP, 1996.

García de León, Antonio. "La Malla Inconclusa. Veracruz y los circuitos comerciales lusitanos en la primera mitad del siglo XVII." In *Redes sociales e instituciones comerciales en el imperio español, siglos XVI y XVII*, 41–83. Edited by Antonio Ibarra and Guillermina del Valle Pavón. Mexico City: Instituto Mora/UNAM, 2007.

Tierra adentro, mar en fuera: El puerto de Veracruz y su litoral a Sotavento, 1519–1821. Mexico City: Fondo de Cultura Económica, 2011.

García Lastra, Leopoldo A. and Silvia Castellano Gómez, *Utopía angelopolitana: La verdadera historia de la fundación de Puebla de los Ángeles*. Puebla: Secretaría de Cultura/Gobierno del Estado de Puebla, 2008.

García Montón, Alejandro. "Corona, hombres de negocios y jueces conservadores. Un acercamiento en escala trasatlántica (S. XVII)." *Jerónimo Zurita* 90 (2015): 75–112.

García Ponce, Daniel. "Indian Slavery in Sixteenth-Century New Spain: The Politics and Power of Bondage." M.A. Thesis. University of Texas at Austin, 2013.

Gerhard, Peter. *A Guide to the Historical Geography of New Spain*. Cambridge: Cambridge University Press, 1972.

"Un censo de la diócesis de Puebla en 1681." *Historia Mexicana* 30, no. 4 (Apr.–Jun. 1981): 530–560.

Gibson, Charles. *The Aztecs under Spanish Rule: A History of the Indians of the Valley of Mexico, 1519–1810*. Stanford, CA: Stanford University Press, 1964.

Gómez, Pablo F. *The Experiential Caribbean: Creating Knowledge and Healing in the Early Modern Atlantic*. Chapel Hill: University of North Carolina Press, 2017.

Gómez García, Lidia E. "Las fiscalías en la Ciudad de los Ángeles, siglo XVII." In *Los indios y las ciudades de Nueva España*, 173–195. Edited by Felipe Castro Gutiérrez. Mexico City: UNAM, 2010.

"El impacto de la secularización de las parroquias en los pueblos indios del obispado de Puebla, siglos XVII–XVIII." In *Palafox, Obra y Legado: Memorias del ciclo de conferencias sobre la vida y obra de Juan de Palafox y Mendoza*, 213–236. Puebla: Instituto Municipal de Arte y Cultura de Puebla, 2011.

Gómez García, Lidia E., Celia Salazar Exaire and María Elena Stefanón López, eds. *Anales del barrio de San Juan del Rio. Crónica indígena de la ciudad de Puebla, siglo XVII*. Puebla: BUAP/ICSyH, 2000.

González, Anita. *Afro-Mexico: Dancing between Myth and Reality*. Austin: University of Texas Press, 2010.

González Obregón, Luis. *Don Guillén de Lampart: La Inquisición y la Independencia en el siglo XVII*. Tours: E. Arrault & Cie., 1907.

Graham, Sandra Lauderhale. "Honor among Slaves." In *Sex, Shame and Violence: The Faces of Honor in Colonial Latin America*, 201–225. Edited by Lyman L. Johnson and Sonya Lipsett-Rivera. Albuquerque: University of New Mexico Press, 1998.

Green, Toby. *The Rise of the Trans-Atlantic Slave Trade in Western Africa, 1300–1589*. Cambridge: Cambridge University Press, 2012.

Gruzinski, Serge. "The Ashes of Desire: Homosexuality in Seventeenth-Century New Spain." In *Infamous Desire: Male Homosexuality in Colonial Latin America*, 197–214. Edited by Pete Sigal. Chicago: University of Chicago Press, 2003.

Hardoy, Jorge E. and Carmen Aravonich, "Urban Scales and Functions in Spanish America toward the Year 1600: First Conclusions," *Latin American Research Review* 5, no. 3 (Autumn 1970): 57–91.

Heywood, Linda and John K. Thornton. *Central Africans, Atlantic Creoles, and the Foundation of the Americas, 1585–1660*. Cambridge: Cambridge University Press, 2007.

Hidalgo Nuchera, Patricio. "Los 'malos usos' y la reglamentación de los temascales públicos mexicanos (1686–1691)," *Anuario de Estudios Americanos* 69, no. 1 (Jan.–Jun. 2012): 91–108.

Hirschberg, Julia. "An Alternative to Encomienda: Puebla's *Indios de Servicio*, 1531–1545." *Journal of Latin American Studies* 11, no. 2 (Nov. 1979): 242–244.

Hoberman, Louisa Schell. *Mexico's Merchant Elite: Silver, State and Society*. Durham, NC: Duke University Press, 1991.

Hoekstra, Rik. *Two Worlds Merging: The Transformation of Society in the Valley of Puebla, 1570–1640*. Amsterdam: CEDLA, 1993.

Holler, Jacqueline. *"Escogidas Plantas": Nuns and Beatas in Mexico City, 1531–1601*. New York: Columbia University Press, 2005.

Hordes, Stanley Mark. "The Crypto-Jewish Community of New Spain, 1620–1649: A Collective Biography." Ph.D. diss., Tulane University, 1980.

Instituto Nacional de Estadística y Geografía (INEGI). "Resultados definitivos de la Encuesta Intercensal 2015. http://www3.inegi.org.mx/sistemas/saladeprensa/noticia .aspx?id=2288

Irwin, Graham W. ed., *Africans Abroad: A Documentary History of the Black Diaspora in Asia, Latin America and the Caribbean during the Age of Slavery*. New York: Columbia University Press, 1977.

Israel, Jonathan. *Razas, clases sociales y vida política en el México colonial 1610–1670*. Mexico City: Fondo de Cultura Económica, 2005.

Karasch, Mary. *Slave Life in Rio de Janeiro, 1808–1850*. Princeton, NJ: Princeton University Press, 1987.

Konove, Andrew. "On the Cheap: The Baratillo Marketplace and the Shadow Economy of Eighteenth-Century Mexico City." *The Americas* 72, no. 2 (April 2015): 249–278.

Krug, Frances and Camilla Townsend, "The Tlaxcala-Puebla Family of Annals." In *Sources and Methods for the Study of Postconquest Mesoamerican Ethnohistory*, 1–11. Edited by James Lockhart, Lisa Sousa and Stephanie Wood. http://whp.uoregon.edu, 2008.

Kuznesof, Elizabeth Anne. "More Conversation on Race, Class, and Gender," *Colonial Latin American Review* 5, no. 1 (1996): 129–134.

Lamikiz, Xabier. "Flotistas en la Nueva España: diseminación espacial y negocios de los intermediarios del comercio trasatlántico, 1670–1702." *Colonial Latin American Review* 20, no. 1 (April 2011): 9–33.

Landers, Jane. "Cimarrón and Citizen: African Ethnicity, Corporate Identity, and the Evolution of Free Black Towns in the Spanish Circum-Caribbean." In *Slaves, Subjects, and Subversives: Blacks in Colonial Latin America*, 111–146. Edited by Jane G. Landers and Barry M. Robinson. Albuquerque: University of New Mexico Press, 2006.

Lane, Kris. *Quito 1599: City and Colony in Transition*. Albuquerque: University of New Mexico Press, 2002.

Lang, Mervyn Francis. *Las flotas de Nueva España (1630–1710): Despacho, azogue, comercio*. Seville: Muñoz Moya Editor, 1998.

Lara Tenorio, Blanca. *La esclavitud en Puebla y Tepeaca, 1545–1649*. Mexico City: Cuadernos de los Centros INAH, 1976.

Lara Tenorio, Blanca and Carlos Paredes Martínez. "La población negra en los valles centrales de Puebla: Orígenes y desarrollo hasta 1681." *Presencia africana en México*, 19–77. Edited by Luz María Martínez Montiel. Mexico City: CONACULTA, 1994.

Lavrín, Asunción. *Brides of Christ: Conventual Life in Colonial Mexico.* Stanford, CA: Stanford University Press, 2010.

Law, Robin. *The Slave Coast of West Africa 1550–1750.* Oxford: Oxford University Press, 1991.

Leicht, Hugo. *Las calles de Puebla.* Puebla: Secretaría de Cultura / Gobierno del Estado de Puebla, 2007.

Lemus, Diego de. *Vida, virtudes, trabajos, fabores y Milagros de la Ven. M. sor María de Jesús Angelopolitana religiosa en el insigne Convento de la Limpia Concepción de la Ciudad de los Angeles, en la Nueva España y natural de ella.* Lyons: Anisson y Posuel, 1683.

Lewis, Laura. "Modesty and Modernity: Photography, Race and Representation on Mexico's Costa Chica (Guerrero)," *Identities: Global Studies in Culture and Power* 11, no. 4 (Fall 2004): 471–499.

Chocolate and Corn Flour: History, Race and the Making of Place in the Making of "Black" Mexico (Durham, NC: Duke University Press, 2012).

Lockhart, James. *Spanish Peru, 1532–1560: A Social History.* Madison: University of Wisconsin Press, 1994.

Lockhart, James and Enrique Otte, eds. *Letters and People of the Spanish Indies.* Cambridge: Cambridge University Press, 1976.

Lohse, Russell. *Africans into Creoles: Slavery, Ethnicity and Identity in Colonial Costa Rica.* Albuquerque: University of New Mexico Press, 2014.

Lokken, Paul. "Marriage as Slave Emancipation in Seventeenth-Century Rural Guatemala." *The Americas* 58, no. 2 (Oct. 2001): 175–200.

Long-Solís, Janet. "El abastecimiento de chile en el mercado de la ciudad México-Tenochtitlán en el siglo XVI." *Historia Mexicana* 34, no. 4 (Apr.–Jun. 1985): 701–714.

López, John F. "'In the Art of My Profession'": Adrian Boot and Dutch Water Management in Colonial Mexico City." *Journal of Latin American Geography* 11 (Spring 2012): 35–60.

López de Velasco, Juan. *Geografía y descripción universal de la Indias.* Madrid: Establecimiento Tipográfico de Fortanet, 1894.

López de Villaseñor, Pedro. *Cartilla vieja de la nobilísima ciudad de Puebla.* Puebla: Secretaría de Cultura, 2001.

Loreto López, Rosalva. *Los conventos femeninos y el mundo urbano de la Puebla de los Ángeles del siglo XVIII.* Mexico City: El Colegio de México, 2000.

"The Devil, Women and the Body in Seventeenth-Century Puebla Convents." Translated by Sonya Lipsett-Rivera. *The Americas* 59, no. 2 (Oct. 2002): 181–199.

"Los artífices de una ciudad: Los indios y sus territorialidades, Puebla de los Ángeles 1777." In *Los indios y las ciudades de Nueva España,* 255–277. Edited by Felipe Castro Gutiérrez. Mexico City: UNAM, 2010.

Love, Edgar F. "Marriage Patterns of Persons of African Descent in a Colonial Mexico City Parish." *Hispanic American Historical Review* 51, no. 1 (Feb., 1971): 79–91.

Lovejoy, Henry and Olatunji Ojo. "'Lucumí,' 'Terranova,' and the Origins of the Yoruba Nation," *Journal of African History* 56, no. 3 (Nov. 2015): 353–372.

Lucena Salmoral, Manuel. *Regulación de la esclavitud negra en las colonias de América Española (1503–1886): Documentos para su estudio.* Alcalá: Universidad de Alcalá de Henares, 2005.

Marín Tamayo, Fausto. *La división racial en Puebla de los Ángeles bajo el régimen colonial.* Puebla: Centro de Estudios Históricos de Puebla, 1960.

Martínez, María Elena. "The Black Blood of New Spain: Limpieza de Sangre, Racial Violence and Gendered Power in Early Colonial Mexico." *The William and Mary Quarterly* 61, no. 3 (July 2004): 479–520.

Genealogical Fictions: Limpieza de Sangre, Religion and Gender in Colonial Mexico. Stanford, CA: Stanford University Press, 2008.

Martínez Montiel, Luz María, ed. *Presencia africana en México*. Mexico City: Consejo Nacional para la Cultura y las Artes, 1997.

McKinley, Michelle. *Fractional Freedoms: Slavery, Intimacy, and Legal Mobilization in Colonial Lima, 1600–1700*. Cambridge: Cambridge University Press, 2016.

Mendes, António de Almeida. "The Foundations of the System: A Reassessment of the Slave Trade to the Spanish Americas in the Sixteenth and Seventeenth Centuries." In *Extending the Frontiers: Essays on the New Transatlantic Slave Trade Database*, 63–94 Edited by David Eltis and David Richardson. New Haven: Yale University Press, 2008.

Midlo Hall, Gwendolyn. *Slavery and African Ethnicities in the Americas: Restoring the Links*. Chapel Hill: University of North Carolina Press, 2005.

Miller, Joseph C. *Kings and Kinsmen: Early Mbundu States in Angola*. Oxford: Clarendon Press, 1976.

The Problem of Slavery as History: A Global Approach. New Haven: Yale University Press, 2012.

Miño Grijalva, Manuel. "¿Proto-industria colonial?" *Historia Mexicana* 38, no. 4 (Apr.-Jun. 1989): 793–818.

Miranda, José. *La función económica del encomendero en los orígenes del régimen colonial* Mexico City: UNAM/Instituto de Investigaciones Históricas, 1965.

Montoya, Ramón Alejandro. *El esclavo africano en San Luis Potosí durante los siglos XVII y XVIII*. San Luis Potosí: Universidad Autónoma de San Luis Potosí, 2016.

Morales Abril, Omar. "El esclavo negro de Juan de Vera: Cantor, arpista y compositor de la catedral de Puebla (florevit 1575–1617)." In *Historia de la Música en Puebla*, 47–61. Puebla: Secretaría de Cultura del Estado de Puebla, 2010.

Morgan, Jennifer L. *Laboring Women: Reproduction and Gender in New World Slavery*. Philadelphia: University of Pennsylvania Press, 2004.

Myers, Kathleen Ann. *Neither Saints nor Sinners: Writing the Lives of Women in Spanish America*. Oxford: Oxford University Press, 2003.

Myers, Kathleen Ann and Amanda Powell. *A Wild Country Out in the Garden: The Spiritual Journals of a Colonial Mexican Nun*. Bloomington: Indiana University Press, 1999.

Navarrete, María Cristina. *Génesis y desarrollo de la esclavitud en Colombia, siglos XVI y XVII*. Cali: Editorial Universidad del Valle, 2005.

Naveda Chávez-Hita, Adriana. *Esclavos negros en las haciendas azucareras de Córdoba, Veracruz, 1690–1830*. Xalapa: Universidad Veracruzana/Centro de Investigaciones Históricas, 1987.

Newson, Linda and Susie Minchin. *From Capture to Sale: The Portuguese Slave Trade to Spanish South America in the Early Seventeenth Century*. Leiden: Brill, 2007.

Ngou-Mvé, Nicolás. *El África bantú en la colonización de México (1595–1640)*. Madrid: Consejo Superior de Investigaciones Científicas/Agencia Española de Cooperación Internacional, 1994.

Olvera Ramos, Jorge. *Los mercados de la Plaza Mayor en la Ciudad de México*. Mexico City: Centro de estudios mexicanos y centroamericanos, 2013.

Otte, Enrique and Guadalupe Albi Romero, eds. *Cartas privadas de emigrantes a Indias*. Mexico City: Fondo de Cultura Económica, 1993.

Owensby, Brian. "How Juan and Leonor Won Their Freedom: Litigation and Liberty in Seventeenth-Century Mexico." *Hispanic American Historical Review* 85, no. 1 (2005): 39–79.

O'Toole, Rachel Sarah. "Danger in the Convent: Colonial Demons, Idolatrous Indias, and Bewitching Negras in Santa Clara (Trujillo de Peru)." *Journal of Colonialism and Colonial History* 7, no. 1 (2006).

Bound Lives: Africans, Indians and the Making of Race in Colonial Peru. Pittsburgh: University of Pittsburgh Press, 2012.

"To Be Free and Lucumí: Ana de la Calle and Making African Diaspora Identities in Colonial Peru." In *Africans to Spanish America: Expanding the Diaspora*, 73–93. Edited by Sherwin K. Bryant, Rachel Sarah O'Toole and Ben Vinson III. Urbana: University of Illinois Press, 2012.

Palafox y Mendoza, Juan de. *Relación de las visitas eclesiásticas de parte del Obispado de la Puebla de los Ángeles (1643–1646)*. Mexico City: El Colegio de México, 2014.

Palmer, Colin. *Slaves of the White God: Blacks in Mexico, 1570–1650*. Cambridge: Cambridge University Press, 1976.

Patterson, Orlando. *Slavery and Social Death: A Comparative Study*. Cambridge: Harvard University Press, 1982.

Paz y Meliá, Antonio. *Nobiliario de conquistadores de Indias*. Madrid: Imprensta de M. Tello, 1892.

Pérez de Ribas, Andrés. *Corónica y historia religiosa de la provincia de la Compañía de Jesús de México*. Mexico City: Imprenta del Sagrado Corazón de Jesús, 1896.

Pérez Fernández, Isacio. *Fray Bartolomé de las Casas, O.P. De defensor de los indios a defensor de los negros*. Salamanca: Editorial San Esteban, 1995.

Pratt, Mary Louise. "Arts of the Contact Zones" *Profession* 91 (New York: MLA, 1991): 33–40.

Premo, Bianca. *Children of the Father King: Youth, Authority and Legal Minority in Colonial Lima*. Chapel Hill: University of North Carolina Press, 2005.

Proctor III, Frank T., "Afro-Mexican Slave Labor in the *Obrajes* de Paños of New Spain, Seventeenth and Eighteenth Centuries" *The Americas* 60, no. 1 (Jul., 2003): 33–58.

  Damned Notions of Liberty: Slavery, Culture and Power in Colonial Mexico, 1640–1769. Albuquerque: University of New Mexico Press, 2010.

Quiroz Norris, Alfonso W. "La expropriación inquisitorial de cristianos nuevos portugueses en los Reyes, Cartagena y México, 1635–1649." *Histórica* 10, no. 2 (December 1986): 237–303.

Ramírez Montes, Guillermina. *Niñas, doncellas, vírgenes eternas Santa Clara de Querétaro (1607–1864)*. Mexico City: UNAM/Instituto de Investigaciones Estéticas, 2005.

Ramos, Frances L. *Identity, Ritual, and Power in Colonial Puebla*. Tucson: University of Arizona Press, 2012.

Rees, Peter William. "Route Inertia and Route Competition: An Historical Geography of Transportation between Mexico City and Vera Cruz." Ph.D. diss., University of California-Berkeley, 1971.

Reséndez, Andres. *The Other Slavery: The Uncovered Story of Indian Enslavement in America*. Boston: Houghton Mifflin Harcourt, 2016.

Restall, Matthew. "Black Conquistadors: Armed Africans in Early Spanish America," *The Americas* 57, no. 2 (Oct. 2000): 171–205.

  Seven Myths of the Spanish Conquest. Oxford: Oxford University Press, 2005.

  "Black Slaves, Red Paint." In *Beyond Black and Red: African-Native Relations in Colonial Latin America*, 1–13. Edited by Matthew Restall. Albuquerque: University of New Mexico Press, 2005.

  The Black Middle: Africans, Mayas and Spaniards in Colonial Yucatan. Stanford, CA: Stanford University Press, 2009.

Restall, Matthew, Lisa Sousa and Kevin Terraciano, eds. *Mesoamerican Voices: Native-Language Writings from Colonial Mexico, Oaxaca, Yucatan, and Guatemala*. Cambridge: Cambridge University Press, 2005.

Risse, Kate. "Catarina de San Juan and the China Poblana: From Spiritual Humility to Civil Obedience." *Confluencia* 18, no. 1 (Fall 2002): 70–80.

Rodríguez Ortíz, Guillermo Alberto. "El lado afro de la Puebla de los Ángeles. Un acercamiento al estudio sobre la presencia africana, 1595–1710," Ph.D. dissertation, Benemérita Universidad Autónoma de Puebla, 2015.

Rubial García, Antonio. *Monjas, cortesanos y plebeyos: La vida cotidiana en la época de Sor Juana*. Mexico City: Taurus, 2005.

Ruíz Medrano, Ethelia. "Los negocios de un arzobispo: El caso de Fray Alonso de Montúfar," *Estudios de Historia Novohispana* 12, no. 19 (1992): 63–83.

 Reshaping New Spain: Government and Private Interests in the Colonial Bureaucracy, 1531–1550. Boulder: University Press of Colorado, 2006.

Rustomji-Kerns, Roshni. "Las raíces olvidadas de Mirrah-Catarina." *Artes de México* no. 66 (2003): 20–33.

Salazar Simarro, Nuria. *La vida común en los conventos de monjas de la ciudad de Puebla*. Puebla: Gobierno del Estado, 1990.

 "Niñas, viudas y esclavas en la clausura monjil." In *La "América abundante" de Sor Juana*, 161–190. Edited by María del Consuelo Maquívar. Mexico City: Instituto Nacional de Antropología e Historia/Museo Nacional del Virreinato, 1995.

 "Los monasterios femeninos." In *Historia de la vida cotidiana en México: La ciudad barroca*, Vol. II, 221–259. Edited by Antonio Garcia Rubial and Pilar Gonzalo Aizpuru. Mexico City: Fondo de Cultura Económica/Colegio de México, 2009.

Salomón Salazar, Mercedes Isabel. "Los Borja: Una dinastía de libreros e impresores en la Puebla de los Ángeles del siglo XVII. Un primer acercamiento." In *Miradas a la cultura del libro en Puebla*, 205–242. Puebla: UNAM/Gobierno del Estado de Puebla, 2012.

Salvucci, Richard. *Textiles and Capitalism in Mexico: An Economic History of the Obrajes, 1539–1840*. Princeton, NJ: Princeton University Press, 1987.

Sánchez Verín, Carlos Arturo Giordano. *Obraje y economía en Tlaxcala a principios del siglo XVII, 1600–1630*. Mexico City: Archivo General de la Nación, 2002.

Sandoval, Alonso de. *Un tratado sobre la esclavitud*. Madrid: Alianza Editorial, 1987.

Schroeder, Susan. *Chimalpahin and the Kingdoms of Chalco*. Tucson: University of Arizona Press, 1991.

Schultz, Kara. "'The Kingdom of Angola Is Not Very Far from Here': The South Atlantic Slave Port of Buenos Aires, 1585–1640." *Slavery & Abolition* 36, no. 3 (2015): 424–444.

Schwaller, Robert. "'Mulata, hija de negro y india': Afro-Indigenous *Mulatos* in Early Colonial Mexico." *Journal of Social History* 44, no. 3 (Spring 2011): 889–914.

 Géneros de Gente in Early Colonial Mexico: Defining Racial Difference. Norman: University of Oklahoma Press, 2016.

Seed, Patricia. *To Love, Honor and Obey in Colonial Mexico: Conflicts over Marriage Choice, 1574–1821*. Stanford, CA: Stanford University Press, 1988.

Seijas, Tatiana. "Transpacific Servitude: The Asian Slaves of Colonial Mexico, 1580–1700." Ph.D. diss., Yale, 2008.

 Asian Slaves in Colonial Mexico: From Chinos to Indians. Cambridge: Cambridge University Press, 2014.

Seijas, Tatiana and Pablo Miguel Sierra Silva, "The Persistence of the Slave Market in Seventeenth-Century Central Mexico." *Slavery & Abolition* 37, no. 2 (Jan. 2016): 307–333.

Shean, Julie. "Models of Virtue: Images and Saint Making in Colonial Puebla (1640–1800)." Ph.D. diss., New York University, 2007.

Sierra Silva, Pablo Miguel. "From Chains to Chiles: An Elite Afro-Indigenous Couple in Colonial Mexico, 1641–1688." *Ethnohistory* 62, no. 2 (April 2015): 361–384.

 "Portuguese *Encomenderos de Negros* and the Slave Trade within Mexico, 1600–1675." *Journal of Global Slavery* 2, no. 3 (special issue 2017): 221–247.

 "The Slave Trade to Colonial Mexico: Revising from Puebla de los Ángeles (1590–1640)." In *From the Galleons to the Highlands*. Edited by Alex Borucki, David Eltis and David Wheat. Albuquerque: University of New Mexico Press, forthcoming 2018.

Sigüenza y Góngora, Carlos de. *Paraíso Occidental*. Mexico City: Cien de México, 1995.

Steck, Francis Borgia. *Motolinia's History of the Indians of New Spain*. Richmond, VA: Academy of American Franciscan History, 1951.

Studnicki-Gizbert, Daviken. *A Nation upon the Ocean Sea: Portugal's Atlantic Diaspora and the Crisis of the Spanish Empire, 1492–1640*. Oxford: Oxford University Press, 2007.

Sue, Christina A. *The Land of the Cosmic Race: Race Mixture, Racism, and Blackness in Mexico*. New York: Oxford University Press, 2013.

Super, John. "Querétaro *Obrajes*: Industry and Society in Provincial Mexico, 1600–1700." *Hispanic American Historical Review* 56, no. 2 (May 1976): 197–216.

Sweet, James H. "The Iberian Roots of American Racist Thought," *William and Mary Quarterly*, 54, no. 1 (Jan. 1997): 143–166.

Domingos Álvares, African Healing, and the Intellectual History of the Atlantic World. Chapel Hill: University of North Carolina Press, 2011.

Tardieu, Jean-Paul. *El negro en el Cuzco: los caminos de la alienación en la segunda mitad del siglo XVII*. Lima: Pontificia Universidad Católica del Perú, 1998.

"Negros e indios en el *obraje* de San Ildefonso. Real Audiencia de Quito. 1665–1666." *Revista de Indias* 72, no. 255 (2012): 527–550.

Terraciano, Kevin. *The Mixtecs of Colonial Oaxaca: Ñudzahui History, Sixteenth through Eighteenth Centuries*. Stanford, CA: Stanford University Press, 2001.

Terrazas Williams, Danielle. "Capitalizing Subjects: Free African-Descended Women of Means in Xalapa, Veracruz during the Long Seventeenth Century." Ph.D. diss., Duke University, 2013.

Thompson, J. Eric S., ed., *Thomas Gage's Travels in the New World*. Norman: University of Oklahoma Press, 1958.

Torres Bautista, Mariano E. "Fulgor y final del Convento de San Agustín de Puebla." In *Estampas de la vida angelopolitana: Ensayos de historia social del siglo XVI al siglo XX*, 63–79. Edited by María de Lourdes Herrera Feria.Tlaxcala: El Colegio de Tlaxcala/BUAP, 2009.

Torres Domínguez, Rosario. "Los colegios regulares y seculares de Puebla y la formación de las élites letradas en el siglo XVIII." Ph.D. diss., UNAM, 2013.

Townsend, Camilla, ed. and transl. *Here in This Year: Seventeenth-Century Nahuatl Annals of the Tlaxcala-Puebla Valley*. Stanford, CA: Stanford University Press, 2010.

"Don Juan Buenaventura Zapata y Mendoza and the Notion of Nahua Identity." In *The Conquest All Over Again: Nahuas and Zapotecs Thinking, Writing, and Painting Spanish Colonialism*, 144–180. Edited by Susan Schroeder. Brighton: Sussex Academic Press, 2010.

Valdés, Dennis N. "The Decline of Slavery in Mexico." *The Americas* 44, no. 2 (1987): 167–194.

van Deusen, Nancy E. "The 'Alienated' Body: Slaves and Castas in the Hospital de San Bartolomé de Lima, 1680 to 1700." *The Americas* 56, no. 1 (July 1999): 1–30.

Between the Sacred and the Worldly: The Institutional and Cultural Practice of Recogimiento in Colonial Lima. Stanford, CA: Stanford University Press, 2002.

The Souls of Purgatory: The Spiritual Diary of a Seventeenth-Century Afro-Peruvian Mystic, Úrsula de Jesús. Albuquerque: University of New Mexico Press, 2004.

"'The Lord walks among the pots and pans': Religious Servants of Colonial Lima." In *Africans to Spanish America: Expanding the Diaspora*, 136–160. Edited by Sherwin K. Bryant, Rachel Sarah O'Toole, and Ben Vinson III. Urbana: University of Illinois Press, 2014.

Global Indios: The Indigenous Struggle for Justice in Sixteenth-Century Spain. Durham, NC: Duke University Press, 2015.

Vaughn, Bobby. "Los negros, los indígenas y la diáspora." In *Afroméxico*, 75–96. Edited by Bobby Vaughn and Ben Vinson III. Mexico City: Fondo de Cultura Económica, 2004.

Vaughn, Bobby and Ben Vinson III, eds. *Afroméxico. El pulso de la población negra en México: Una historia recordada, olvidada y vuelta a recordar.* Mexico City: Fondo de Cultura Económica, 2004.

Van Young, Eric. "Social Networks: A Final Comment." In *Redes y negocios globales en el mundo ibérico, siglos XVI–XVIII*, 298–308. Edited by Nikolaus Böctcher, Bernd Hausberger, and Antonio Ibarra. Vervuert: Instituto Ibero-Americano, 2011.

Vasconcelos, José. *La raza cósmica.* Madrid: Agencia Mundial de Librería, 1925.

Vega Franco, Marisa. *El tráfico de esclavos con América (Asientos de Grillo y Lomelín, 1663–1674.* Seville: Escuela de Estudios Hispanoamericanos/Consejo Superior de Investigaciones Científicas, 1984.

Velázquez, María Elisa. *Mujeres de origen africano en la capital novohispana, siglos XVII y XVIII.* Mexico City: UNAM/INAH, 2006.

Ventura, Maria de Graça Mateus. *Negreiros portugueses na rota das Índias de Castela (1541–1556).* Lisbon: Ediçoes Colibri, 1999.

Vetancur, Fray Agustín de. *Theatro Mexicano. Descripción breve de los sucesos ejemplares históricos y religiosos del nuevo mundo de las Indias.* Mexico City: Editorial Porrúa, 1982.

Vila Vilar, Enriqueta. *Hispanoamérica y el comercio de esclavos.* Seville: Escuela de Estudios Hispano-Americanos, 1977.

Villa-Flores, Javier. *Dangerous Speech: A Social History of Blasphemy in Colonial Mexico.* Tucson: University of Arizona Press, 2006.

"'To Lose One's Soul': Blasphemy and Slavery in New Spain, 1596–1669." *Hispanic American Historical Review* 82, no. 3 (Aug. 2002): 465–466.

Vinson III, Ben. *Bearing Arms for His Majesty: The Free-Colored Militia in Colonial Mexico.* Stanford, CA: Stanford University Press, 2001.

"Estudiando las razas desde la periferia: las castas olvidadas del sistema colonial mexicano (lobos, moriscos, coyotes, moros y chinos). In *Pautas de convivencia étnica en la América Latina colonial (Indios, negros, mulatos, pardos y esclavos)*, 247–307. Edited by Juan Manuel de la Serna. Mexico City: UNAM / CCyDEL / Gobierno del Estado de Guanajuato, 2005.

Viqueira, Carmen and José Urquiola. *Los obrajes en la Nueva España, 1550–1630.* Mexico City: CONACULTA, 1990.

von Mentz, Brígida. *Trabajo, sujeción y libertad en el centro de la Nueva España: Esclavos, aprendices, campesinos y operarios manufactureros, siglos XVI a XVIII.* Mexico City: CIESAS, 1999.

Walker, Tamara. "'He outfitted his family in notable decency': Slavery, Honour and Dress in Eighteenth-Century Lima, Peru." *Slavery & Abolition* 30, no. 3 (Sept. 2009): 383–402.

Wheat, David. "The First Great Waves: African Provenance Zones for the Transatlantic Slave Trade to Cartagena de Indias." *Journal of African History* 52, no. 1 (Mar. 2011): 1–22.

"Garcia Mendes Castelo Branco, fidalgo de Angola y mercader de esclavos en Veracruz y el Caribe a principios del siglo XVII." In *Debates históricos contemporáneos: Africanos y afrodescendientes en México y Centroamérica*, 85–107. Edited by María Elisa Velázquez. Mexico City: INAH, 2011.

Atlantic Africa and the Spanish Caribbean, 1570–1640. Chapel Hill: University of North Carolina Press, 2016.

Yanes Díaz, Gonzalo. *Desarrollo urbano virreinal en la region Puebla-Tlaxcala.* Puebla: BUAP, 1994.

Zavala, Silvio, ed. *Ordenanzas del Trabajo, Siglos XVI y XVII.* Mexico City: Editorial Elede, 1947.

Index

For EU product safety concerns, contact us at Calle de José Abascal, 56–1°,
28003 Madrid, Spain or eugpsr@cambridge.org.

www.ingramcontent.com/pod-product-compliance
Ingram Content Group UK Ltd.
Pitfield, Milton Keynes, MK11 3LW, UK
UKHW010250140625
459647UK00013BA/1775